THE LAND AND THE BOOK

Israel: the Perennial Nation

Geoffrey Ashe

THE LAND AND
THE BOOK

ISRAEL:
THE PERENNIAL
NATION

Collins
ST JAMES'S PLACE, LONDON
1965

A translation in Chapter Two is taken from James
B. Pritchard, *The Ancient Near East*. Some
portions of the text, chiefly in Chapters Six and
Thirteen, are adapted from contributions of
my own to the *Sunday Express* and
the *Jewish Chronicle*

TO ARNOLD WESKER

CONTENTS

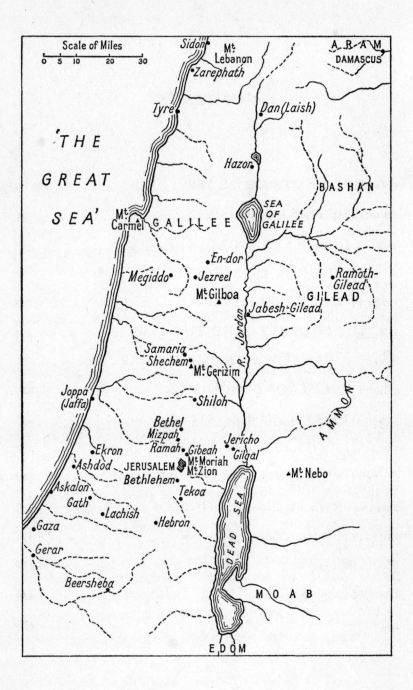

Scale of Miles

0   5   10   20   30

'THE GREAT SEA'

Sidon
Mt Lebanon
Zarephath
Tyre
Dan (Laish)
Hazor

A R A M
DAMASCUS

BASHAN

Mt Carmel
GALILEE

SEA OF GALILEE

En-dor
Megiddo
Jezreel
Mt Gilboa

Ramoth-Gilead
GILEAD
Jabesh-Gilead

R. Jordan

Samaria
Shechem
Mt Gerizim

Shiloh

Joppa (Jaffa)

AMMON

Bethel
Mizpah
Ramah
Ekron
Ashdod
JERUSALEM
Bethlehem
Gibeah
Gilgal
Jericho
Mt Moriah
Mt Zion

Mt Nebo

Askalon
Gath
Lachish
Tekoa

DEAD SEA

Gaza
Gerar
Hebron

Beersheba

MOAB

E D O M

CHAPTER ONE

THE ROOTS OF ISRAEL

Modern Israel is a very young state, fortified by a sense of being old. Paradoxically, both adjectives fit. But most Gentile onlookers (and even some Jewish ones) see only half the paradox. They see Israel's youth without its age. The Republic, they are apt to suppose, is a recent makeshift of politicians. It had its origins in a rescue operation, providing a haven of last resort for persecuted Jews not assimilable where they were. It still carries on after the persecutions, because . . . well, perhaps because millionaires have put money into it?

Yet to the true champions of Zionism, and to many spokesmen and supporters of the Republic to-day, this notion of a mere improvised refuge has never been acceptable for an instant. In their eyes Israel is the outcome of an historical process antedating all Fuehrers and Tsars; an organic process which can be traced without a break, all the way from the biblical past to the un-biblical present. The movement of Jews everywhere to a land of their own expresses a political character which has always been latent in them—whether assimilated or not. Pogroms were a spur, an occasion, but not a cause. In that spirit an Israeli Minister of Education[1] has spoken of the Jews as "the only people whose continuous national memory has comprehended the full cycle from ancient prophecy to modern science," and declared that one of the aims of resurrecting the Hebrew language is to nurture the sense of "lineal descent from ancient Israel," the ancestral biblical nation.

---

[1] Mr. Abba Eban. The Chapter Bibliographies give more precise references for most citations in the text.

Pogrom: An organised riot, usually against the Jews

Furthermore, the main body of Zionist pioneers never regarded their goal as a land in general, an undefined anchorage for the dispossessed. They meant the ancestral place Palestine, and nowhere else. Jewish continuity through something like thirty centuries was held to have consisted, to a large extent, in the constancy of that local claim. Theodor Herzl, the organiser and publicist of Zionism during the 1890's, did offer a plan for a Jewish colony in Uganda instead; and it was thrown out by the angry votes of the Russian ghetto-dwellers whom he conceived himself to be saving. Rather than turn away from Palestine, they preferred to cling to their unassimilated identity, and go on being trampled.

Chaim Weizmann, who led Zionism after Herzl and became President of Israel, writes in his autobiography of the way in which he stated his case to Balfour and others. "The Jewish people," he told them, "would never produce either the money or the energy required in order to build up a wasteland and make it habitable, unless that land were Palestine. Palestine had this magic and romantic appeal for the Jews; our history has been what it is because of our tenacious hold on Palestine. We have never accepted defeat and have never forsaken the memory of Palestine. Such a tradition could be converted into real motive power, and we were trying to do just that." In other words the People—somehow—are linked with the Land, and have been so for a prodigious time. But how? and why? The long continuity is affirmed; it is not explained.

Weizmann speaks of Zionism in the same passage as "a deep religious conviction expressed in modern political terms." If we pass from Jewish nationalism to Jewish religion, we do find related views. They are not held unanimously, but they are held widely, and they have gained ground since the Republic's birth. Thus Dr. David Polish, President of the Chicago Rabbinical Association: "A central aspect of Judaism's life-style . . . is the irrefragable relationship of Israel to its land. In fact, this relationship can be adequately understood only as one of the crucial elements in the covenant. It is impossible to interpret Jewish history except in terms of a passion to be restored to the homeland, in fulfilment of a divine promise, often repeated and more often recalled. . . . Like the tropism of a living organism which instinctively gravitates toward the sun, the Jewish people, despite the tortured convolutions of its history, constantly reoriented itself toward Palestine."

One could multiply examples. For many distinguished teachers of Judaism besides Dr. Polish, the Faith also is linked with the Land . . . and has been so for a prodigious time. Some synthesise both beliefs, to a point where religion and nationalism, both flowing the same way, blend into one. Ahad Ha-am, Zionism's great literary voice in its years of struggle, affirmed that "the Law, the Land, the People, the God, the sense of destiny," are the essence of the Jewish historical fact. Martin Buber, the philosopher, speaks of the unity of People with Land as embodying a mission: it is a holy mystery, and if the Jews renounce the mystery, they "renounce the heart of reality itself." Dr. Norman Bentwich even refers to "the Messianic vision which has inspired the re-establishment of the nation in its old home."

As a respectful, indeed a reverent outsider, I wish to examine the ground for such ideas. I am not attempting a mere impudent exercise in social dissection. The problem is, I believe, of immense relevance and importance, not only to Jews but to myself and many others. What is the logic, if any, that connects the planting of "Israel" in contemporary Palestine with the planting of a grotesquely different "Israel" during the Late Bronze Age? If the Jewish people were always spiritually linked to the Land, even through centuries of absence, how was this link forged and what was its nature? If the mystique of Palestine was part of their religion, why did many Orthodox Jews oppose Zionism, and many irreligious Jews favour it? On the other hand, if the mystique was not part of their religion, why did it persist among Jews dispersed all over the world, who apparently had nothing but religion in common? If Zionism was only the active expression of something that was there all along, what was the "something"? How did it have the power to effect, against monstrous odds, one of the most unlikely political successes on record: a success which the agnostic Koestler has trouble in distinguishing from a miracle?

2

But of course these questions immediately provoke yet another. What is a Jew, and who in fact are we talking about?

The point is far from academic. Israeli immigration officials have had to face it, and their answers remain provisional. Dr. Bentwich is right to speak of the Jewish people as a "nation" in some sense, because otherwise the nationalism that made Israel could never have been generated. But the sense is not ordinary, and if the word creates an impression that it is, then one had best avoid it. To speak of the Jews simply as a nation is to collide at once with their ability to be national wherever they are—to be English in England, French in France, or American in America, and to change in moving from country to country. The Israeli population was formed out of a mixture of Russians, Germans, displaced persons from all over Europe, and refugees from the Arab states. Civilised Berliners of high attainments received medieval Yemenites who were afraid to board a bus. Many of the immigrants were as much foreigners to each other, in every ordinary sense, as human beings could be. The second-generation "Sabra" are more homogeneous, but at the same time less like the known Jewish stereotypes. They are a novel phenomenon which cannot be read back into the past, or projected to places outside the Israeli borders.

This multiple nationality, which always seems to hold something in reserve, is so puzzling that it has prompted essays in direct exorcism. Hilaire Belloc insisted that the Jews actually were a nation, and that all the trouble sprang from a failure to recognise them as such. Once recognised, they would become resident aliens with their own culture, and the problems would at least diminish. But since they have gone on for so many centuries without a land of their own or a common vernacular, any such nationality would have to be a matter of race. And race does not work. There are white Jews, brown Jews, yellow Jews, black Jews. There are

Jewish communities descended from converts, with no blood-relationship to the tribes of Israel. Even among Europeans the supposed physical type is a doubtful proposition. Tests prove that the Jewish "look" is hard to tell from an Italian or generally Mediterranean look. If we study the faces of ancient peoples in statuary and relief, we glimpse the look more often among the non-Semitic Hittites than among the Jews' own Semitic forebears. Its antecedents lie in mixture rather than purity.

The notion that the Jews are a race is not only wrong, but disruptive of the religion which is bound up with their identity and endurance. It annuls that religion's chief tenet by making it tribal. If a person without Jewish blood cannot become a Jew—at least a kind of honorary or associate Jew—the God of Israel is not what he is said to be, the God of all mankind. Can we shift the ground, then, and put the definition on a confessional basis? Is a Jew nothing but an Englishman or Frenchman or such-and-such practising the Jewish religion?

A manifest drawback is that he very likely doesn't. Nevertheless the idea is familiar, and more helpful. Herman Wouk, in his much-read popularisation of Orthodoxy, affirms outright that faith is the crucial thing. But faith in what? Plenty of Jews, including some outstanding ones, have been so by birth and cast of mind without being so by religion. Baptised Jews like Heine and Disraeli, atheists like Marx and Freud, must somehow be fitted in. The Israeli Republic has never imposed a religious test, and the record of the return to Palestine would make nonsense of it. The most ardent Zionists, the most intensely and idealistically Jewish Jews, have often been strangers to religious practice. The Liberals who have laid most stress on religion as their special mark have tended to disavow any others, thereby reducing themselves to sectaries. Moreover the Hebrew language has no word for religion at all, in the doctrinal sense.

Faith, then, if a clue, is a risky one. The obverse of the definition by creed is the definition by persecution ascribed to Sartre: "Jews are the victims of anti-Semitism." This however simply leads to the question, "Why the persecution?" or to be more precise, "What is the distinction which Jews everywhere have persisted in hanging on to?" If we can isolate a common factor, we can search there for the connection with Palestine. The word "faith," though insufficient, points the right way.

All Jews in all countries have inherited one possession: the Hebrew sacred literature, meaning chiefly the Bible, or in Christian terms the Old Testament. Whatever else they may be, they are the People of the Book, archetypally, pre-eminently. Christians and Moslems too have their books, but they have their territories as well. The Jews alone have survived (against all human probability) with a book only. Not that this possession explains everything, or anything, in itself. But at least it is a common factor. Inquiry into Jewishness can start from here, as it could not start from such attributes as dark pigment or acquaintance with Yiddish, which not all Jews have.

To say so is not to uphold the religious theory after all. A Jew's relationship to his Bible need not imply anything about his religion. He may be Orthodox or Reformed or Liberal . . . or Christian. He may value Scripture only for Zionist inspiration, or for the ethical wisdom of the prophets. He may criticise it or totally reject it. Yet he stands in a certain relation to it. Whatever his Bible may be, its successive strata are a record of experience, the collective experience of the Israelites who made it. That experience has been kept alive and prolonged ever since through a solid catena of heredity and conduct, commemorative ritual and biblically-based teaching, down to his own generation—however grim the consequences. The corporate memory, the awareness of history, is unremitting. In that sense at any rate there is no break between the Jewish communities of to-day and the Jewish community of the past that assembled the Old Testament; or between that and the ancient Israel before it.

Every Jew shares in an experience that stretches back into antiquity. He may not be conscious of it except in its late phases. All the same, his Bible is his family history. Its characters are his own people. He can identify himself with them. He will often find, whatever his religious belief, that the ancient Hebrew sayings and stories are supremely apt to express his own thoughts. The persecution which his ancestors suffered resulted from the history that the Bible contains. Among modern Israel's Sabra, for whom the ghetto is irrelevant and the synagogue often worse, the Bible's fascination has grown rather than lessened.

This is a continuity which can be discussed with fair precision: the continuity of what Dr. Polish calls a life-style, going back to a common source in the Old Testament. It might be urged that sharing in the Jewish experience—in the living, portable, communal past—is exactly what constitutes a Jew; that to be Jewish is to be conditioned by that, directly or indirectly, and no other definition is needed.[2] Perhaps. But at any rate we have a point of departure. We can take hold of something which all Jews had before they were last scattered from Palestine early in the Christian era, and which they have clung to everywhere in dispersal. We can approach the problem of the bond between Palestine and all Jewish groups by studying Scripture to make out what experience it really embodies.

Even at a glance, it is encouraging to see how much the Bible has to say about an ancestral title to the Land. But its words, in themselves, do not make sense of Zionism or the Republic. Religious commands cannot account for the actions of agnostics, and secular facts are not intelligible motives at such a distance of time. Arabs gibe at "a claim thousands of years old." In the context of any normal nationalism, they are right. The English feel no interest in Schleswig-Holstein, and would not dream of resettling it, though they are descended from colonists who left it more recently than the Jews' ancestors left Palestine. We have to ask what it was

---

2 Cp. Cecil Roth in *The Guardian*, 16th March, 1962: "Surely the 'Jewish mind' is the outcome of historical experience, stimulated by the traditional intellectual preoccupations and religious precepts?" Similar definitions by "experience" are indicated by James Parkes (*The Foundations of Judaism and Christianity*, p. 243) and Chaim Weizmann (*Trial and Error*, p. 108).

that burned on from the biblical world through those millennia. Somehow, the biblical experience generated forces that kept the claim vital and made it potent in the politics of the twentieth century. Somehow, at last, collective memory inspired an ardent vocation that burst the religious matrix itself.

3

Our task is to re-create this experience which, in its formative phases, the Old Testament preserves. To see whether the claim to Palestine actually was a key factor in the growth of Jewish life, so closely intertwined that it could not and still cannot be torn away.

I believe this view to be correct. The "tropism" was not something added to a cult or nation already in being, which could afterwards revert to existence without it. Around the Land, on the contrary—around attempts to reach it, attempts to hold it, attempts to fathom what was involved in holding it—the entire experience took shape. It is the consequent mass-conditioning, sometimes overt, sometimes latent, that we witness in what has happened since. The conditioning is so deeply stamped that it can still be active when the synagogue is abandoned; as the irreligious Japanese are still governed in their conduct by habits due to Confucianism and Zen.

But before studying the data, let us note what the Bible is, and how extraordinary it is. No other society has produced anything like it. Because of its unique nature, no other society has the Jewish capacity for collective memory, or can open up its own past with such fullness.

As a rule, explorations into the antique world, or into national beginnings in general, are beset with hazards. Almost every society outside Israel (I am speaking now of historical Israel, not the Republic) has suffered from a kind of amnesia. This is not so much a lack of records as an incoherence of records. Experiences are not fused together. The deposit of the remoter years is a miscellany. We find heroic sagas and sacred texts and myths, chronicles and poems and dramas, all distinct from each other and often connected only by the frailest of links and cross-references. The creators of a national literature do not work within a single convention, or clearly illuminate each other. Greece, for instance, has left a marvellous literature, everlastingly valid as such. Yet the gaps between its various branches, not only at the start but at the climax, make the vision of Greece astonishingly hard to bring into focus. We cannot, to any fruitful extent, use Thucydides to interpret Homer, or Euripides to annotate Xenophon. We cannot form a reliable idea even of one of the greatest Greeks of all, Socrates; nobody knows how far Plato's protagonist is the real Socrates, how far he is a character invented by Plato. Aristotle was Alexander's tutor, and in all his writings he never mentions him. Hellenic civilisation is fragmented; and to compare eighteenth-century notions of it with some of those current to-day—to compare, say, Winckelmann with Robert Graves—is to appreciate what a shaky basis for historical statement even such a rich literary legacy can be.

But the Jewish people are different. Their collective memory stands in sharp contrast to the amnesia of others. The experience of ancient Israel in Palestine is knit together and made intelligible, not only by the literature that preserves it, but by the structure of that literature.

When the Old Testament was compiled, something happened among the Jews that never happened among the Greeks. Their representatives decided which of the surviving writings were of prime importance, from far-off generations to what were then recent times. This collection was set up as a single canon of Scripture for the people's unification and instruction. It was not their whole literature, but it did cover the whole normal range. It comprised traditions and chronicles, mythical matter and legendary matter, law codes and ritual handbooks, verses and meditations and dialogues. But together, not separate. Here in the Jewish Bible, and here alone in the whole known career of mankind, these things are not dispersed but assembled, and woven into a single historical scheme. Here alone a people's experience is put on record, facts and dreams and aspirations and all, without division. Everything lights up everything else—because everything is placed in relation to a belief about the presence of God throughout Israel's life.

The Old Testament is a national literature, bound up into one volume as a sacred book. But because of its inner organisation, whether the religious reason for that is sound or not, it is also more than literature. The editors who defined the canon were not solely or even mainly responsible; they set the seal on a development which had been going on for generations. Biblical cross-references and internal overlaps are many and complex. Thus a number of the hymns called Psalms are ascribed to a king, David, whose biography we are given. A number of the maxims called Proverbs are ascribed to another king, Solomon, who plays a leading role in the nation's economic progress. Prophetic poetry is related to foreign policy. Laws are fitted into a narrative about the first lawgiver. In the *Book of Job* theology is presented through drama, and in the *Song of Songs* it is presented through love-odes. While the Old Testament is hardly to be read straight through like a novel, its interlocked unity makes it, in a sense, one story— a tragic epic unfolding a concept of divine law in the world, with ancient Israel for its hero.

To quote Professor Butterfield, what was unique about the Israelites was "their historiography rather than their history." The Hindu sacred epic *Mahabharata* is also a mixture of diverse elements, but its unity comes from metaphysics and not from history, which the Hindus never conceived till alien influences began to affect them. Among Gentiles the deposit of the past has been scattered. Among Jews it is hoarded as a single treasure, made so by the conviction that Israel's experience has eternal meaning.

The Old Testament, of course, is not a scientific treatise or an objective register of events. The history which it furnishes is experience passed through a mill of imagination. Its many accounts of miracles and marvels cannot be assessed by simply asking "What really happened?" True or half-true or (literally speaking) false, they are devices by which the authors symbolise some state of

affairs, or convey the atmosphere surrounding some great occasion.
From early times even the most orthodox Jewish commentators,
convinced that all Scripture was inspired, nevertheless taught
that there were different levels of inspiration; that different inspired
authors had different outlooks and methods of expressing themselves; that each passage had to be construed in terms of its adaptation to audiences who would ask "What is the point of this?"
rather than "Did this actually happen?" Most of the commentators
allow that while Scripture must be taken as history, it can be taken
in a variety of ways. Truth may be communicated by myths
and parables and legends, as well as by bald reports. A distinction
of four "senses"—the literal, the allegorical, the didactic, and the
esoteric—is probably as old as the canon itself. Recognition of the
façon de parler, of the use of metaphors and symbols to describe an
event, is well established. No Jew is obliged to believe that Elijah
flew physically to heaven in a fiery chariot.

Nominal Christians may find these facts surprising. They still
tend to view the Bible in a Fundamentalist light, and accept it or
reject it accordingly. To the consistent believer (they are apt to
fancy) it is a volume dropped from the clouds, not occurring under
human conditions, and showing neither development nor variation
in texture; all literally inspired, all literally true. Even the Modernist,
it is thought, only picks and chooses, hanging on to some bits as
true, and throwing the rest away. But the Jews who compiled the
canon did not regard it thus. Nor indeed did the Fathers of the
Church. Right through the Middle Ages, Christian exegetes
recognised the Jewish "four senses of Scripture" and added more of
their own. Fundamentalism began only when the Bible, translated
into foreign tongues, was divorced from the traditions of interpretation, and set up by itself as the infallible basis of Christian faith.[3]

3 In *A Path through Genesis*, which bears the Imprimatur, Father Bruce
Vawter writes: "*What the author intended to teach* is the meaning. . . . Any
interpretation of Scripture that contradicts a known fact of science we
may be very sure is no true interpretation. . . . 'Fundamentalism' or
'literalism' has never had a home in the Catholic Church."

This error produced the absurd Victorian rearguard action against evolution and the Higher Criticism. The agnostics' attack was deadly. But most of the battles need never have been fought. To-day, anti-biblical pamphleteers like Ingersoll look as archaic as Bishop Wilberforce. The difficulty in dealing with people who still talk that language is not so much to refute them as to make them see that there is little in their words to refute. Archaeological finds which bear out Scripture have helped to keep Fundamentalism alive, by prompting some rather misguided books of the "Bible-is-True" type. Archaeology has certainly put the Bible on a much firmer basis, by showing that the main narrative does not have to be vaporised into myth and allegory. But its results must be placed in the context of a deep understanding as to the layers of meaning in the various documents. Such an understanding the Jews, in principle, always had, and it has remained with them. Not with all, since narrowness and superstition are not Gentile monopolies, but always with a fair proportion of the best minds.

To sum up, the Old Testament supplies a marvellous opulence of matter, with a concentration and unity which allow boldness in probing. Guided not only by scholarship but by traditional Jewish insight, we can sometimes risk generalisations that would hardly be better than guesswork if extracted from the records of other peoples. At the near end of a long time-scale is the unique phenomenon of the Republic of Israel. At the far end, plainly, there is a corresponding uniqueness. Let us approach the Republic through the Bible, and so try to define the bridging relationship which Zionist and Israeli spokesmen assert.

CHAPTER TWO

THE FIRST ZIONISM

Israel appears first in undisputed history on a piece of stone—a triumphal stela from Thebes, now in Cairo at the Egyptian Museum. The inscription, to be dated between 1230 and 1215 B.C., commemorates a victory won by the Pharaoh Merneptah over the Libyans, and lists several Near Eastern nations as cowed into submission by his grandeur. The phrasing is largely conventional panegyric. It is the single famous name that captures attention.

> . . . The princes are prostrate, saying "Mercy!"
> Not one raises his head among the Nine Bows.
> Desolation is for Tehenu; Hatti is pacified;
> Plundered is the Canaan with every evil;
> Carried off is Ashkelon; seized upon is Gezer;
> Yanoam is made as that which does not exist;
> Israel is laid waste, his seed is not.

Israel's début, despoiled and sorrowing at the hands of a mightier power, is strangely characteristic. So is the unwise boast of the victor. Merneptah's propaganda is echoed by the Egyptian communiqués of 1948.

Here then is a distinct nation "Israel" in the late thirteenth century B.C., apparently viewed by the Egyptians as troublesome. The next step is to sort it out from the complexities of a confused age.

Egypt in those days was still an empire, and had long exercised a vague and variable protectorate over the lands neighbouring on the east. In Canaan, afterwards Palestine, she ruled the coastal cities. Meanwhile her administrators were carrying on a drawn-out struggle to tax and police the interior, though their final failure was imminent. The library of dispatches known as the Tell el-Amarna tablets reveals some of the difficulties they had long been contending with. Beyond, round the fertile crescent of Syria and Mesopotamia, and far north toward Asia Minor, roaming masses of Semites presented an unsolved problem several centuries old. About 1730 B.C. a predominantly Semitic host had overrun most of Egypt itself and set up a dynasty of "Hyksos" (Kings of Foreign Parts, mistranslated as Shepherd Kings), who reigned in the Nile Delta till a revolution expelled them. This Hyksos invasion left its mark on Egypt. Semitic personal names became current there; Semitic gods were worshipped; Semitic words infiltrated Egyptian literature, and flourished long after the foreign kings were no more.

Associated in some way with the Hyksos conquerors was a mongrel swarm of people called Habiru, or in Egypt, 'Apiru. They flit through ancient records over a wide area and a long stretch of time: as dwellers in Babylonia before Hammurabi, as mercenaries serving the Hittites of Asia Minor, as slaves east of the Tigris, as guerrillas and bandits on a large scale in Canaan, as workmen under the pharaohs.

When these Habiru were first discovered by archaeologists, their name was equated with "Hebrew" and attempts were made to bring them into relationship with the Bible. The philology is correct, but the identification with the Israelite Hebrews is only partly so. It would seem that between 2000 and 1700 B.C. the loosely-linked Habiru included a cohesive group of Semites with desert origins, who held to an old tribal organisation and semi-pastoral mode of life. Roaming with their flocks through the same regions as the rest, aloof from civilisation and strong enough to avoid subjection, they made their homes in the Canaanite uplands away from the sea. These alone were the real Hebrews.

Some centuries later at any rate, the Chosen People traced their ancestry to a Hebrew patriarch named Jacob or Israel. Between his time and theirs the "children of Israel" had been serfs in Egypt. The actions of their patriarch were credibly invoked to account for this fact. In seasons of famine, Semites of the desert had been accustomed for many generations to cross the Egyptian frontier in search of grain and richer pastures. The Egyptians despised them and dubbed them "sand-ramblers," but a memo has been preserved which shows that the border officials sometimes let them pass. The Hyksos reign in Egypt naturally encouraged the drift while it lasted. Jacob-Israel, we are told, made such a move from Canaan with eleven of his sons and their households, aided by a twelfth son, Joseph, who had risen to a position of trust in Egypt. Instead of going back to Canaan they all settled in Goshen, east of the Delta. There they multiplied till Jacob's progeny made up an appreciable fraction of the inhabitants. It was from that stock, from the "twelve tribes," that the nation of Israel was constituted.

Goshen, during the latter part of the second millennium B.C., was possibly bi-lingual and undoubtedly much affected by Semitic penetration. But these very humble residents could not have been a nation in any true sense while they were actually in Egypt. We must picture them as a collection of families with hazy tribal pedigrees, united chiefly by a common language and a tradition of common origin.[1] Neither of these possessions could have given them any special interest for others. They hover in the reconstructive imagination as backward and undistinguished, a thoroughly petty group, a subdivision of a subdivision of a subdivision. There is no certain contemporary allusion, and no good reason why there should be. Israelite insignificance by all ordinary standards is a vital thing to grasp; and the Goshen families' best-informed descendants remained well aware of it.

Israel's launching in the biblical narrative is initiated by a single event, the Exodus. Egyptian policy toward the alien serfs is said to have altered and grown harsher. They were driven into compulsory labour as builders and brick-makers. At last their burden became too heavy to endure. Enabled to free themselves, they fled together into the isthmus of Sinai and received laws there.

---

[1] It is uncertain what the common language was. The Israelites may have adopted or evolved what is called "Hebrew" after their Egyptian phase.

Then, making a huge slow circuit, they broke back into their ancestral homeland of Canaan by capturing Jericho, and re-conquered and re-colonised it over a series of generations. The Israel of Merneptah's stela would be this repatriated horde at some stage of its national evolution.

That is the essence (on the human side) of the Bible's account. While it was not given its present form till long after the actual flight, portions of it are contemporary, and it can safely be accepted as historical in its main drift. Israel's later career, indeed, is hard to understand except on the supposition that the nation was forged by some most impressive train of events; and there is no trace of any such events other than the Exodus, with its sequels. Archaeology confirms that Israelite tribes did at least enter Canaan very much as the Bible says, and offers nothing to suggest that they had been living anywhere but in Egypt.

Admittedly myths along the same lines have been spun out of nothing or next to nothing in other cases. An autocracy can get such a myth widely believed, as Hitler did with the Aryan theory. But successful fables like this always look back to inaccessibly remote ages. To suppose that the priests or princes of Israel could have faked an Exodus-and-settlement history coming down perilously close to their own day, and then forced it on the populace without either dictatorship or mass-media, when every authentic tradition would have clashed with it . . . that is too much. The Old Testament never hints that anyone was disposed to challenge the approved narrative. Its writers have no scruples about mentioning other subversive trends, but they never so much as glance at any in that respect. Even *prima facie* the Exodus must have happened, if only because its denial means postulating behaviour as foreign to human nature as the miracles of Scripture are to physical nature.

However, to fix a date for the opening movement of Israel's formative adventure—namely the mass escape from Egyptian bondage—is a hard job. In the Old Testament itself our solitary direct clue is a statement that King Solomon began building his Jerusalem Temple in the four hundred and eightieth year after it occurred (*I Kings* vi:1). In view of Solomon's own date, this would push the Exodus far back into the fifteenth century B.C. Such a period used to be thought acceptable, mainly because of a Tell el-Amarna letter from an Egyptian governor in Canaan, complaining of 'Apiru overrunning the country. Support was also adduced from excavation, which allegedly placed the fall of Jericho about the same time. These evidences, however, have crumbled. The governor's 'Apiru are unlikely to have been Israelites, the Amarna rulers' names are different from the biblical ones, and Jericho's fall has turned out to be later. Actually, in any case, there is no real ground for treating the interval in the *Book of Kings* as authentic. The Greek version known as the Septuagint gives 440 instead of 480, a strong hint that the tradition underwent literary tampering. Probably it was revised in the interests of an artificial scheme which divided Israelite history into equal periods. If so, the text reflects a kind of cryptographic symbolism rather than genuine chronology, and no one can tell what number of years was originally recorded.

Confusion may have arisen from a first minor migration far in advance of the main body. But, for various reasons, an Exodus in the thirteenth century before Christ now looks plausible. Merneptah's stela gives us that glimpse of enmity between Egyptians and Israelites somewhere about the 1220's. Moreover, while other political units named on the same monument are defined by geography—Ashkelon, Gezer and so forth—in this instance the name is that of a people, not a place. It appears that the tribes were not yet regarded as a settled nation with a recognised territory; hence, that in the latter half of the thirteenth century they were not long out of Egypt and not established in Canaan.

The Bible portrays them as having hostile dealings with Edom, Moab and Ammon, kingdoms which did not come into existence till the same period. On the other hand it never portrays them as fighting against Egyptians in central Canaan itself; and Egypt's grasp on the area did not relax enough to account for that absence till after Merneptah. The *Book of Joshua* speaks of iron, which was not introduced into this region till the thirteenth century. Finally, the archaeology of the towns captured by the invaders points in general to a lengthy campaign extending from the middle thirteenth century into the twelfth. Several exhibit traces of violent sacking about this period.

The *Book of Exodus* distinguishes two Egyptian pharaohs. Under one the Israelites are oppressed, under his successor they are delivered. It also says (i:11) that they built the treasure-cities Pithom and Raamses. The first is Pi-tum, largely a thirteenth-century work. The second is Tanis, reconstructed by Seti I and his son, Rameses II, Merneptah's father, who called it "The House of Rameses" and employed workmen described as 'Apiru in its construction. These two pharaohs are doubtless the two in question. At Pi-tum it has been observed that some of the bricks are made with straw and some without. Exodus v depicts the second pharaoh as ordering the Hebrew brick-makers to gather their own straw while maintaining output, a demand which they were unable to fulfil, and which might well have led in practice to the furtive manufacture of strawless bricks in an effort to make up the quota.

Rameses II was one of the ablest pharaohs. He succeeded to the throne in 1290 and reigned for fifty-six years. In Herodotus's *History* he figures, exaggerated, as the mighty conqueror Sesostris, and it is noteworthy that the Greek author refers to his use of alien slaves on public projects. One of these was the celebrated temple at Abu Simbel. The Bible implies that the Israelites' struggle to break free began soon after his accession but was not successful at once. The departure from Egypt may therefore be fitted loosely into the decade between 1290 and 1280. Any dating whatever presents difficulties, but this one presents by far the fewest.

2

The Hebrews' flight would never have acquired any special interest if it had not been part of an extraordinary series of happenings. All the tradition of these comes down to us focused on a leader,

Moses. In spite of everything that has happened since, he remains imperishably Israel's creator, on whom Jewish life and faith depend; the axiomatic hero, founder of a nation and a religion. As to whether he really existed, it seems sufficient to point out that such achievements as the Exodus do not happen without leadership, and that to dispute whether the Hebrews' leader was Moses or someone afterwards called so by story-tellers is to split hairs. We may stress his role as a prophet, or (in the manner of Conrad Noel) as a kind of Spartacus, the organiser of a successful brick-makers' strike. But there he stands, immovable and colossal.

Through much in the Bible that is strange, and much that is exceedingly dark, a living personality still asserts itself. There is nothing facile or obvious about it. Moses, who is to teach all Israel so copiously, is not a rhetorician but "slow of speech" and diffident. The masterful grandeur which he attains is the result of an imposed discipline. But he has the resources for it, and, one gathers, the physique. Quite apart from Michelangelo it is hard to think of Moses as small. He is shown to us as enduring and powerful, a match for several opponents in his youth, active and hale in extreme old age.

Spiritually at any rate, Moses towered so high above the rest of his people that the whole Pentateuch—the series of five books with which the Bible begins—is in effect a record of his doings with an explanatory prologue. It used even to be attributed to him as sole author, or nearly so. In its existing form it most certainly is not. It is a medley of "tribal reminiscences, folk-tales, legal and ritual enactments, and moral and religious teaching," built up over nearly a thousand years. Later we shall dissect it in more detail. What matters for the moment is that in the Pentateuch we have, not history in the modern sense, but *Heilsgeschichte*: a body of real events interpreted, weighed, imaginatively expanded, so as to symbolise their inner truth. Sometimes we can reason our way to the bare fact, sometimes only to an idea which the writer is trying to communicate. Nevertheless the story presses through in both cases; and it should never be supposed that the view we take of it must depend entirely on our religious belief or disbelief. If the Bible is a divine revelation, it is none the less a revelation occurring under human conditions, through human experience. Always there is a datum of event or tradition or interpretation which is the same whether we believe or not. Sometimes the difference consists mainly in this—that when scholarship has done all it can to establish what a biblical writer meant to convey, the believer will add "and essentially (by God's aid) he was right," whereas the unbeliever perhaps will say otherwise. Here our primary task is to find the datum.

The story which presses through in the *Book of Exodus* and its sequels is, by any intelligible standard, one of the great stories of the world. It describes events almost contemporary with those of another great story, the Trojan War. Indeed, the mystery that surrounds Moses may arise in part from his being not so much an early figure of Israel as a late figure of another society now largely lost. Both in the Aegean and in Egypt, civilisation slid downhill after 1200. But before that, Moses could probably have talked to King Priam.

His name—in Hebrew, "Mosheh"—is Egyptian, a component of names like "Thutmose" and "Ahmose." The fact may be accounted for by the biblical statement that an Egyptian foster-mother re-named him, yet in one place (*Exodus* ii:19) he is unequivo-cally called an Egyptian himself. A legend avers that there was doubt as to his true origin. The biblical version gives room for this and other opinions. It says that the first of its two pharaohs (presumably Seti), who had taken alarm at the Hebrews' growth in numbers, imposed crushing labours on them and then ordered a massacre of their male children. The infant prophet, placed by his mother in a basket and concealed among the reeds of the Nile, was rescued and adopted by the Pharaoh's daughter. As a courtier he would certainly have learnt much that most Hebrews did not—Egyptian ritual, theology, notions of divine government. But to trace a connection between these things and his subsequent career is to tread on perilous ground.

After he grew up (*Exodus* continues) he went out to look at the sordid world of slave-labour which the nobles doubtless averted their eyes from. He saw an Egyptian beating a Hebrew, and promptly killed him. The act was discovered. Moses fled out of Egypt into Midian, in the south-east of the isthmus of Sinai. He halted at a well used by the daughters of a priest named Reuel or Jethro, and protected them when some shepherds tried to drive them away from the water. The grateful priest invited Moses to visit him. In due course the exile married one of the daughters, Zipporah.

For some years the narrative leaves Moses living quietly in Midian tending his father-in-law's flock. And then comes a momentous interview, in which the chief character of the Old Testament—it has been said, the only character—discloses himself. It will be necessary to inquire rather carefully what the incident implies, and who this character is.

One day when Moses leads the flocks westward in search of pasture, he comes to Mount Horeb.

And the angel of the Lord appeared to him in a flame of fire out of the midst of a bush; and he looked, and lo, the bush was burning, yet it was not consumed.

And Moses said, "I will turn aside and see this great sight, why the bush is not burnt."

When the Lord saw that he turned aside to see, God called to him out of the bush, "Moses, Moses!" And he said, "Here am I."

Then he said, "Do not come near; put off your shoes from your feet, for the place on which you are standing is holy ground."

And he said, "I am the God of your father, the God of Abraham, the God of Isaac, the God of Jacob." And Moses hid his face, for he was afraid to look at God.

Then the Lord said, "I have seen the affliction of my people who are in Egypt, and have heard their cry because of their taskmasters; I know their sufferings.

And I have come down to deliver them out of the hand

of the Egyptians, and to bring them up out of that land to a
good and broad land, a land flowing with milk and honey,
to the place of the Canaanites. . . .

Come, I will send you to Pharaoh that you may bring
forth my people, the sons of Israel, out of Egypt."

(Exodus iii:2-10)

What shall we say of this meeting which provides the slaves
with a God to rescue them, a God who asserts an ancient relationship
with Jacob and other tribal ancestors? What in fact is supposed to
have happened?

Here at least the claim that Moses wrote *Exodus* himself has a
certain force, for apparently no one else was with him to tell the
tale. Either the episode is symbolic (the real author's extended
metaphor of his hero's vocation), or it is history of a kind, derived
from the words of Moses himself. On either hypothesis the same
point stands out. If the incident is a later fiction, the author is
allegorising the dawn of Israel's freedom in a visionary experience
of a type often recorded by the nation's prophets. If it has an
authentic basis in the shape of a report by Moses, that experience
is still there and still crucial. Legend may have added to it, or we
may after all be getting the seer's own account of it, but there it
remains. The constant factor in every interpretation is the prophetic vision itself, the burning bush with a Voice issuing from the
blaze.

How such visions actually came—as apparitions or hallucinations
or ecstatic reveries—is a problem best deferred. But the prophetic
books show that they did come, and that descriptions of them were
always acceptable as statements of religious insight. The scene on
Horeb is not an isolated freak or a savage's fancy. Moses indeed
might have misunderstood some natural sight, such as a "gas-bush"
or dittany accidentally lit. But it does not matter, whereas the
conformity to prophetic style does. The passage evokes a profound
experience marked by a peculiar mixture of the awe-inspiring and
the grotesque that runs through much of the Old Testament.
Imagery of this type does not fade away with advancing maturity.

On the contrary, it is as vital as ever in those very authors who carry Hebrew thought to its apex.

To Victorian rationalists such visions were so comic and shocking as to bring Israel's whole testimony into contempt. (You couldn't imagine Mr. Herbert Spencer talking like that.) They urged that if God had ever spoken at all he would have enunciated great truths in fine language. Dated as they make it sound, the complaint must be faced if one proposes to take the Bible seriously. At least as a dogma, however, it is not merely dated but outdated. Psychology and anthropology, and advertising for that matter, have done too much to support Scripture in this respect as by no means an implausible rendering of the ways of a wise deity to men: men being what they were, and are.

Revelation must be adapted to the recipient. It should be plain in any case that in Moses' time communication would only have been possible through concrete imagery, because nothing else would have been grasped, except by a few; but the principle is permanent. Lofty abstractions in themselves are regrettably lifeless and unpersuasive, giving no sense of contact with any compelling reality. We are gripped far more readily by the vivid, the homely, the incongruous. The authors who conceive God as seizing hold of human minds in queer haunting disguises are not to be dismissed as purveyors of childish superstition with no message for an adult people. Since the chord which they strike is fundamental, there is surely no absurdity in their notion of a superior Being striking it in order to rouse some chosen soul. They do not *ipso facto* discredit themselves.

The divine Speaker in the fire, so strangely and peremptorily presented . . . who is he?

For Jewish and Christian orthodoxy he is the One True God of monotheism, and the speech unfolds the will of the Creator himself. However, it is proper to ask whether Moses saw him in that light, and what theological level the folk of the Exodus actually attained. Their leader brought them a new deity, or rather a new revelation of an old and partly-forgotten one. But was he perhaps only a tribal deity still, a fierce little tutelary spirit not so different from any other idol of city or clan? This of course is the liberal progressive view. Its upholders allege that a minor God of Moses evolved slowly through about half a millennium into the exalted God of the Prophets, and that the Pentateuch, which does affirm monotheism, was put together in retrospect under their influence. Moses was thereby turned into the first and greatest of them, a mouthpiece for teachings which were not his.

While the theory in this extreme form has lost ground, to some extent it is attractive. The Old Testament books do show progress, especially in ethics. It is not a question of religious orthodoxy or otherwise. God might have appeared early in a way which primitive people could understand, and then have guided their development. The question is purely of historical fact—how the God of Israel really was pictured when he presided over the Exodus.

Provisionally assuming his crudity and evolution, let us see if we can reconstruct him, or it.

Difficulties arise at once. To begin with, if this growth of God occurred, it was not simply one instance of a familiar or classifiable process. It was unique. Anthropology utterly explodes the notion that ancient Man normally made a linear progress from polytheism to monotheism or from small gods to great ones. Hebraic monotheism has very few parallels of even a superficial kind, and these did not "evolve." The Pharaoh Akhnaton's famous cult of the sun-disc was the fad of an eccentric ruler, wholly against the grain for his subjects, who forgot it as soon as he was dead. A supposed growth of the God of Israel cannot be taken for granted as if the word "evolution" explained everything.

Exclusiveness might seem a promising clue. Certainly this God was always jealous and possessive. Was he then distinguished from other gods in the sense that his spokesmen tried from the beginning to suppress those gods in the minds of the laity, and sublimated him at last into a Supreme Being who did blot out the rest and stand alone? Perhaps; but this is still no solution. Many gods of the ancient world were exclusive. Among the Greeks each city had its own, and visiting strangers were sometimes forbidden to join in their ceremonies. But the meaning of this exclusiveness was merely that each local divine protector had his own citizenry, his own jurisdiction. Their spheres were allocated. None of them was exclusive against other gods. Few even began to grow toward monotheistic status.

To judge from history, a god thus restricted to a place or a group will not ordinarily be aggressive and devouring, he will be (if anything) weak and expendable. When the non-Hebrew mind did press toward monotheism, what usually happened was not that one of the local gods annihilated his rivals, but that all the local gods were made out to be different manifestations of universal ones. In Egypt, Ammon became Jupiter-Ammon; in Britain, the Celtic godlets Belatucadrus, Rigisamus and Cocidius were all revalued as aspects of Mars. Few of the small gods anywhere grew into great ones, and no god at all, not even the mighty Vishnu, grew in the sense of gradually squeezing out others to reign alone. So the supposed evolution of Israel's God remains a puzzle.

Apart from all this, there is the further difficulty of picturing what he was before he started evolving. If a tribal fetish, what sort of fetish? No biblical strata, not even the oldest and most barbarous, preserve this God-in-embryo for us. He has to be fitted together like a dinosaur from fossil scraps of alleged evidence, and he has in fact been fitted together in several different shapes. One reconstruction makes him a djinn inhabiting a volcano. Another makes him a spirit of the storm. Admittedly God is portrayed in *Exodus* and elsewhere with the kind of physical imagery that would have struck Hebrew imaginations: fire, smoke, tempest, rain. The elements attend and obey him, wind fulfils his word, and so forth. But he is never baldly and unambiguously a god of the wind or any other element. If he cannot be pinned down by attributes, can he be pinned down by area? Was he a god of the Midianites or, as they are called elsewhere, Kenites with whom Moses lived during his exile? Was he the genius of a particular spot: Kadesh, as some have argued? Again there is no sign that he was ever *only* such a thing, and if he was, it is odd that the later Israelites never came back to pay their respects.

These efforts to whittle the God of Moses down have led always to unconvincing results. Doubtless early material that would have borne one of them out could have been re-written or expurgated before the biblical canon was fixed. The point is, however, that none can be proved or even strongly supported from the text as it stands. They are strictly speculative, and they tend to cancel each other. The most that can be allowed is that the Old Testament does speak of many entities called "gods," and that there are traces of a territorial limitation of some sort on Israel's God himself. But both facts, as we shall see, are open to several interpretations.

Failing other clues, the wise course is to turn back to *Exodus* and observe further how God is represented to Moses.

Then Moses said to God, "If I come to the people of Israel and say to them, 'The God of your fathers has sent me to you,' and they ask me, 'What is his name?' what shall I say to them?"

God said to Moses, "I AM WHO AM." And he said, "Say this to the people of Israel, 'I AM' has sent me to you."

By English standards the first phrase is somewhat indefinite. It can mean "I am wont to be what I am wont to be" or "I will be what I will be." God, at all events, is here expounding the name YHWH by which he is habitually known in the Old Testament; the name translated "the Lord."

This was pronounced "Yahweh" ("Jehovah" is a late Christian corruption) and was regarded as the true Name, the sacred Tetragrammaton, all others being substitutes or periphrases. It was sometimes shortened to "Yahu" and may have been adapted from an older divine name; a Canaanite cuneiform tablet long prior to Moses has "Yahu" scratched on it. The Israelites, however, transformed its meaning. At first they used it freely. It occurs as a Palestinian place-name from the thirteenth century B.C. Later its holiness made utterance unlawful, except at a few solemn ceremonies. As "Yahweh" it is certainly derived from a verb, and Jewish

tradition follows *Exodus* in connecting it with the verb "to be."
"Yahweh" is supposedly a special, perhaps archaic way of saying
"He Is," which the *Exodus* writer puts into the first person when
God is the speaker. Another interpretation is "He Causes To Be."
Given the stress on activity which marked the Hebrew language,
there need not be much difference. "To be" is to be positively there,
to produce effects.

The last point is of some importance, because of the objection
that "He Is" does not sound right for the people and the period.
It seems too close to academic philosophy. In keeping with the
progressive view, attempts have been made to show that "Yahweh"
originally stood for a narrower and more naïve concept. The God
of Israel has been explained as "He Blows" (i.e. sends the wind),
"He Makes Fall" (i.e. the rain, or, perhaps, Israel's enemies), and
several other things, with the fallacious refinement "He Is" coming
in as a priestly afterthought. These guesses depend on doubtful
etymology, and the fact that they are all equally good—or bad—
tells against the acceptance of any one. True, the formula "He Is"
savours of medieval debates about self-existence and the ontological
argument, wholly foreign to the Pentateuch. But its application by
schoolmen to an abstract Pure Essence does not preclude its having
once had a more urgent meaning.

Exodus does imply that. The Being who talks to Moses is not
a metaphysical wraith in a void. He "is" in an active sense, expressing and manifesting himself according to his own will. To repeat
"He Is" with a full, strong, meditative stress on the verb is to appreciate the power of the phrase. Yahweh is an inescapable Presence
blazing alone like the desert sun. You cannot get away from him,
or reckon without him, because he is always there. Fly to any
distance of space or time, reach back in imagination to the silence
before the world was made, and still . . . there he is, relentlessly
asserting his own majesty, self-sufficient and inextinguishable.

There is no reason why the primitive Israelites should not have
had such a deity. The nearest thing to an independent parallel
occurs in the religion of an Australian tribe more primitive still.

But to allow that they could have is not to swing over to a mistake made by Renan, and infer that the idea of Yahweh grew by a natural process out of the sun-drenched simplicity of life in a wilderness. Desert peoples in general were grossly polytheistic. They never discovered the path on which Moses set Israel; they never even turned towards it, except belatedly under Israel's influence. To protest that the path is obvious, or that the definition of Yahweh is a truism, is only to betray the extent of that influence on ourselves. Because of our biblical inheritance we think of God as necessarily something like this, the Eternal, no less. But the pagans outside Israel did not think in that way by any means. Comparison of Yahweh with his divine rivals reveals a distinctive set of ideas even at the oldest levels.

To trace Moses further is to begin to see the contrast.

3

Disclosure of the Name does not end the interview. For Moses, his commission to go back to Egypt and arrange with Pharaoh for the Hebrews' release is distressing in the last degree. He argues. This motif of contention with heaven, of a relation of striving rather than meek submission, is to be characteristic of Israel. Moses urges that the Israelites may not believe him; the Lord pledges miracles in support, and works two on the spot. Then Moses pleads that he lacks eloquence; the Lord tells him to use his brother Aaron as deputy and spokesman. Moses acquiesces, though without saying so. He walks away from the mountain in thunderstruck silence. Not, however, away from Yahweh. The Voice henceforth is with him inwardly wherever he goes, ordering and explaining and commenting.

Meanwhile there have been changes in Egypt. A new Pharaoh is on the throne (presumably Rameses II) and the lapse of time has removed any risk of Moses' arrest for murder. He returns to collect Zipporah and his sons, and they set off. At an inn on the way "the Lord met him and sought to kill him," because he had neglected to circumcise one of the boys in keeping with Hebrew custom. As to how the assault is to be pictured, we are given no clue. Zipporah performs the operation and the journey continues.

Aaron comes to meet them, and accepts his charge. On arrival in Goshen they summon the Hebrew elders and tell them of the Lord, of his special care for the Israelite people, and his intention of bringing them back to Canaan where their ancestors lived. The elders—for the moment—believe. The First Zionism is launched, though with more emphasis on escaping from Egypt than on going anywhere in particular. While it may be questioned whether "Zionism" is a fair translation of any term actually found in Scripture, we shall see to what an extent the facts justify it, and are illuminated by using it.

Moses, accompanied by Aaron, obtains an audience at court. Nothing is said as to how he manages this, but we may reasonably assume the good offices of his foster-mother, the new Pharaoh's sister. He presents Pharaoh with the Lord's demand as he has been instructed to state it. The careful reader will notice a curious feature in this and all subsequent exchanges between them. Their negotiation is never at any stage a genuine discussion of the real issue. Both of them are puppets deviously manipulated from above. Moses does not ask leave for the sojourners of Goshen to return to Canaan, he asks that they be allowed to travel three days' journey into the wilderness to sacrifice to the Lord. This modest request looks like a device to get Pharaoh talking with a view to winning his consent and tricking him later. But that never happens. Pharaoh does not talk—at least not coherently. He zigzags through a series of vacillations and "hardenings of the heart" explicitly stated to be caused by the Lord, who is the true sovereign of this affair, guiding it from a higher level toward a goal which becomes terrifyingly apparent.

Pharaoh, who has never heard of the deity mentioned, rejects the first petition. He accuses Moses of distracting the Israelites from their work, and gives his taskmasters the notorious order that the brick-makers at the cities of "Pithom" and "Raamses" must gather their own straw and still produce the same number of bricks; a measure intended to keep them out of mischief. Moses becomes heartily unpopular with them, and can no longer get a hearing.

Thus far we are more or less in contact with external evidences. The reversal of fortune which leads to Israel's deliverance is another matter. The only non-biblical account of it is a version written a thousand years later by an Egyptian priest, Manetho, as part of a long survey of Egypt's history. This (understandably) is a retort to the Bible, and claims that the Egyptian government drove the Israelites out when they became diseased. But Manetho, where he can be checked, is most unreliable. He helps to establish that the Exodus happened, because, if his researches had given him any cause to suspect that it had not, he would surely have denounced it as an invention, rather than go to the trouble of composing a weak and verbose parody of it. However, he is no use here as an historian. We can only proceed along the biblical track.

Moses and Aaron are now commanded by the Lord to give signs of his power. They start with a very small miracle, one of those promised on Mount Horeb. Aaron flings down a rod in Pharaoh's presence and it turns into a snake. Pharaoh is not impressed; he produces magicians who do the same. Then Aaron, with a more grandiose gesture, whirls his rod over the surface of the Nile, and the water changes into blood. Again the magicians manage to do a similar trick. A week or so later, masses of frogs overrun the land. Still the proof is inconclusive; the magicians' arts attract other masses of frogs, and Moses has to appeal instead to the frogs' dying when he gives the word. However, more prodigies ensue, in a quickening tempo and in the same style of public calamity as the fouling of the water and the frog invasion. Whereas these two plagues were predominantly demonstrations, the rest are predominantly afflictions, designed to make the Egyptians wretched and wear down resistance. There is a logical progress in them. When swarms of gnats settle on man and beast, the magicians admit defeat. They cannot copy this effect. Next come swarms of flies, but the land of Goshen is exempt—the first clear sign of a special providence at work. The fifth plague passes from the troublesome to the fatal; it is a disease which kills livestock, again sparing the Israelites. Boils, hail, locusts and darkness follow.

These chapters supply a brilliant example of the way in which biblical history transfigures events in order to impress their meaning. Egypt's plagues are too realistically Egyptian to be pure fiction. The reddening of the water is due to a micro-organism. The various insects and epidemics are nearly all plausible, especially at the end of the Nile inundation. Yet the series is not likely, humanly speaking, to have occurred in quite this manner. As the literal basis we might almost accept Winwood Reade's rationalisation: that whenever there was a public disaster Moses ascribed it to the wrath of his deity, and a run of bad luck played into his hands. But to stop here is to miss the impulsion of the tale, the titanic issues latent in it, the epochal nature of the clash. Precisely by dramatising, by systematising, by working up a sense of purpose and climax through a ding-dong battle, the authors of *Exodus* convey these things and thereby give us history which the rationaliser lets slip.[2]

During the plagues Moses pursues his equivocal bargaining with Pharaoh, who talks sometimes of concessions, but withdraws his words as soon as the current plague is over. The Lord, as promised, is hardening Pharaoh's heart, and his aim is to avert any feeble compromise. Here also the movement is progressive, not simply oscillatory. Though the hints are always revoked, they become more generous in tone. Step by step the Egyptian does retreat. He tries saying, "Sacrifice inside Egypt." Then he says the Israelites can go into the wilderness, but not far. When Moses threatens him with the locusts, he offers, on the advice of his counsellors, to let the men go; their women and children must stay behind. Moses of course refuses. The plague of darkness

2 I first realised that traditional Jewish religion is not Fundamentalist when an Orthodox acquaintance dismissed the Egyptian plagues airily as simply the author's "De Mille effects," and seemed surprised that anyone should think them a problem.

reduces the acknowledged gap between them still further. Pharaoh asks only that the flocks and herds stay in Egypt. But Moses is inflexible. "Then Pharaoh said to him, 'Get away from me; never see my face again; for in the day you see my face you shall die '." (x:28)

The negotiation seems to have collapsed on the brink of success. But in any case it was hardly more than a feint. The Lord's real object is to make the triumph as spectacular and crushing as possible, and ensure that the Egyptians will not only want the Israelites to go but never want them to return. He has one more plague in reserve, a tenth. "About midnight I will go forth in the midst of Egypt; and all the first-born in the land of Egypt shall die." The Israelites are to smear their doorposts with the blood of slain lambs, and then death will pass over them.

In Jewish ceremony the annual recollection of this last night is the chief and archetypal instance of ritual story-telling, the chief act of memory. Frazer considered that the one certain thing about the Passover was that it had its origin in a massacre. On the other hand, the actual commemoration always had much in common with the ancient spring-festival of the Near East. The Israelites' connection of the massacre with the festival was due perhaps to nothing deeper than a coincidence of date. But the point is that in adapting the festival they transformed it. A theme based on the impersonal cycle of Nature gave way to a theme based on a single awe-inspiring occurrence in the life of the people. Thus it acquired a fresh meaning, a fresh moral, as a perpetual reminder of the Lord's justice and of Man's right to liberty. We have not heard the last of this principle of transformation in Israel.

For the moment it is enough to record the end of the struggle, whatever construction we choose to place upon it:

At midnight the Lord smote all the first-born in the land of Egypt, from the first-born of Pharaoh who sat on his throne to the first-born of the captive who was in the dungeon, and all the first-born of the cattle.

And Pharaoh rose up in the night, he, and all his servants,

and all the Egyptians; and there was a great cry in Egypt, for there was not a house where one was not dead.

And he summoned Moses and Aaron by night, and said, "Rise up, go forth from among my people, both you and the people of Israel; and go, serve the Lord, as you have said."   (xii:29-31)

4

Throughout this duel there has been no conflict whatever between Yahweh and the Egyptian gods. Pharaoh produces wizards, not priests. The mighty pantheon which we know to have existed—Ptah, Anubis and the rest—never takes the field at all. In one verse of doubtful interpretation (xii:12) the Lord speaks of executing judgment upon the gods of Egypt, but they have not taken an active part against Moses as the gods of Troy fight against Agamemnon. They are negligible.

This absence must be construed theologically. The whole tradition is moulded by the teaching of Moses himself, and with Moses the huge intellectual step from "the gods" to "God" has already been taken.[3]

The question whether Moses was numerically a monotheist is not the main issue. Dim notions of a High God, not alone but supreme over all others, seem to have been current during the Bronze Age over a large part of the Near East. The currency of such ideas might have helped Israel in formulating its own; and since, everywhere else in the Near East, the vision afterwards faded and lay dormant, this possibility favours an early rather than late date for Israelite monotheism in some sense. However, it neither explains it nor sheds much light upon it. The innovation was not a mere reduction in the number of gods, but a radical change of concept.

3 I have based this section mainly on Yehezkel Kaufmann, whose concept of the "metadivine" is the key to the difference between the God of Israel and all other deities.

Yahweh IS . . . but the gods of paganism?

In the first place, they are never defined by "being" but by limitation. Their characters arise from attributes which narrow them down. They are associated with special things: sun and moon, natural phenomena, mountains and islands. While above us in power, they are not unlike in essence. The distinction is blurred. Thus various heroes of Greek myth are the offspring of gods and mortal women, or of goddesses and mortal men. One of them, Hercules, is promoted to Olympian rank by apotheosis. Again, many nations have regarded their kings as divine; while the Hindu doctrine of metempsychosis declares that men may be reborn as gods, or gods as men.

The gods are pictured mythologically. They have life-stories and life-cycles. They are sexually begotten; they are born; they have family relationships; they are acted upon by other gods and by impersonal forces (Tammuz and many more are wounded and slain); they fight among themselves (as in the Trojan War and the upheavals of pre-conquest Mexico), or against previous divine generations (as the Olympians fought the Titans), or against independent daemonic beings (such as the giants of Nordic myth, or the dragons of Babylonian). They can go to sleep (as Zeus is made to do in the *Iliad*); they can decline (as in the Gotterdämmerung) and even die. When a missionary spoke to an Eskimo about the God who made the world, the Eskimo remarked that that one must have died a long while ago.

But still more significant than the gods' limited and mutable nature is the reason for it. Essentially there is only one reason, which distinguishes them all from Yahweh. You could not make up the God of Israel even by combining them, because no pagan deity anywhere is ultimate.

Every god is rooted in an impersonal Something transcending him, a "metadivine" order which is not itself a god. These divine beings invariably have a background. Therefore they are contingent, subordinate. The background may be conceived in several ways—as Primal Matter, the Universe, the Nature of Things; but as the uncreated context of gods and men, it eternally exists. Paganism always affirms that-which-is, never he-who-is.

Geography may be prior to the gods. Zeus is born in a Crete which was there before him. Creation-myths attempt to go back behind the world, yet a pagan creator never makes the world out of nothing with an imperial "let there be." He shapes pre-existing materials that come to his hand, or begets creatures upon a pre-existing female in a pre-existing environment. Even in the highest pagan religions you can always go past the gods to the more fundamental Something. The priests of Memphis, who experimented with monotheism in Egypt, held that Ptah made all things according to his own desires. But they thought of the primordial abyss, Nun, as prior to him, and thought of Ptah himself as more like an energy in Nature than a divinity outside it. Zoroaster, again, spoke of Ahura Mazdah as creating by his own mind. But the act took place within a sort of eternal and pre-ordained polarity of Right and Wrong, Truth and the Lie, which affected the whole structure of creation. In Hinduism, the One Reality Brahman may be regarded as a Supreme God in its "lower" aspect, but the "higher" Brahman is . . . other. Buddhism takes a similar view. Indian thought in general insists that the spiritual explorer must press beyond gods to a point where he can only murmur "Not so, not so."

To the pagan mind, gods as well as men are always *inside* something, a system. This controls them negatively by imposing rules which they cannot break and boundaries which they cannot cross, *fas et nefas*. It may also control them positively, steering their destinies. In the latter case such ideas as Fate and Cause, Law and Necessity are potent. The universe, very often, is made out to be cyclic, in keeping with the rotation of skies and seasons. A fixed series of ages returns upon itself and cancels itself. Life passes through endless futile destruction and renewal. The gods themselves are bound to the wheel. They do not make things happen in any coherent sequence or with any finality.

In contrast with all these deities, hemmed in by alien powers and entangled in webs of myth and doom, the God of Israel as he appears throughout the Old Testament is absolute. We cannot dig down anywhere to a primitive Yahweh who is *a* god in pagan terms. Yahweh stands above the world and distinct from it, freely determining events that occur in it. While he intervenes in the system below, he is not enclosed in any system above. He has no metadivine background and he is subject to no necessity.[4] He never undergoes mythological treatment. There is no account of his birth, no theogony; he is simply there. He has no life-history, he is never coerced by Fate or by other gods, no predestined succession of ages or cycles sweeps him along. He goes through no phases; his "changes" such as repentance arise from the exercise of his own judgment. He has no family or sex-relations. The gulf between himself and other beings cannot be bridged—no image can represent him, no apotheosis can put a man on a level with him, no ritual can make a king divine in the same sense. Yahweh is a solitary supreme Will.

And this view of him is constant. Granted, Israel advances in moral insight, in exaltation of ideas. Still there is nothing to show that its God evolved from *a* god, or could have done so. Moses may not have taught strict monotheism. Nevertheless he arrived, by an unanalysable leap, at a concept which could not fail to become so when clarified. While other so-called gods might exist, the glare of Yahweh shrivelled them up. They did not count and they could not contend with him. The Lord is variously portrayed in the Old Testament, sometimes childishly, sometimes magnificently. But always and everywhere, he is *the only Higher Power that matters.*

5

The Hebrews of Goshen packed and left. *Exodus* gives a tantalising hint (xii:38) that other subjects of Pharaoh took advantage of his

4 Louis Finkelstein (*The Jews*, p. 1749) quotes a rabbinical saying: "In God is the universe fixed, not he in it."

surrender to slip out of Egypt with them, but the hint is not followed up. The alleged number of Israelites (about 600,000 men, besides women and children) is far too large, and quite incompatible with an earlier statement that they were all served by two midwives —a statement which is probably well-founded, since the midwives' names, Shiphrah and Puah, are genuine Semitic names that occur elsewhere. The inflated number may be due to a simple misunderstanding. The word which has come through as "thousand" may originally have meant "tent" or "family." If so, the actual total was at most five or six thousand, and the entire movement so petty, quantitatively speaking, that its absence from known Egyptian records is no problem—especially in view of the rather humiliating circumstances. The slaves would not have had much in the way of a baggage train; they are said, however, to have carried off some valuables more or less extorted from the Egyptians. Also, the hallowed bones of Joseph, the ancestor who had arranged their settlement in Goshen, were reverently borne along in the caravan.

Assembling under the hateful walls of the city of Rameses, they set out on the first stage of their migration. They did not take the direct route toward their forefathers' country. For Moses it was the Lord's will that he should lead them south-eastward into Sinai, to the mountains where he had received his commission. Here he was to enrol them in Yahweh's service. Whether or not they grasped his aim, they had little choice. Their beasts of burden were asses, not camels, and could not survive a long trek between oases. Only the roundabout route into the angle of the isthmus held out any prospect of finding water-sources at short enough intervals. Also they had to pasture their flocks and herds.

Their march soon brought them to the edge of what is popularly supposed to have been the Red Sea. The biblical text, however, is dubious, and this body of water was more likely the shallow "sea of reeds" or Papyrus Lake on the Suez Canal route. As they encamped on the shore, a frightening report came in. Pharaoh had regretted his weakness, a military force was rushing to intercept them.

The people of Israel lifted up their eyes, and behold, the Egyptians were marching after them; and they were in great fear. And the people of Israel cried out to the Lord;

And they said to Moses, "Is it because there are no graves in Egypt that you have taken us away to die in the wilderness? What have you done to us, in bringing us out of Egypt?" . . .

And Moses said to the people, "Fear not, stand firm, and see the salvation of the Lord, which he will work for you to-day; for the Egyptians whom you see to-day, you shall never see again." (xiv:10-13)

Night fell, and a fog rolled between the pursued and the pursuers. For hours all was in suspense.

Then Moses stretched out his hand over the sea; and the Lord drove the sea back by a strong east wind all night, and made the sea dry land, and the waters were divided.

And the people of Israel went into the midst of the sea on dry ground, the waters being a wall to them on their right hand and on their left.

The Egyptians pursued, and went in after them into the midst of the sea, all Pharaoh's horses, his chariots, and his horsemen. . . .

Then the Lord said to Moses, "Stretch out your hand over the sea, that the water may come back upon the Egyptians, upon their chariots, and upon their horsemen."

So Moses stretched forth his hand over the sea, and the sea returned to its wonted flow when the morning appeared; and the Egyptians fled into it, and the Lord routed the Egyptians in the midst of the sea.

The waters returned and covered the chariots and the horsemen and all the host of Pharaoh that had followed them into the sea. . . .

Thus the Lord saved Israel that day from the hand of the Egyptians; and Israel saw the Egyptians dead upon the seashore. (xiv:21-30)

Given the shallows, the great wind suddenly shifting, confusion in the half-light, a stupid Egyptian commander who did not reflect that his chariots would become bogged . . . in essence it is credible. A ford which could be passed on foot when the wind pushed the water the right way could have become a trap for heavy wheeled vehicles when it changed, and panic and trampling might account for the rest. The marvel is not so much the thing's happening as its happening at the moment of need; and the effect is instant and overwhelming. "Israel saw the great work which the Lord did against the Egyptians, and the people feared the Lord; and they believed in the Lord and in his servant Moses." (xiv:31)

And here we touch the very root of the Bible. Joy burst out spontaneously in a song. Like a Negro spiritual, like a work-song, it virtually composed itself. Moses and Aaron had a sister Miriam, and she took a tambourine in her hand and sang, while the women followed dancing:

"Sing to the Lord, for he has triumphed gloriously;
The horse and rider he has thrown into the sea."

(xv:21)

This is probably the oldest verse in the Bible, and contemporary. It actually is what Miriam sang.[5]

Israel's faith was born in an act of logic. As we shall see, this was the first such act in a series. A question was irresistibly posed:

How did we escape from Egypt?

The climactic wonder of the crossing settled what the answer must be:

We were delivered by miracles. No man, not even a magician, could have worked them. They were performed by Yahweh, the God of Moses. Plainly he is the Supreme Power ruling over events . . . at least as they concern us.

---

5 The Egyptians had no cavalry, but "rider" can mean "chariot-rider." See Vaux, *Ancient Israel*, p. 224.

CHAPTER THREE

COVENANT AND CONQUEST

With the Gulf of Suez on its right, the procession plodded south-eastward into the isthmus. An Amalekite tribe which was already roaming there tried to block its advance, but after defeat in a pitched battle the enemy survivors withdrew. Thereafter, despite the scale of their intrusion, the Israelites were left alone. *Exodus* glorifies their march with more wonders like the plagues of Egypt. The Lord went before them in a pillar of cloud by day and a pillar of fire by night. When they were hungry, he sent a flock of quails, and then rained "manna" on them in sweet white flakes—a gift which need not be taken as altogether miraculous: manna is a gum exuded by the twigs of the evergreen tamarisk. Again, when they were parched with thirst, he told Moses to strike the rock with his staff, whereupon water gushed out. That too is a phenomenon not unknown in Sinai, where the fracture of a limestone cliff-face may occasionally uncover a spring.

Moses had learnt the supreme art of leadership, but he had yet to learn the ancillary arts of management. He found himself overwhelmed with business. The people, fresh from slavery and unfitted to make their own decisions, brought him endless disputes to be arbitrated. It was a weary man who greeted his father-in-law Jethro as they neared Jethro's country. The old sheikh listened with interest and delight to the tale of Israel's escape. Then he gave Moses some sound advice, rightly singled out by the American authorities Mooney and Reilly in their history of administration. He taught him to delegate.

Moses gave heed to the voice of his father-in-law and did all that he had said.

Moses chose able men out of all Israel, and made them heads over the people, rulers of thousands, of hundreds, of fifties, and of tens.

And they judged the people at all times; hard cases they brought to Moses, but any small matter they decided themselves. (*Exodus* xviii:24-26)

Freed from the treadmill of routine, Moses led the tribes on and on into the wilderness where he had been before. They passed through lonely storm-swept regions of rock, of bluish granite and purple porphyry, scarred here and there by man-made workings, where miners in Egyptian employ had extracted copper and malachite and gems. After two or three months of journeying they pitched camp at last near the foot of the mountains where Moses had heard the Voice. It was time for them to do what Moses had spoken of to Pharaoh—worship Yahweh in the desert. But few Israelites foresaw what this worship would entail, or how they were to be made a nation.

What follows in the narrative is the centre of the whole faith of Israel. It is a weird, almost surrealist story, unforgettable yet hard to bring into focus. For the crucial parts of it there are no fitting words but the Bible's own, in *Exodus* xix and xx. First:

Moses went up to God, and the Lord called to him out of the mountain, saying, "Thus you shall say to the house of Jacob, and tell the people of Israel:

You have seen what I did to the Egyptians, and how I bore you on eagles' wings and brought you to myself.

Now therefore, if you will obey my voice and keep my covenant, you shall be my own possession among all peoples; for all the earth is mine.

And you shall be to me a kingdom of priests and a holy nation. These are the words which you shall speak to the children of Israel."

Moses retraced his steps and summoned the elders. After listening they answered unanimously: "All that the Lord has spoken we will do." He took the message back to the Lord, who replied that the people must now be ceremonially cleansed. On the third day he would appear to them. Moses must lead them to the base of the mountain, but not up it, on pain of death.

On the morning of the third day there were thunders and lightnings, and a thick cloud upon the mountain, and a very loud trumpet blast, so that all the people who were in the camp trembled.

Then Moses brought the people out of the camp to meet God; and they took their stand at the foot of the mountain.

And Mount Sinai was wrapped in smoke, because the Lord descended upon it in fire; and the smoke of it went up like the smoke of a kiln, and the whole mountain quaked greatly.

And as the sound of the trumpet grew louder and louder, Moses spoke, and God answered him in thunder.

And the Lord came down upon Mount Sinai, to the top of the mountain; and the Lord called Moses to the top of the mountain, and Moses went up.

And the Lord said to Moses, "Go down and warn the people, lest they break through to the Lord to gaze and many of them perish."

The warning given, Moses fetched Aaron, and the brothers ascended unaccompanied. But before they had gone far up the slope, the Voice halted them.

God spoke all these words, saying,

"I am the Lord your God, who brought you out of the land of Egypt, out of the house of bondage.

You shall have no other gods before me . . ."

And so through the Ten Commandments.

Let us set aside for a moment all speculation as to what happened, and simply try to conceive what the impact of such words would have been. In the retrospect of three thousand years they may sound platitudinous. Would the Eternal have begun by reeling off a string of copy-book maxims about respect for one's parents and abstention from theft? But that feeling is the measure of the spiritual change which Sinai itself has caused. To the Israelites, or almost anyone alive then, a God who spoke thus would have been a soul-racking novelty. They might have expected Yahweh to give instructions for some improved magical ritual to make their flocks flourish. They might even have expected him to add a few incidental hints about the right conduct to go with it. But to strike brutally and repeatedly and exclusively at their moral habits, and invest these with cosmic value! to imply that the echo of that thunder would pursue them through every twist and turn of day-to-day living! "All that the Lord has spoken we will do" . . . what was this burden they had so carelessly agreed to shoulder?

Even when the tenth Commandment was finished, and the anathema against covetousness pronounced, no respite came. The nightmare grew more appalling.

> When all the people perceived the thunderings and the
> lightnings and the sound of the trumpet and the mountain
> smoking, the people were afraid and trembled; and they
> stood afar off,
>
> And said to Moses, "You speak to us, and we will hear;
> but let not God speak to us, lest we die."
>
> And Moses said to the people, "Do not fear; for God
> has come to prove you, and that the fear of him may be
> before your eyes, that you may not sin."
>
> And the people stood afar off, while Moses drew near
> to the thick darkness where God was.

It must be stressed at once that no other literature contains anything like the Sinaitic encounter. Fear is its ruling characteristic, but a holy and purging fear that casts out lesser fears. Yahweh himself is so overpowering that all ordinary perils look faint and feeble; the only terror in the world is the divine wrath. The description suggests a volcano, and further on we are informed that "the appearance of the glory of the Lord was like a devouring fire on the top of the mountain." No volcanoes were then active in the isthmus of Sinai. Arabia had a few on the far side of the Gulf of Aqaba, and it has been suggested that some at least of the Israelites wandered farther afield than the Bible indicates, the name "Sinai" being an indefinite regional term that has narrowed since. Another suggestion, perhaps less drastic, is that the authors of *Exodus* used eruptive imagery to symbolise the violence of God's bursting into the world from beyond. But the passage scarcely has an air of mere poetic contrivance. It is too passionately graphic. Among the Greeks, Aeschylus himself failed to make anything like this out of Etna.

The passage records a tremendous experience of some sort; but what? One strange feature is the combination of extreme vividness with extreme vagueness. Even apart from guesswork about Arabia, it is quite impossible to be sure where the biblical "Mount Sinai" was, and what was its relation to "Horeb" where Moses saw the burning bush. Not only is the location uncertain, it seems to have become uncertain to the Hebrews themselves, after they settled in Canaan. Moreover they were not interested. In spite of their looking to Sinai as a sacred point of origin, we have no scrap of evidence that they ever made pilgrimages there, or maintained a shrine there, or took notice of the mountain in any way after they had left it. In all the rest of the Bible only one Israelite goes back to that region, the prophet Elijah, and he goes as a hunted exile. It has actually been surmised that the adventure at Sinai did not happen to Moses' expedition at all, but to some other body of Hebrew ancestors coming from a different quarter altogether. If so, the mystery is still more mysterious. A tremendous joint experience, conveyed by tremendous imagery, and so alien that it is afterwards left alone like a dream, unreverted to: we can hardly be more precise. Rabbinic commentators have dropped curious negative hints. "It need not be insisted that God was present through a literal sensory phenomenon . . . All Israel stood before Sinai, only Moses heard the Voice."

As for the specific Commandments of the Decalogue, they define Yahweh's nature and lay the basis for all that comes after. Their style, in Hebrew, is curt and telegraphic. They establish that

Yahweh is "the only Higher Power that matters." Other gods are worthless. The moral precepts forbidding murder, adultery and so forth summarise the ethical norms of mankind and are not unique. What the Lord does is to set his seal on them, and make it clear that their observance concerns him. Separate from these and in a class by itself is the command to keep the Sabbath. This is unparalleled. Israel, alone in the world, is to have a day of recollection at short regular intervals to forget work and remember God.

But in the torment of revelation at Sinai, no reminders are needed. The people shrink back, and Moses climbs toward the terrible cloud. God speaks to him again. However, the next series of utterances brings an anti-climax. The towering theophany is over, and we plunge into a section of *Exodus* (xxi-xxiii) where God's promised Covenant with Israel, the *b'rit*, is embodied in laws for the community. Before we grasp where we are, the Lord is heard giving rules about slave-holding and burglary and assault. The bathos is purely literary, perhaps even scribal. It is very proper that the application of the Decalogue should be worked out in more detail, and a few lines of preface would have bridged the gap. But they are not supplied, or else they have dropped out. For an instant (no more than an instant) a reader may recall Kipling's story telling how an Indian sorcerer raised a spirit most uncannily and convincingly, and how the spell was then broken by the spirit demanding that the sorcerer's fee be raised.

To ask how much of this "Book of the Covenant"—or indeed, how much of the Decalogue itself—has come down to us literally from Moses, is to ask an almost futile question. There seems no reason to doubt that he did teach the Ten Commandments, in whatever way they were given to him, but no one knows whether he taught them in this order or in this wording. The Covenant-Book in its present form is no older than the ninth century B.C., but Moses may well have given prophetic sanction to a previous version. Comparison with other codes of the ancient Near East suggests that it is a digest of a Hebrew text on the same lines as the codes of Hammurabi, the Hittites, and the Assyrians. These all belong to the second pre-Christian millennium, but they are more sophisticated. The Hebrew is simpler and makes no provision for urban life. One would guess that its original was, if anything, earlier rather than later.

Analysis in relation to the non-Hebrew legal documents uncovers points of likeness and points of divergence. For example, the Covenant when spelt out in full has an interesting kinship in structure to contemporary treaties. Two types have been preserved and distinguished, parity-treaties between equal powers, and suzerainty-treaties between a protecting power and a vassal. Yahweh's Covenant belongs to the second type, especially in its Hittite form. Such a treaty begins with an identifying phrase, "Thus says the Great King." The monarch then enumerates his past acts of goodness. Next, the duties of the vassal are specified, sometimes with a veto on his forming other alliances. Provision is made for the filing of the treaty and its periodic re-reading. Blessings and curses are invoked according to whether the vassal honours it or breaks it. Yahweh, in his dealings with Israel, is shown behaving very much like a Great King.

As to the framing of the laws, some are conditional or casuistic ("If A happens, then B shall be done"), while some are direct orders. The casuistic laws follow the Near Eastern norm; Hammurabi's are like this. But the apodeictic—the direct orders, positive and negative—are more strictly Israelite and less easy to parallel, though again echoes can be caught in the Hittite treaties.

The cluster of laws in this basic Covenant-Book leads on to others, hundreds of them, scattered through the rest of the Pentateuch with frequent repetition and overlap. Mnemonic groupings suggest oral transmission. Fewer of these subsequent laws have the casuistic phrasing, and they bear, in general, a more deeply Israelite stamp. But throughout, the major contrast with foreign codes lies in the method of promulgation. From the Covenant-Book onward, the laws are all presented as dictated at various times by God to Moses, who transmits them to the tribes. Thus they all claim divine authority, mediated through Moses as the inspired Lawgiver of Israel. Many are far later than his time, and reflect the life of a settled agricultural nation, not a band of nomads. Yet it is hard to pick out strata, or draw lines between basic texts and interpolations. The laws that can be ascribed credibly to Moses in person lead on logically to the ones that are doubtful and to the ones that cannot. There are some awkward transitions, but no glaring discrepancies or changes of tone. Jewish tradition holds that Moses' teaching was developed afterwards by an unbroken succession of disciples and sages. If so, all the laws really are, in a sense, his.

Those which govern civil and economic relations are not very notable in themselves. Many of them resemble other ancient laws in content as well as form. Thus the *lex talionis*—"eye for eye, tooth for tooth"—occurs in the code of Hammurabi. The most striking feature of the entire series, perhaps, is an absence. Nothing is said about a king or any other despotic authority. Israel is to be the Lord's commonwealth. Israelites are to show mercy to the poor, protect the widow and orphan, and treat the slave justly and the stranger hospitably, because they themselves were slaves and strangers in Egypt. Such ideas have a potentiality of ethical progress which is lacking in the edicts of human monarchs.

Much is commanded about the cultus of Yahweh. He is to be worshipped by sacrificing unblemished beasts. Before Moses the idea of sacrifice was common enough throughout the East, but usually with a crude notion of physically feeding the gods. Israel's Law makes it emblematic, a stylised gesture of expiation or devotion. Idolatry is of course forbidden. So in general is the worship of other divine beings than Yahweh, however conceived; the only specific example is sacrificing to "satyrs," a species of demon. Impiety extends to witchcraft (a capital crime), and its avoidance is a likely motive behind various vetoes which do not look religious at all. Thus the well-known ban on seething a kid in its mother's milk probably has something to do with paganism. That motif recurs in a Greek text about an initiatory rite.

In fact the whole spirit of the code is religious, because all the laws branch out from the single Sinaitic purpose, the setting-apart of Israel as the Lord's pure and consecrated people. Where the death penalty is laid down for a crime, the aim is not so much punishment or vengeance as amputation; what matters is not the sinner but the holy community which his deeds threaten to poison. The special practices and ceremonies which have remained the mark of Orthodox Jews to this day must be regarded in the same light. They are not primarily concerned with health, though some of them, medically, do make good sense. Nor are they magical, though Israelite superstition may long have thought them so. Circumcision, the diet rules, and the rest, are parts of a huge complex ritual by which Israel must discipline itself to be different from the nations, to be separate. That theme pervades every passage. It accounts for some apparently grotesque laws against mixture, such as sowing a field with two kinds of seed, or wearing a garment made of two kinds of stuff.

The heart of this dedication to difference is the Covenant, the *b'rit.* Yahweh, by his own sovereign choice, has offered friendship to a certain body of people. Their acceptance binds them to him in unity of purpose. If they sin, he can withhold his favour. But there are genuinely two parties to the contract. In moments of crisis it is legitimate for a spokesman of Israel to remind the Lord of his Covenant, and urge that his own honour requires him to save his Chosen. Israel as a formally-defined entity has its origin in a religious event, not a political arrangement. Its members are all those and only those who have taken part in the event—they and their descendants, who were there potentially. The definition of a "descendant" can change, can become spiritual rather than hereditary, but the idea is constant. "All the generations of Israel were present at Sinai." The event not only determines them as a community, but determines them in keeping with its own nature. After Moses (not before) mankind is split by a cleavage between the true God and false gods, which corresponds to a cleavage between Israel and "the nations." Israel is, precisely, the solitary people that has come face to face with the true God, and this tragic privilege is the cause of the split.

God's choice is an historical act, and his commandments are embedded squarely in history. He grounds them on appeals to the past and the future, beginning in the Decalogue. "I am the Lord your God, *who brought you out of the land of Egypt.*" "Honour your father and your mother, *that your days may be long in the land which the Lord your God gives you.*" The latter verse affirms continuity. Honouring one's parents is the basis for tradition, hence for the perpetual memory and consciousness of God's dealings, with all that they imply for one's own generation and the next. And the first result of the divine choice is to be the planting of Israel in that Land which the commandment mentions, the Promised Land called Canaan, which will be Yahweh's sanctuary. There alone can the Covenant bear flower and fruit.

"Behold, I send an angel before you, to guard you on the way and to bring you to the place which I have prepared . . .

If you hearken attentively to his voice and do all that I say, then I will be an enemy to your enemies and an adversary to your adversaries . . .

I will drive them out before you, until you are increased and possess the land."

This programme is fundamental. It links Israel's spiritual character and territorial claim. No part of it can be left out, nor can the extent of its application be a matter for debate or dispute. The psychological meaning of Sinai must be firmly held on to. For the Hebrew mind as it emerges from these stresses, Israel is not a collection of individuals but a collective individual. In addressing his people Yahweh is portrayed shifting repeatedly from the plural "you" to the singular "thou"—they are interchangeable. Any single Israelite exists in a contingent way, as a member of the chosen community. Israel itself, however, exists in its own right as a complete unit, "a people dwelling alone, and not reckoning itself among the nations." If terms of modern jargon are excusable here, Israel after Sinai is a corporate "existentialist," finding vocation not in abstract rules but in an intense and illuminated awareness of what he is and how he has come to be so; a corporate "outsider," poignantly cut off from those round him by a shattering insight.

So the tribes accepted a future in Canaan. There was, indeed, nowhere else they could go. Some of those who knew the map hoped for a more splendid domain than was ever lastingly achieved. The ideal Land which they expected God to give them stretched from the Red Sea to the Euphrates, taking in the agreeable coastal strip along the Mediterranean.[1] They were disappointed, and so were their children and their children's children. It would be unjust, however, to picture Moses as luring his followers on with false dreams of empire. At Sinai a question was posed and answered, and with its answer the Israelites took a second logical step. They had already accepted their leader's explanation of the escape from Pharaoh. Now he carried them further.

Why did Yahweh deliver us from Egypt?

To bring us back to our ancestors' home, Canaan. The Covenant is a divine title-deed to the Land.

2

Between the Covenant's first announcement in outline and its augmentation with the rest of the laws, Scripture itself recognises a gap. After the first colloquy, we are told, Moses "wrote all the words of the Lord" (*Exodus* xxiv:4) and built an altar at the foot of the mountain. Sacrifice was offered, and he sprinkled the people with the victims' blood. He also read the Lord's words aloud to them. By reiterating their assent they ratified the Covenant.

1 The texts defining the Promised Land (*Genesis* xv:18, *Exodus* xxiii:31, *Deuteronomy* i:7 and xi:24) give frontiers which were never actually established. They mention the Euphrates, which is too far north, and they omit the trans-Jordan territory which Israel did in fact conquer. Hence they are unlikely to be late inventions; they go back to a prophecy of the Exodus period or earlier. See Kaufmann, *The Religion of Israel*, pp. 201-2.

When the ceremony was finished, Moses led his brother and seventy elders up the mountain, where they "saw the God of Israel" in a simultaneous vision. Then he dismissed them and waited to be called again.

The glory of the Lord settled on Mount Sinai, and the cloud covered it six days; and on the seventh day he called to Moses out of the midst of the cloud.

Now the appearance of the glory of the Lord was like a devouring fire on the top of the mountain in the sight of the people of Israel.

And Moses entered the cloud, and went up on the mountain. And Moses was on the mountain forty days and forty nights.

To be further instructed. He came down at last carrying two tablets of stone with the Commandments engraved on them. But he came down to an evil sight. The people had given him up for lost and besieged Aaron clamouring for a god, a visible god. Aaron had complied—he, the leader's own brother and assistant. Collecting a stack of golden ear-rings, he had melted them and made a calf. Moses descended the mountain on its festal day. The camp was full of singing and dancing and orgiastic excitement. Furious, he flung down the two stone tablets and broke them; then he ground the calf to powder, poured the powder into water, and made the worshippers drink it; then he summoned a party of his own tribe of Levi, the men most devoted to him, and ordered them to draw their weapons and cut down all the worst offenders.

The main point of this affair (which in substance looks perfectly and indeed depressingly authentic)[2] is that Israel was still far from understanding its prophet or his terrific God. Aaron's role confirms what archaeology would suggest, that the Calf was not meant as a fetish supplanting Yahweh, or even as a symbol, but as a pedestal or mount for Divinity. Aaron would not have set up a vulgar idol. For him, says Scripture (*Exodus* xxxii:5), the festival of the

---

2 At least to the extent that some sort of heresy occurred. The Calf itself may be a retrospective symbol; but see Vaux, *Ancient Israel*, pp. 333-4.

Calf was "a feast to the Lord." But even he was mistaken in fancying that he could attract the Presence with a sort of lightning-conductor, and the mass of tribesmen probably had no notion what he was talking about. The task of Moses, after restoring order and praying for the guilty, was to schematise his revelation so as to exclude such vagaries. The added commandments, and a regular cultic practice, were the natural sequel.

Moses as depicted giving these to Israel is subtly altered. His Lord, it appears, grew more remote and less accessible to anyone else. He himself was more completely alone when the awful confrontations took place. Even animals had to be kept away. Meanwhile the communion between them was becoming more familiar. Yahweh spoke to Moses "face to face, as a man speaks to his friend." Possibly the Levite purge had left Moses with few other friends. It had taken him far on the road to the loneliness of absolutism. After it he lived in a private ecstasy, returning from his next trip to the mountain with an unearthly change in his face, which he covered with a veil. He produced a duplicate pair of stone tablets to replace the first. Armed with these, and his new sets of divine precepts, he began to organise his people.

Israel's relationship to its God now found expression not only in laws but in institutions and concrete objects. Moses' tablets were put in an acacia-wood box called the Ark of the Covenant, about four feet by two by two. The Ark had rings on the sides, through which poles could be passed so that a couple of bearers could carry it in the manner of a litter or sedan chair. When the tribes resumed their march, the Ark went ahead with an advance party. When they pitched camp, it was housed with other cultic appurtenances in a portable temple, the Tabernacle. The Tabernacle was a huge tent of bright-coloured fabrics, blue and purple and scarlet. Both Ark and Tabernacle are described in *Exodus* with a wealth of detail. Some of it is hardly credible at face value. But both are genuine, not inventions of religious romancers living long afterwards. They are nomadic holy things which can be paralleled among the Arabs, but not closely among sedentary peoples in the ancient

Near East. The Tabernacle was served and the sacrifices offered to
Yahweh by a corps of priests, headed by Aaron as chief and prototype, despite his lapse in the matter of the Calf. This Hebrew
priesthood seems to have been almost entirely a Mosaic innovation.
The order itself, and the robes and pectorals worn by its members,
probably owed something to Egypt. Aaron had custody of certain
tokens called the Urim and Thummim, through which the Lord's
will was investigated by some kind of lot-casting, although such
practices were frowned on among the laity. Whatever these
objects were, they operated like the toss of a coin, giving the
answer A or B, yes or no. Consultation on any complex matter
therefore had to go through a process of elimination which might
take a long time.[3]

Exodus closes with an account of the making of Ark, Tabernacle
and furnishings, by a group under the presidency of the master
craftsman Bezalel. All the people assist with offerings of various
kinds. When the work is finished, the Lord shows his presence
over the Tabernacle in the shape of a cloud by day and fire by
night.

The next book, *Leviticus*, is a medley of laws and regulations
which take the actual story no further. The book of *Numbers* which
follows begins with a census of the adult male Israelites. It gives
the fabulous total of 603,550. The figure is almost certainly symbolic. It nearly corresponds to the phrase "all the congregation of
the people of Israel," which, when its Hebrew letters are given
the value they bear as numerals (like the Roman v for 5), yields
603 and 551. The rest of the book contains still more ordinances
and judgments. They include a command that all priests shall be
of the tribe of Levi like Moses and Aaron. This at first was a statement of preference rather than a rule. It was enforced later, but
not so early.

The legal material, however, is here interspersed through a
fairly direct narrative which takes us to the gates of the Promised
Land. Not by a smooth path. *Numbers* is predominantly a record

3 See *I Samuel* xiv:18-19, 41-2.

of crises, of a season of trial which partially destroys the achievement. Soon after the marching column has left Sinai, Moses has to face a complaint which every leader of change has to face at some point: "We were better off before." The Hebrews, stricken with famine, yearn for the good old days in Egypt when they ate "fish and cucumbers and melons, leeks and onions and garlic." A providential wind blows in more quails from the sea, and hunger is appeased. Thirst produces similar murmurings. Again Moses taps a rock with his staff, and again water flows. Hunger and thirst may be satisfied, but they are not the only afflictions. Plagues thin the ranks, and mutinies break out. Even Aaron and Miriam protest at their brother's high-handed conduct, and at his marrying an Ethiopian woman. Every revolt is crushed by some divine judgment.

Moses, perhaps, is seeking more trustworthy helpers. He has already persuaded some of his first wife's kinsfolk from Midian to join the expedition. It is not clear how he attaches them to the Israelite body: only as guides, we gather, since there is no hint of a religious affiliation. Aided at any rate by these Midianites or Kenites, Israel reconnoitres the southern slopes of Canaan. Scouts go forward to spy out the country. Among them are Caleb and Joshua, a young warrior in Moses' personal service. They find the Promised Land a delicious contrast with the desert (the famous phrase about its "flowing with milk and honey" is a proverbial hyperbole occurring in other literature), and pluck a huge bunch of grapes to show to the tribes, together with figs and pomegranates. However, the nations already installed look formidable. Frightened at the prospect of war with them, most of the scouts paint a dark picture of Israel's chances. The men, they declare, are bigger: "we seemed like grasshoppers." Their words provoke a fresh clamour and an outright demand for retreat to Egypt. When Joshua and Caleb present (so to speak) a minority report, they are threatened with stoning. Moses desperately intercedes with the angry Lord as he has done before, using, this time, an almost blackmailing tone. "If thou dost kill this people as one man, then the nations who have heard thy fame will say, 'Because the

Lord was not able to bring this people into the land which he swore to give to them, therefore he has slain them in the wilderness'."

Moses' plea is only partly successful. His faint-hearted followers have at last condemned themselves in God's eyes. Divine sentence is pronounced. Of the generation that left Egypt, all but Joshua and Caleb will perish in the desert. Their children will attain the goal of the Exodus . . . forty years after it. Doom falls first, and swiftly, on the scouts whose cowardice caused the trouble. They fall sick and die. The rest of the Israelites are awed into penitent submission and agree to push on. Sentence, however, has been passed, and even the family of Moses is not exempt. Miriam dies, and so does Aaron.

A premature raid into the southern Canaanite hill-country is a failure. Moses applies to the king of Edom for leave to trek eastward through his land, but meets with a rebuff. So the Israelites make a detour round the Edomite territory and the Dead Sea, appearing finally near the east bank of Jordan in the area of Mount Nebo. Victories over the Amorites and Og king of Bashan (a giant with a huge bedstead made of the new-fangled metal iron) give them a wide hold on that side of the river. The neighbouring Moabites are alarmed, and their king Balak sends for a man called Balaam to pronounce curses on Israel.

This Balaam is evidently a seer and enchanter with mantic powers. He expects a fee for his services, and his curses are incantations which harm their victims. He undertakes to come, but finds himself moving to an accompaniment of uncanny omens. As he rides his donkey an invisible angel scares it till it sinks down in terror. Balaam beats the animal to make it get up, and it speaks with a human voice in reproof. He learns that if it had not halted, he would have perished at the angel's hands. Balaam realises that the God of Israel is close upon him. On arrival, to Balak's fury, he refuses to curse. When his speeches grow more and more favourable to Israel, the king tries to stop him from talking altogether, and hustles him from one mountain vantage-point to another in search of an auspicious locale. But Balaam looks out over the Israelites, and with God prompting him he can only bless.

> How fair are your tents, O Jacob,
>   your encampments, O Israel!
> Like valleys that stretch afar,
>   like gardens beside a river . . .
> God brings him out of Egypt;
>   he has as it were the horns of the wild ox,
> He shall eat up the nations his adversaries . . .
> A star shall come forth out of Jacob,
>   and a sceptre shall rise out of Israel;
> It shall crush the forehead of Moab . . .

For Balak, who is king of Moab, this is doubtless the last straw. A few verses later we are told that "Balaam rose, and went back to his place; and Balak also went his way"—without further comment.

Balaam's oracular sayings have analogues in Canaanite poems and are among the oldest things in the Bible. As Miriam's song is a contemporary witness to the marvel of the escape from Pharaoh, so this heathen's prophecies are a contemporary witness to a similar charged atmosphere surrounding the other end of the march. However, the final advance is delayed for several decades. The tribes go on living pastorally as semi-nomads in the border zone across Jordan, north-east of the Dead Sea. Moses, knowing that he himself will never complete the journey, appoints Joshua as his deputy and successor. He climbs to the summit of Mount Nebo, gazes westward, and sees all the Promised Land spread before him. (This is perfectly possible; no miracle is required.) Then he dies and is buried, though the place of his grave goes unmarked and unremembered. And under Joshua's leadership Israel girds for the invasion.[4]

---

4 *Deuteronomy*, which gives the story of Moses' last days, will require separate discussion.

3

The Land which God gave may conveniently be called Palestine, though nobody called it so at the time of the Israelites' return. To desert wanderers it might well look rich. By the standards of most other folk it was poor, and fitted for peasants but not for really civilised people. Lacking the rivers that fed Egypt and Babylon, it depended for the bulk of its water supply on a not too reliable rainfall. Even this had to be supplemented by springs; areas without springs were largely without inhabitants, and the economy could be crippled by drought. Its sandy coastline, unbroken except for the bay north of Mount Carmel, offered no natural harbours and discouraged seafaring. Its mineral resources, except for a little iron, were scanty. In the virtual absence of commodities to export, its trade was small.

Northern Palestine and the coast had fair agricultural land. The southern area away from the sea, later known by the name of the tribe of Judah, was high and comparatively arid; as it is still. A Jewish legend says that in the dawn of creation God sent an angel with a bag full of stones to distribute through the world, but as he was flying over Judah the bag burst. Because of this rocky crust the relics of the past are meagre, and the improvement as you go north is not very striking. Biblical archaeology does in general concur with the Bible; it does administer a final repulse to various attacks grounded on literary dissection and textual speculation; but it does not often go far enough to confirm a particular detail, or the existence of a particular person.

Palestine's history or prehistory seems to have been roughly this. Parts of it were inhabited from very primitive days indeed. Jericho, for instance, is one of the oldest cities on earth, and one of the few places where deep-level excavation shows the change from nomadic to stationary life actually in progress. But, as a bridge between more populous centres rather than a centre in its own right, Palestine always had a miscellaneous air. Its Early

Bronze Age ended in chaos about 2300 B.C. with a wave of invasions. The first phase of its Middle Bronze Age, beginning three or four hundred years afterwards, saw two principal nations in possession: the Semitic Amorites chiefly in the inland hill-country, the Canaanites chiefly in the more fertile coastland, but spreading out and imprinting their culture at many points. Scattered over the uplands in that era there must have been a sprinkling of Hebrews, the ancestors of Israel. About 1730 the Hyksos poured across into Egypt. When the Egyptians shook themselves free a century and a half later, they followed up their victory by annexing Palestine with its tangle of communities—the Canaanites, the Amorites, the Hyksos remnants, and other Semites. Egyptian control was at first half-hearted, then, after a campaign by Thutmose III, a great deal more ruthless.

Palestine under the Pharaohs had a dual administration. It was a medley of city-states ruled by local princes. The Egyptians insisted on describing these harassed dignitaries as "governors"; the princes co-operated by phrasing their correspondence with their divine overlord in the most servile terms, referring to themselves as his "dogs" and his "footstools." Egyptian inspectors descended on them at intervals and extorted tribute. Apart from this, the paramount power did little constructive beyond maintaining the roads, which the inspectors needed to travel on. Understandably the country grew poorer rather than richer. The Amarna letters cover a period when the Egyptian system was being shaken by Canaanite disaffection, Amorite revolts, interference from the Hittites away northward, and massive Habiru raiding. Seti I more or less restored order for a moment, but the rotten fabric was inexorably falling apart. When the Israelites entered, they advanced into a confusion. There is no evidence that they had to fight any Egyptian patrols or garrisons.

The population which they did have to fight, left to its own devices by Egyptian withdrawals, was by now still more of a mixture. It was mainly Semitic but not entirely so. Its religion was a jumble of cults; its imports, though not plentiful, came from every quarter, including the Mycenean world of Homeric epic; and it spoke several languages. Palestine had five different methods of writing, namely Babylonian cuneiform, Ugaritic cuneiform, Egyptian hieroglyphs, a syllabic script from Syria, and a tentative version of the alphabet. There were settled Palestinians and semi-nomadic ones. The settled variety were mostly Canaanite. Their tongue resembled Hebrew. The feudal patricians lived in well-built houses, with rows of rooms enclosing a spacious court, and efficient stone-lined drains. However, they were not wealthy: Egypt had bled them white; and Canaanite artistic achievement was feeble. Petty wars and marauding invasions had promoted the growth of defensive architecture. The cities were ringed with circuits of cyclopean masonry. Hence in part the nervousness of the Israelite scouts, who scampered back with reports not only of "taller people" but of "cities fortified up to heaven." Yet the enemy's shortcoming slowly became apparent. His best military organisation was defensive, and its very strength on that side reflected a more profound weakness. The city-kings distrusted each other. They could not combine except in leaderless *ad hoc* coalitions that seldom survived a bad defeat, and Joshua's troops had a flair for stratagem which enabled him to inflict such defeats.

For the Israelite conquest and settlement we have a mass of traditions in the books of *Joshua* and *Judges*. These furnish many valuable details, but are not so clear as to the overall nature of the process. The dating, forty years after the Exodus, may or may not be meant literally; though we are left in no doubt that the wilderness period was long, since none of the men born in Egypt enter Canaan except Joshua and Caleb, a tiny remnant preserving continuity and linking promise with fulfilment. Of the two books which deal with that fulfilment, *Joshua* (xi:23) suggests a fairly thorough triumph in Joshua's lifetime, *Judges* a gradual and piece-meal occupation with heavy setbacks. The two can be harmonised. Able generalship may have carried Israelites quickly into many parts of the Land, while a Sisyphean task of consolidating and pacifying followed. But it is as well to grasp that the need for harmonisation exists.[5]

Whatever the truth about possible attempts to invade from other directions, the main body skirted the Dead Sea on the north and crossed Jordan. The crossing is said to have been effected dry-shod, a non-miraculous possibility, because the river near El-Damieh has clay banks which can subside and block the channel, forming a rough temporary bridge. After setting up a stone monument Joshua led the host toward Jericho. This exceedingly old city, far down in a quasi-tropical valley, had an adventurous history. Its fortifications had been remodelled more than a dozen times. It had been wiped out by some other army in the disorder of the Hyksos retreat, and then, after a gap, re-occupied. According to *Joshua* vi the Israelites marched round it and blew their trumpets and shouted, whereupon the walls collapsed. It is a fact that at some stage in Jericho's career its walls did collapse, doubtless owing to an earthquake. Archaeologically the problem is to decide whether they did so for Joshua. The only safe statement is that positive datings very much earlier can no longer be insisted upon. A debacle within a decade or two of 1250 appears fairly acceptable. Excavation confirms other biblical assertions about Jericho—that the walls were double, with connecting beams that supported dwellings; that there was only one gate; that the catastrophe occurred suddenly without prior undermining; that the town was burnt but not looted; and that it was not rebuilt for many years afterwards.

At any rate, Jericho succumbed. From its neighbourhood the road to Jerusalem winds upward through a sandy desert. But the tribes did not immediately go there. For the moment their future capital remained in the hands of another people, the Jebusites. Instead, traces of what appear to be their campaigns emerge from the subsoil farther north. Between 1230 and 1220 at least four cities were overrun. Prosperous Bethel was destroyed by fire,

---

5 Careful reading refutes the assertion sometimes made, that *Joshua* implies complete victory in a single campaign. See xi:18, xiii:1 ff.

leaving a deposit four or five feet thick. The ramparted stronghold of Hazor was stormed and sacked; Mycenean pottery lay shattered among the wreckage. Lachish and Tell Beit Mirsim suffered the same ruin.

Strokes like the fall of Jericho must be seen, as Egypt's plagues must be, in their theological context. At the time and *a fortiori* in retrospect, Israel's wars were Yahweh's wars. The Lord was in every action that hastened victory—devastation, assassination, massacre. He aided his warriors with marvellous interventions, not only hurling down city walls, but, on another occasion, stopping the sun so that Joshua should have some extra hours of light to defeat his foes. (Again the miracle can be rationalised. In mountainous country it is possible to go through gathering darkness along the floor of a valley and then come out into the sunshine of a late afternoon. A more intriguing theory connects the event with a celestial rain of stones mentioned just before: meteor showers may be accompanied by a prolongation of twilight, due to dust-particles in the stratosphere.) Despite his activity, however, Yahweh is never described as fighting against the Canaanite gods. They are contemptible idols scarcely worth speaking of, and Yahweh is "the only Higher Power that matters" in Israel's warfare as in any other field.

What would be fascinating to learn is the attitude taken to the incoming zealots by their own kinsmen, the descendants of the Hebrews of Canaan who had never gone into Egypt, and were still living in the ancestral home. That such folk existed there cannot be much doubt. Probably they were in the north-central region, about which the conquest narratives have little to tell us, and were absorbed by intermarriage into the conquerors' religious and ethnic system. *Joshua* xxiv may give us a confused tradition of their formal acceptance of the Covenant. But how far, after all those years, did their culture harmonise? How much re-education was necessary? To what extent were these clans' myths and customs digested by the new Israel which Moses had moulded? Nobody knows.

In one way or another the Israelites steadily extended their holding. They spread through Gilead and Bashan on the east side of Jordan, into the south of Palestine, and into the north, though they failed to win control of the coastal plain, where Egyptian power lingered and their opponents could use chariots to full advantage (*Judges* i:19). The Canaanites and others among the hills were not all killed or expelled. Many were left in enclaves, sometimes explicitly protected by treaty, though as serfs. But between the old society and the new the break was abrupt. The Israelites did not care as yet for the urban amenities of their more polished victims. Apart from a certain amount of camping and improvisation, they were slow to take over the captured towns for their own purposes, and allowed some of the ramparts to crumble into disrepair. They did occupy the big Canaanite houses, but with a difference. Whereas the former owners had lived upstairs, keeping the ground floor for storage and slaves, the Israelite pioneers huddled downstairs in the storage space. Their own style of building was a crude heaping of unshaped stones on stones, with pebbles stuffed into the crevices. Their crafts were bluntly utilitarian, their arts non-existent.

However, even in these squalid beginnings there were points on the credit side. Thus a major reason for the decay of public works was simply that free tribesmen could not be forced to do anything about them. Furthermore, the Israelites were far from unenterprising after their fashion. Instead of clinging to a pastoral life they brought fresh land under cultivation, cleared patches of forest, founded villages, and, by exploiting the recent invention of cisterns lined with lime plaster for storing rain, succeeded (unlike the Canaanites) in colonising districts that lacked springs. Repatriated Israel multiplied fast.[6]

Each tribe acquired a territory, although the early borders were not those of the ultimate map. The twelve groups (if indeed all twelve were distinguished at this stage) did not form a political unit but a loose federation, like the Greek amphictyonies of petty

6 There are interesting parallels with the Anglo-Saxon conquest of Britain.

states grouped round a central shrine. The sole semblance of a capital was Shiloh, a place of assembly and communal worship where the Ark was kept. Government was vested in "judges," helped by councils of elders. Despite much trouble with neighbouring nations, and a chronic need for strong leadership, trends toward monarchy at first made no headway. Unity was derived entirely from the cult of Yahweh and the great shared adventure, now augmented with countless glorious tales of the wars.

CHAPTER FOUR

THE BOOK OF BEGINNINGS

However conclusive the entry into Palestine looked, it was not, after all, the end. Presently Israel's cult began to work upon Israel's experience. The appeal to the past for authority—"your God who brought you out of Egypt"—was the mainspring of Decalogue and Covenant. This grew steadily more potent in the inner life of the federation. Hebrew tribal mythology was taken up by poets and priests. It was re-assessed, re-interpreted, and woven into a sort of cosmic chronicle. This traced Yahweh's action in history not merely back to the Exodus but back through a line of patriarchs, Israel's ancestors, to the very birth of the world, which (since no other deity counted) Yahweh must obviously have created himself. The chronicle of the Lord and his deeds was recited as a liturgy cementing the unity of the tribes. From expansions and improvements of it there developed at length the book called *Genesis*, meaning "beginning" or "origin."

If we ask why Israel's history should have come to be prefaced thus with a pedigree of events going back to Creation, the answer is given with perfect frankness by Rashi, the medieval master of Jewish commentators. The object was to prove an incontrovertible right to Palestine. As a modern scholar has put it, the theme of *Genesis* in conjunction with the subsequent books to *Joshua* is as follows: "God, the Creator of the world, called the patriarchs and promised them the land of Canaan. When Israel became numerous in Egypt, God led the people through the wilderness with wonderful demonstrations of grace; then after lengthy wandering he gave them under Joshua the Promised Land."

Here then was a third step in Israel's logic. The initial prompting doubtless came from a feeling of incompleteness and insecurity. We are told in *Judges* ii:14-23 how the tribes had to struggle endlessly with their enemies and could not enjoy the Land in peace. It became necessary to be sure, to be very sure indeed, that they did belong there and had not been guilty of an appalling error. Hence another question and answer:

Couldn't our title to the Land be challenged—say by the Canaanites who were here before the Covenant and whom we have treated so harshly?

No, because Yahweh made the world and his will is supreme. He has been active in history from the beginning, though not fully revealing himself, to bring about our possession of this country. The Covenant was a reaffirmation of his pledges to our remote ancestors. There is no appeal from that. He is God.

For its cosmic apologia Israel had a wealth of saga to draw upon— material stored in the vast memory of a mainly pre-literate people, celebrating past events conceived as decisive. By the judges' era a fair amount of it may have been written down, as several Canaanite sagas had already been written down. The Hebrew words could have been carved on stone, as in *Exodus*, or engraved on tablets of clay or lead. Egyptian papyrus also came to be used in Israel after 1100. If we have few specimens, that is probably because it perished in a less dry climate.

Genesis in its present form is a late compilation. The text has been jigsawed together by choosing pieces from three previous bodies of material, overlapping but distinct. They extend through *Exodus* also, and *Leviticus* and *Numbers*. This combining of several documents accounts for the discrepancies (or near-discrepancies) and the repetitions. The backbone of *Genesis* is a narrative now known as "J", ascribed to an author or editor called "the Yahwist" because he uses the Name of God as revealed to Moses. Intermingled with it is an "E" narrative. In "E" God is usually "Elohim," a puzzling title which is plural in form and means "spirits" or "divine beings," though it normally takes a singular verb. J and E may well

73

be two adaptations of a common original, a folk-epic. However, as they stand, J would seem to have been composed in or near Jerusalem during the tenth century B.C., and E farther north and perhaps a little later. The third source, P, consists of matter written by priests after 600. These dates of "finalisation" imply nothing as to the age of the contents, which are far older in substance than P or E or J itself.

Whatever share Moses had in person, the essential work must have been done within the two or three centuries from his time onward. In the text of *Genesis* as we have it, the presiding genius is the Yahwist, who organises the J matter received from his predecessors. His interpretation of history is the summing-up of a long literary process. He adopts a number of traditions which reach him in versions too well-beloved to tamper with, but manages to fuse these into a cogent synthesis, an exposition of divine purpose underlying events. His writings, indeed, are the first in which humanity breaks away from passive acceptance of the cycle of Nature into a realm of thought where past, present and future run in sequence and real change is possible. In keeping with Mosaic theology he ignores notions of destiny, and makes God's will the law of the universe. The "E" sections scarcely do more than supplement him, though they do it ably. The Priestly authors systematise and define, adding, for example, a scale of years which sets the story in a chronological frame. Broadly speaking the Yahwist's mind is focused on Man and history, guilt and salvation, the back-and-forth dialogue between human beings and a Lord who is present in their lives; while the Priestly text is more doctrinal, stressing God's august exaltation in language that is concise, measured, and most carefully phrased. Together they leave a deep impression of richness and variety in Hebrew thought—despite the wretchedness of material culture—during the formative age that furnished the elements of both.

2

Let us see what Israel made of its remote past, and of the world's.

Genesis opens with a prologue of ten and a half chapters, which must be traversed before there is so much as a glimmer of anything peculiarly Israelite. The prologue sketches a national mythology with motifs which are not hard to fit into the Near Eastern context. Yet because Yahweh is unique, the motifs are transmuted.

A prior understanding is perhaps needed about the terms "myth" and "legend," especially the former. "Mythical" tends to be a synonym for "untrue." But in dealing with stories told by people at the early biblical level (as Jewish teachers have always recognised) the rigid true-false polarity is anachronistic. Far more important is the story's intention. Roughly one might say that a "legend" is regarded as more or less historical; the story itself is what counts. A "myth" is more or less symbolic; its value lies in its meaning or moral. A "myth" in practice probably is fictitious or mainly so, but the word must not be allowed to prejudge the issue, or lay stress where it was never meant to be laid. If we want to emphasise that a story is not literally true, we shall do better to use some other term such as "fabrication" or "fantasy."

In practice human imagination can easily "mythify" actual happenings and real persons. So it was with the Exodus, and so it is, in a famous literary instance, with *Faust*: Goethe's plot is almost pure myth, yet it can be traced back to an obscure German conjurer who did exist—yet (again) it makes no scrap of difference whether he existed or not.

A nation's amalgam of myths, legends, traditions and so forth may therefore be spoken of as its mythology without question-begging. To refer to Israelite mythology as one refers to Greek is not to imply that either is necessarily a tissue of falsehood, only that both must be evaluated by other standards besides literal truth. A myth may be related in some way to a ritual. It may be a kind of spell, supposedly having magical powers when recited. It may express what is held to be an insight into the cosmic order. It may seek to solve some quite humble problem, such as the origin of a place-name, or the reason why the serpent crawls on its belly.

To revert, then, to the mythology of the region where Israel was born, the ancient Near East and the adjacent part of Europe. How does *Genesis* fit in?

Three basic myths can be traced with many variants throughout the whole area. One is the story of Creation, describing, in essence, the conquest of chaos by a god who fixes the heavenly bodies in their stations and gives shape to the Earth. Another is the Flood story, describing the wiping out of humanity by a deluge of water, and a fresh start by a surviving remnant. The third is the Tammuz-Ishtar myth in its numerous forms. A young king-god is assailed by demonic enemies and imprisoned in the underworld, where a goddess goes to seek him, finally escorting him back in triumph to the land of the living. This last is certainly a ritual-myth connected with ideas of fertility, the rotation of the seasons, and the killing of actual kings representing the god.

If we set aside Tammuz for a moment, we are left with two myths of inception or at least renewal. Several further themes are attached to these in different ways. We find such motifs as the Beginning of Mankind; the Primary Ancestor, who may be either the first man himself or a god prior to him; the Superhuman Early Race, often regarded as giants; the Paradisal State of Ancient Humanity; the Origin of Earthly Evil (an event that is blamed more than once on women, like Pandora); and the Origin of Knowledge and Useful Arts, sometimes carrying a suggestion of danger, and of divine wrath against those who, like Prometheus, presume too far. Since none of the mythologies have come down intact, we cannot say whether all these themes were originally present in every one of them. Some systems are more fully preserved than others: the Israelite best, the Greek a close second, probably in versions closer to the primitive forms. The Israelite stories in the first eleven chapters of *Genesis* are not derived from the Greek. Nor are they Egyptian or Canaanite, except perhaps in incidentals. Comparison shows that despite the tribes' long residence in Egypt and Canaan, they had a folklore from an older home still. The nearest parallels in fact are Mesopotamian.

Beside Tigris and Euphrates, a thousand years before Moses, there had been an empire of Sumerians and Akkadians. The dominant Akkadians were a Semitic people like the Hebrews, the Sumerians were of a non-Semitic stock. From these came Babylon. The mixed culture was rich in mythology. Tammuz—the authentic archetypal Tammuz—was the Sumerian god Dumu-zid-abzu, Faithful Son of the Subterranean Ocean, and liturgies in his honour are extant. The actual myths came chiefly from Sumerian ritual; the Akkadians gave them a more literary turn. It is largely to this fund of ideas and imagery that the first part of *Genesis* can be traced. The Israelites' ancestors must have gleaned what they did in Mesopotamia itself, at a very early time, long before the Egyptian captivity. Their re-workings of Mesopotamian myth may derive, here and there, from intermediate Canaanite forms; here and there, they may owe something to the Babylon of a later era; but they cannot be explained adequately except by far-off beginnings in the country itself. Many of their ingredients are strange, primordial, out of key with the Bible-making Israel of kings and prophets, which would simply not have adopted them as they stand. They are the legacy of an alien past, made sacrosanct solely by immense age.

To review their Mesopotamian analogues is to realise what sort of changes the Hebrews made, and how the themes were adapted to a practical, even political style of thinking about the world and human destinies.

With the Babylonian Creation Epic, which priests recited at the Spring New Year Festival, the first thing one notices is that it does not begin "in the beginning." Primeval chaos is not mere formlessness but an unexplained kingdom of night ruled by monsters and dragons, the chief being Apsu and Tiamat, the universal ocean-mother.

Through some obscure process the gods are formed "within"

these beings, and rebel against them. Tiamat's foes choose the youthful Marduk, otherwise Bel, as their leader. He kills Tiamat and disperses her followers. Creation itself is an accidental result. Our world is made by Marduk out of the corpse of Tiamat. He splits her into an upper and lower half, and we are all inside her. After he has set up the heavenly bodies to light her immense interior, he makes Man for the service of the gods. They build a tower in Babylon, assemble there, and confirm Marduk as lord of the universe, hailing him as "the Son, our avenger." Thus the triumph of order is confirmed.

That is the Mesopotamian Creation. The Flood-myth survives in more than one version. It excels most of the numerous other Flood-myths in vividness and detail, largely because it includes the folk-memory of a real inundation, a monstrous and traumatic shock for a people living away from the coast. The disaster seems to have occurred about 3000 B.C. Sir Leonard Woolley uncovered some signs of it in the lower part of the country toward the Persian Gulf. Digging down through layers of clay with scraps of pottery in them, he came at last to an eight-foot stratum with no human traces at all. Below that he found pottery again. The barren clay between had been laid down by a huge rush of muddy water. Probably the cause was a rare coincidence. A tidal wave swirled up from the Gulf with a following gale, at the same moment as unusually heavy spring floods from the mountains were pouring down the rivers. The collision was fatal.

Woolley's discoveries did not prove that the Flood was widespread, nor did excavations in other districts. But a spectacular sweep over a densely peopled area would have been enough to inspire stories about the drowning of "the world" (i.e. the known world) and their incorporation into mythology, pointing a moral about Man's ultimate helplessness in the face of awful and unpredictable powers.

There is an early Sumerian Flood-narrative about a king named Ziusudra, which is found both on tablets and in a work by Berossus, a Babylonian priest of the third century B.C. But a better version is in the Akkadian epic of Gilgamesh. In quest of the secret of immortality Gilgamesh visits the principal survivor of the Flood, now called Utnapishtim, who is living far away from the rest of humanity. Utnapishtim describes how the god Ea warned him against the schemes of the god Enlil, and urged him to build a ship. In due course the Flood covered the land. For six days the winds blew and the waters tossed. Finally a calm fell. Utnapishtim sent out a dove and a swallow which found no resting-place, and then a raven which did. The water subsided and the passengers came out. Having told his tale, Utnapishtim gives Gilgamesh a magical plant that makes its owner deathless. Gilgamesh, however, loses this on the way home when a snake steals it from him.

3

Inspection of *Genesis* reveals an eloquent co-existence of likeness and unlikeness.

About the Hebrew saga or whatever it was which the writers used, only the most general statements can be made. It was not adapted from the Mesopotamian myths as they are now known to us, but drawn from the same sources, and related in a cousinly way. In *Genesis* the myths come through entirely transformed by the Israelite idea of God. This transformation may have been rapid, or it may have been gradual. All we can say for certain is that even in the earliest portions it has gone a long distance—a decisive distance. The text has few traces of development in the sense of a qualitative change. Yahweh is always as he appears in *Exodus*: the only Higher Power that matters, the God who makes things happen, the inescapable Presence behind events. He is not accounted for or given a setting. He is simply there.

One result is a shift in context. The Mesopotamian stories, like most non-Israelite mythology, are not pictured as happening in historical time. They happen in what Australian aborigines expressively call the Dream Time. A few details like place-names link them with the world we live in. But the gods' activities go on in an alien realm, and even the alleged earthly events are not seriously dated—nor (and this is crucial) does it matter whether they are or not. Their significance lies outside the sequence of history. The Israelites, on the other hand, having made a fresh start from the historical fact of the Exodus, went on along the same path. They fitted everything as best they could into time and space as we experience them, simply because they conceived nowhere else. There was no Otherworld of the gods for anything to happen in, because Yahweh was alone. All myths had to be combined with chronology, and lined up with human affairs. It was this rearrangement that made the scheme of *Genesis* possible.

How the transformation worked out in practice begins to appear at once in the chapter on Creation. This was composed by a "Priestly" author and affixed to *Genesis* as prologue. Though the date of composition is late, the chapter is an outcome of centuries of reflection on the same theme under the influence of the same ideas, discernible throughout the Old Testament.

Since the God of Israel has no predecessors or colleagues or background, the long Mesopotamian preliminaries have gone. God cannot be an actor like Marduk in a drama with characters existing before himself. The beginning of the prologue is the beginning of everything, and there is no "before." Time itself is created. The gibe "What was God doing before he made the world?" is meaningless.[1] Whether he creates out of a total vacuum is open to debate. At the very least, *Genesis* make him solely responsible for every actual existence, everything you can put a name to.

He starts with The Deep, which is more or less the Babylonian Tiamat, but de-mythologised. It is not a monster with an evil life of its own, but simply . . . ocean: a sterile fluid mass. When God acts, he is not fighting dragons or disposing of the by-products of an irrelevant process. His own will is the single force at work, and he proceeds by a series of commands, not, as some gods do, by

1 Bertrand Russell (*History of Western Philosophy*, p. 373) acknowledges the effectiveness of this answer.

sexual generation or the budding off of bits of himself. From his deservedly famous first sentence "Let there be light," he goes on through six days. He makes a firmament—a transparent dome or vault—with an air-filled space under it, in the middle of the waters of chaos. This dome is the lower heaven, the sky. It is made fast to pillars. Beneath is a flat expanse of sea, while above, and showing through, are the azure abysses of what must now be called the heavenly ocean. The upper realm is the source of rain, snow and hail, which fall through openings in the dome when these are unstopped.[2]

Under the dome, by some sort of precipitation, a solid mass of land appears. It rests on columns rising through the water below. This is what is designated in Hebrew the *tebel*, the single continent surrounded by ocean which all ancient geography assumes—the Greek Oecumene or inhabited world, the Roman *orbis terrarum*. Earth, and the encircling sea, God fills with vegetation and animal life. On the sixth day he says, "Let us make Man in our image," and does so: Man is to rule all creatures. On the seventh day God completes his work and rests. The completion consists in the rest itself. Without phases of quiet and renewal, life would be imperfect. The Sabbath, the weekly pause which Israelites observed and Gentiles did not, was justified by an appeal to this divine hush.

Meanwhile, the Mesopotamian pantheon has vanished. Or nearly so. It has left one vestige, with weighty implications. God does not say "in my image" but "in our image." There are no gods indeed, or none who count. But there are celestials of another order, exalted beings with a divine likeness. They figure elsewhere in the Bible as *elohim* or *seraphim* or "sons of God." One shrinks from the word "angel" because of its connotations in bad art. However, it means simply a messenger, and the Hebrew belief was that the Lord employed these rapid and splendid spirits as his envoys under the dome of heaven. They are nowhere mentioned as being

2 Some of the cosmological details are not in *Genesis*, but elsewhere in the Bible. For references see Pedersen, *Israel: its Life and Culture*, vols. I-II, pp. 453-4.

created; Jewish tradition usually assigns their creation to the first day, perhaps comprised in that of the primal light.

Israel's theology has turned the pantheon back to front. Instead of being a late-comer promoted by senior divinities, the Creator stands alone at the point of origin, and all other celestials are as much his creatures as everything else—like him, but infinitely inferior. As for the dragons and sea-fiends of the Mesopotamian chaos, they are by no means absent. Elsewhere in the Bible, Yahweh can still be glimpsed quelling them, as Marduk does. "Thou didst crush the heads of Leviathan." "The Lord will slay the dragon that is in the sea." (*Psalm* lxxiv:14, *Isaiah* xxvii:1.) But again the monsters are his own creatures—turbulent, frightening, but subject to him. They are to be reckoned among the aquatic beasts of *Genesis* i:21. Evil is regarded, not as an independent anarchic force, but as insubordination by God's creatures in a world which (as the Creation-story repeatedly tells us) he has created good. It cannot be anything else. He alone IS.

4

In the middle of the fourth verse of *Genesis* ii, we pass from Priestly to Yahwist writing, and from a grandiose to a restricted scene. The paragraphs that come next were composed earlier, and the more primitive atmosphere is what might be expected. Their ruling ideas are the same. God throughout remains the supreme and solitary Creator. However, the panorama does narrow down, the focus does shift to ground level. First we saw Man from outside as the climax of the cosmic process, now we begin to see the world through his eyes.

The name "Adam" which is given to the first specimen means "Man" pure and simple. It echoes another Hebrew word that means "earth," and Adam in fact is made of earth. The idea of a link between humanity and the soil is found in several mythologies. *Genesis* enlarges its implications. In the Israelite context, it suggests a link between a special human group and the special soil allotted to it.

God makes Adam and transports him to a beautiful garden, "in Eden in the east." There he shapes a woman out of Adam's rib. The pair live together in a happy instinctive innocence. This phase in the garden without clothing or complications is the Israelite version of the Paradisal State. But the notion of a mere lazy idyll, an invertebrate South-Sea-Island romance, is misconceived. Adam has to work for his living; he must "till and keep the garden." Moreover he is not a placid beast of the field, but a rational and responsible being. That is the whole point of his having been made at all. Though he lives at first in keeping with the Lord's will, he can elect to do otherwise. The faculty is given exact statement in a special veto. The tree of the knowledge of good and evil grows in the garden, and God forbids Adam to eat its fruit. The same veto applies to his still anonymous wife.

What follows is familiar. Dangerous thoughts are planted in the woman's head by the subtle serpent. She eats the fruit, and, a true Pandora, induces Adam to do likewise. Promptly innocence goes. The forbidden fruit does not represent knowledge in the abstract, but knowledge through experience. "Knowledge of good and evil" means a sort of unbridled sophistication about things-in-general, and the sin is an unfilial adventure, a presumptuous experiment in living. *Genesis* employs symbols of a highly fundamental kind. The story involves food, and has a sexual tinge, while the serpent himself is a formidable cult-figure of widespread potency; the exegesis that makes him the Devil in disguise is fully in keeping. These images of food, sex and religion stamp the Fall with a perennial character. Guilt strikes at the heart of life. Man, colloquially, gets off on the wrong foot. He throws away the privileges that go with the garden, of which immortality seems to be one—filched from Adam as from Gilgamesh, by a snake. God responds with acts of judgment. Henceforth men will have to drudge to wrest a living from an unfriendly soil, and women will be subject to male dominance and bear children in pain. The serpent himself is condemned to degradation. In some way which only time can reveal, his victim humanity will defeat him.

The Fall establishes the nature of moral evil in Hebrew eyes, as a refusal of responsible creatures to comply with God's will. God is absolute, therefore anything wrong *must* have the nature of revolt against him, or at least estrangement from him. But evil is not the fault of Man alone. He has been drawn into a prior revolt of non-human beings. Jews explain this eventually, though after the composition of *Genesis*, as the rebellion of Satan and his angels—a motif which brings the Mesopotamian War in Heaven into the system after all, but with a different meaning.[3]

Adam and Eve (as his wife is now called) are exiled from the garden. Their first children are Cain and Abel. Both brothers sacrifice to God. Abel receives favourable omens, his brother's are adverse. Cain is angry and kills Abel; God again intervenes to judge, and sends the murderer off with a curse on his head. Six generations of Cain's descendants are traced, with a suggestion of multiplying violence and lawlessness. (The origin of Cain's wife, by the way, is sometimes paraded as an insoluble conundrum. Actually it was faced by Jewish commentators well over two thousand years ago. Their answer is that she must have been his sister, one of Adam's daughters who are mentioned in the next chapter. The uncanonical *Book of Jubilees* puts a name to her, Awan. It is a fair answer. At that stage there would have been no ban on incest, and no reason to avoid it, in view of the parents' presumed soundness.)

Contrasted with Cain's villainous progeny are the descendants of Seth, another son of Adam. A chapter by a Priestly contributor traces this line with indications of date as far as Noah. One of the Sethites is Enoch, whom God takes mysteriously away to himself. In later literature a great deal more is said about Enoch. He becomes,

---

3 Some examinations of Judaeo-Christian religion, notably Jung's, are weakened by a delusion that it lays the whole blame for evil on Man. It does not. It recognises other subversive forces, and that recognition remains whether these are regarded as malign spirits or as personifications. The alienation of creatures from God, resulting from the autonomy he has willed for them, is a collective thing in which Man is involved.

as we shall see, a leading figure in the crisis uprooting Israel from its Land. But the brief passage in *Genesis* is cryptic—though in a list of mythical Babylonian kings, which has parallelisms with the Seth pedigree, the king who corresponds to Enoch is a favourite of one of the gods. Apart from Enoch, nothing calls for immediate comment but the vast length of the lives, up to 969 years, and the late age of begetting. Prolonged virility and vitality mean superiority. The human span may be assumed to have dwindled after these patriarchs because of sin and degeneration.

A contrast, in fact, is to be inferred between an evil population associated with Cain, and the line of virtuous and long-lived Sethites. It is brought to a head by another divine judgment, the Flood. "The Lord saw that the wickedness of men was great . . . so the Lord said, 'I will blot out Man whom I have created'." Only the upright Noah is saved, with his wife, his three sons Shem, Ham and Japheth, and his sons' wives. Obedient to God's instructions, Noah builds his ark and fills it with animals. Then the waters of chaos pour into the hollow universe through the firmament and from underneath. The narrative is a mixture of Yahwist and Priestly matter, in some ways very close to the myth of Utnapishtim (as in the sending of the birds) and in others remote from it.

With this rescue of only eight persons for righteousness' sake, we have the first clear occurrence of a further biblical theme: that of the Remnant. The historical trend is seen as double. A human society—usually, but not always, God's chosen society of Israel—may grow and extend its influence and be blessed in doing so. Yet with growth comes a falling away. A faithful minority has to be distilled out, so to speak, to embody the group's true vocation and save (if possible) the backsliders. Later we shall encounter the idea of the Remnant several times. The whole theory of Jewish identity arose from it.

Noah's Ark comes to rest "upon the mountains of Ararat," in the Armenian highlands. Noah emerges, and God commissions him to re-people the world and rule over the beasts. It is a second, less glorious Beginning. After it comes an ugly anecdote about

Noah planting a vineyard and getting drunk. The nucleus of this is a curse in which he condemns "Canaan," the ancestor of the natives of that country, to be a slave to Shem and Japheth. The curse is intended to justify the Canaanites' subjection. Canaan has not been mentioned before. However, the author fits him in as a son of Ham, whose insult to Noah is responsible. With this episode the long stage-setting is almost completed. Israel's possession of the Land begins to gleam on the horizon, mythology begins to slide into historical fact.

In the first chapters of *Genesis*, besides noting what myths are present, it is worth noting what myth is absent. Of the three major themes of the Near and Middle East, only two appear. Creation occurs, and the Flood occurs. The cycle of the death and resurrection of Tammuz does not. Israel came in contact with this, and we have not heard the last of it at all. But in *Genesis* it leaves no trace. The gap is due to its being doctrinally unmanageable. Israel's God can be thought of as making the world and as flooding it. But being eternal, unsleeping, subject to no eclipse or removal, he cannot be thought of as dying and returning to life. The transforming logic is all-pervasive.

As for other Creation-stories and Flood-stories, the first chapter of *Genesis* is most creditably different from all rival Creations on two counts: its magisterial movement and progress; and its august simplicity. The writer knows nothing of evolution. But he does picture Creation as growing through a series of distinctions and definitions, and he makes Man a climax. His evolutionary outlook in this sense is not a belated plea of modern believers trying to save something from the wreckage. It was noticed by early commentators, whom, indeed, it was apt to distress. If Almighty God wanted to produce Man and other creatures, why should he do it in instalments? Hugh of St. Victor, a twelfth-century scholar who worked closely with Jews, offered an interesting answer. God willed the process as well as the products. He created the raw materials all at once, but then built up his work successively as an object-lesson, to teach his rational creatures that they must advance in self-improvement by stages. Men are to see themselves in relation to the entire growth of Nature, and think and act progressively. This idea is not so far from the "Evolution becoming conscious of itself" asserted by Sir Julian Huxley. Certainly Israelites conceived time and the world as going forward, not rotating in futile cycles.

Also, the concise and simple Creation went with a particular habit of thought among them. It freed them from a stifling swarm of capricious powers and conflicting destinies. Israel's best minds, having decided that one all-wise Deity was behind all that happened, inferred that it was possible to make sense of the world, and strove persistently to do so. Though they achieved nothing in the physical sciences, they did grasp that a quest for general laws would not be in vain. They applied this mode of thinking to history. Others were to extend it. After the decline of classical civilisation, nearly all pioneers of science arose in cultures which had the Bible or its derivative the Koran; very few in India or China or Mexico, till these countries came under the influence of Christians or Moslems.[4]

Comparison of the biblical and Babylonian Flood-stories shows what form Israel's "making sense of the world" inevitably took. The tale of Utnapishtim is much finer as literature, and in spite of the curious plottings among the gods, it is not, as sometimes alleged, totally amoral. But *Genesis* makes morality central. The God of Israel causes the Flood himself, to destroy creatures that have turned from him into wickedness, and himself makes Noah the exception. His will, his judgment on human action, is the single key to events.

5

The sons of Noah take us into a new set of origins, out of which

4 Cp. the conclusion of Koestler's *The Lotus and the Robot*. C. S. Lewis, citing Whitehead in *Miracles* (pp. 127-8), observes that the orderly Newtonian world-picture was constructed by believers in the biblical God, while the emergence in recent physics of a less rational, less determinate cosmos coincides with his rejection.

Israel is presently to come. Chapter x is an impressive attempt to trace the descent of all nations from that one family in the Ark. Each is given an ancestor bearing its own name, like Canaan.

First come Japheth's sons and grandsons. Among them "Javan" stands out. This is "Ionian," denoting the Greeks—the same word, "Yavana," means a Greek in Sanskrit. "Gomer" is the ancestor of the Cimmerians in the Ukraine, "Madai" is the ancestor of the Medes. The other nations descended from Japheth are mostly in the Caucasus, Asia Minor, and the nearer Mediterranean islands. Their distribution suggests that Israelite mythology is linked at this point to Greek, and that Japheth is the Titan Iapetus. Iapetus was an ancestor, through Prometheus and the Greek Flood-survivor Deucalion, of all mankind. The human race or *genus Iapeti*, as known to the early Greeks, comprised roughly the same peoples as *Genesis* credits with a Japhetic ancestry. As for Noah's other sons, they account for Canaan, Babylon, Nineveh and so forth, Shem being the ancestor of "Eber" and therefore of the Hebrews themselves. The basis of the list is not ethnic but political. Japheth is the father and type of "good" Gentiles with whom ancient Israel had no quarrel; Noah, in his prophetic utterance after the vineyard affair, says that Japheth will dwell as a friend in the tents of Shem. These two are opposed to Ham, who is the father of Israel's enemies.

Noah's wandering descendants arrive in Shinar or Babylonia. They propose to settle there as a group instead of spreading over the earth, and to build a city with a brick tower reaching up to heaven. God, however, humbles this Promethean pride. He resolves to "confuse their language, that they may not understand one another's speech." Soon the builders are chattering back and forth without comprehension. Linguistically torn into shreds, mankind drifts apart. Work on the city is suspended. It is called Babel, "Confusion."

A piece of folklore about the diversity of languages has been combined here with a Mesopotamian legend of a divine tower, as at the end of the Creation Epic. Towers of a religious nature were typical Babylonian structures. Built of brick, they were known as *ziggurats*, and took the form of stepped pyramids with stairs leading up. The ascent to heaven was symbolic, and the flat top enclosed a shrine where the deity was supposed to alight and rest. If the Tower of Babel is any particular *ziggurat* it is probably the Etemenanki in Babylon itself. The cosmopolitan city is seen through the disdainful eyes of a desert-bred visitor.

Hitherto the divine judgments have been accompanied by touches of mercy or mitigation. Babel is not; the failure of mankind seems final, and the Yahwist author says nothing about a Remnant. A Priestly contributor does add a genealogy of descendants of Shem, leading to a man named Terah. This is the solitary link between one part of *Genesis* and the other.

6

A ritual formula commemorating the gift of the Promised Land, preserved in *Deuteronomy* xxvi:5-11, required the Israelite to say "A wandering Aramaean was my father." The word "Aramaean" is a gesture in a north-easterly direction. *Genesis* from xi:10 onward glosses it at copious length. Here Israel's tribes assert, through the literary spokesmen, their beliefs about their own making. They are the Righteous Remnant whom the Lord saved, after all, from the disaster of Babel; but by a slower and subtler process than the rescue of Noah.

All twelve are traced back to a single family, and to a tree of patriarchs beginning with Abraham, originally called Abram. He is the son of Terah, and the grandfather of Jacob or Israel. These patriarchs are none too easy to bring into focus. Heroic figures of the same type have existed in more recent times among similar peoples, such as the Arabs, and they occupy a strange borderland between fact and fiction. A strong leader gathers his kin together, and others join him; the assemblage acts as a unit under his name; and even after his death he is still present, taking part in the affairs of the tribe so that its acts are his acts. Moreover, any newcomer who marries into the tribe adopts him as ancestor. Hence he may come to have numerous official descendants who are not literally so. Likewise with the patriarchs or "fathers" of Israel. They have touches of myth about them, and to some extent they personify groups. In one case at least (Benjamin) a tribe may have existed in some form before its supposed ancestor. But the differentiation of group from individual is far less rigid than it is in civilised societies. Israel's fathers are neither simply individuals nor simply personifications. Merely to be understood they must be construed as great men around whom legends have clustered, men whose saga has grown, men who have been magnified into symbols. Whether such persons actually lived and underwent such transfiguration is, of course, a further question. A fictitious person can be subjected to treatment of the same kind. The classic twentieth-century example is Sherlock Holmes.

In marshalling and editing the saga matter about their forebears, the Israelites indulged no fancies of racial purity. The Priestly pedigree which alone connects Abraham with the pre-Babel world includes one name, Arpachshad, which is not even Semitic. The narratives speak of marriages implying Canaanite, Egyptian and other foreign factors in Hebrew heredity. Faith and vocation count for more than blood. With them, rather than genealogy as such, the tale of Abraham and his folk is concerned.

The line from Shem is traced through Eber, Peleg and Serug (among others) to Terah. Terah, we are told, lived at Ur of the Chaldeans—i.e. Babylonians. He had three sons, Abram, Nahor and Haran. This last died at Ur leaving a son of his own named Lot. Terah and the rest left Ur, and travelled up the Euphrates with the object of migrating to Canaan. They stopped, however, in northern Mesopotamia or Paddan-aram, at the city of Haran. The repetition of this name is a little confusing, but significant, as we shall see.

After a time the Lord spoke to Abram, telling him to complete the journey. "I will make of you a great nation . . . and in you all the families of the earth shall be blessed." Here, at the very outset of Israel's story and in a tradition which is certainly early, is a plain indication that Yahweh's purpose transcended all tribal limits;

though it was to be many years before Israel saw how. Abram, taking his wife Sarai, his nephew Lot, and servants and animals, set out and arrived at Shechem in central Palestine. There the Lord appeared to him, saying: "To your descendants I will give this land." Abram built the Lord an altar, and then moved southward along the central range to a hill just east of Bethel, where he pitched his tent and set up a second altar. Still he did not settle, but wandered on south toward the Negeb. During a famine he went to Egypt. The Pharaoh saw Sarai and desired her. Abram pretended that she was his sister, and flourished on Pharaoh's generosity till the deception was found out and Sarai was expelled from the palace.

The party returned to their encampment near Bethel. Abram was now wealthy, and there was not enough pasture for Lot's herds as well as his own. Lot therefore left him and went down into the lush Jordan valley, and along to the neighbourhood of Sodom, afterwards covered by the Dead Sea. There he stayed.

But the Lord said to Abram:

"Lift up your eyes, and look from the place where you are, northward and southward and eastward and westward;

For all the land which you see I will give to you and your descendants for ever.

I will make your descendants as the dust of the earth; so that if one can count the dust of the earth, your descendants also can be counted.

Arise, walk through the length and the breadth of the land, for I will give it to you."

Accordingly Abram went south again. He halted at Hebron by the oaks of Mamre, and built a third altar.

A war broke into his life (*Genesis* xiv). The rulers of Sodom, Gomorrah and three other cites, which had been tributary to distant Elam beyond the Tigris, revolted. The King of Elam with three powerful allies marched in to restore order. After crushing the rebels they departed northward with many prisoners, including Lot and his family. "Then one who had escaped came and told Abram the Hebrew," who mustered three hundred and eighteen warriors of his own household, and recaptured his relatives from the invaders' rearguard. He went to meet their protector the King of Sodom to hand them over. The meeting took place on ground that belonged to another local prince, Melchizedek of Salem. Melchizedek "brought out bread and wine; he was priest of God Most High." He gave Abram his blessing.

Up to this Melchizedek scene, the whole story has been non-ethical and scarcely theological. Abram seems to regard God as a tutelary spirit whose commands refer only to his movements, and whom he obeys in hopes of reward. One gets an unhappy impression, which the commentators fail to dispel, that the foundation of his fortune consists in his wife's immoral earnings in Egypt.[5] But Melchizedek blesses him in the name of "God Most High, maker of heaven and earth, who has given the foe into his hand." This blessing clarifies for the first time who Abram's Deity is, and Abram refers to him immediately afterwards in the same words. When God speaks to him again, Abram complains of having no children; God tells him to look up at the night sky and repeats that he will have descendants, as numberless as the stars; and Abram's trust in this pledge is "reckoned to him as righteousness"—the first phrase with any moral allusion. The train of thought starts from God and proceeds to faith in him. Actual righteous conduct on the part of the worshipper is the expression of this faith.

God's reiterated promise of posterity and the Land is made more detailed and confirmed by a covenant, with an uncanny primitive apparition of a torch in darkness. But still no heir is born. Abram (the narrative goes on), being childless after a long time in Canaan, took Sarai's Egyptian maid Hagar as a concubine. At first Sarai approved, but when Hagar actually became pregnant Sarai dismissed her. An angel, however, appeared to Hagar in the desert and assured her of the Lord's mercy. Her son was Ishmael, the ancestor of the bedouins. He and his mother were allowed to go back and live with Abram.

5 It is claimed in palliation that Pharaoh was forestalled from actually consummating the arrangement.

When Abram was ninety-nine years old the Lord came to him with the words "I am God Almighty; walk before me, and be blameless." God went on to reaffirm the gift of the Land to the patriarch and his people, "for an everlasting possession." Abram's name was altered to Abraham. From being "exalted father" he thus became "father of a multitude." Sarai's name was altered to Sarah, "princess." Again a son was promised to them. Abraham laughed; but he obeyed God's command that in token of the compact between them, he and all his tribe should be circumcised. In the Bronze Age and for some time after it, circumcision was widespread and not distinctive. However, as a Hebrew religious custom, still observed when other nations had given up the practice, it did become so.

While Abraham was sitting outside his tent by the oaks of Mamre, the Lord approached him in human form attended by two angels. After eating with the patriarch, and telling him that Sarah's son would be born soon—at which she laughed like her husband, being ninety herself—he and the two angels walked on toward Sodom. Abraham went with them. The Lord was about to execute judgment on the sins of Sodom and Gomorrah. He took Abraham into the secret: "Shall I hide from Abraham what I am about to do? ... No, for I have chosen him, that he may charge his children and his household after him to keep the way of the Lord by doing righteousness and justice; so that the Lord may bring Abraham to what he has promised him." (*Genesis* xviii:17-19.) Thus moral conduct enters as the condition of having a great posterity in possession of the Land.

Abraham pleaded for Sodom, and after much bargaining the Lord consented to spare it if even ten righteous citizens could be found there. However, they were not. The two disguised angels went down into the city and were threatened with homosexual assault. Fire and brimstone from heaven laid the area waste. Lot, who had given the angels refuge, was permitted to escape. His wife looked back and was turned into a pillar of salt—a myth purporting to account for a peculiar rock formation. Lot himself survived to become the ancestor of the Moabites and Ammonites. Israel's opinion of these nations is reflected in a story that they were descended from two boys whom Lot sired on his own daughters when drunk. It is our parting glimpse of him.

Abraham meanwhile, aged a hundred, was at Gerar in southwest Palestine. Here Sarah's long desired son was born, and called Isaac or "Laughter" as a reminder of his parents' amused scepticism at the thought of his arriving at all. Sarah sent Hagar and Ishmael away into the wilderness, this time for good. Ishmael's death from thirst appeared imminent; but again an angel rescued them. Their expulsion, which Abraham had disliked but not prevented, was followed by an agonising test of the patriarch himself. Jewish commentators connect the two incidents. God ordered Abraham to take Isaac to the hill of Moriah and sacrifice him as a burnt offering. Abraham passed the test; he was just drawing his knife when an angel checked him. He sacrificed a ram instead. The angel praised his faith, and reaffirmed all the promises.

Again he lived in the south, sometimes at Beersheba. Sarah died at Hebron, and he bought a nearby field from the local Hittites as a burial place. There was a cave in it which became the family sepulchre. When Isaac grew up, Abraham sent a servant to Paddanaram to seek out a wife in his brother's family. The servant went to the city of Nahor (another duplication of personal and local names) and brought back Isaac's cousin Rebekah, whom Isaac married. Abraham himself married again, begot more children, and did not die till he was a hundred and seventy-five.

Isaac is transitional. The traditions about him are very early, but he remains tenuous. We hear of him as living at Gerar, where the divine promises are repeated to him; as sowing and reaping there, and digging wells; and as moving to Beersheba like Abraham. His sons are Esau and Jacob. Jacob cheats Esau out of his birthright and blessing. Esau marries two Hittite women and becomes the ancestor of the Edomites.

The next episode is the saga of Jacob, relating how he fled from the anger of Esau. He retraced his grandfather's migration, to live with his uncle Laban in Paddan-aram. On the way, at Bethel, he had his famous dream about the ladder to heaven, in which he in turn heard the promises—"the land on which you lie I will give to your descendants," and so on as before. He stayed for a long time in the neighbourhood of Haran, marrying Laban's daughters Leah and Rachel, and becoming rich by outwitting his uncle. On his return to Palestine, his way was blocked at a ford by a man who wrestled with him and lamed him. The man said: "What is your name?" He said, "Jacob." The man replied: "Your name shall no more be called Jacob, but Israel, for you have striven with God and with men, and have prevailed." The implication is that "Israel" means "he who strives with God." Its original sense, however, was probably less thought-provoking, "may God rule."

Jacob-Israel entered the Land again and was reconciled to Esau; together they buried Isaac, when he died aged a hundred and eighty. Jacob lived at Bethel and then near Shechem. He had twelve sons, the ancestors of the tribes of Israel, all but the twelfth (Benjamin) born in Paddan-aram.

The last part of the patriarchal history explains the captivity of Israel's people in Egypt. His best loved son was Joseph, to whom he gave a rich robe in token of affection. Joseph's brothers resented the favourite. He annoyed them further by his interpretation of dreams, from which he derived omens of his own future over-lordship. They sold him to a caravan of "Ishmaelite" traders who took him to Egypt as a slave. His master was Potiphar, an officer of the royal guard. Trouble with Potiphar's lustful wife caused Joseph to be put in prison. There he interpreted the dreams of the Pharaoh's chief butler and baker, who were fellow-prisoners; the butler, he said, would be restored to favour and the baker executed. At the ceremonies on Pharaoh's birthday, both prophecies were fulfilled.

Pharaoh too had a dream, which his soothsayers could not expound. The butler recollected Joseph, who was sent for from prison. He said that Egypt would have seven years of plenty followed by seven years of famine. Therefore he advised Pharaoh to set aside a surplus from each harvest, so as to be prepared.

Pharaoh, satisfied, appointed Joseph himself to superintend the task, invested him with a ring and chain of office, and gave him the second royal chariot to ride in.

When the famine came, Joseph's measures saved Egypt, but adjacent lands suffered grievously. His own brothers came to buy corn. After various misunderstandings, Joseph forgave them and arranged for the whole family to come and settle in Goshen as protected immigrants. "All the persons of the house of Jacob that came into Egypt were seventy." *Genesis* draws toward its close with a series of oracular blessings pronounced by the aged Jacob over his sons, and over Manasseh and Ephraim, Joseph's sons by an Egyptian wife. These blessings of course apply to the tribes sprung from them. When Jacob and Joseph die, their bodies are embalmed in the Egyptian manner.

7

In view of the rash claims which are sometimes made, it should be admitted at once that none of this is directly confirmed by outside evidence. On the other hand there is no reason why any of it should be. The only character who is a prominent public figure, and thus worth searching for, is Joseph; and his career falls within the Hyksos epoch, for which we have few Egyptian records, and indeed few records anywhere in the Near East. What we can do to get *Genesis* in perspective is to ask whether it is viable, whether it shows enough knowledge to command respect, whether any of it can be proved wrong as a good deal of "ancient history" can.

First, as to the main geographical sites and movements. The story opens with a pastoral family, dwelling in a civilised area yet not of it. Terah and his sons are introduced at Ur, near the eastern horn of the Fertile Crescent that stretched round from Palestine to the Persian Gulf. There is no doubt that such pastoral families did wander into the Crescent, along the rivers, and across to the Mediterranean. Ur itself has been amply excavated. The city flourished as a metropolis of the Sumerian-Akkadian culture, under its third dynasty, from about 2060 B.C. It was four miles long by a mile and a half wide, with walls and gates. Most of its brick houses were low and flat-roofed, but a temple of the Moon at its heart was eighty feet high. Its royal tombs were made of stone transported from thirty miles away. Grave-goods unearthed by Sir Leonard Woolley—golden cups and headdresses, jewelled statues, mosaic-ornamented harps and inlaid gaming boards—testify to the splendour of the court. Terah and his family, neither able nor willing to be permanent citizens, would probably have camped on the outskirts.

Genesis gives no motive for their migration to Haran. But they could in fact have had a very strong motive: about 1950 the Elamites attacked Ur and destroyed it. As for Haran, that too was a civilised centre, and at the right time. It belonged to the kingdom of Mari which bestrode the upper Euphrates. The inhabitants were Hurrians, a mainly Semitic nation that had absorbed Akkadian culture and spoke a language akin to Hebrew. Their royal archives have been recovered and deciphered. These tablets reveal a level of prosperity between 2000 and 1800 which might well have induced Terah to change his plans and settle. They also take us a step farther along Abraham's route, since they mention a contemporaneous drift of nomadic tribes from north-western Mesopotamia toward Palestine. Abraham's people could have been among them.

Palestine itself may wait for a moment. The other major movement in the history is the descent into Egypt at the end. On this only two points need be made. Joseph's rise to the post of chief minister appears to coincide with the early phase of the Hyksos invasion, when Semites arriving in the Semitic conquerors' wake might naturally have enjoyed favour. Also, the small number of Abraham's descendants who go to Goshen (no more than seventy, after many years for increase and multiplication) accords with the evidence that there were really many Hebrews who did not accompany the migration, but stayed in Canaan and were reunited with their kinsmen when these returned under Joshua's leadership.

If we check *Genesis* more closely by scrutinising the proper names, the effect is no less impressive. They fit extremely well, and they belong not only in the right countries but in the period indicated—the Palestinian Middle Bronze Age, about 2100 to 1550 B.C.

"Abraham" (or "Abram") is the same as "Abarama," which is scratched on a Babylonian tablet recording a rent payment by a small farmer so called. In the Haran area several more names answer to *Genesis*, if sometimes unexpectedly. The Hurrians are palpably the biblical Horites. Abraham's relatives bear names sounding like cities that are mentioned in the Mari tablets. His pedigree includes "Peleg" and "Serug," his father is "Terah," his brothers are "Nahor" and "Haran"; the tablets refer to places called Phaliga, Serug, Til-Turakhi, Nakhur, and of course Haran itself.

Abraham breaks away from his Mesopotamian background as a "Hebrew" (*Genesis* xiv:13). This, as we have seen, may be equated with the word "Habiru" which covered many semi-nomadic groups not absorbed into the rooted communities. In Old Testament usage it is suitably an early term, marking a distinction between the Chosen People and foreigners; the last people who utter it are aliens, in *I Samuel* xxix:3. The Hebrews of *Genesis* are depicted passing to and fro over a map which corresponds to the Middle Bronze human topography.

Genesis xiv supplies a whole host of names, with a sweeping geographical range. Some are enigmatic, but others can be identified. Among the four rulers who attack the rebels, "Arioch" is equivalent to Arriwuku, which occurs in the Mari archives; "Chedorlaomer" is Kudur-Lagamar, i.e. slave of Lagamar, an Elamite god; "Tidal" is the Hittite Tudhalia.[6] King Tidal's subjects the "Goim" are heathens—the word *goy* still means a non-Jew. The town of Ham (verse 5) is mentioned in Thutmose III's inscription about his Palestinian campaign. The kings' line of march through Gilead and Moab follows a route well trodden by merchants in the copper trade before 1700 B.C. Salem or Jerusalem, where Mel-

6 But Amraphel is apparently not Hammurabi. See Gerhard von Rad, *Genesis*, p. 171.

chizedek reigns, figures as "Urusalim" in a Tell el-Amarna letter, and perhaps on a Canaanite fragment as far back as 2000.

In the saga of Jacob and his sons, some of the characters are doubtless tribal personifications, but again several names are traceable, if not with the biblical reference. "Jacob" itself is a widespread contraction of "Ya'quob-el," "may El protect," "El" being a term for deity. It is found in the Mari documents, on a Babylonian contract tablet, as a Hyksos name, and as the name of a Palestinian place or tribe in Thutmose's list. "Joseph," also, occurs as a place-name. There are Mari allusions to the Banu-yamina, arguably the tribe of Benjamin. "Potiphar" in the Joseph romance is Egyptian.

It might be thought that the odd way in which some of these names appear outside the Bible tends to be adverse rather than favourable to its truth. But that need not be so. The interchange of names, or bits of them, among gods and places and persons has always been so complex a process that inferences beyond the bare facts are risky. In some biblical genealogies names of villages replace names of ancestors. To cite a modern instance, Lincoln the town is prior to Lincoln the man, whereas Washington the man is prior to Washington the town. And in neither case should it be judged that the man is fictitious because the town exists. If a writer in some distant future were to bring a "Washington" and a "Lincoln" into a book about the formation of the United States, it would at least be certain that he was not totally ignorant.

As for the society portrayed in these chapters—the customs, the religion, the "picture" and atmosphere in a broad sense—this too is usually plausible. Victorian charges that *Genesis* is full of manifest rubbish can no longer be sustained. Abraham himself, simply as a character in the known setting of Habiru dispersal, carries conviction. He is a prosperous chief with great flocks (but, correctly, no horses). He wanders through the highlands away from the more civilised coastal strip, intervening in local wars and imposing his will on local princes, yet without becoming deeply involved. This credible image is purely Hebrew; *Genesis* conveys hardly anything of the bustling Canaanite life going on near by; but its very absence helps to show that the story is created from Hebrew tradition, not from eclectic fancy.

For the patriarchs' life in Palestine archaeology offers little, but what it does offer is again mostly favourable. Their mixed nomadic and agricultural habits—in xxvi:12 Isaac takes to "sowing" for the first time—agree with a known pattern. The holy places associated with them are all in the borderland between pasture and arable. Tablets found at a Hurrian colony in Mesopotamia called Nuzi or Nuzu show that the social norms of the narrative are in fact largely Nuzian. They shed light, for instance, on such curious topics as Laban's family gods or *teraphim* (xxxi:19, 34-35), which have Nuzian counterparts. The account of Abraham's purchase of the field and cave of Machpelah from a Hittite (xxiii) has parallels in early Hittite and Babylonian contracts, and in nothing later. The "Field of Abraham" itself is noted in an inscription at Karnak dealing with a war in the tenth century.[7]

A few other Palestinian touches are also effective. Thus, while Jerusalem does figure, its role is minor and properly so. A fantasy concocted in ignorance after Jerusalem became supreme would have made far more of it. The fire and brimstone of Sodom led a geologist, Xiel Federman, to prospect for oil and natural gas in the Dead Sea neighbourhood, and his success would seem to imply concrete facts behind the biblical imagery.

With the shift of focus to Egypt the accumulation of details grows thicker. Chapter xl, which concerns Joseph in prison, is especially fruitful. The titles "chief of butlers" and "chief of bakers" both occur in Egyptian records. Celebrating the Pharaoh's birthday was habitual, and so were attempts to interpret dreams; though Joseph, unlike pagan seers, significantly has no technique for doing it—God inspires him (xl:8, xli:16). An Egyptian provincial governor's tomb credits its occupant with storing up wheat in seasons of plenty for distribution in famine. Moreover this task of admin-

---

7 However, the Philistines of xxvi:14-15, and the camel of xxxi:34, are anachronistic.

istering food supplies is known to have been partly in the hands of Semitic officials. The chariot of xli:43 is a Hyksos vehicle, unheard-of on the Nile before the foreign kings' advent, but made familiar by them. The Pharaoh's gifts of a signet ring and gold chain are correct as Egyptian tokens of honour.

When Jacob and his household enter Egypt in search of food, and settle in Goshen, they are doing what countless other Semitic tribesmen did. A mural at Beni-Hasan, dated 1892 B.C., shows thirty-seven such folk arriving. They are Amorites from the land east of Jordan. The men are sandalled, the women shod. All wear woollen tunics of many colours, like Joseph's. One has an eight-stringed lyre. Their weapons are bows, javelins and throw-sticks; their beasts are asses, not camels. Nor was this Amorite move an isolated case. The admission of "sand-ramblers" was so frequent that, as we have seen, the Goshen of Rameses II abounded in Semitic names and was perhaps bi-lingual. In the reign of Merneptah, the Pharaoh who exulted over nascent Israel, permits were still being issued to Edomite bedouins to come to Goshen and "keep themselves and their flocks alive in the territory of the King."

One other item of interest is Joseph's embalming, in conformity with Egyptian, not Israelite practice. We are informed afterwards that the Israelites buried his venerated remains at Shechem (*Joshua* xxiv:32). A tomb at Shechem, traditionally alleged to be Joseph's, was found when opened to contain a body mummified in Egyptian style with an Egyptian sword of office.

Lastly, as to the vital question of religion and religious mythology. All Israelite legends are linkages between Man and God: they disclose God, they gather round great men. But in *Genesis*, what is that relationship made out to be, and are the authors right?

To begin with, the harmony between Abraham's career and its scriptural prologue is perfect. The transformed Mesopotamian mythology in *Genesis* i-xi demands a folk-origin in Mesopotamia such as Abraham provides. *Joshua* xxiv:2 draws the strands together: "Your fathers lived of old beyond the Euphrates, Terah, the father of Abraham and of Nahor; and they served other gods." The patriarchal tales themselves include several further ingredients which have the same air of immense and almost frightening age. Most memorable is the sacrifice of Isaac, a grim scene set forth with the sternest economy, which has disturbed endless commentators in more civilised eras. The sacrifice of the firstborn was in fact a Canaanite custom, often observed at the foundation of a new house. Abraham's three celestial guests who promise him a son recall the visit paid to Orion's father in Greek myth by Zeus, Poseidon and Hermes. Jacob's opponent in his wrestling may have been originally a god of the country, whom he had to vanquish before he could take possession.

In the handling of the patriarchs' own religion there is an eloquent confusion, which our habit of reading in the light of later belief tends to cover up. Each patriarch has dealings with one God. However, this Being is not always plainly Yahweh. The Yahwist author views all the manifestations as aspects of Yahweh, but the "E" author does not. On the whole the "God of the Fathers"— sometimes called El Shaddai, a non-Israelite title construed as God Almighty—is rather baffling. Furthermore the concept changes. In the chapters on Abraham, God walks visibly into mundane affairs. A man can meet him as a friend, talk to him, even argue with him. In the chapters on Joseph, God has withdrawn to a more sophisticated remoteness. He is a secret Voice, an overruling Providence. What is conspicuous above all is that at no stage does *Genesis* give that feeling of tension and conflict between the worshippers of true and false deities, which pervades the rest of the Bible. The cleavage is still to come. With all their faith Abraham and Isaac and Jacob are seekers rather than finders, aspirers rather than achievers. They have no priests in their train. They are not enlightened as Moses is enlightened, with a vision of the Eternal that cuts them off sharply from the heathen. *Exodus* vi:3 says as much.

And this ambiguous effect, of people as it were under a clouded sun which fitfully breaks through, agrees with the probabilities as well as anything in the book. Anthropology is wholly against the notion that monotheism evolved by abstraction from many gods, and that the early Semites of Abraham's stock must therefore have been polytheists. They are more likely to have been what *Genesis* makes them: worshippers of a vague awe-inspiring Chief God, not defining him very strictly, or excluding lesser gods, or condemning the gods of others. The believer, Jewish or Christian, is entitled to maintain that the true Lord chose to speak through one such accepted mask in order to make contact with men alienated from him. As usual, we have an historical kernel here which is independent of belief or unbelief.

Notable in this respect is the unsolved riddle of Chapter xiv, of the battle of four kings against five, and Melchizedek. With all its wealth of detail the passage is bewildering rather than informative. It cannot be assigned to any of the main sources, J, E, or P. Its incidents cannot be dated, though some of the allusions would fit the eighteenth century B.C. The war is a blend of the weirdly accurate and the weirdly incomprehensible. Yet one thing does emerge. Melchizedek is a priest of the same God as Abraham. If we explore his probable antecedents, we strike two facts which the Bible does not give. The title "God Most High," not employed elsewhere in *Genesis*, is the Canaanite "El Elyon." Zion, the sacred hill of Salem where Melchizedek lives, is also called Safon, and Safon in Canaanite myth was a kind of earthly paradise.[8]

The episode is no mere invention. A primeval Something has intruded into the stream from outside and become a theological point of departure. Nor does it vanish. It is a seed that grows in the body of Israel. Eventually that growth bursts out again into the world beyond.

---

8 God is called "Most High" by another early non-Israelite, Balaam (*Numbers* xxiv:16). Israel's investiture of Zion with the mystique of "Safon," which the Canaanites located elsewhere, is paralleled in Britain by the pinning-down of the pagan Celtic "Avalon" at Christian Glastonbury.

8

Clearly the indisputable factor in all this is a tribal memory of unique strength and scope. If it could be shown that the patriarchs were non-existent and that their stories were only instructive fiction, it would still remain true that the authors show amazing knowledge in contriving the fiction. They score again and again— on the plausibility of events, on the aptitude of names and phrases, on the sureness of colouring. They are seldom downright wrong on a verifiable fact. Until very recent times, few historical novelists could have claimed as much, with all the added resources at their command. In antiquity there is no parallel at all. Homer himself scarcely does better with Mycenean society, and he composes or compiles his epics after a much shorter interval. Certain essays in archaism by Babylonian scribes are so clumsy that experts can tell them at a glance. The evidence for Abraham and Isaac and Jacob may be open to question. The evidence for a wide-ranging, tenacious, factual tradition about the Middle Bronze Age, intelligently used by Israelite authors after Moses, is conclusive. Israel's claim to the Land was anchored, and known to be anchored, on a real and therefore unalterable past.

Even the Priestly time-scale is less irresponsible than it looks. The leading personages, of course, are given fantastically long lives. Yet if we pick out or compute periods counting backward from Moses, some of the results are arresting. Thus Jacob's household moves into Egypt under Joseph's auspices 430 years before the Exodus, while Abraham leaves Haran 215 years before that. Relying not on Scripture, but on the rough Exodus date of 1290 to '80 suggested by impartial research, we have 1720 to '10 for the descent into Egypt, 1935 to '25 for Abraham's departure from Haran. And both these dates are acceptable. The migrations, first from Ur to Haran, then from Haran to Canaan, fit into the troubled period from 1950 when Ur fell and the Elamites made their inroads into Mesopotamia. The rise of Joseph in Egypt, and the special welcome extended to his relations, fit equally well into the very first phase of Hyksos rule after 1730. At that stage the Semitic kings might well have employed Semitic viziers and actively fostered Semitic settlement.

Efforts have been made to fix the dates of Israelite history by counting generations and ignoring the numbers of years. Every clue suggests, however, that the right method is the opposite. The priests who devised the chronology did know a few major intervals of time, but they did not know enough names to fill them. Hence, the long lives are due fundamentally to stretching. The chronological frame preserves the large periods correctly, and then assigns durations for human lives and for shorter periods in a quite artificial way. Some of the by-products are astonishing. Shem, Noah's oldest son, outlives Abraham and does not die till Jacob is adult.

The artificiality, however, is far from random. For example, there are simple proportions between some of the periods, such as the 215 and the 430. There are traces of numerology. Back beyond Abraham, Enoch lives on earth to the age of 365, the number of days in the solar year—and the corresponding king in Babylonian myth was a favourite of the Sun God. Noah is 600 during the Flood, and 600 was a Babylonian unit, the *ner*. Later on Joseph lives to be 110, and "living 110 years" was an Egyptian proverbial expression for "living long and prosperously." Running through *Genesis* is probably a subtle cryptography of times, to which the key has been lost. The single outstanding constant is that long life is a sign of superiority. The authors make the patriarchs attain incredible spans partly because they can thereby show reverence to them. On the other hand, by beginning with lives such as Adam's verging on a thousand years, and dropping gradually down to a century or so, they also convey a sense of degeneracy. The pedigrees echo the Fall, underlining Man's plight and the need for God's help.

If the Priestly chronologists display knowledge and energy of mind, the Yahwist displays genius. By his skilful fusion of traditions, he sketches out the embracing theme within which Israel's thought will henceforth develop. He connects the territorial claim with the creation of the world. He knits the twelve tribes into a close unity by stressing their common and archetypal ancestor, Abraham, through whom God's promise descends to every Israelite. Moreover, in his portraits of the patriarchs, he has a genuine literary flair, as indeed has the "E" author whose contributions are mixed with his. They are not idealised into dull paragons. They are not made consistently virtuous or praiseworthy. They are fallible human beings, each with a character of his own, through whom God's purposes are worked out under human conditions. Their life-stories are convincing enough to be expounded, debated upon, returned to as a source of comfort and strength.

After Israel consolidated its hold on Palestine, there was temporarily less cause to think of these far-off matters, except in liturgical recitation on feast days. The patriarchs are seldom mentioned in the books that follow the Pentateuch. But in a subsequent age of fear and upheaval, the Chosen were to fall back on their gigantic reserves, rediscover their "father Abraham," and rekindle their faith.

CHAPTER FIVE

A WORLD BY ITSELF

During the centuries that laid the basis of *Genesis*, Israel fades entirely from general history. The literary remains of other nations give no word of its presence among them. There are few traces of trade; the Israelites had so little to trade with. For this period the Bible itself is the sole documentary source, though archaeology supplements it as usual, as do various non-biblical records which interlock without directly confirming. Such a long silence, taken up with the building of an imperishable mythology, might suggest a phase of peaceful withdrawal. But whatever else this period was, it was not peaceful. Throughout most of its course, Israel's life was stormy; Israel's career was the career of a small nation battling fiercely with nations like itself. Sceptics have made much of Israel's insignificance and cultural backwardness with a view to discrediting its religion. But to do so is merely to throw the mystery into bolder relief, to underline the startling discrepancy between Israel's legacy to the world and that of its superficially similar neighbours. The Bible's claim that Israel was different from Moab and Edom is proved by its own existence. We have no Bibles from the Moabites or the Edomites.

On a secular level, the idiosyncrasy of Israel consisted partly in a feature quite easily defined: its method of government. The judges who ruled its people in the two hundred years after the conquest of Canaan were neither despots nor hereditary office-holders. They were "charismatic" leaders, supposedly chosen by Yahweh and visited by the breath of his *ruach* or Holy Spirit. They governed with the aid of the elders, voices of a primitive democracy.

The judges' power was regional rather than national. Scripture gives the impression that Israel normally had a supreme judge as a kind of king. No doubt one or other of the senior judges did often have precedence, a primacy of honour. But except in crises demanding a special unity, it is unlikely that he ever had more. The reigns ascribed to successive judges must be allowed to overlap if a credible chronology is to be worked out at all; and the story of Abimelech, who tried to be king, shows how anti-monarchical the tribesmen were.

Early Israel was an amphictyony. The Greek term remains the aptest, though Greek amphictyonies had permanent councils for matters of common interest, and Israel lacked even that. Its bond was the religion grounded on the common experience. Its unifying symbol was the Ark of the Covenant. This was kept at several recognised sanctuaries—at Shechem, Bethel, Gilgal—before being lodged at Shiloh, in the heart of Palestine. Here assemblies were held when national business had to be transacted. Here the chief priests sacrificed to Yahweh. Here the tribesmen came together to join in the common liturgy, to make their offerings of firstfruits, and to recite the confession of faith in *Deuteronomy* xxvi:5-11, recalling the Lord's mighty deeds with their climax in the gift of the Land.

The tribesmen . . . of what exactly? The famous number "twelve" was part of the institution, and perhaps rather artificial. The Blessings of Jacob supply the full list, together with some cryptic hints at the character of each tribe. Reuben, Simeon, Judah, Zebulun, Issachar, Dan, Gad, Asher, Naphtali and Benjamin, all have territorial associations. Levi has not: the Levite families supplied priests to all Israel, and lived everywhere. The tribe of Joseph was split into two half-tribes, Manasseh and Ephraim, tracing their descent to Joseph's two sons. Much is said in the books of *Joshua* and *Judges* about the allocation of living space, and indeed the main lines of settlement probably were laid down by treaty. However, some of the tribes wandered for a time before actually settling. Their freedom to do so was a result of external politics.

Egypt was now declining fast and could no longer interfere. Furthermore, before that decline began, a pact between Rameses II and the Hittites of Asia Minor had temporarily stabilised the Near East enough to prevent any other power from moving in at once to fill the Canaanite vacuum.

Into the apex of the Land, between Jordan's head-waters and the coastal strip which the Carmel promontory breaks, four tribes managed to crowd: Asher, Zebulun, Naphtali, Issachar. Part of Manasseh lived to the south of them, and part of it across Jordan. Ephraim occupied the centre including Shiloh, with Gad as its trans-Jordanian neighbour. Judah and Simeon held ill-defined areas west of the Dead Sea. Reuben was on the Dead Sea's opposite side. In the process of parcelling-out, the small tribes of Dan and Benjamin were almost lost. Benjamin finally squeezed in between Ephraim and Judah. As for the Danites, they tried to make a home for themselves on Ephraim's western border, but later migrated to the extreme north near Mount Hermon. There they captured Laish and re-named it Dan. (Hence the phrase "from Dan to Beersheba"; Dan was the Israelite John o' Groats.)

The struggles of Dan and Benjamin cut a swath of debatable country across the middle of the Land. Judah lay to the south of this. Judah was originally a minor grouping. However, it rose in importance, drew in fresh blood, absorbed Simeonite elements, and eventually took Benjamin under its wing. "Judah" in the Bible is often spoken of as distinct from "Israel," partly for reasons arising from later politics, but not altogether. It was always a little aloof from the northern Israel beyond Benjamin. This division, and the disruptive geography of the country itself, led to border fighting between tribes. The disputed town of Bethel was four times destroyed.

Civil strife kept the martial spirit alive during stretches of external peace. But external peace was the exception rather than the rule. Though the retreat of Egypt did not immediately bring the entry of another major invader, the petty border kingdoms became more active. Moabites, Midianites, Ammonites, all made inroads to carry off slaves and loot, and sometimes established a brief local ascendancy. Therefore Yahweh had to remain a War God, a Lord of Hosts. An aura of holiness, of crusading, continued to surround the Israelite warrior, whose wars were still Yahweh's wars.

Internally these wars had achieved their main object. Generally the Canaanites and kindred pre-conquest peoples no longer resisted. In some places they had been massacred, in others they had been forced out. Elsewhere an appreciable number survived. A wedge of free Jebusites persisted in the debatable centre; most, however, were in the north. As yet their assimilation had scarcely begun. Those whom the Israelites had succeeded in fully dominating were treated as "sojourners" in the Land, not equal citizens, and made to work. Under various conditions various groups kept their identity, and here and there on the frontiers they still fought back. The coast around Tyre, claimed by the tribe of Asher, slipped out of Israelite control.

By Canaanite standards, Israel's culture was poor for a long while after the conquest. The reason lay not so much in any lack of talent or energy as in diversity of outlook. The tribes did gradually learn from their neighbours—more and more as the generations passed. But their history is not only a record of what they learned, but conspicuously of what they declined to learn, or were slow to learn, or learned and radically altered. Yahweh was associated with desert simplicity, and that persisted as an ideal. The Hebrew language took many metaphors from tents and pastoral life. Commerce and industry were suspect as being Canaanite. All the oldest relics of Israelite culture are egalitarian. We find no signs of any concentration of wealth, or of large-scale building. Huts and enclosures and crude stockades simply go on and on, for two or three full lifetimes. Peasant plots of land were privately owned, pasture was held in common and not by large landlords. While polygamy was allowed, monogamy was the norm, because very few men could afford more than one wife. Slavery was restricted by law.

An interesting social symptom is the form and use of the Hebrew alphabet. Its ancestry can be followed from Syria down to Sinai before Moses, and thence back into Palestine. Alphabets were democratic: they made writing easy, and broke the monopoly of the priestly scholars who alone had had leisure to master ideographs and hieroglyphs. Israel therefore found such a script congenial. Its alphabet had twenty-two letters. Whether Moses employed these we do not know. The first characters which we do know bore no resemblance to the square Syriac of to-day. They were based on sketches of objects. The list reflects the rustic simplicity of the life this alphabet served. Seven of the letter-names are parts of the body (head, back of head, eyes, mouth, teeth, hand, palm). The others refer to domestic things (house, door, window, fence); to animals (camel, fish, snake, oxen); to weapons and implements (goad, hook, fish-hook, support, spear). There is a letter-name meaning "water," and one meaning a "cross" used as a mark.

The earliest Hebrew text thus far discovered is a tenth-century inscription on a limestone plaque, the Gezer Calendar. This gives a sort of Thirty-Days-Hath-September jingle about the peasant's year—"two months of ingathering, two months of sowing," and so forth. It must be repeated, however, that in the judges' era the Israelites were almost certainly writing down a serious literature. What some of that was like, the older parts of the Pentateuch attest. But Scripture itself, on its own showing, gives a selection only. It cites other books: the "Book of Jashar," the "Book of the Wars of Yahweh." They were probably saga compilations in verse. In this field Israel borrowed from Canaan, whether admitting it or not. The fact is proved by discoveries at Ras Shamra or Ugarit, a coastal town away to the north opposite Cyprus. Here a store of inscribed tablets has revealed the secrets of Canaanite mythology, and the nature of the chief foreign models behind early Hebrew poetry. Incidentally it also confirms that the poetry actually is early. Its own date is in the second millennium B.C., and Hebrew authors would hardly have faked imitations of it a thousand years later.

This Hebrew verse which took literary shape after the conquest was composed in short lines, with a free rhythm of sense rather than sound. The lines were linked in couplets and triplets and little stanzas, not by rhyme, but by parallelism and iteration.

> Let God arise, let his enemies be scattered;
>   let those who hate him flee before him!
> As smoke is driven away, so drive them away;
>   as wax melts before fire,
>   let the wicked perish before God!
> But let the righteous be joyful;
>   let them exult before God;
>   let them be jubilant with joy!
>
> (Psalm lxviii)

The folk-ballad was seldom far in the background, and Israelite songs are scattered up and down the Old Testament. The first and simplest may be prior to Canaanite influence. Such are Miriam's song, Lamech's song in *Genesis* iv:23-24, and a work-song about a well in *Numbers* xxi:17-18. But the more polished productions, such as Moses' song in *Exodus* xv, are clearly derivative.

Poetic development was also religious development. The spontaneous hymns of the pioneers—their "spirituals"—led on to the prayers and psalmody and ritual story-telling of their descendants. The liturgy grew round Miriam's cry of triumph. A Hebrew poet could thus be a charismatic person with the Spirit upon him. Presently certain bards of Israel begin to come into focus as a momentous new multiple phenomenon. We begin to hear of the *nabhi* or prophet.

In English the word "prophet" is ambiguous. For one thing it suggests predicting the future. That meaning, however, is secondary. The implication in the Old Testament is not prediction but a special relationship with God. Even within the Old Testament, the English word has been made to cover several kinds of relationship. Abraham is referred to as a prophet simply as being the Lord's friend. Moses and Aaron are referred to as prophets, Miriam as a prophetess; they form, in fact, a prophetic family, all receiving intimations of the Divine Will and passing them on. But the *nabhi*, the forerunner of those prophets whose names appear on so many books, was psychically out of the ordinary. With him, "prophecy" was a peculiar condition, and the condition tended to overshadow its victim.

The word *nabhi* means "someone who is called." Such a prophet was the Lord's chosen messenger. He had no special qualification; he might be anybody. Prophecy was something that seized him from outside—or seemed to. He was blown upon by a mighty wind, the Spirit of Yahweh. It turned him into a sort of dervish. He became ecstatic in the true sense of the word, standing outside himself. His feeling of identity was dissolved in a soaring excitement; he danced and saw visions; he blurted out oracular chants and songs, which listeners revered as communications from Yahweh. Some were prone to the seizure, and it engulfed them frequently. In other cases prophecy was a rare event, a holy fit attacking a man habitually balanced and responsible. A man, or a woman. Scripture speaks respectfully of prophetesses, a striking point, since women were not much honoured in ancient Israel. (A husband could easily divorce his wife. A wife could not divorce her husband.)

Prophecy of this kind was not only violent but contagious. Ecstasy could leap from person to person in a Pentecostal uproar. The *nabhi* phenomenon is first mentioned in *Numbers* xi:24-29, where the Spirit of the Lord radiates from Moses to seventy others, and Moses voices a wish that "all the Lord's people were prophets." Later (*I Samuel* xix:18-24) we hear of men being infected against their will, flinging off their clothes and rolling on the ground for hours. Happenings of this type were by no means confined to Israel. Possession by the gods was becoming a recognised occurrence in several parts of the Near East. It took place among the Canaanites, though the sole instance which is anywhere near as early as the first Hebrew prophets concerns only an isolated fanatic about 1100. A closer parallel is the Dionysiac frenzy which swept from Asia Minor to Greece, accompanied by alleged wonder-working. Euripides' *Bacchae* has some odd echoes of the Bible, such as miraculous milk and honey, and water gushing from a rock struck by a staff. It is uncertain where prophecy began, in Israel or in Canaan or in Asia Minor. It could have spread, like the medieval dancing mania, in any direction. The Canaanites were in touch with the Aegean world; at Ras Shamra there was a colony of Aegean traders. If the passage in *Numbers* is correct—and it is known not to be a late addition—one could argue that Hebrew prophecy was the original, and Canaanite and Dionysiac prophecy were pagan offshoots.

All this is speculative. As a fact, however, Israel made *nabhi* prophecy an institution. Prophets and "sons of the prophets" acquired an accepted status as Yahweh's minstrels. They combined in societies or guilds. *I Samuel* x:5-13 gives us a glimpse of one of these. The professional *nabhi* wore a mantle of skin and a leather girdle. He played an instrument—a harp, a flute, a tambourine. His credentials perhaps were not always of the best. Sometimes he prophesied for pay, supplying "inspired" utterances of a useful sort in return for presents and hospitality. A living could be made in this manner, since generosity to prophets was thought to bring luck. Under the circumstances one might ask whether a *nabhi* was really different from a soothsayer or medium. Superficially he often was not. Babylonian diviners consulted their gods through dreams and omens; Delphic priestesses gasped out Apollo's messages in a temporary madness. But an essential difference did exist. Hebrew prophecy was an experience held to be sent by Yahweh when he saw fit, whereas soothsaying in all its forms was a human procedure leading to knowledge or decision, initiated by privileged people versed in the method. The *nabhi* could perform actions to make himself receptive, and did, but he could not compel the Spirit. The soothsayer practised a mantic science which gave him his answer. Even if the process involved possession by a god, that state was induced by incantations or drugs. The Bible describes interpretation of dreams, but with no hint of any technique for doing it. Joseph in Egypt says it is God alone who shows him the meaning of the dreams he explains.

Hebrew prophecy, therefore, always depended on a divine

factor apart from any merely mantic entanglements. Moreover, since God was not as the gods, the ecstasy which he sent could differentiate itself from all other ecstasies, such as the Dionysiac. It could grow into an exalted form of spiritual and moral insight. It was slow to do so, but the potentiality was always there. And in the end it gave Israel the only nationalism which the world has found indestructible.

While the *nabhi* was a custodian of Israel's faith, he was never, of course, alone in that. The priest or sanctuary-servant—the *kohen*—also had his holy concerns. On the whole, the priest was the humbler figure; he was simply a functionary, not "called" as the prophet was. Between the two there was no sharp rivalry. *Nabhi* guilds indeed used to attach themselves to particular sanctuaries. It has been suggested that priest and prophet were specialised variants of a primitive soothsayer or seer who was both at once. The Arabic word *kahin*, cognate with *kohen*, does mean a soothsayer. However, the Canaanite *kahin* meant a priest. The Arabic meaning may reflect a later debasement rather than a prehistoric survival.

2

Priests and prophets expounded the same religion: the desert Covenant-faith planted in Canaanite soil, and thereby both enriched and endangered. A necessary step in approaching this is to sum up, as succinctly as may be, the main features of the Israelite mind and the way it worked.[1]

As we have noted, in contemplating the nation to which he belonged, an Israelite saw not so much a collection of persons as a collective person. The Covenant had brought this person into existence, and a single life infused the whole body. Israel could digest this view as a religious principle, partly because Israel carried over a habit of purely primitive minds into its own society. Savages have less sense of individuality than civilised people; the individual

[1] In this section I have drawn heavily on Pedersen's *Israel: its Life and Culture.*

115

is part of the total life of his tribe. So in Hebrew consciousness, the distinction between the community and any one member could not be rigid and was hardly even real. The Hebrew language itself was deficient on the point. It could not strictly discriminate between a species and a member of the species. "A lion" and "the lion" were the same. Any particular lion was, in effect, "the lion-species here." In much the same manner, each Israelite was a local manifestation of his own family, and all the families formed a single great family, that of Abraham in whom all were united. One result was a basic social equality going deeper than the accidents of economics. No Israelite was superior to another, as the deified rulers of the Gentiles were superior to their subjects. Another result was a careful attention to the treatment of exceptions: the "sojourners," not part of Abraham's stock, who were to be dealt with justly because the Israelites themselves had been sojourners in Egypt; and the widows and orphans, who received special solicitude as having no close family to knit them to the body of Israel.

The minds which thought like this were integrative rather than analytic. When an Israelite did pick out an individual human being, he did not regard him as a composite of body and soul. Adam in *Genesis* is not "given" a soul, he "becomes" one, a unit of life. The body is distinguishable in the Old Testament only as the soul's visible aspect. Moreover, the soul is not self-contained; external relations are part of it. To take the most familiar instance, a man is apt to be spoken of as "X the son of Y." His soul in fact is the full potentiality of his nature, comprising whatever he is now and whatever he can become. And it is the man's environment— chiefly, God and other people—which alone can draw this potentiality out and enable him to fulfil his vocation. So he is simply not to be thought of as isolated. We come back to the collective again. A human being cannot truly exist except as a member of a community, the Israelite of course as a member of Israel, as Israel-here. Within that frame his growth to full selfhood depends on a certain harmony, the community's *shalom* or peace.

In general, when mentally organising any part of their world,

Israelites tended to fasten upon the main pattern rather than details. A Hebrew sentence is a totality-structure. The event or fact is hit off, frequently by a verb, and then ingredients are curtly filled in. Where English would say "the man kills an ox," Hebrew says "kill-man-ox." Hebrew description is impressionistic, a curious blend of the vivid and the vague. Scenes in the Bible have inspired thousands of artists without giving them any precise directions as to what they should draw. Even so simple an object as Noah's Ark remains hazy. Again and again something is intensely and unforgettably there, yet we cannot quite picture it.

Likewise with the Israelites' logic. This was not in the spirit of Aristotle or Euclid, and it led them to no major discoveries in science or mathematics. It was a practical "logic of the situation," foreshadowing one of the best-known administrative theories of recent times.[2] We find no word in ancient Hebrew meaning exactly "to think," in the sense of consecutive investigation, or the rational solution of abstract problems. Rather, the Hebrew mind takes hold of a state of affairs, and then sorts out whatever is apposite and crucial within it. The notion of an event having or requiring an assignable cause is only loosely grasped. When a scriptural author says "therefore," the sentence thus introduced sometimes gives the feeling of a *non sequitur*. What the word really implies is "under these circumstances." Causation is not analysed, but compressed and symbolised. Hence a great deal of narrative which by our own standards is fictitious or inadequate, as when the whole Law is accounted for by a few lengthy revelations to Moses, and when decisions arrived at through what must have been strenuous debate are summed up in a phrase indicating that the Lord put such-and-such into So-and-So's head. Israelite insight perceived trends and resultants rather than linkages of fact at close range. Israelite argumentation was not so much a process of reasoning as an attempt to induce a state of mind by images and repetitions. The arguer tried to evoke the situation in such a way that others would see its inherent tendency as he himself did, and draw the

2 Mary Parker Follett's.

same moral. (Look, for example, at *Amos* iii:3-8, or many of the Psalms, or most of the speeches in *Job*.)

Ancient Hebrew was an active language, with hard consonantal tones and few abstractions. Its weakness on the last score was not part of a universal weakness. Egyptians and Sumerians could express concepts like "truth" and "virtue" as far back as we can verbally trace them. But Israelite thought did not incline that way. The term for "a good person" did duty for "goodness." Between words and facts, the tangible data of experience, there was no divorce. The name was the essence; hence the significance given to the true Name of God, Yahweh. The word meaning "word" itself could also refer to an action or a happening, and Yahweh's creative utterances in *Genesis* should be construed in that light. Hebrew had no word for "will" in quite the modern sense. "Will" implies a distinction between intention and act which was not clearly drawn. In one biblical story a character is threatened with death for breaking a prohibition of which he knew nothing. Yet his defence is merely that the violation was trifling, not that he never heard of the ban and "didn't mean to do it." (*I Samuel* xiv:24-27, 43.)

Israelite thinking was scarcely ever internal or theoretical, scarcely ever detached from the demands of the current situation. When it went beyond fleeting images it was always concerned with guidance, with the direction of the soul in the world-context. Wisdom was the capacity to think to some purpose: the steersmanship of life. Knowledge of the Lord himself came through experience rather than reflection. Even memory was a practical function. To remember was to recall something with a view to acting on it. The exhortations of prophet and priest to remember the deliverance from Egypt always meant—and for Jews still mean— "Be mindful of it, act with that lesson perpetually at heart." Israel's preoccupation with history (the point must be insisted on here as elsewhere) never had the slightest tincture of antiquarianism. Its theme was not the-past-in-itself-for-its-own-sake, but the-past-in-the-present-determining-the-future.

Every soul had to rely, for its ability to fulfil its vocation, on a power called its "blessing." Each tribe as a whole had its vocation too, and a blessing to correspond. So of course and pre-eminently did all Israel. The blessing was a gift of the Lord, who could send it or withdraw it. He could also mediate it through inspired spokesmen: thus the blessings of the tribes are pronounced by Jacob, not simply as oracles but as having a divine power to produce effects. Israel's corporate blessing descended from Abraham. It was so mighty that it was destined to spread—in some way not at first explained—to "all the families of the earth."

The Covenant pursued the same theme. To conserve its blessing, Israel had to be pure. This purity was not negative. It was no cramping refusal of desirable things arbitrarily forbidden. The aim of the Mosaic vetoes was to delimit a goodness of a positive sort, the field of the community's right action. In Israelite minds, good was the norm and evil a deviation and deprivation, an off-centre condition. Sin was a hateful caricature of rightly ordered behaviour. It disintegrated the soul and society. As has been remarked before, the real object of the death penalty, as of the laws against unclean-ness, was protection of the community—protection against a poison, against the curse of evil that could sap the great blessing and unnerve Israel for its tasks.

Although evil was a negation, and not the work of an alien Tiamat-monster independent of God, Tiamat still existed imper-sonally as a region of outer darkness. Sinners slipped, as it were, into this gulf and become contaminated, able to infect others. The outer darkness was not only figurative but physical. It was an actual anarchic realm or non-world to which the sinner traitorously gave his allegiance. Israel's blessing was bound up with Israel's Land, interfusing the soil as well as its appointed owners; and the Land was literally the *place* of good, the centre of the world and of life.[3] To sin was to defile it and weaken the blessing. To move

3 The idea of Israel being at the geographical centre is not explicit in early writings, though it becomes so later (cp. *Ezekiel* v:5, xxxviii:12). But the idea of a "vital" centre, so to speak, can be traced far back.

away was to move into a peripheral zone where the blessing faded. Within were law, welfare, peace of soul. Outside were deserts, idols, demons. As you left the Land behind, you came nearer and nearer to that surrounding ocean of chaos which God had thrust back to make a sunlit cell for his creatures. Its waters were the waters of gloom and death.

Death itself belonged to the outer region. Here we confront one of the major mysteries of the Bible. Early burials with grave-goods suggest that the primitive Palestinian Hebrews honoured the dead and believed in an after-life for them. But the religion of Yahweh, as it bit deeper, reduced their status and turned them into weak shades and ghosts, like all but a favoured few of their Greek counterparts. Their abode was Sheol, the grave: not any particular grave but the-grave-in-general, below and away, the underworld to which the corpse was committed. If a man lived well his state after death was tranquil and holy, and he could still be dreamily present among his kinsfolk. However, he had no more to do. All that mattered of him was absorbed into the blessing of the living. Death therefore was an evil, despite the duty of resignation to it. Sheol was of the non-world, and its darkness crept into the world's light and into the souls of the wicked. In view of later Jewish beliefs about immortality, and earlier Egyptian ones, much bewilderment has been voiced at the virtual absence of direct teaching on the subject in the Old Testament. The reason perhaps is that the creative spirits of Yahweh's cult could not visualise any kind of after-life without imitating the mythical charivari of Egypt. Therefore they played the topic down, and acquiesced in a minimal folklore. Only centuries of growth could prepare Israelite minds to conceive anything else.

A situation, then, was given: Israel pursuing its vocation at the heart of God's light, in the blessed Land which he had bestowed. This was the Land of the patriarchs whose bodies lay in its soil. From them, life flowed to the swarm of their descendants, an organic whole in communion with Yahweh.

3

Yet the situation contained a riddle. The Land itself did not possess that unmarred purity which its role seemed to require. While it harboured Yahweh's people and the Ark of his Covenant, it also harboured less hallowed people and things: namely the surviving Canaanites and other previous occupants, with the damning emblems of their alienation from the Lord. A command to wipe them out, ascribed in Scripture to Moses himself, had not been obeyed even if given. The point of that ruthless order—whether authentic or an editor's afterthought—lies in the motive behind it. When the writer concerned said the settlers should have "saved alive nothing that breathed" in the Canaanite cities, the reason he subjoined was that the citizens were liable to teach Israel the "abominable practices" which they "did in the service of their gods." The pollution within, the heathen impurity still rooted where all should be pure, was a perennial threat.

What were these practices? Wherever the Israelites penetrated Canaan they stumbled on traces of them. The typical pagan shrine in the hill-country was an unroofed enclosure on high ground, not too far from a water supply. It had an altar mound, a sacred stone as a male symbol, a tree as a female symbol. A small building, or a cave if any were handy, housed a priest or two and perhaps a modest treasury. Down near the coast were larger sanctuaries with more elaborate endowments, but these the invaders failed to reach. The fearful chariots drove them back. As a result their acquaintance with Canaanite cultus was chiefly at a rustic level. Israel encountered, not the major gods in their full panoply, but a type of worship that was disseminated by their myths and their attributes.

From the Ras Shamra tablets and the remains of various sacred objects, we can form a notion of the coastal religion that set the tone. It was a variant of the normal Near Eastern pattern, with special stress on a particular aspect. At the head of the pantheon stood El, *the* god (the Israelites themselves, it will be remembered, adapted the titles El Shaddai and El Elyon). El's consort was Ashirat, the scriptural Asherah. Another deity was the weather king Haddu, elsewhere called Hadad, as in the name Ben-Hadad. Two unpleasant goddesses held exalted roles, Astarte and Anath. Anath was the prototype of all *femmes fatales*. Her devotees imagined her naked and voluptuous yet perpetually withheld by ever-renewed virginity; as a source of life, yet also as a destroyer who massacred mankind and waded in blood. Both goddesses concerned themselves with fertility. This was a leading motif in most religions of the Near East. The Canaanites, however, emphasised it so much that their own tended to be a cultus of sex. It included the common Tammuz theme of the death and resurrection of a young Nature-god. But its rites ran to sensual and sadistic extremes, such as mystical prostitution, and the sacrificial killing of children.

Haddu himself was the Canaanite Tammuz, under which aspect he was known as Baal. That ominous title is the most notorious point of contact between the Old Testament and paganism. But it is strictly a title, not a name, and it applies to other gods. It means "the owner," a deity with a claim on a specified bit of earth. Baal-Haddu was not the same as the Tyrian Baal-Melkart, who reached Israel after the judges' era. "Baal" to an early Israelite usually meant neither Melkart nor Haddu, but one of the lesser inland baals—local male powers of nature, worshipped in Canaanite style against the Canaanite mythological background. These might be regarded by their worshippers as manifestations or representatives of the royal Baal in the sky. Asherah had a fairly secure footing up-country. However, what Yahweh's people in practice lived alongside was not so much an array of rival gods as a rival system of thought and behaviour. The apparently inexact use of the generic "Baal" brings out a profound constancy. "Baal" in the Bible really stands for the system, which, under various divine masks, was unchanging.

It was a widespread system, and the Canaanites merely subscribed to one form of it. Our review of the myths will have indicated its shape. Men and deities, El or Haddu or whatever their names, were

all pictured as enclosed in an impersonal Nature that went round and
round for ever. There was a cycle of creation which began with the
powers of life and order defeating the powers of death and chaos.
Within that, and occurring thousands of times as it elapsed, there
was the cycle of the seasons with a similar conflict annually repeated.
Paganism did not accept time as a significant reality, because everything fell back and returned. Its ritual worked largely through
that eternal and inscrutable Metadivine which encompassed the
machine, gods and all. The priest explored its secrets by reading
omens. Or he tried to influence the cycle for human welfare by
incantations and imitative magic. Sacrifice to the darker deities
might propitiate them; sacrifice to the friendlier kind literally
fed them, keeping up their strength and life-giving virility. Women
were made fruitful to make the earth do likewise. In Babylon
liturgical chanting of the Creation Epic was a spell to revivify the
world's resistance to chaos. But Canaanites took more interest in
the year than the aeon. Nature, with them, was both worshipped
and—theoretically—controlled. In their calendar of festal observances, ethical concepts had no part. Canaanite orgies and cruelties
did not make Canaanite religion immoral. It was not necessarily
the business of such a religion to have any morality. The customs
of Canaan were doubtless more degrading and less defensible than
those of the Babylonians or Greeks. They supplied a ready target
for Israelite preachers, a justification for fierce language. But the
rejection that prompted the language went beyond.

Because Israel's cosmos was utterly other than this, the Canaanite
presence in the Land was unclean and alien. To stay pure and act
aright as a living organism, Israel had to set its face against the whole
order of Canaanite ideas. Yahweh in his sovereign wisdom was
absolute, not moulded by any metadivine processes, not caught in
any mythical web. He could be prayed to but not controlled. His
rule made sense of the world and Israel's history; his power made
nonsense of all supposed cycles. The law of the Lord broke through
the automatisms of pagan mankind. He gave commands about
conduct, not secrets for making crops grow. You could not elude

him or circumvent him, by magic or any other means, and if you tried to do so you sinned and courted disaster: sin consisted precisely in that—desertion, evasion, rebellion. Yahweh as the source of all law and righteousness could never be wrong, and no law that clashed with his could ever be right. By deposing Nature and keeping a personal Being firmly at the summit of things, Israel made its universe moral, intelligible and purposeful. The Canaanite universe was amoral, incomprehensible and aimless.

Of course the Israelites could hardly help drifting toward Canaanite religious practice. To a large extent it was a Semitic norm which an unsophisticated Semitic people could not reject. A solution emerged which was neither complete refusal nor compromise. It was transvaluation. The trappings, the forms, the calendar of annual ritual were all copied. But they were given fresh meanings and a kind of fulfilment, just as the primordial myths had been. Israel's tradition already had an adaptability which the Bible by itself does not fully disclose. The Mosaic system had digested the patriarchal inheritance; and it must also have digested the religion of those Hebrews who had never gone into Egypt, and had been re-absorbed by their returning kinsfolk. A cultic scheme now succeeded in growing up which could satisfy the tribes' needs without yielding to the assaults of the non-world.

The first Israelite sanctuaries were like those of the Canaanites. Trees and wells, stones and pillars were ordinary features. The Hebrew priest looked like any other priest. The chief Canaanite festivals were observed . . . but they were observed with a new reference, to History as well as Nature, indeed to History above Nature. Israel's cementing liturgy was a liturgy not of myths in dream time but of events in real time. The national festivals took shape as re-enactments of those events. Canaan's spring-festival became Passover, and recalled the Lord's triumph over Pharaoh, which had happened in spring. The summer-festival became the Feast of Weeks, Pentecost, and recalled the giving of the Law. The autumn-festival of ingathering became Tabernacles, and recalled the wanderings in the wilderness.

Hence, the seasonal cycle was observed, but not for its own sake. There was no question of the priests trying to affect it by combating evil powers or reinforcing good ones. They recited prayers, not spells. Their sacrifices were gifts expressing communion with Yahweh, not meals to keep him in health. Furthermore, the dethronement of Nature shifted emphasis to Man as well as to God. Man was regarded, not as struggling through a sort of cosmic jungle, but as active and clear-eyed in relation to a Maker who had given him earthly dignity; as a being who could strive and seek and rebel.

It may be asked: was this the religion of the tribesmen in general, or just an official orthodoxy that did not permeate all Israel till centuries afterwards? As in a previous context, is the Old Testament largely a work of hindsight? These are disputed questions. We have plenty of proof in the Old Testament itself that the Canaanite species of religion—worship of "Baal"—appealed to many Israelites as more congenial. Yet we should not jump to the conclusion that such waverers were familiar with foreign gods, and consciously served them. It is surprisingly difficult to decide how far the Israelite populace in fact gave any recognition to other gods, and to what extent any of them confined Yahweh in their imaginations to the role of a local genie whom they could get away from.

They certainly recognised other nations' gods as existing in some fashion. So indeed did the priests and prophets themselves. Explicit monotheism was still latent. But there is no proof that any Israelites of this early time saw their own God as anything less than the only Higher Power that mattered, at least to Israel. One or two passages do raise minor perplexities. In *Judges* xi:24 Jephthah says to the King of the Ammonites, "Will you not possess what Chemosh your god gives you to possess? And all that the Lord our God has dispossessed before us, we will possess." Also, *I Samuel* xxvi:19 implies that a banished outlaw must "serve other gods." Yet it is not easy to reconcile the idea that such gods were respected as sovereign entities with Israel's manifest ignorance of them.

Though their names are cited in a few cases, their attributes and myths are not. It might be argued that everything of that kind which the biblical literature once contained has been censored out. But the Bible never even denies the foreigners, or attacks them in any detail, or portrays them as fighting Yahweh. They are null—astonishingly so.

If the early Israelites were ever inclined to defect to them, we would expect warnings in plainer terms. Yet the only beings whose worship the Law specifically forbids are minor Hebrew demons, the "satyrs" of *Leviticus* xvii:7. All others are comprehended under broad bans on idolatry and "sacrificing to any god save the Lord only." The inference with regard to these other gods is that most Israelites knew practically nothing about them. They were aware that pagans outside their own territory bowed down to idols, which had names and were foolishly supposed to have autonomous power; but they thought of these as scarcely more than fetishes. While the allusion to Chemosh sounds like a confession of his genuine godhead, it need not be more than an *argumentum ad hominem*, a remark framed so that the barbarian listener can take it in.

To Israel in its age of creative isolation, foreign gods apparently were not personal deities with a real jurisdiction. They were the ju-jus of the blinded heathen, with at most a baleful half-life, a clinging aura of bad magic. An exile could be forced under their spell. Not however because Yahweh had any frontiers, for he was God of all the world; but because the Land was his earthly dwelling-place, the region of his manifestation. In the impure realms outside, it was impossible to make contact with him. One was cut off.

When passages in the *Book of Judges* denounce Israel's treason against the Lord, they would not seem to be referring to a deliberate service of other gods, whether by apostasy or by polytheism. The target of their complaints is a mental confusion—a cultus of indigenous baals as guises or deputies of Yahweh, and kindred lapses toward the foreigner's Nature-worshipping pattern.[4] The scriptural "Baal"

4 Later, the evidence for the worship of Yahweh as Baal is explicit. See *Hosea* ii:16.

means an image under which the cosmos was apprehended, rather than a single god. Its generic sense of "owner" or "lord," and its Canaanite association with a god who sent storms, made it usable in connection with Yahweh. Israelite personal names give a sidelight here. We find many with "Yahweh" in them, as "Jo" at the beginning or as "-iah" at the end; we also find "Baal" names; and in the judges' era and for long after, the names give no evidence of a factional split or a direct Yahweh-Baal clash. In *Judges* vi:11-32 the same man has a Yahweh name and a Baal altar, with a tree for the lady Asherah. His son wrecks the altar and cuts down Asherah's tree, whereupon the father abandons the cult as pointless. But there is no suggestion of a sustained conflict or a radical conversion. This Baal was probably thought of as a fertility spirit in the Lord's service.

Elsewhere the Old Testament speaks many more times of respect being shown to goddesses, perhaps as wives of Yahweh. It also adumbrates a bull-cult (as in the matter of Aaron's Calf) and a serpent-cult. It has stories of occasional human sacrifice (as in the tragedy of Jephthah's daughter) and of what may be ritual prostitution. Above all, it has numerous allusions to "high places," hill-shrines on the Canaanite model devoted to mixed and probably zestful ceremonies. But a doubt remains as to how much of this irregularity actually went on, and the high places, at first, were not condemned at all. None of the tampering with Yahweh went so far as to negate the Mosaic view of him. The temptation to commit the arch-blasphemy—to make him frankly a common Nature-god, dying and reviving as the Canaanite Baal did—was opposed with energy and success. Orthodoxy was always the norm, baalism a perversion: alluring, but certainly never triumphant, and shown chiefly in superimposed superstition rather than a downright divergence—in unhallowed offerings, in wild carnivals, in the prizing of amulets, in spell-weaving and divination and necromancy. To sum up: in attempts to have it both ways. A good parallel is the semi-paganism of Mexican Indians, who keep the older cults alive without ceasing to be Catholic.

In the light of comparative religion, one would expect more. One would expect to see Israel settling into a cult that came naturally, a Hebrew variant of the Semitic norm. Israel had nothing tangible to bias it otherwise. In fact the Bible shows plainly that the slide toward baalism, whatever its true extent, was persistent. All surrounding peoples had religions that grew out of their culture and situation; and Israel was continually trying to have one. But it was continually being dragged back against the grain. The voice which recalled Israel to Yahweh was a voice from the past, that of the generation which entered into the desert Covenant. This voice never lost its authority. It could always renew itself. There were the priests and prophets. There were ardent conservatives who lived in tents like their forefathers. There were dedicated men called Nazirites, athletes of Yahweh, who drank no wine and observed the Law austerely. Again and again eyes and hearts were trapped in the kaleidoscope of misconceived Nature. Again and again a fiery minority drew the rest back, in the face of all likelihood, to the Lord of History—to the vision of an intelligible world of men and events, sustained and morally ordered by the blessing of God.

Where the restraining power came from, believer and unbeliever may debate as they please. The point is that such a power did exist. No other nation of antiquity was ever similarly bent against its own character and conditions of life. Israel displayed, and continued to display, the spectacle of a prophetic few and a recalcitrant mass, the few for ever hauling the mass into an extraordinary stance of eternal dissent.[5] And the background of that dissent, in the judges' era, was a mental process which amounted to a fourth step in Israel's logic.

5 I would like here to record a tribute (and indeed a debt) to my great-grandfather, Dr. Isaac Ashe, who, in his essay *The Divine Origin of Christianity*, enlarged on these and related facts with an insight far ahead of his time. The essay won a prize, but seems never to have found its way into bibliographies; perhaps because its author was a physician, and therefore an amateur.

A World by Itself

Why did God do so much to plant us here in the Land?

To create a nation in a special relationship with himself, living by his laws in a special territory, and knowing and affirming him in a manner superior to the heathen. His promise of the Land to Abraham and Moses was conditional on "righteousness"; and he made that condition because he desires righteousness, just as we desire this country to live in.

4

It followed that when the tribes' tenure of Palestine was so long imperilled by enemies, a belief grew that religious falsity was to blame. Yahweh was punishing his people for not living up to their vocation. Whether or not one accepts this retributive idea, every weakening in the solidarity of the common faith must have lowered morale and exposed the settlers to fresh danger. The *Book of Judges* is a record of conflict.

Israel's tribulation was only part of a vaster upheaval over-spreading half the known world. Nations were on the move. The advance of the Iron Age was undermining the social order, some-what as the advent of longbows and guns undermined feudalism. A commoner with iron weapons could kill a Homeric knight. In the thirteenth century B.C. it had been possible for the Hittite-Egyptian entente to pacify the Near East. In the twelfth, any such omnibus arrangement was out of the question. The immediate sequel of this change was a dark period of disruption. Several civilisations, such as the Mycenean, succumbed. Hordes of wander-ing clans from the Balkans and Greece and Asia Minor surged over the Levant. The Egyptians called them Sea Peoples, and many raiders did cross the Mediterranean in pirate fleets. Others, with all their families and goods, pushed along the coasts in wagons. Names which occur in an Egyptian account at Medinet Habu suggest that some of Homer's Achaeans took part in the adventure; but any such elements must have been decadent and barbarous. The Sea Peoples poured down to within a few miles of Egypt. They did not repeat the victory of the Hyksos. Rameses III defeated them in

1196 and drove them back. But he could not prevent large numbers of them from making their homes along the Palestinian coast (which was thus finally lost to Egypt) and in the nearer hinterland. These remained there, ostensibly under Pharaoh's protectorate, in practice independent.

They may have had something to do with the displacement of the tribe of Dan from its original holding. However, their first serious collision with Israel took place about 1125. A chief who had established himself at Hazor, in what is now Upper Galilee, sent an army into the strategic plain of Jezreel beneath Megiddo. The fertility and ease of communication in this area held out an alluring prospect. The name of the general in command, Sisera, indicates that he was of Sea-People descent, with forebears perhaps from as far away as the Adriatic; and if he was, then probably many of his warriors were. Sisera was opposed by several thousand Israelites who momentarily reversed the trend of the times by defeating his chariots. Owing to a rainstorm, the river Kishon overflowed and the war-vehicles were useless. The tribesmen had never got the better of chariots before, and their victory was an elixir. Sisera himself did not escape. He was decoyed into a trap by a Kenite woman, who murdered him in his sleep with a mallet and tent-peg.

In this campaign we hear of a prophet as supplying inspired leadership. The prophet is a woman, Deborah. She is said to have been a judge as well. A forceful triumphal ode attributed to her is old enough to be authentic. Its repetitive climactic effects belong to the early poetic school.

> Most blessed of women be Jael . . .
> She put her hand to the tent-peg
>   and her right hand to the workmen's mallet;
> She struck Sisera a blow,
>   she crushed his head,
>   she shattered and pierced his temple.
> He sank, he fell,
>   he lay still at her feet;

At her feet he sank, he fell;
   where he sank, there he fell dead.

Like the *Exodus* authors, Deborah has not a word to say about foreign gods opposing Yahweh. Her sole hint at other non-human powers ranges them on the side of the Lord who made them. "The stars in their courses fought against Sisera."

The rout brought Israel no lasting peace. Judges such as Gideon and Jephthah are depicted struggling again and again with various interlopers. But all other enemies are eclipsed by the entry of the Philistines. In the Egyptian record at Medinet Habu, the Philistines are called Pulasati and counted among the Sea Peoples. They were a nation of complex ancestry, formed by the union in Crete of streams of marauders from several regions—Asia Minor, the Aegean, perhaps mainland Greece. They may have been the attackers who destroyed Knossos and the Minoan empire, about 1400 B.C. If so, they stayed on among the ruins intermarrying, till the wave of the twelfth century hurled them forward again. Their apparent archaeological linkage with Crete is supported by *Amos* ix:7, where they are stated to have come from Caphtor—that is, in all probability, Keftiu, the Egyptian name for Minos's island. In the Sea Peoples' vanguard that squatted on the Canaanite littoral, the Philistines were the strongest group, already on the way to absorbing the rest. On the sites of Canaanite towns burnt in the invasion they built five cities of their own. The chief was Askalon; the others were Ashdod, Ekron, Gath and Gaza. These cities were allied but autonomous. The Philistines were a crude race with little inventive talent. They acquired some Canaanite culture, and gave their Aegean gods Canaanite names such as Dagon. Their only contributions to their adopted country were the general use of iron and, most ironically, the name "Palestine" itself. The renascent Greeks of a later day, who knew the coastland long before they knew the interior, called it Philistine Syria.

For about a century Philistine and Israelite lived side by side without clashing. Then, doubtless owing to economic pressure, the people of the coast began to thrust inland. Mercenary service under the Hittites and Egyptians had given them a strong military tradition, and they of course had iron weapons and chariots. The Israelite judge Samson, a Nazirite, who was on friendly terms with them during phases of truce, tried to resist them when they domineered. They captured and blinded him. Legend afterwards made him a superhuman Hercules, but one has the impression of a lonely leader and a supine nation, weary of fighting and acquiescent for the moment in alien overlordship. Through the middle of the eleventh century the Philistines were in the ascendant. To strengthen their hold, they forbade subject Israelites to work in metal. Tools, theoretically at least, had to be taken to Philistine smiths for sharpening (*I Samuel* xiii:19-22). Weapons of war, apart from bows and slings, were hard to maintain. Swords existed, but must have been either crude makeshifts or expensive imports.

Philistine domination reached its first climax in the time of the judge Eli, who was also head priest at Shiloh. Israel by then was in one of its deeper troughs of failure. After a defeat, some of the elders took the Ark out of its sanctuary and into the camp, superstitiously hoping that it would act as a talisman. In a second battle a few miles west of Shiloh, the Philistines won again and captured the Ark. The news broke Eli's heart; the Philistines marched farther inland and burned Shiloh itself—a blow not recorded in the biblical history, but glanced at by the prophet Jeremiah. Israel was reduced to a leaderless and centreless rabble holding out in the hills and desert fringes. The Philistines restored the Ark, which a plague had caused them to regard as an unlucky object, and it was set up in a private house at Kiriath-jearim. But years passed without any sign of revival. No name of a judge has been preserved from this abject anarchy.

Fresh leadership eventually came from Samuel. His story, like so many in the Old Testament, is a blend of various traditions. He seems to have been the last great Israelite on the undifferentiated pattern of Moses, combining all roles. We see him as a prophet in the broader sense, receiving messages from Yahweh; as a priest, officiating at sacrifices; as a judge, governing; as a commander, helping to organise campaigns; and even as a humble seer, supplying useful information for pay. It is quite credible that he did all these things.

He began life as a servant of Eli. After Shiloh fell, he wandered among the pockets of guerrilla resistance, preaching that the disaster was a divine judgment and that Israel must return to the Lord. Finally he managed to draw together an assembly at Mizpah, where his recognition as judge ended the interregnum. A Philistine expedition lost its nerve in a storm and withdrew, leaving Samuel in control of a nucleus of free territory, though a very small one. His home was at Ramah, and his annual circuit took him only to Mizpah, Bethel and Gilgal. As to the condition of the rest of the Land, we have no direct knowledge. But Philistine rule was probably slack enough to allow a quiet recovery, here and there, under Samuel's influence. In his old age he was able to appoint his sons as judges in Beersheba, an act implying the liberation of much of the south. This liberation may have been the work of the tribe of Judah, which thereby rose to prominence and established its claim in all that area.

The elders of the people, however, had no confidence in Samuel's sons. They precipitated a crisis by waiting on him at Ramah and asking him to appoint a king. The primary need was for stable and united authority. Only the rule of one man could organise the overthrow of the Philistine.

Scripture gives two versions of the birth of the monarchy, reflecting the ambiguity which it always had in Israelite eyes. The first treats it as a mistake, the second as a divine ordinance. Yet the two are squared. The Lord, we are told, did not approve the elders' request. Accordingly Samuel, who doubtless knew something of the despotisms around, gave the deputation a solemn warning. It was no good pretending that a king could be merely a commander-in-chief. He would set up a court, and maintain it by requisitioning land and labour. He would take away the best of Israelite youth to work on his estates, serve in his army, cook for his household. Also, monarchy had a heathen air. The people were "rejecting the Lord from being king over them"—and, we may add, embracing an institution which tended elsewhere to deify human beings. Samuel's protests were vain. The elders repeated their demand. Again he sought guidance, and the Lord (here is the reconciling link) replied that having done his duty, he should give way. "Hearken to their voice, and make them a king." In the upshot, as the sequel discloses, the Lord showed him how to turn the situation to good account.

Samuel was inspired to choose a Benjamite king. Benjamin being the smallest tribe, the choice would avoid arousing jealousies among the larger. Also, the late-settling Benjamites had not acquired much land of their own, and therefore had a restless and predatory spirit which could be harnessed for war. The election fell on Saul, the handsome, very tall son of one of the better-off peasants. He came (it is said) to ask Samuel about a lost herd of asses. Samuel invited the bewildered visitor to a feast, and anointed him with oil to be sovereign of Israel. As a sign of good faith, the old king-maker predicted that when Saul went on his way he would meet a party of *nabhi* prophets playing on their musical instruments. Saul did meet them; the fever seized him and he prophesied with the rest. The spirit of Yahweh now dwelt within him.

Saul made Gibeah his capital and raised troops at once. His immediate opponents were not the Philistines, but the Ammonites beyond Jordan who were threatening the Israelite town of Jabesh-Gilead. The royal summons called for warriors to follow "Saul and Samuel," a form of words answering to his doubtful and makeshift office. He was still no more than a paramount chief, a leader of patriotic irregulars. However, a victory over the Ammonites strengthened his position. Retaining a picked force, he began to probe the Philistine outposts. A war of stratagem and surprise was clearly Israel's best chance. His son Jonathan scored the first success by overwhelming the Philistine garrison of Geba.

Hope was returning. On a hill at Gibeah—perhaps converting a Philistine depot—Saul built himself a stronghold. It was to be his sole monument, and not a durable one at that. Later in the reign his enemies partially destroyed it. Excavation, however, has uncovered the plan of a crude but formidable rectangle, with four corner towers and at least two stories. Its walls are double, the outer being six feet thick. The external measurements are 169 feet by 114. In the inner enclosure many sling-stones and bronze arrowheads have been found, and some pottery, very rough and undecorative.

Long before the fortress was finished, Saul had to face a Philistine counter-attack. He mustered a new army in the Jordan valley and waited at Gilgal for Samuel to arrive. Morale was low. As the Philistines approached, the Israelites began to desert, hiding in caves or slipping across the river into Gilead. The weakness of the dual command became evident. Saul and Samuel were both appointed by Yahweh, but for different tasks. Saul fought; Samuel prayed, and offered sacrifice for the army. At Gilgal there was a hitch. Samuel's coming was delayed. What was Saul to do? The steady trickle of desertions went on; the Philistines might appear through the hills at any moment. It was imperative to advance and forestall them, yet impious to move without sacrificing to the Lord. After waiting an anxious week the King assumed the priestly duty himself, and made a burnt offering. Then Samuel came at last, and told him that by acting independently he had forfeited divine favour. His descendants would not succeed him.

Argument at such a crisis was futile. Saul led the army west again, and an ambush contrived by Jonathan gave him victory. But he still had no rest. To maintain any living space at all, he had to lead repeated wars against every neighbouring nation, Ammonites and Moabites as well as Philistines. No doubt, by this time, Israelite smiths were supplying their countrymen with good swords and spears. Little by little Saul gained ground. However, an attack on the Amalekites led to a final breach with Samuel. For reasons arising out of past history, the prophet placed them under a *herem* or ban, meaning "no quarter." In the Lord's name he forbade Saul to take prisoners or carry off animals. The single aim of the war was

extermination. When Saul reappeared with the pick of the Amalekites' sheep and oxen, making the unconvincing excuse that he had
saved them as sacrificial victims, Samuel declared roundly that the
Lord would transfer the crown elsewhere. The King, in fact, had
lost the blessing which effective kingship required. The partnership
dissolved; the junior partner's character deteriorated; and the
senior carried out his threat.

Samuel set up another king. According to the Bible he acted
secretly. The tale is too familiar to need much recalling. It relates
how Samuel went to Bethlehem, to the house of a landowner
named Jesse, of the tribe of Judah. There he anointed Jesse's youngest
son David, who was tending the sheep. Thus the prophet transferred
the charisma from Saul to David. The youth was a poet and musician. Saul had become subject to fits of melancholia, and David
was invited to play on the lyre to soothe him. For a while David's
time was divided between his home and the court. When a fresh
Philistine host entered Israelite territory, he won Saul's favour by
killing the giant champion Goliath with a sling. He became a
close friend of Saul's son Jonathan, married one of Saul's daughters,
and led a contingent of his own. But he was so successful and
popular that the King scented a dangerous rival, and tried to have
him murdered. For some years David was hounded from place
to place, together with a band of devoted outlaws who shared the
secret of his kingship. At first he was befriended by Samuel; then
Samuel died, and the precariousness of his life increased. He even
enrolled as a mercenary in Philistine service, out of the presence of
the Lord.

When the Philistines threatened Israel yet again, Saul had no
one to turn to for advice. In desperation he took unlawful means,
consulting a woman medium at En-dor. Samuel's shade appeared,
and told him that he had no more to hope for. He would fall in
battle and David would be king. The armies met at Mount Gilboa,
far to the north and far inland, and the Israelites were totally routed.
Saul and Jonathan both perished. David—who had had no part
in the fighting—mourned for them in a song of lamentation, one

of the surviving poems attributed to him, of which there are many more in the *Book of Psalms*. Saul had another son Ish-bosheth, who inherited his title, but David openly asserted his own claim, and was recognised by his tribe of Judah. He reigned in Hebron. After seven years of confusion Ish-bosheth was assassinated and David became the monarch of all the tribes.

5

With David the Israelite kingdom properly starts, and the possession of the Land is given political and dynastic form. The record of his doings has an impetus which is hard to resist. Although it has been compiled from several sources, a little roughly here and there, it presents few difficulties of detail. Few, at least, that cannot be credibly resolved. Thus the hero's famous musical gift is sometimes alleged to be a later interpolation which makes the story stumble. Admittedly Saul seems uncertain who David is on the day of Goliath's challenge, when he is supposed to have already had him performing at court. But boys in the East grow up and change rapidly. Saul may not have been able to "place," in a different and distracting context, the youth who had sung for him some time earlier. David may have drifted back almost entirely to the family flocks, and grown a beard in the interval. To speak more generally on this point, the strangeness of a warrior being also a poet and lyre-player is an argument in favour of authenticity rather than against it. Such artistic accomplishments are not of the sort which Semitic nations regarded as virile. It is more likely that David actually had them than that heroic legend falsely ascribed them to him. He must have been versatile; but if anyone insists on being given a trustworthy parallel, we need not look further than Winston Churchill.

Criticism here cannot destroy, but it can revalue, by putting the data in their setting. David's connection with Judah marks him as an Israelite of a slightly abnormal kind. He belonged to a tribe which was late in putting itself into shape, and more heterogeneous than most. The *Book of Ruth* indeed gives him a partly Moabite ancestry. Even his name is odd. No one else bears it in the Bible, but it occurs in the Mari archives as *dawidum*, meaning a commander. Was David in reality named otherwise, but remembered only as "The General"? or had his family adopted a foreign rank as a personal name, as dark-age Welshmen turned the Roman "tribune" into the name "Triphun"? On either showing, one gets a hint of something a trifle curious, and it is surely more than a trifle curious that David of all people should have "served other gods" and fought loyally for the Philistines. He may have been a man of hybrid heredity and culture, who threw himself into public affairs with a special impact. So perhaps was Moses, "the Egyptian," before him. So were others after him. In this case the outstanding parallel is not Churchill but Napoleon.

Evidently when Saul's forces collapsed at Gilboa, toward the end of the second millennium B.C., the Philistines recovered the whole country. They may even have pushed across Jordan and won control of the caravan routes beyond. The political result was a division of the conquered area into subject states. David, at Hebron, ruled his own southern tribe as the Philistines' vassal—a pretender enthroned by outside aid. Saul's son Ish-bosheth (or rather Ish-baal; the name is a scribal euphemism) held the north on similar terms, if with less complicated antecedents. Between them was a patch of ground still occupied by the non-Hebrew Jebusites, and these also must have come under Philistine mastery. David, however, had served the conquerors himself, and he saw that their achievement was hollow. The five coastal cities had no single head and no common plan. They could not maintain a joint empire, or prevent their puppet in Judah from reverting to his natural patriotism. Whenever he chose to assert himself, their system proved ineffectual. The northerners rallied to the bold Israelite who acted as if there were no Philistines about, and did it with complete success. David, on his accession as their new king, was anointed separately. For the moment the sole secular bond between the northern and southern tribes was this personal one. David was monarch of all Israelites as James I was King of England and

Scotland before their union. For the moment that was enough.

The Bible makes clear the vigour and purpose of his next steps. Although the Philistines were still nominally his suzerains, they had not interfered. He was already independent. Now, doing what no previous Israelite had done, he occupied the Jebusites' enclave and took their chief town by cutting off its water supply. This town was Jerusalem. The Amarna letter which calls it "Urusalim" proves its considerable age; Abraham's meeting with Melchizedek, and his binding of Isaac on the hill of Moriah, would seem to give it a semi-historical character several centuries further back still. Having captured the place, David made it his royal city and capital, not incorporated into the tribal scheme. This was an astute move, showing both political and strategic sense.

Jebusite Jerusalem must have been a mere village. David's creation, in his own lifetime, was still small. Essentially the site consists of a block of elevated ground formed by two ridges. David appears to have built where his Jebusite precursors built, on the easterly ridge called Ophel. To a part of the ridge (then, though not to-day) the name "Mount Zion" was given. This was the hill that grew so richly symbolic, the heart of Israel to which the thoughts of the wanderer always turned, and which stood mystically for the entire Land as Yahweh's dwelling-place. On the east of Ophel is a cleft, the valley of the Kidron, and across Kidron is an abrupt ascent to the Mount of Olives, which is part of a much higher ridge overlooking the city. Yet Jerusalem itself is high, half a mile above sea level. When one approaches it along the road leading upward from the Dead Sea and Jordan, at the bottom of their crack in the earth's crust, the freakish twists of landscape set Jerusalem on the skyline. Though desert presses in close, the district itself is comparatively kindly, at least in spring when white almond-blossom and red anemone have pleased the eye from time immemorial. Jerusalem's summer is parched by the *khamsin* wind, but absolute drought has seldom been its worst affliction. For three thousand years there have always been weary travellers to whom the sight of David's city is a joy and relief.

As soon as Jerusalem was ready, David sent for the Ark of the Covenant (which had been kept in its home-made shrine at Kiriath-jearim since the ruin of Shiloh) and escorted it into his capital with a grand procession, dancing in the festivities himself. Some of his sons were made priests, though they were not Levites. Also he brought Goliath's head—or skull, one would suppose, by this time—and set it up as a trophy.[6]

He had learnt other things among the Philistines besides a correct appraisal of their imperial strength, or lack of it. He had learnt the secret of the strength which they did possess: their ability to win battles. Instead of relying on *ad hoc* levies of rustic militia, they employed professional soldiers such as David himself had been. One of his first concerns was to form an army of his own under picked officers, and enlist foreign mercenaries. When the Philistines did at last try to crush him, he drove them back and confined them to a strip of coast. The tables were turned, and finally. They could still make trouble on the border, but they never penetrated Israel again.

The victory was not an end but a beginning. David happened to be a great man in an age of dwarfs. By a coincidence of chances, all the larger nations had passed into eclipse at the same time. Egypt was governed by a dynasty of nonentities. The Hittite and Babylonian states had dwindled away. The kingdom of Assyria, formed by a revolt against Babylon, had lost momentum and could not oppose a Palestinian ruler. David's foreign policy consisted chiefly in profiting by these facts. He extended his frontiers on all sides, till a solid belt of annexed borderlands was yielding him revenue and holding potential challengers at arm's length. Success attended him everywhere. Pushing past the Dead Sea, he conquered Moab and made it a dependency; then he invaded Ammon, to the north of Moab, and had himself proclaimed king; then Edom, to the south, where he planted garrisons and appointed a military governor. The Aramaeans of Syria menaced his flank, but he routed these

6 The bringing of Goliath's head is mentioned in *I Samuel* xvii:54, out of place.

also and occupied Damascus, their capital. Inside Palestine he suppressed the last tiny Canaanite city-states, and refortified some of the cities.

Israel's forward surge created a new empire stretching from the Gulf of Aqaba to the Euphrates, or nearly so. It was a composite structure containing a medley of peoples. Its only unity was in the person of David, and its power of survival depended on the quality of his heirs. Israel easily dominated the complex. Yet the assimilation of the Canaanites meant a subtle reinforcement of their internal influence. Furthermore, David embarked on trading and diplomatic relations with the Phoenicians of Tyre, whose king, Hiram, sent him cedar wood from the forests of Lebanon. There too was a threat to Israel's integrity, though it took time to develop.

An interesting figure among David's officers is Uriah the Hittite. "Uriah" looks like a Yahweh name, "the Lord my light," suggesting that this alien had adopted the worship of Israel's God; not as the first to do so, to judge from *Ruth* i:16, but very nearly. The biblical Hittites are elusive. They are mentioned living in Canaan, as when Abraham buys the field and cave of Machpelah, and when Esau marries two Hittite women. *Numbers* xiii:29—certainly an early text—places them in the hills. But although the Hittite monarchs of Asia Minor were once capable of treating with the Pharaohs as equals, we have no direct evidence that they ever colonised Canaan. The most that can be said is that there may have been small settlements of emigrants. If not, the Pentateuch's Hittites must be a different nation. In any case the empire collapsed before David's time. It was succeeded in Syria by petty "Neo-Hittite" kingdoms of mixed culture. When the later books of the Bible speak of Hittites (as in *II Kings* vii: 6) they seem to mean Neo-Hittites. Uriah could have been one of these.

In the Bible he is David's unwitting nemesis. David wanted Uriah's wife Bathsheba. During the campaign in Ammon, he arranged for Uriah to be placed in an exposed position and then deserted. The King married the widow. This crime of David's was the beginning of a decline and a partial loss of divine favour.

The prophet Nathan denounced him, and he was duly penitent. But he kept Bathsheba. He lived henceforth under a cloud. His son Absalom rebelled, and while David came through unshaken, Absalom's death was a tragic loss for which nothing could compensate. Toward the close of his reign he ordered a census of all Israelites, which is said to have revealed that the north had 800,000 able-bodied men and the south 500,000; these figures, however, are questionable; it is unlikely that the whole population was much above a million. David's census was a sin in the Lord's sight, and judgment came in the form of a plague. He made atonement by buying a plot of ground on Moriah, the threshing-floor of Araunah the Jebusite, where, just outside the wall of his infant capital, he put up an altar as the nucleus of a permanent temple. Here Israel's vocation was to be brought to a focus. Here the work begun in Egypt was to be finished at last.

David is in many respects an Israelite ideal. But in the books of *Samuel* and *Kings* he is conspicuously not idealised. The court annals used in these books were probably assembled within the lifetime of eye-witnesses, and written down on the recently invented papyrus. Compared with anything else from the monarchies of ancient Asia, they are amazingly frank and realistic. Moreover (to sum up on the main historical issue) they can be trusted in all essentials, if only because the attempt to treat them as fiction would raise far greater problems than any it solved. If the events did happen, the writer need not have been too extraordinary a genius. If they did not, he becomes an almost incredible literary freak. There is nothing like his work in contemporary royal annals; but there is nothing like it in fiction either—unless we allow Homer an improbably early date.

From this court history, and some supplementary points in *I Chronicles*, David emerges as an Israelite ruler of a new kind. He has Yahweh's blessing, and is personally devout. However, he does not rely on inspiration, or special divine interventions. He is a statesman, although his statesmanship is consecrated; a man of intelligence, although his intelligence is directed to translating Yahweh's will into human terms. Around him we see a new system growing up to hold the nation together—an administrative class, a standing army, an embryo civil service. Eloquent touches like a reference to iron nails attest Israel's progress. And the honesty of the account brings out the resultant stresses. Already there is a prophet on the scene who dares to rebuke the King. Already there is an undercurrent of resistance. The sin of the census is that it encroaches on freedom. David's aim in taking it was undoubtedly to compile a sort of Domesday Book. With his subjects registered, he could tax them more efficiently, and conscript them for war and labour service.

The truth is that Israel was still socially and constitutionally unlike its neighbours. Monarchy had been superimposed on the distinct tribal communities, and each had its special customs, its laboriously developed sense of its members' rights. The Hebrew tribesmen had strong ideas about property and the dignity of the subject; the divine commandments supported them; and the King, a late-comer, had to move cautiously and could never be absolute.[7] In the affair of Bathsheba, the surprising feature is not David's conduct but the condemnation in which it involves him. Any oriental despot might have behaved as he did. No other oriental people would have reproved him for it, or put the reproof on record.

Israelite monarchy matured in this atmosphere of adjustment and tension, both during David's reign and afterwards. The King had certain tasks to do, and no one challenged his right to do them as he saw best, provided that he stayed within bounds. He was commander-in-chief. He dispensed justice. Also he performed various ritual duties as a kind of priest. The last matter was delicate, and remains obscure. Throughout the Near East and Egypt, as anthropologists have exhaustively shown, kingship had a "sacral"

7 Here again there is a parallel with the Anglo-Saxons, and with the peculiar growth of monarchy in England. I have gone into this a little in *From Caesar to Arthur*, pp. 260-7.

character. Normally the sovereign was descended from gods. He incarnated a god himself, and led annual festivals in this role. His health and fortunes furnished the index of national prosperity, and, indeed, affected it. The Israelites were disposed to see their own sovereign in the same light, as they were disposed to copy their neighbours in other ways; indeed that temptation has left its marks on the biblical text. But actually they watered the concept down, first because of the aforesaid social restraints, and secondly because Yahweh and the King could not be fused. The King could not *be* God or descended from God. His sacral character could consist only in being God's agent, duly anointed by a priest, solemnly enthroned and homaged in a holy place. Israel's true King was always Yahweh, and the people could appeal to him if their human monarch failed them—by losing a war, for instance. When David praises God in the Psalms, he is not hymning himself. The gap between creature and Creator is always there.

David's religious acts are entirely human in their nature. As a king-priest he conducts the Ark into Jerusalem. It is a pious deed; it is also a fine stroke of policy, which annexes the history of Israel to the monarchy and the royal city. Soon after it, we are told, David received through Nathan the Lord's promise that "his house and his kingdom would be made sure," that "his throne would be established for ever." This combination of divine purpose with dynastic principle was to be momentous. So was the act which carried centralisation further, David's purchase of land for an immediate altar and a prospective temple.

David died within a few years, one way or the other, of 970. His chosen heir was Solomon, his son by Bathsheba. Notoriety has clung to his deathbed order to Solomon to kill two men whom he had spared himself. But this order was grounded on ancestral beliefs about guilt and curses; it implies no malice or cruelty beyond the norms of the age. The succession was not smooth. Another prince tried to effect a coup. However, Solomon carried out a swift purge and was in due course enthroned.

6

Solomon's name is etymologically linked with *shalom*. Despite the initial murders, most of his reign was peaceful enough to fulfil the implied omen. David's son held the empire securely, and continued David's work. The story of the dream in which God offered him a boon, and he asked for wisdom, marks the full transition from inspired leadership to deliberate rule. Solomon's wisdom is to be construed chiefly as a practical Hebrew gift, "an understanding mind to govern the people," shown in the celebrated tale of the disputed baby. However, the King is also credited with a rare knowledge of natural history, and with the composition of three thousand proverbs and a thousand and five songs.

His main religious concern was to institutionalise the cult in a temple on David's site. Israel had no engineers or architects equal to his ambition. He turned, therefore, to David's correspondent Hiram, the King of Tyre. All the stretch of coast from Mount Carmel northward was by this time under Phoenician control. To appreciate what Solomon's move meant, one must realise that the Phoenicians were, in effect, the Canaanites recrudescent. Thrust under by Israel and the Sea Peoples, a remnant had spread out northward, enriched themselves with new blood, and made a brilliant recovery. They had grown into a people of immense if narrow vigour and skill, great traders and seafarers; the form of the letters in the Hebrew alphabet owed something to them. In due course they were to open up the western Mediterranean, found Carthage and Tartessus or "Tarshish," and circumnavigate Africa. Their civilisation was the Canaanite carried further, with a more refined and arbitrary governing class, a more flamboyant and cruel Nature-worship.

To these dubious friends the King of Israel applied. First he asked for building materials. In return for annual shipments of wheat and oil, Hiram ordered the felling of more cedars in Lebanon, employing lumberjacks of his own and admitting Israelites to work alongside them. The logs were hauled down to the coast and floated along in raft formation to a point as near Jerusalem as possible. But Phoenician help was not solely material. Hiram sent a master metal-worker of mixed Israelite and Tyrian parentage—also confusingly named Hiram—to superintend the Temple's bronze. It is no shock to learn from archaeologists that this Israelite house of worship, as portrayed in the Bible, sounds very like a Phoenician one.

Solomon's labourers and craftsmen took seven years to finish it. Yet it was quite small, even cramped. Its internal dimensions were about ninety feet by thirty, with a ceiling forty-five feet high. These figures are not taken from excavations (nothing visible is left, and the mosque on the site precludes digging), but from the plain statement of the biblical author. Shelley's lines in "Queen Mab"—

> There once old Salem's haughty fane
>
> Reared high to heaven its thousand golden domes—

betray an unpardonable ignorance of the very Scripture which the poem professes to refute.

As to details, we have the customary difficulty about picturing anything whatever from a Hebrew description. But it seems that the Temple ran from west to east. Its walls were of stone, and had side-chambers or chapels along the outside. Entry was by way of a porch at the eastern end. All the interior was lined with wood. The floor was of fir or cypress; the walls were of cedar, carved with floral designs, and embellished with gold. The main nave or Holy Place, into which the porch led, was sixty feet long and contained an altar where perfumes were burnt. Doors of carved olive wood opened from it into the residual space at the western end, thirty feet each way. This was the windowless inner shrine or Holy of Holies; a raised floor and perhaps a lowered roof made it a perfect cube. Inside it stood two "cherubim," symbolic winged sphinxes. Made of olive wood like the doors and plated with gold, they were fifteen feet tall, and their outspread wings measured fifteen feet from tip to tip, so that the two pairs of wings reached from one wall to the other and touched in the middle.

Round the Temple was a court as a place of assembly for the laity. Hiram, the metal-worker, set up two hollow bronze columns with ornamented capitals, one on either side of the porch. These were called Jachin and Boaz, and were about twenty-seven feet high. He also provided the east portion of the court with a circular bronze tank or "sea" supported by twelve images of oxen. Other ritual apparatus included ten bronze trolleys and many pots and bowls. These served an outdoor altar for burnt offerings, not far from the porch. But the Temple's finest furnishings—its lamp-stands and cups and dishes—were made of gold.

On an autumn day when the Temple was complete, Solomon summoned all his chief subjects. Priests carried the Ark through the porch and nave into the dim Holy of Holies, and set it down beneath the wings of the cherubim, finally at rest with its precious tablets of stone. "The Lord," Solomon declared, "has said that he would dwell in thick darkness," and so it was. Standing by the outdoor altar before the crowd, Solomon offered up a prayer, which he followed by sacrificing sheep and oxen in huge numbers.

Henceforth the Temple was Israel's sanctuary. Its priests sacrificed daily. On a table inside they laid out the shewbread, a batch of twelve loaves renewed each Sabbath, symbolising the tribes. The head priest with his rich vestments was a splendid figure; he alone had the right to enter the Holy of Holies. From all over the Land, pilgrims came regularly by thousands for the annual ceremonies.

The dedication gave Israelites a sense of fulfilment. They felt that they had at last, so to speak, "arrived." Yahweh had rescued them from Egypt, granted them the Covenant, established them firmly in the Land. Now they had given him a permanent home and would live happily ever after. It was probably in Solomon's reign that the Yahwist author composed his narrative which supplies the Pentateuchal backbone. The chief Elohist may have been busy too, though his "E" matter was undergoing revision for some decades or even centuries afterwards. Both writers drew on the corpus of tradition which had gathered round the liturgy of the tribes. If there was an earlier single epic, it may have been divergently expanded in north and south when the Philistine occupation reduced contact, so that the Yahwist used a southern form and the Elohist a northern.

Though the Yahwist shows no sign of a wish to flatter Solomon, his work has one partial parallel—the legend connecting Rome with Troy, which Virgil gave epic form as a mythos for Augustus. But in spite of a genuine traditional pedigree, the saga of Aeneas and Jupiter's plans for him had neither popular roots nor the authority of a large enough faith. It was too much a literary contrivance to have any serious bearing on the vast affairs of the Empire. As a real influence the Yahwist's work stands alone, and there is little doubt that the other Pentateuchal sources, "E" and "P," both owe him a debt.

With the Temple launched, Solomon put other schemes into effect. Just south of it he built an administrative block including a palace for himself, covering a much greater acreage. For this operation the King of Tyre gave further help. When his new halls were safely finished, Solomon ceded Hiram twenty cities in Galilee. Hiram came to inspect them and had the impression that the Israelite had overreached him. In spite of Hiram's grumbles the buildings stood. With them looming alongside, the Temple of the Lord must have acquired the look of a royal chapel. Certainly it was under royal control, and the corps of Levite priests were functionaries of the King's household and paid by him.

Solomon's centralisation of religion was simply one aspect of his centralisation of government. Pursuing a policy which David may have begun, he broke up the kingdom into twelve districts which did not always coincide with the domains of the tribes. Where a territory was split in this way, the tribe as a whole could no longer have any voice. The overshadowing royal power was based on taxes in kind and new forts, garrisoned by professional troops. They were equipped with chariots—those devilish engines of the heathen which even David had never introduced, except experimentally. Solomon's "chariot city" covering a hill at strategic Megiddo has been laid bare by excavation; including later additions, it provides stalls for fully 450 horses. Solomon imported these from Kue, i.e. Cilicia, in south-eastern Asia Minor.

To execute his public works, the King built up a system of forced labour. For the Temple itself he conscripted thirty thousand Israelites into short-term service, reserving the right to make levies of the same kind again. Many of his non-Israelite subjects were reduced to virtual slavery and employed on other projects, military and civil. The tangible grandeur that resulted was at first almost confined to Jerusalem; Solomon's capital contrasted jarringly with the country. However, he did promote some economic activity outside. Thus a refinery at Ezion-geber, on the Gulf of Aqaba, smelted iron and copper ore from his much-romanticised mines in Edom and Sinai. The designers ingeniously arranged it so as to catch a draught from the prevailing north wind rushing down the cleft from the Dead Sea.

Nor were Solomon's relations with the Phoenicians confined to the matter of the Temple. He learned what those masters had to teach about trade, diplomacy and negotiation. His buyers, for example, not only purchased horses for him, but traded in them profitably as agents for the Neo-Hittites of Syria. While he had no good port on the Mediterranean, Israelite ships joined in trading expeditions with Hiram's. Near the Ezion-geber refinery he built a port of his own, and launched a fleet with Phoenician instructors to train the crews. It was this fleet that sailed down the Red Sea to the Indian Ocean, and transported gold from that mysterious place Ophir. No doubt it also took Solomon's fame to the Queen of Sheba, in southern Arabia, who came to Jerusalem with "a very great retinue, with camels bearing spices, and very much gold, and precious stones." Perhaps her unspecified desire which Solomon granted was for a trade treaty.

In the view of later generations, Solomon became an equivocal person. He was proverbial for wisdom and glory. Yet he was also the anointed fool whose errors had ruined his people. The clue to the paradox lay in a sad conviction that his glory and wisdom were incompatible; that the first had undermined the second.

We cannot get any glimpses of him through non-Israelite eyes, because we are still in the phase of isolation. The area where he counted is still one which contemporary records ignore. To Israelites, however, Solomon's contacts with the nations manifestly gave him an alien air. Legend made him a magician, and his wisdom largely an occult wisdom, a mastery of spells and genies. But a more discerning tradition fastened on the cosmopolitan harem which he acquired. He married the Pharaoh's daughter and "Moabite, Ammonite, Edomite, Sidonian, and Hittite women," collecting, it is said, seven hundred wives and three hundred concubines, though there would not have been room for anything like such numbers in his palace as described. They were allowed their own gods, who were installed on a hill east of Jerusalem, probably the Mount of Offence which is part of the same ridge as the Mount of Olives. This importation of gods-in-law from abroad, and the respect which Solomon had to pay to their priests, injected a new potentiality into Israel—the plantation of foreign cults beside Yahweh's, not merely as sources of heresy, but as rival religions in outright competition with his.

For a time no major defection occurred. The wives were not missionaries, and few Hebrew converts climbed the Mount of Offence. But the cultivation of pagan courts and pagan alliances cleared the way for more perilous invasions. Even Solomon's piety had doubtful results. By building the Temple in Phoenician style, with a royal priesthood, he provided a ready setting for the imitation of pagan divine kingship, and the introduction of pagan ritual to suit royal whims and policies. There are biblical hints at the existence of a puritan party who saw this, and opposed the Temple altogether. Israel never actually stooped to king-worship. But a series of psalms extolling the monarch show that an insidiously different atmosphere was seeping in. It was seeping in also at other levels. Commerce and industry, once disreputable, were now accepted things; and the growth of a wealthy governing class was warping the old equality far out of shape.

Disruption had already started while Solomon reigned. Both causes, the economic and the religious, were at work in it. The King put a young Ephraimite, Jeroboam the son of Nebat, in charge of the forced labour programme in northern Israel. As Jeroboam was on his way from Jerusalem to take up the appointment, a prophet named Ahijah approached him. The Lord, Ahijah said, was angry at Solomon's dalliance with idols. If Jeroboam were to lead a revolt in the north, the enterprise would have divine blessing on it. Thereby a conspiracy was set on foot. Solomon found out, but Jeroboam escaped to Egypt and placed himself under the Pharaoh Shishak's protection.

As Solomon's grip weakened, the Davidic empire began to crumble. Edom revolted, and Damascus became the capital of a separate Aramaean kingdom of Syria, which was henceforth a constant threat to Israel. Then a far more serious crisis tore apart Israel itself. The fault lay with Solomon's heir Rehoboam. On his father's death, which occurred somewhere about 930, he made a state visit to Shechem to be proclaimed king by a national assembly. At this function the exile Jeroboam reappeared, and asked in the people's name for guarantees that the burdens imposed by Solomon's régime would be lightened. Rehoboam consulted his senior advisers, who urged him to be moderate. However, he preferred the younger officials, the creatures and beneficiaries of the system; and these advised firmness. When he met his subjects' deputation, he told them that he would intensify Solomon's measures rather than relax them. "My father chastised you with whips, but I will chastise you with scorpions." At once the northern representatives refused their allegiance, and withdrew into a camp of their own.

To restore order Rehoboam sent (of all people) his chief overseer of forced labour. The indignant rebels stoned him to death. The northern tribes seceded and made Jeroboam, as the popular leader, their king. David's insufferable grandson was left presiding over Judah.

Monarchy had produced its own contradiction. It had split the community which it was meant to hold together. The tribes could not go back to their old federal unity, because they were now committed to centralised rule. The kings had supplied a personal link superseding the amphictyony. Now this link was snapped, but there could be no return. The outcome was not a federalist reaction. It was a division of the tribes between two kings, and of David's empire into two monarchies.

All the people were still Israelites, with the same traditions and the same faith. Confusingly, however, the northern state appropriated the name of Israel, giving that consecrated term a narrower political meaning. As for the south, which kept Jerusalem and the dynasty, it was naturally called Judah; though when conditions were stabilised it included rather more than the tribe of Judah, because it took in most of Benjamin. The northern tribes continued to be reckoned as ten, or nine and a half, on the ground that they included Simeonite remnants and most of the Levites. However, the discrepancy of size was not so great as the disparity in number of tribes would suggest. The frontier ran from the neighbourhood of the Dead Sea's northern end in the general direction of what is now Tel-Aviv. Judah stretched southward from this line to Ezion-geber. Israel extended northward to Lebanon; but the strip of Phoenician coast made its extremity very thin. Gilead and Moab beyond Jordan, and resentful Edom to the south-east, were not yet finally lost. Both kingdoms succeeded in holding land in these areas.

Lacking the Temple, and afraid that his subjects would be seduced if they went there to worship, Jeroboam took a step which damned him for ever in the judgment of the orthodox. At Bethel near the frontier and at Dan in the extreme north (both associated with Jacob) he set up golden bull-calves, or more exactly, gold-plated wooden ones. These stood for Yahweh. To serve them he founded an irregular priesthood. The calves were perhaps suggested or authorised by some northern tradition current among descendants of Aaron. They were not fetishes, but thrones or pedestals for the Lord's presence. Little bull-images of the same type were mounts of an unseen storm god among the Hittites and other nations. However, Canaanite gods had sometimes taken the form of bulls. Jeroboam was fostering ambiguity.

Surveyed by hostile authors who knew the sequel, the northerner's act was blatant idolatry which brought a curse on his realm. The undoubted secular fact is that the northern kingdom was made for trouble. It was born in revolt, and therefore contained the seeds of further revolt. Its first king was an upstart, and the circumstances of his rise were a standing invitation to other upstarts. Deprived of royal legitimacy, the north had no safeguard against palace revolutions and soldiers' coups. Judah, by contrast, kept the Davidic succession. It also kept Jerusalem and the Temple and the Ark. With all these assets it was inherently far more stable. Also, the forces making for orthodoxy were stronger. There was a genuine popular tendency to appear to conform. For instance, the percentage of names with "Baal" in them dwindled. Judahite parents did observe that propriety toward Yahweh, at least in the same way as modern parents take their children to church to be christened.

But all such gestures were soon to change in meaning.

CHAPTER SIX

THE PROPHETS AND THE LAW

After those enclosed centuries, Israel's people at last enter the historical mainstream. Almost at the same time as their entry, and partly because of it, their religion bursts into amazing florescence. The collective logic which seemed to have reached its term springs forward again in a giant stride. For the trend's inception, though not for its culmination, we must look to the schismatic north. Precisely because it possessed neither the Temple nor the Davidic lineage, precisely because of its instability, it was more liable than Judah to be shaken and shocked into fresh creation.

The annals of nearby monarchies begin to interlock with Scripture late in the tenth century. Shishak of Egypt, according to *I Kings* xiv:25-26, raided Jerusalem in the fifth year of Rehoboam and plundered the Temple. An Egyptian inscription at Karnak commemorates this raid. The god Ammon is shown leading Semitic captives, and some biblical place-names can be picked out, including the "Field of Abram." But the first individual Israelite to impress himself on his neighbours was Omri, the commander of the northerners' army, who became king in 887 and left an enduring fame behind him. In Assyria, well over a hundred years afterwards, the northern kingdom was still inaccurately referred to as the Land of Ben-Omri—of the House of Omri. Yet here at the actual point of convergence, the difference between biblical and ordinary history stands out starkly. The Bible itself disposes of Omri's distinguished reign in six verses, of which only a couple give any solid information about him. By Israel's standards he is bad, and that alone is the determining factor. The writer is conscious that he was, in the normal sense, an important king—one who "showed might"—but deliberately leaves out his important acts.

With a single exception. Omri "bought the hill of Samaria from Shemer for two talents of silver; and he fortified the hill, and called the name of the city which he built, Samaria, after the name of Shemer, the owner of the hill." This new capital, founded in 880, was the only city which the Israelites ever did found. The site was strategically chosen; Omri was a soldier. Excavation has uncovered the scars of his walling and levelling, and of similar operations by his son Ahab, who succeeded him in 875. Ahab built himself a palace which the Bible calls "the ivory house." The ivory portion has been unearthed. It consists mainly of decorative panels. They portray lilies, lotus-flowers and papyrus plants; bulls and lions and deer; sphinxes and Egyptian gods. On the backs are letters in Hebrew-Phoenician script. It is interesting to see how poverty-stricken Hebrew art was, owing to the dearth of myths in the usual sense, and the fear of idolatry. There is no sign of a native tradition in the carvings. Everything pictorial had to be copied from foreign artists, or perhaps even executed by them.

Samaria's opulence reflects the character of King Ahab's realm. The northern kingdom was opening out; "Ahab the Israelite" figures in contemporary inscriptions beyond his borders. The beasts and blooms on the ivory plaques are cosmopolitan, derived largely from Egyptian art, yet treated in a style that is more Phoenician. Ahab maintained his standing among the rulers of the Near East with the professional army and civil service which had originated with David, and taxation to match. He enlarged Solomon's chariot-city at Megiddo and sent out expeditionary forces. Also he made his mark in diplomacy, negotiating for trading-posts in Damascus.

Town life was flourishing. An embryonic currency in the form of weighed-off metal lubricated the economy. Many crafts were plied: we hear of fullers and weavers, millers and bakers, locksmiths and barbers. Carpenters worked with iron axes and saws, hammers and chisels. The citizens used a quickly-made functional type of pottery on Phoenician patterns. They had cheap but showy jewellery. Women wore anklets, bracelets and ear-rings, and fastened their clothes with safety-pins; they improved their eyelashes with *kuhl*, and their eyelids with greenish copper ore.

Outside in the country, the peasants were of course very poor. Yet they were not so abjectly primitive as their forebears. When Jacob's sons went reaping they would have carried sickles of wood edged with flint. Peasants under Ahab had sharp sickles of iron which could reap fully twice as fast. Their wives ground the grain in their own cottages with a stone pestle and mortar. Home furnishings were simple—coarse goat-hair rugs, pottery lamps, wooden platters and leather mats to put them on. The usual dress of men was practical but not wholly undecorative: a short stocking cap, a long fringed tunic with a fringed mantle which could be worn over it, leggings and high boots with turned-up toes.

Judah was a smaller state and not so advantageously placed. Its distinctive possessions proved in the end to be more important than anything else. But it lacked the north's immediate contact with Phoenicia, and with the Aramaic kingdom of Syria, centred on Damascus, which lay north-east. It withdrew into its shell. While the same developments occurred, they occurred in a minor key. City life remained somewhat plainer, not progressing so far or so fast. Jerusalem always had the air of being a town in the country. Its little green valleys were full of irrigated orchards and vegetable gardens, and the opposite hillside was warm with grapes and figs, almonds and pomegranates.

The peace between Judah and the north was uneasy and often broken. Fortifications at Gibeah and elsewhere attest the dread which the weak sovereigns of Jerusalem felt when they contemplated their Israelite neighbours. During and after Ahab's reign the upper classes in both states did well out of the warfare and tension. Soldiers, officials, profiteers made their fortunes. But the peasants and craftsmen, burdened with taxes and military service, failed to score any corresponding advance. The social gap widened. Ahab's Phoenician fraternisation was a source of benefits, but also dangers. His rashest act added an ideological threat. He married the Princess Jezebel of Sidon. She arrived in the capital, gorgeously dressed and meticulously made up; and she brought her god with her.

In the Bible this deity is called simply Baal. However, he is not to be equated with any of the petty baals of the judges' era. He is the mighty Tyrian Baal, Melkart, "King of the City"—probably the underworld. Temples were dedicated to him as far off as Spain; the Greeks for some reason thought he was the same person as Hercules, whence perhaps the myth of Hercules' trip to Cadiz on his tenth labour. With Melkart came Asherah, in a new guise as his consort. Queen Jezebel was a sincere missionary, by no means content to pray in a private shrine like the wives of Solomon. She imported a mob of priests and medicine-men, loud-voiced, corybantic and dandified. At her request Ahab put up a temple for Melkart in Samaria, and himself adored the sophisticated interloper.

Ahab did not desert the Lord altogether. He tried to maintain both cults. His children were given names with "Yahweh" in them. But the royal sponsorship of a great pagan god was a graver menace to Israel's faith than the lingering popular confusion of Yahweh-worship with Nature-worship. Its ultimate effectiveness is hard to assess. On the whole Melkart seems to have remained chiefly a court institution. The Bible gives us two clues: that Ahab had only seven thousand subjects who did not "bow the knee to Baal"; but also, that a few years after his death the solitary Samaria temple could hold all the Baal-worshippers in the northern kingdom (*II Kings* x:21). These statements need not conflict. It may well be that while Ahab and Jezebel were in power, very few had the fortitude or conviction to "contract out." Most citizens, one supposes, observed such occasional conformity as would please their sovereigns, while still clinging to Yahweh and seldom crossing the threshold of the rival chapel. As soon as royal sponsorship ceased, Melkart lost the time-serving majority. His support dwindled to his committed sectaries.

Archaeology shows nothing that is against this reading. But it reveals more clearly than Scripture what the context of the episode was, and how Ahab fostered disintegration. The foreign cult in Samaria created an atmosphere and started fashions in devotion. There were trees of Asherah—more than ever in the past—and altars of pagan incense. Sculptors sold female fertility-statuettes of Phoenician type, wearing veils and carrying tambourines. In the northern kingdom (not in the southern) personal names with "Baal" in them became more and more popular, till there were fully half as many of these as there were of "Yahweh" names. Once ambiguity had firmly entrenched itself, the suppression of any single cult could not evict it; and gradually other alien practices crept in or resumed encroachment, such as star-worship, goddess-worship, ritual prostitution. Jezebel's missionary effort appears under scrutiny as the leading wave in a series undermining the Yahwist citadel. It has been put on record in Scripture, where most of the rest are merely indicated, for two reasons. First, because Melkart invaded Israel ostentatiously as a court favourite, whereas the astral cults and so forth progressed quietly at lower levels. Also, because the Queen unintentionally founded another movement besides her own.

2

One day a man strode into Ahab's court. His rough tunic and leather belt were in violent contrast with the finery round him. He was the Tishbite prophet Elijah, from Gilead. He announced in the Lord's name that the rain of heaven would cease and Israel would be afflicted with drought.

Elijah was an associate of those guilds of *nabhi* prophets which had been active for several hundred years. But he was more than a *nabhi*. Prophecy hitherto, we must recall, had been largely a sort of contagious exhilaration. The prophet went into ecstasies and capered and sang; he gave answers (or what professed to be answers) to hard questions; often he performed for pay. In fact he did just what many other dervishes and soothsayers were doing all over the Near East and the southern Balkans. The difference was that the power controlling him was believed to be the Holy Spirit of

Yahweh. Therefore, however self-deluded he might sometimes be, he was at least open to influences of another kind. Hebrew prophecy could detach itself from its root. Given the right stimulus, there was always the possibility that a prophet would begin to speak without the frantic accompaniments and in a more serious, authoritative, connected style.

A few had already shown signs of doing so. Elijah, however, is the first who stands out as an original and commanding figure. The crucial stimulus came from Jezebel, who had not only installed her Baal with a train of prophets of his own, but had seen fit after a while to persecute the prophets of Yahweh.

Here is Elijah's story, as narrated in the *Books of Kings*, I xvii-xxii and II i-ii.

After giving his warning about the drought, the prophet retired to a hermitage in the valley of the Kerith, a small tributary of Jordan. When the drought spread over the land and food began to fail, he ate scraps of bread and meat brought to him by ravens, and drank water from the brook. But a day came when the brook itself dried up.

Divinely guided, he made his way through the stricken country to Zarephath near the Lebanese coast, where a widow lived who had not submitted to any alien gods and would be willing to shelter him. Seeing a woman gathering sticks close to the gate, and suspecting her to be the one, he asked for food. He was not mistaken, since she answered with a phrase invoking the God of Israel. But she had no food to offer, she said sadly, only a last handful of flour in a barrel, and a drain of oil in a jar. The wood was for one final baking for herself and her young son. After that they would starve.

Elijah promised that if they shared with him they would never go hungry while the drought lasted. Accepting his assurance, she gave him lodging. Days passed and meals were eaten, yet there was always oil in the jar and flour in the barrel. This wonder-working frightened her, and when her son fell sick and stopped breathing she blamed Elijah. However, he laid the boy on his own bed, prayed, and threw himself forward on him several times.

Breathing resumed, and the mother was convinced that Elijah was a man of God.

The drought became intolerable. To save the kingdom's livestock, Ahab organised two foraging parties to gather wild grass. He led one group himself and gave charge of the other to Obadiah, his steward. Obadiah was friendly to the persecuted prophets of Yahweh and was supplying some of them with food while they hid in a cave. On his tour he met Elijah, who had left Zarephath. Somewhat reluctantly Obadiah agreed to take a message to Ahab.

The King, who had been searching for Elijah to keep him under supervision, advanced to meet him and accused him of "troubling Israel." Elijah retorted that Ahab himself was to blame because of his apostasy, and demanded a public conference, which the King, alarmed at the drought and fearful of divine judgment, consented to summon. On the heights of Mount Carmel, the ridge close to Haifa, he assembled representatives from all over the northern kingdom, together with the four hundred and fifty elegant prophets of Baal. Elijah addressed the people. He declared that they must make a decision. "How long will you go on limping with two different opinions? if the Lord is God, follow him; but if Baal, then follow him." There was no response. Then Elijah pointed to the prophets of Baal. Let the rival deities be put to the test, he said. Let Baal's prophets cut up a bull's carcass for sacrifice and put the pieces on firewood, and so would he. Whichever god sent fire to consume the offering should be acknowledged by Israel.

Baal's prophets tried first, behaving in the normal way of such people. All the morning they chanted incantations and danced round their altar without effect. At noon Elijah mockingly urged them to call louder: Baal, he suggested, was in conference or away travelling, or perhaps he was asleep and needed to be woken up. The prophets did call louder, and gashed themselves with knives till they streamed with blood. But the afternoon lengthened towards evening and no fire came.

Then Elijah told the people to stand closer. He took twelve stones, one for each of the sons of Jacob, and built an altar for himself and dug a trench round it. He piled up wood and arranged his joints of meat on top. Lastly he had buckets of water poured over the offering and into the trench. He prayed to the God of Israel; and the offering was wrapped in a sheet of flame that seemed to burn the altar itself and dry up the water in the ditch.

The people prostrated themselves and worshipped. Elijah's shouts brought them to their feet, and they rushed at the prophets of Baal. Ahab could only watch helplessly. Led by Elijah, the rioters easily won the fight, which ended in a massacre of the prophets below the hill. While the nonplussed King was at supper, Elijah climbed up again and sat with his face bowed between his knees waiting for the rain that he foresaw would break the drought. Seven times he sent a servant to scan the Mediterranean, and the seventh time the servant reported seeing a tiny cloud rising above the horizon like a hand. The sky grew dark, the wind mounted, and a storm rolled in from the sea. Ahab left hastily for his palace in Jezreel and the prophet ran alongside his chariot.

Jezebel of course was enraged. She sent Elijah a message threatening to have him executed; by giving him a chance to escape she hoped to avoid making a martyr of him. Aware that there was no hope of the brief revolt going on or spreading, Elijah fled into Judah and trudged on for forty days till he reached Sinai and Mount Horeb. There he withdrew to a cave and awaited fresh guidance. One day as he stood near the entrance a fierce wind sprang up, followed by an earthquake and flashes of lightning; "but the Lord was not in them." Then, with no more disturbance than a gentle breeze or a soft footfall, there came a "still small voice" and Elijah recognised God's presence.

"What are you doing here?" said the voice. Elijah replied that Israel was forsaking its faith and he was left alone, a refugee under sentence of death. But the voice urged him to take heart and return. Hazael, the next King of Syria, would be the instrument of divine vengeance, and Jehu son of Nimshi would be King of Israel and complete the overthrow of Baal. Seven thousand remained, and would remain, who had not bowed to Jezebel's idol. Meanwhile

Elijah must appoint a new prophet, Elisha, as his successor. So Elijah went back. He found Elisha on his farm ploughing, and threw his mantle over the peasant's shoulders in token of spiritual adoption.

Ahab meanwhile was worried. Elijah seemed to have disappeared, but other prophets, who sounded like emissaries of his, kept visiting the court with disturbing messages. King Ben-hadad of Syria was raiding the country. The prophets predicted that Yahweh would give Ahab victory as a proof that he was the true God. Ahab won two battles and granted Ben-hadad peace on lenient terms. At once another prophet told him that by letting the heathen marauder go in friendship he had brought doom upon himself.

Near Ahab's palace at Jezreel was a vineyard belonging to a certain Naboth. Ahab wanted to join it to his own land, and offered Naboth another vineyard or compensation in money. Naboth, however, refused to give up the family property. As Israelite law stood, he could not be compelled. (David had bought the threshing-floor of Araunah, Omri had bought the hill of Samaria, from consenting owners.) While Ahab lay on his couch sulking, Jezebel ridiculed him, saying that any ruler worth the name could crush a subject who made such difficulties. The Queen undertook to dispose of Naboth herself. She sent letters sealed with Ahab's seal to the city elders telling them to proclaim a fast—and with this order went some other confidential instructions. The fast was proclaimed, and Naboth was given a conspicuous place at the ceremony. Two hired witnesses promptly accused him of blasphemy and treason. Without allowing any defence, the elders had Naboth led out of the city and stoned to death. Jezebel informed her husband and he took possession of the vineyard.

This piece of pagan absolutism drew Elijah again into the foreground of affairs. He approached Ahab as he walked in the vineyard superintending its conversion into a herb-garden.

"Have you found me, O my enemy?" the King exclaimed guiltily.

"I have found you," the prophet answered. "You have sold yourself to do what is evil in the sight of the Lord." Ahab, he said, would come to a disastrous end, his family would die out, Jezebel's corpse would be food for dogs. Ahab, shaken, tried to atone by wearing sackcloth and going about with bowed head.

But the close of his reign was near. He made an alliance with King Jehoshaphat of Judah for the recapture of Ramoth-Gilead from the Syrians. Jehoshaphat agreed, subject to favourable omens. Ahab collected four hundred *nabhi* prophets, who swore that Ramoth-Gilead was his for the taking; one of them put on iron horns to show how the King would toss his foes. Jehoshaphat, however, doubted their qualifications. Another prophet named Micaiah announced a vision of Yahweh which was much less encouraging. Ahab imprisoned him and the two armies marched on Ramoth-Gilead. The King of Israel fought in disguise, and his ally's royal insignia diverted attention from him; but a random arrow passed between his breastplate and collar. Propped upright, he stood for hours in his chariot covering it with blood, and died defeated at evening.

Jezebel lived on, and their son Ahaziah became King of Israel. He continued Baal-worship, and when injured by a fall he sent messengers to a pagan oracle at Ekron to inquire whether he would recover. Elijah met them and asked sternly whether there was no God in Israel? Ahaziah would never leave his bed, and they could go back and tell him so.

With Ahab's family in decline, it began to be rumoured that Elijah was going away. He walked down from the hills toward the Jordan, accompanied by Elisha. Fifty prophets of the Jericho guild followed, mystified, at a distance. Elijah struck the stream with his rolled-up mantle and it divided, allowing the two to cross. On the farther bank Elijah begged his master to confirm him in the succession to his mission. But the prophet's reply sounded like a riddle. Suddenly, through the glare and heat, a fiery chariot and horses came careering between them, and Elijah rode upward in a whirlwind. His disciple was left holding the mantle. The fifty watchers saluted him as his master's heir, and he returned to take up the war against Baal. A search party explored the desert; but no one ever saw Elijah again.

How much of Elijah's saga is literally true, nothing is to be gained by asking. It is more to the point to notice what sort of stories have attached themselves to him, constituting the real meaning of his Scriptural portrait.

Elisha calls him "the chariots of Israel and its horsemen" (*II Kings* ii:12). The chariot is a war-vehicle. Elijah symbolises the nation's true strength, which is drawn from Yahweh. The miracles that cluster round him, after a stretch of biblical narrative where miracles are few, convey what he is. Some of them can be rationalised. He may have revived the boy by artificial respiration. He may have lit the fire with a burning-glass and oil. But the aim of all these marvels is to reveal him as a God-possessed man. He is not a wizard performing feats by his own secret spells, nor does he take payment for anything that he does or says. The miracles are worked by God. They are tokens that God is with him and in him, and acts through him as formerly through Moses. Even if he did use a burning-glass, or some other unfamiliar method of fire-lighting, his special knowledge would still be regarded as divinely instilled in him.[1]

Yet the signs and wonders are subordinate. What is primary is the hidden presence, the indwelling imperative of the Lord. At Horeb Elijah witnesses much the same cataclysms as Moses—but God is not in them; God is in the hush that follows. Nothing distracts attention from the divine voice itself, which is clear and uncompromising. Elijah has heard it before and he will hear it again. His own inspired words are always relentless in their simplicity and quite free from *nabhi* intoxication, which only his opponents display. He is an Either-Or man, not, like most of his compatriots, a Both-And man. He insists that issues be faced and that

---

1 Carmel, as a matter of fact, was one of the first places where glass was made. The sand on the beach below the mountain was exceptionally suitable.

an elementary choice be made. He takes it for granted that there is only one God who matters, and that the Israelites know this in their hearts. The true Lord is *either* Yahweh *or* Baal, and they must make up their minds. They cannot have it both ways.

The Either-Or drives Elijah to the verge of despair, because (in Israel as in general) so few people do make up their minds. The voice on Horeb tells him how many have done so in his favour: seven thousand. Here we have the theme of the Righteous Remnant again, as already in the cases of Seth's family, Noah's family, Abraham's family, and Joshua and Caleb. Its combination with the idea of a Righteous King, who will purge the realm and leave the Remnant triumphant, is the first hint of a view of history which is destined to become extremely important.

Elijah's action in the affair of Naboth is of a piece with this conception of justice and cleansing. God permits no exceptions, even for a sovereign's benefit. The space which the author of *I Kings* devotes to Naboth typifies the moral atmosphere of the whole story. He cares much more about the shocking assault of absolutism on a subject's rights than he does, say, about the glories of Omri. Outside the Hebrew tradition, a similar view of relative values would not be easy to find at that period.

The dramatic heavenward flight without death associates Elijah with Enoch. Hebraic legend has much to tell about these two mortal-immortals. Elijah, however, is more of a living figure, and he is said to have often revisited the world below. His translation ranks him with a number of favourite non-biblical heroes —King Arthur is the best known—who are supposed never to have died, and to be waiting to return in the hour of need. The Old Testament closes with this expectation (*Malachi* iv:5-6), and it is mentioned several times in the New as a commonplace among the contemporaries of Jesus, though for him at least it is metaphorical (*Matthew* xi:14, xvii:10-12; *Mark* vi:15, viii:28; *Luke* i:17; *John* i:21).

With Elijah, then, a distinctive Hebrew prophecy fully dawns. But the incident of Micaiah and the council of war (*I Kings* xxii) should not be hurriedly passed over. Here already is an abrupt and obvious differentiation of the new from the old. The *nabhi* seers consulted by Ahab are "false" prophets, reassuring spell-binders who strengthen the morale of the royal forces. Micaiah is a "true" prophet who speaks intrepidly whatever Yahweh puts in his mind, however unwelcome it may be to authority.

Even with Elisha the emergence of the authentic prophet from the shaman stereotype is not quite complete. The account of his ministry is a series of marvels, some of them, like the notorious tale about the bears, childish and barbarous. On the other hand he is very angry when his servant surreptitiously collects a reward for his services. He carries on the political activity of Elijah and Micaiah, pronouncing dooms or inspiring others to pronounce them. One of his miracles, the healing of the leprosy of the Syrian general Naaman, is a semi-political act which teaches a heathen the superiority of the God of Israel. Among Elisha's successors in this vein is Jonah, who, in *II Kings* xiv:25, makes his sole appearance outside the book named for him.

After the early demise of Ahaziah, Ahab's second son Jehoram reigned in the north. He abandoned the cult of Baal (*II Kings* iii:2). But in 842 Elisha, emulating Samuel, sought out the army officer Jehu and had him anointed king instead. Jehu led a successful rebellion, personally slew Jehoram, and flung his body into the field of Naboth. He then drove his chariot (which he handled with a dash that became proverbial) to the palace where the Queen-Mother Jezebel was. Her painted face peered out at the window; Jehu called to his friends inside, and some of the eunuchs threw her down to the pavement below, where she was trampled and torn apart by a mob. Jehu consummated his revolution by beheading the rest of Ahab's male issue, gathering the surviving Baal-worshippers in the temple at Samaria, massacring them all, and turning the temple into a latrine.

So expired the house of Ahab. Jehu had reinstated Yahweh. But he still did not destroy the golden calves at the shrines of his kingdom. He still, in the eyes of the biblical historian, "did not turn from the sins of Jeroboam, which he made Israel to sin." Hence, a number of severe Syrian attacks by King Hazael were regarded as divine punishment fulfilling the promise made by God to Elijah (x:32, xiii:22). There are several external witnesses to all this phase of Israel's affairs. Ahab's dealings with Syria are recorded by the Assyrian Shalmaneser III, whose inscriptions also portray Jehu as humble and submissive. The "Moabite Stone" sheds further light on the middle ninth century. This is a black basalt slab, three and a half feet by two, which was found at Dhiban in 1868. The text consists of 260 words in old Hebrew characters, and is a communiqué of King Mesha of Moab. He speaks first of inroads made into Moab by Omri and Ahab, then relates how the god Chemosh enabled him to recover his land from Ahab toward the close of the Israelite's reign. The army of Moab took three cities by storm, killed the inhabitants, and carried off sacred objects dedicated to Yahweh. Apparently the Syrian wars were seriously draining national military resources even during Ahab's lifetime.

The northern kingdom, in fact, drifted on; sometimes successful, sometimes hard pressed. The calf-cult of Jeroboam persisted, and so did popular paganism in various forms, though Jezebel's attempt at outright conversion had failed. Jezebel's campaign had a passing effect in Jerusalem through Ahab's daughter Athaliah, who married into the southern royal house and reigned in person from 842 to 836. Her modest temple of Baal with its single priest was overthrown in a coup. Jehoash, whom the coup set on the throne, followed up this victory over court paganism by equipping the Temple with the first recorded collection-box. In Judah too, however, the older popular worship stayed alive in the "high places."

3

Although (to judge from *II Chronicles* xxi:12) Elijah could write, he left no permanent writings. During the eighth century, however, his work was taken up again by prophets who did. Literary prophecy began in the northern kingdom and spread rapidly to the southern. Like the mission of Elijah himself, it was a growth out of *nabhi* enthusiasm. But its exponents seldom belonged to the *nabhi* guilds, or prophesied for pay. They were free-lances of various origins and occupations, through whom the Holy Spirit, the *ruach* of Yahweh, breathed and spoke with power. They were brave, turbulent, and often in trouble. If any single prophet had stood alone, he would soon have been silenced and forgotten. But they arose in roughly contemporary quartets—Amos, Hosea, Isaiah, Micah; Zephaniah, Habakkuk, Nahum, Jeremiah—and achieved immortality together. Re-discovered and re-stated by them, the religion of Israel began to free itself from the trap of ritual, and to advance into an ever-broadening landscape. Yahweh himself became, through their impassioned definitions, the unequivocal One Righteous God of Jewish faith . . . and Zion became far more than a hill.

The collections of their verses and visions are, as finished books, among the oldest in the Bible. Earliest of all is the revolutionary pamphlet of Amos. It was once widely believed (as we had occasion to note in connection with Moses) that this fact was the key to Scripture in general. Israel's religion was not merely purified by the prophets, but invented by them. The historical books from *Genesis* to *II Kings* were romances constructed as an afterthought out of a few barbarous legends, to give the prophets' teachings a weightier pedigree. Moses, if he existed at all, was a tribal witch-doctor; in the Pentateuch he was artificially inflated into a prophet, the first and greatest, to supply a precedent for the others. Similarly in the medieval stories of Arthur, dark-age Britons were transformed into courtly knights.

This theory launched a spate of rash and complicated conjectures about the text, which has now ebbed. In its extreme form it could not stand up against the archaeology which proved the historical books to be far more than the fantasies of a later age. Anyone who is inclined to belittle this should try digging up comparable support for Malory; he will soon see the difference. But in any case the two bodies of writing, historical and prophetic, are not enough alike in spirit or content for the former to be a by-product of the latter. The histories scarcely mention their supposed inspirers, whom we would expect to be prominent: there is nothing at all in them about Amos, for instance, or Hosea. Again, their version of events does not always reflect the prophets' own judgment: thus we are told of sweeping reforms during the lifetime of Jeremiah, which Jeremiah himself seems to think hardly important enough to notice. Above all, the religion of the historical books is not as close to that of the prophets as it would be if the afterthought theory were correct. In their present form they were admittedly compiled later. But their use of ancient materials reflects the prior tradition.

That tradition is not the same as the prophetic, yet it is lineally related. The prophets never speak as innovators; they never sound like innovators; and their strength lies in the fact that they are not innovators. They can appeal historically from a false Israel in the present to a true Israel in the past, and be understood. For their success, even for their existence as prophets, we have no explanation but the Bible's, that there was something there for them to spring from and work upon. What that "something" was, we have seen. It was a religion that contained most of the prophetic motifs, but only potentially. It was the same religion as theirs at an earlier stage, narrow and exclusive and bound up with local cultus. With no stronger nourishment, Israel under the kings might well have petered out like other small nations. But its heritage had a glowing core of vitality: Yahweh himself, his action in Israel's history, his moral commandments. This was infinitely more potent than the forms which confined it; and this the prophets blew into flame. A succession without parallel, they lifted Israel's faith into a new phase.

Their prophesying was an outcry of public conscience. In this likewise they were not innovators, but revivalists of a less diseased past. They looked away from the gilded kingdoms to the authentic Israel of old—to the Israel of slaves triumphant over their masters; of desert tent-dwellers assembled at the mountain in holy dread; of free peasants living frugally under crownless judges. With those memories in the background they assailed the wealth and oppression around them. They were radicals, but they were Tory radicals. The type is rare in the modern English-speaking world. Cobbett perhaps is the best example. Among Socialists William Morris, with his Utopian medievalism, stands closest to the Hebrew prophets.

In the light of this fiery sequel the role of Elijah as archetype becomes clearer. He is a second Moses, a Moses of prophecy. He too goes to Horeb, his forty days' journey corresponding to the forty years' wandering. He too has a revelation there. It is the Mosaic revelation turned round so as to bring its moral aspect exclusively to the fore. The storm and blaze of Yahweh's theophany give way to the still small voice in the heart. With the prophets henceforth it is the moral law, the utterance of Israel's conscience, that matters. The elemental terrors remain, but they are transmuted into poetic symbols. Most of the things related of Elijah—his voluntary poverty, his war against a bejewelled paganism, his attack on the tyrants and their tame priesthood, his protest at the judicial murder of a small landowner—set the tone in one way or another for the prophets who follow.

Elijah at Horeb knows that he stands almost alone and that the mass violence on Mount Carmel meant very little. He pours out his sorrow in hyperbolic language at the lack of response: "I have been very jealous for the Lord, the God of hosts: for the people of Israel have forsaken thy Covenant, thrown down thy altars, and slain thy prophets with the sword; and I, even I only, am left; and they seek my life, to take it away." All the prophets were "jealous" like Elijah, and Yahweh as they portrayed him was essentially the jealous God of the Mosaic commandment against idolatry. Prophecy spurned the indifferentism of the present, and called back the more heroic tradition of early Israel in the desert.

The heart of that was the Covenant, which, being prior to any cult or ritual, implied an ethical factor in all Israel's fortunes.

Prophecy ranged itself on what was at first the popular side, against monarchy, or, at least, against corruptions which monarchy had brought—the rich officialdom, the foreign alliances, the heathen marriages of state. Monarchy went with urban society, affluent and hungry for ostentation. The leaders of the old Israel of the Covenant had never dreamed of living like that. Their austere ways were certainly not a nostalgic or propagandist invention of the prophets themselves. The ideal had been preserved or revived by a sect called Rechabites, who drank no wine, cultivated no land, and lived in tents. They helped Jehu, and seem to have been un-yielding champions of Yahweh, hereditarily linked with the mysterious Kenite tribe into which Moses married.[2] Distinctively Hebrew prophecy may owe a debt to these Rechabites. However, it left them far behind. The prophets challenged the whole idea of material grandeur. Israel, they reminded their audiences, was a puny nation and comparatively speaking a thing of yesterday. Except by the special fiat of God it could not be otherwise. Even its existence was most precarious, and depended on a divine favour which might be withdrawn.

Closely connected with the system of monarchy were two sinister trends in religion. One was the spread of paganism, not in the former sense of a blurred confusion of Yahweh with this or that local baal, but in the sense of substitution. Jezebel's Melkart, as Elijah had pointed out on Mount Carmel, was meant to replace the God of Israel. Thoughtless Israelites might pay their respects to both, but the two were distinct. A choice had to be made. The cults of the goddess Asherah, and the "host of heaven," and the vegetation-god Tammuz who died and rose every year, were stealthily growing into competitive religions. Against all these the prophets naturally stood firm. Also they condemned the long-equivocal "high places." They admitted no excuse for surrender to a fertility-worship or star-worship which left Man a puppet of

2 See *II Kings* x:15, *I Chronicles* ii:55, *Jeremiah* xxxv.

inscrutable forces. Such forces not only drove their victims into particular evils such as degraded sex-rites and the sacrifice of live children, they sapped human responsibility in general. The prophets affirmed God as the intelligible world-ruler, and Man as made in his image: not subject to any capricious demons, not chained to any seasonal or cosmic cycle, not coerced by any Fate. It is no use trying to dismiss them as dirty fanatics railing at a superior culture. Apart from any question as to what that culture was really like, history has shown that it was not superior. Tyre, Nineveh, Babylon are dust. The spiritual descendants of the prophets live on.

A second, subtler threat lay in the Temple cultus itself and its northern outgrowths, all royal in origin. The paganisation of Yahweh-worship had reappeared in a new form. Solomon and Jeroboam had both imitated pagan models. Under feebler successors the liturgy was always in danger of degenerating into a magical calendar, with Yahweh acquiring attributes of Tammuz, and the king playing a semi-divine part.[3]

Here also the prophets found a theme for their indignation. The inference has been drawn that they revolted against the Temple as such, and were perpetually at feud with its priests. This view is much too harsh. Some of them belonged to the Temple staff. We hear of the association of priest with prophet, and important instances of priests who were prophets themselves. Modern notions about a conflict have been prompted chiefly by the prophets' denunciations of ceremony, by the eloquent contrasts which they draw between futile offerings at the altar and the righteousness which God truly requires. However, to set the one against the other is to impose on Israel a kind of Protestantism alien to it. None of the prophets condemned ritual as wrong in principle. Their target was ritual that had become mechanical, and was conceived as a magic process taking effect *per se* like the Tammuz drama, irrespec-

3 The theory that the monarchies were actually pagan, or nearly so, is less popular than it used to be. Kaufmann hints that its vogue among Christian writers was a subtle form of anti-Semitism. Still, as to the Temple's potentialities there can be no doubt.

tive of the worshippers' conduct. Condemning this, they insisted upon morality instead of cult as the essence of the Covenant.

In this case as in others, prophecy meant the recovery of the right emphasis rather than a fresh departure. Even within the moral field it is a mistake to oppose a "simple," "sublime" ethic taught by the prophets to a "dull," "complex," "legalistic" ethic taught by the priests. Many of the Psalms, composed as Temple hymns, have the same noble piety and clarity as poems by Amos or Isaiah. Conversely, where practical conduct is concerned, "simple sublimity" itself is nearly always a mirage, and the prophets were wise enough to know it. Would-be simplifiers are fond of quoting Micah: "What doth the Lord require of thee, but to do justly, and to love mercy, and to walk humbly with thy God?" Alas, it is only necessary to recall—without going past the first injunction —that the endeavour to define "justice" involved Plato in a literary project of cosmic scope which still leaves us uncertain what justice is. The intention of Micah or any other instructed Israelite in such a saying appears from a fuller version of it which is put in the mouth of Moses in *Deuteronomy* x:12-13: "What does the Lord your God require of you, but to fear the Lord your God, to walk in all his ways, to love him, to serve the Lord your God with all your heart and with all your soul, and to keep the commandments and statutes of the Lord . . . ?" In other words, to keep the Law. As St. Augustine put it long afterwards, love is all, but virtue is the ordering of love—*ordo amoris*.

The prophetic restoration consisted in bringing out what was already latent in Israel's religion, and polishing till it shone. But the latencies were so tremendous that the prophets' action in doing so was revolutionary. In all the ferment of protest and troubled conscience a fresh question was framing itself.

If God planted us in the Land on the understanding that we should live and act in a certain way, doesn't this imply that our tenure is conditional on living and acting as required?

And the prophets answered:

Yes, it does. We must keep our side of the bargain. God still rules over events. The Covenant would be pointless if he relinquished control. And the rise of this most dubious monarchial system, with its wealth in a few hands, its paganised ritual, its foreign cults, is a standing menace. God in his righteous anger may allow other nations to conquer or even dispossess us.

Thus Israel's logic took a fifth step, and a crucial one. Since the reign of Solomon it had been in danger of stopping short. David's wise son, with his Temple and his trade and his visible glory, had had that air of completion about him. Yahweh's goal seemed fully attained. Here were his people dwelling unchallenged in the Land, with a stable constitution, duly venerating their God at a worthy altar. Abraham and Jacob, Moses and Joshua, were now very far away. The unity which Yahweh-worship had fostered during the amphictyony was achieved. Even the subsequent split was no more than a recognition *de jure* of a distinction *de facto* which the personal union under the first kings had disguised. Progress, not collapse, followed the schism. Ahab's contemporaries and successors in both kingdoms (or at least the privileged few who were in the saddle) felt that there was nothing more to worry about. Yahweh had given them the Land to enjoy. So long as he received his honours from the court-priests, he would relax and let them enjoy it.

Confronted with this complacency the prophets rebelled, and went on rebelling. The ruling class, they cried in reign after reign, was not only wicked but desperately shallow. They forced their hearers to take a longer view, looking backward and forward. Yahweh's acts in the past were a warning that he could act in the future. Magnates and courtiers might fancy that they could exploit the Land in security if they paid for sacrifices to the God whose care for their fathers had placed them there; but it was all blasphemous nonsense. The Covenant must be kept in letter and in spirit. Yahweh, who had so imperially put it into effect, was still on the throne of heaven. He was, as ever, the sole Higher Power that mattered. He could always take back his gift, if Israel failed to abide by its terms.

Through their insistence that the building of the Israelite commonwealth was not a *fait accompli*, but a continuing process with ethics at its heart, the prophets moved toward a philosophy. They extrapolated the Exodus. The God associated thus far with a single series of events grew in their teaching into the Lord of all history, reigning over events in general for as long as the world should last. That conception was implicit, as we saw, in the cult, and rather more than implicit in the Yahwist Pentateuchal material. But it could not be realised while the belief prevailed that there was nothing tangible left for Yahweh to do. The prophets drew it out and enlarged on it. Only Yahweh among the gods of mankind could have been pictured in this way, because only Yahweh was absolute, not subject to Fate or competing divine agencies.

4

All these men who were successively commissioned by Yahweh are called "literary" prophets. However, it would be wrong to picture any of them as scribbling away in a study like a modern author. They were primarily speakers, and public speakers. Their language was everyday and energetic. They told stories, they played on words, they made up verses and songs. They harangued crowds in the Temple precinct and in the streets. Some of their utterances they did write down, or dictate; but others were preserved only through the care of disciples, and most were lost altogether. The books that we possess are simply collections of surviving fragments with or without a biographical framework. These were transcribed on sheets of papyrus in parallel columns from right to left, sometimes during the prophet's life, sometimes afterwards; the sheets were glued side by side to form a continuous roll. The classification into "major" and "minor" prophets is not based on relative importance or value. It is quantitative. More was preserved of the "major" than of the "minor," and the scrolls were correspondingly bulkier.

Besides talking, the prophets acted and were acted upon. To

drive their preaching home, they performed symbolic gestures like shattering a pot in token of a city's destruction. Also they saw visions and heard voices. The records of these incidents are mostly in prose, and may be notes taken by disciples to whom the prophets described what they had undergone. Such items (like Moses' burning bush) raise the whole puzzling question of the way in which revelation actually came. When the Lord spoke to a prophet, or through him, what happened?

One would gather that as a rule it was not anything plainly out of the ordinary. Ideas or sentences entered his mind, with a sense of conviction and inspiration which he could not gainsay. They seized him and never let him go till he had poured them out. In other words his experience was much like that of any other creative person. To determine on purely psychological grounds whether a given prophet was or was not inspired from outside himself would involve knowing far more about his native gifts than we ever do.

As for the visions and the voices, these also can be discussed and perhaps "explained" in terms of psychology, in this case abnormal psychology . . . or mere physical disorder. Regarding mysticism in general, Bertrand Russell has alleged that we can draw no objective distinction between the man who eats too little and sees heaven, and the man who drinks too much and sees snakes. If we take these two in isolation at the instant when the apparition occurs, Russell may be right. But with Hebraic prophecy, as with so much in the Hebraic tradition, to treat it thus is to falsify it. Prophecy takes place in a context. The visionary experience is always more than a private excitement. It is a factor in the life of Israel, to be judged by its results, by the depth and durability of the prophet's insights, by his whole career and its effect on his contemporaries and on posterity. Here alcohol fails. The verdict of psychology may or may not be worth seeking. It must be inconclusive, because, in any event, abnormality may open doors which normality keeps shut. On a more mundane level, Byron's poetry is not invalidated by its debt to his club foot. What matters chiefly is that whereas the psychological approach to prophecy can have only a secondary usefulness, the historical approach is vital.

In the earlier group of literary prophets—Amos, Hosea, Isaiah, Micah—Amos is the prototype. Born at Tekoa near Jerusalem, he moved into the northern kingdom, where he was active about 760. He was a penniless shepherd and day-labourer belonging to no *nabhi* guild, and denied being a prophet at all in that sense. His inspiration caught hold of him independently. "The Lord took me from following the flock, and the Lord said to me, 'Go, prophesy to my people Israel'." When he arrived the northerners were enjoying a spell of outward success. King Jeroboam II was winning victories over his neighbours. But against the civilised prosperity round him the immigrant shepherd set his face firmly. His sayings, mostly in verse, have a left-wing tone, which thus appears for the first time in any literature.

Amos's attacks on the upper class are unsparing. Though concerned mainly with the north, he glances back across the frontier; Judah is not so different.

> Thus says the Lord:
> "For three transgressions of Israel,
> and for four, I will not revoke the punishment;
> because they sell the righteous for silver,
>   and the needy for a pair of shoes—
> They that trample the head of the poor into the dust
>   of the earth,
>   and turn aside the way of the afflicted.

> "Woe to those who are at ease in Zion,
>   and to those who feel secure on the mountain of
>   Samaria . . .
> Woe to those who lie upon beds of ivory,
>   and stretch themselves upon their couches,
> And eat lambs from the flock,

and calves from the midst of the stall,
Who sing idle songs to the sound of the harp . . ."

(ii:6-7, vi:1, 4-5)

Among other scandals the prophet mentions the merchants' use
of unequal weights, heavy ones for buying and light for selling.
Two such weights, made of polished red stone, have been found in
a water cistern at Tell el-Nasbeh. Both are an inch across and half
an inch thick, but one has lead in the bottom and the other has
not.

Samaria's religion is assailed on two counts. Amos refers to
the growth of paganism in the form of star-worship (v:26), but he
is much more deeply concerned with the decadence of the true
cult itself. God speaks:

"I hate, I despise your feasts . . .
Even though you offer me your burnt offerings and
cereal offerings,
I will not accept them . . .
Take away from me the noise of your songs;
to the melody of your harps I will not listen.
But let justice roll down like waters,
and righteousness like an ever-flowing stream."

(v:21-24)

The Lord sends Amos menacing visions—locusts and fire, and
autumn fruit symbolising the nearness of a long winter. He recalls
how he led Israel out of Egypt in triumph; his people's very
afflictions are the chastisement of love; but the result of all his care
had been that they think themselves secure, and free to pursue the
same sort of aggrandisement as the Gentiles. They are fools.
Israel is puny. God, in a most impressive passage, sets his children
for the first time against the world background. He brought them
into the Land, yes. But he has governed the movements of other
nations too, even their oppressors, and Israel's fortunes are just as
mutable: "Are you not like the Ethiopians to me, O people of
Israel? Did I not bring up Israel from the land of Egypt, and the

Philistines from Caphtor and the Syrians from Kir?" (ii:9-10; iii:2; vii:2, 5; ix:7.)

Amos introduces the theme, afterwards much enlarged upon, of the Day of the Lord. This formerly meant an autumn harvest-festival marking the turn of the agricultural year. But, like other festivals which the Hebrews adopted, it was transposed into histori-cal terms. There seems to have been a current patriotic hope for a coming Day which would witness the final ruin of Israel's enemies. Amos warns that the divine judgment, if it comes, will not be so flattering.[4]

> Woe to you who desire the day of the Lord!
>   Why would you have the day of the Lord?
> It is darkness, and not light.
>
> "On that day," says the Lord God,
> "I will make the sun go down at noon,
> and darken the earth in broad daylight.
> I will turn your feasts into mourning,
> and all your songs into lamentation."
>
> (vi:18; viii:9-10)

The prophet in fact sees doom hanging over the northern kingdom, the Calves wilting and the luxuries popularised by Ahab crumbling away.

> "On the day I punish Israel for his transgressions,
>   I will punish the altars of Bethel,
> And the horns of the altar shall be cut off
>   and fall to the ground.
> I will smite the winter house with the summer house;
>   and the houses of ivory shall perish,
>   and the great houses shall come to an end," says the Lord.

4 Compare the old Prussian toast to *Der Tag* which would usher in the ascendancy of *Kultur*. One of Bernard Partridge's cartoons of the Kaiser, "The Day of Reckoning," inverts this hope in precisely Amos's manner.

Because you trample upon the poor
   and take from him exactions of wheat,
You have built houses of hewn stone,
   but you shall not dwell in them;
You have planted pleasant vineyards,
   but you shall not drink their wine.

(iii:14-15; v:11-12)

Naturally Amos aroused opposition. Amaziah, a priest at Bethel, accused him of foretelling a violent death for the King. Ordered back to Judah, he took his leave talking more ominously than ever.

Next comes Hosea, the only literary prophet to arise in the north itself. A man of higher standing than Amos, he seems to have flourished between 750 and 725. A special feature of his message is his startling exploitation of the symbolic act. He tells how at God's command he married a prostitute. Their whole troubled relationship, including the naming of their children, becomes a complex emblem of God's relationship with Israel. The use of sexual depravity as a spiritual image recurs elsewhere in the Bible, and Hosea's marriage sublimates a pagan conception of the bond between deity and worshipper. That the prophet does regard it as a metaphor and no more is proved by another passage where he portrays God speaking of Israel, not as his bride, but as his son (xi:1).

Hosea's main topic is religious corruption, including ritual prostitution (iv:14). He condemns the Calves (viii:5-6). But in one noteworthy poem he achieves the distinction of being the first in recorded history to denounce military power-politics, which Jeroboam II had made an issue. Jeroboam's troops were efficient and well equipped: besides the normal archers and slingers, he had armoured infantry carrying swords, pikes, and light lances like the Roman *pilum* which could be thrown as javelins. It is in reference to their campaigns that Hosea coins the phrase "sow the wind and reap the whirlwind." All the King's strategy and diplomacy, his foreign leagues and his hiring of mercenaries, the prophet scornfully dismisses as worse than futile. However, he has gleams of hope. Israel may repent, and live in peace with the Lord again.

Of these four prophets Isaiah is the greatest. He flourished in Jerusalem between 742 and 701, and became a court adviser to King Hezekiah of Judah. He was well circumstanced and well educated, a professional teacher perhaps. According to legend he was put to death. The book bearing his name is drawn from several sources. None of the original prophet's work, or hardly any, appears after Chapter xxxix, and even the earlier portion is thickly interpolated. Where Isaiah's real sayings can be picked out they show a rare eloquence. His account of his calling as a prophet (vi:1-8), in an ecstatic experience in the Temple, goes far beyond the curt jottings of Amos. Isaiah has a profound sense of awe before the Lord, whom he speaks of as "the Holy One of Israel." The themes of his prophesying are largely the same as those of his predecessors. We find, as before, the denunciations and threats and hopes, the visions and the symbolic acts, the application now being mainly to Judah. Isaiah marries a "prophetess" and, like Hosea, gives his children significant names (vii:3 and viii:1-4; this is where the famous name Maher-shalal-hash-baz occurs). He goes about naked in public to show how the Egyptians must be despoiled and led captive by the King of Assyria (xx:1-6). The chief difference from Amos and Hosea lies in the more elaborate style. However, two points may be singled out.

The first is that the prophet is already less a popular spokesman, more an outsider preaching at a nation which has yielded *en masse* to materialism and superstition. Isaiah finds it necessary to attack "false" prophets, who proclaim comforting things to order. This idea is pursued by Micah—a younger contemporary, and more or less a continuator—in a fierce assault on the charlatans who, for pay, beguile Zion with spurious inspiration.

Secondly, besides appealing to Israel's past, Isaiah takes a hint from his two precursors and looks ahead. By so doing he sets a fashion which his successors follow. From this chiefly we derive our debased notion of a prophet as somebody who foretells. But an Isaiah would never have concerned himself with frivolous forecasts of the Old Moore type. Prophetic anticipation is always related to choice and conduct, to the proper guidance of Israel. Moreover, some of it is conditional rather than absolutely predictive. The divine message may be that "if present trends continue, so-and-so will happen"; whereas if the people repent, something else will. Failure to grasp the conditional nature of a prophecy has sometimes led to bewilderment and disappointment. There is an instance in the Bible (*Jonah* iii:1-10, iv:1).

Gazing out over their world, the prophets all faced what is now called an international situation, heavily charged with danger. The small Hebrew states were forced into a perpetual awareness of realms and empires all around; of Egyptians, Assyrians, Babylonians, Medes, resurgent after the pause in David's time. Waves of warfare swept back and forth, always threatening to engulf them. The prophets lived in an age of crises with no clear progression or direction, more like the twentieth century than the nineteenth. They struggled to understand these forbidding events, at least as affecting the two kingdoms, and it was one of their glories that they never despaired. They made catastrophe creative and drew fresh insight from it, discovering spiritual resources such as no other people had. They did not merely complain at the foreigners; they asked how Israel itself had gone wrong, and tried to interpret the marches and countermarches as divine judgments. The inference was obvious. If God's people went on sinning, then sooner or later he might enable some enemy to triumph, and destroy their hold on the Land altogether. Thus the ethical meaning of history was extended. It now applied not only to the tribes but to the neighbouring world, and not only to a few special happenings in the past but to the details of the present and future.

Hence that fifth step in the logic of Israel. Hence also a sixth which followed rapidly. The further question was this:

If God can bring conquerors against us, doesn't this imply that he rules over other nations as well as Israel, and should be their God too?

And the prophets answered:

Yes, it does. At present they are simply his puppets—they do not know him. But the veil that hides him is of our own making. If we keep the Covenant to the full, the consequences will be so splendid that all men will honour him, and us. The Land will become holy for them also, and they will let us, to whom he has given it, possess it in safety.

In fact it is through these efforts to rationalise a baffling world that the latent ethical monotheism of Yahweh-worship at last begins to come out into the open. The plain statement that there is no God but the Lord is still not made. However, in all these classical prophets, it is on the brink of being made. The only Higher Power that matters to Israel is now unambiguously the only Power that matters at all, anywhere. God's "bringing Israel out of Egypt," for Amos, can be paralleled by his bringing "the Philistines from Caphtor, and the Syrians from Kir." Even imperial Assyria, for Isaiah, is "the rod of God's anger" to be wielded against a nation of hypocrites and laid aside at his pleasure.

The prophets declare that God will govern events in the future as in the past. Frightening as the near prospect may look, it can serve to shake Israel out of self-sufficiency into repentance and re-thinking and the quest for love behind wrath. And the love is there. The passage of time will justify all God's dealings. The atonement of his people will some day bring their salvation, or, at least, the salvation of the Righteous Remnant.[5] This is not an otherworldly salvation. It is the peace of the Lord's community, on earth, in time. Israel's enemies will fall. Warfare will pass away. A glorious king coming from Bethlehem like David (*Micah* v:2) will succeed to the throne of David. There will be a new Jerusalem and a golden age.

> It shall come to pass in the latter days
>   that the mountain of the house of the Lord
> shall be established as the highest of the mountains,
>   and shall be raised above the hills;
> and all the nations shall flow to it,
>   and many peoples shall come, and say:

5 As to the continuing idea of the Remnant, see *Isaiah* x:20-22.

"Come, let us go up to the mountain of the Lord,
    to the house of the God of Jacob;
that he may teach us his ways
    and that we may walk in his paths."
For out of Zion shall go forth the Law,
    and the word of the Lord from Jerusalem.
He shall judge between the nations,
    and he shall decide for many peoples;
and they shall beat their swords into ploughshares,
    and their spears into pruning hooks;
nation shall not lift up sword against nation,
    neither shall they learn war any more.

                      (*Isaiah* ii:2-4)

Yahweh then is to be reverenced by all mankind. Yet the Land of Israel will still, as ever, be the place of his manifestation. Indeed, the *Micah* version of the same prophecy indicates that other gods will continue to be worshipped in other countries (iv:1-5). While an ampler faith is dawning, it is no abstract theology. It is still grounded in the known patterns of human living. It still invokes collective experience, the Exodus and all the rest. Its supreme hope is a transfiguration of the past in the future.

With the new vision, finally, comes a new burden. If God—being infinitely wise and just—presides over everything that happens, then everything that happens, even the most appalling disasters, must somehow make sense. The prophets, holding that faith, ventured far and boldly in the pursuit of cosmic sanity. They also sharpened the pain of generations of sufferers who accepted their doctrine but lacked their genius in applying it. After Isaiah, Job.

5

But while Isaiah was still exhorting Jerusalem, the doom which Amos had seen overhanging Samaria descended.

From 784 to 744 the northern realm had expanded and prospered under Jeroboam II. Yet even he, we are told, persisted in the sins of his namesake. He was succeeded by a string of nonentities who did the same. Nothing but a mighty spiritual and material effort could have kept the kingdom afloat much longer, and that was not forthcoming. Away to the east lay the empire of Assyria creeping closer and closer.

Its heartland was the region round the upper Tigris and Euphrates; its capital was Nineveh. Assyria had originated more than five hundred years earlier as a Babylonian outpost, and its culture and religion were largely copied from Babylon. But the colonists had revolted and overthrown the parent kingdom. Now, after several turns of fortune, the Assyrian monarchs had at last succeeded in dominating the Near East. They were military despots, and all their nobles were warriors. These Semites with their thick curled beards and imposing head-dresses were in fact utterly dedicated to power, and their thorough-going brutality has scarcely been equalled till modern times. From ponderous palaces embellished with winged bulls and lions, they rode out to wage a warfare of unprecedented competence, using heavy cavalry and siege-engines. The conquests which they generally achieved were recorded in complacent reliefs portraying captive kings being tortured, prisoners being flayed and impaled, civilian populations going away into bondage, and hordes of identical-faced slaves toiling at public works under the lash.

Such was the enemy that loomed on the horizon of Israel. The line of able commanders on its throne—the Shalmanesers and Sargons and Tiglath-pilesers—showed no sign of breaking. For a while the Aramaic state in between acted as a buffer, and Assyrian strength served Israel's interests. With a threat on the other frontier, Damascus dared not exert much pressure on Samaria. But little by little that advantage trickled away. The net effect of each shift was an Assyrian gain. In 734 Tiglath-pileser III invaded Israel and carried off many of the inhabitants. After the war he kept control of Galilee and Gilead. Through an alliance with Judah he had conquered Damascus too, so that the buffer was gone. A conspiracy prompted by these reverses placed a certain Hoshea on the northern throne. His foreign policy was reckless. He accepted the status of an Assyrian vassal, paid an annual tribute for a few years, and then began conspiring again—with Egypt—while withholding the tribute. Assyrian troops arrested him and laid siege to Samaria.

The siege was pushed to its conclusion by Sargon II, whose army occupied the city. He marched down through Palestine and drove back Hoshea's Egyptian allies, then returned to blot out what he regarded as a nest of brigands. In 721 Samaria was devastated, the mansions torn down, the best ivory panels carted off for Sargon's own palace. In keeping with Assyrian precedent, the King resolved on a wholesale transfer of populations. He uprooted many Israelites and "placed them in Halah and on the Habor, the river of Gozan, and in the cities of the Medes." Then he brought other subjects "from Babylon, Cuthah, Avva, Hamath and Sepharvaim," and settled them in the former Israelite territory.

Their advent had a strange sequel. At first they met with difficulties. They were beset by wild beasts, which had grown bold and multiplied in the anarchy of war. Blaming this plague on their ignorance of the local god, the colonists persuaded Sargon to send back an Israelite priest, who re-established the cult of Yahweh for them. But they naturally did not want to give up their own gods. So the Babylonians worshipped Yahweh, and Succoth-benoth; the men of Cuth worshipped Yahweh, and Nergal; the men of Hamath worshipped Yahweh, and Ashima; the Avvites worshipped Yahweh, and Nibhaz; the Sepharvites worshipped Yahweh, and Adrammelech (for whom they burned their children alive). All the Lord's priests after the first were recruited from Sargon's settlers and their descendants. A debased cult unalleviated by prophecy became the norm. And this was not to be the end of the story.

The true scope of the Assyrian deportation is doubtful. An inscription refers to the removal of 27,290 Israelites, numerically a mere fraction. While this may have been only one instalment of several, it is unlikely that even the relentless Assyrians would have gone to the trouble of totally emptying a country. But certainly they took all the aristocratic and wealthy elements, and most of the city-dwellers in general: everybody who, in the vulgar sense, counted. The Israelite population that stayed behind was poor, rustic, scattered, and leaderless. The King's colonists moved into the ghost-towns forming a new administrative stratum, and spread out through the rural districts. Racial mixture over the years filled northern Palestine with a mongrel "Samaritan" stock practising the debased Yahweh-cult. So the strain of the ten tribes did not die out in the Land. But more colonists reinforced the first wave, and after a very few generations hardly any Samaritan can have been a pure Israelite with a convincing pedigree.

More interesting, at least to minds of a certain type, is the fate of the Hebrew deportees. They lived on in Media, and still had a recognisable identity when *II Kings* was written, since the author says (xvii:23) that they are there "to this day"—i.e. the sixth century B.C. But canonical Scripture does not pursue them further. According to legend they moved on, wandering for a year and a half into another country. Their cousins of Judah believed firmly that God had condemned them. Yet some also believed that northern Israelite groups remained in existence and might not be permanently lost. In the first century A.D. the Jewish historian Josephus locates these groups vaguely beyond the Euphrates. The Jewish-Christian *Epistle of James* is addressed to all twelve tribes. St. James's hope, if that is what he implies, has never quite perished. During the Middle Ages a stir was caused by a person named Eldad who professed to belong to the tribe of Dan. Fresh legends told of a secret retreat cut off by the mysterious river Sambatyon. As we shall see, there is even yet a lingering rabbinic notion that the northerners will re-emerge in the end. But it is not pseudo-scientific or speculative. No rabbi seriously attempts to guess where they are, or in what disguise they have been hiding so long. They are ignored, or rather left to God.

The notorious Lost Ten Tribes problem which has inspired so

much conjecture is a recent phenomenon, outside the Jewish tradition. Most of the zealots of the quest have been Christians, and some have been vocally anti-Jewish. Their normal point of departure is not in ethnology but in extreme Fundamentalism. They fail to grasp (in spite of the *Book of Jonah*) that biblical prophecies can be conditional, and (in spite of much else) that the sense of biblical terms can change. One or two of the prophets do hint briefly at a prospective reunion of Israel and Judah; so these infallible sayings must some day be literally fulfilled. No "if," no concession to poetry, no diversion of spiritual descent can be admitted. "Israel" must always mean exactly what it meant when the distinction of Israel and Judah was first drawn, i.e. the complete northern tribal system. Therefore the complete northern tribal system must still exist somewhere . . . because the destined reunion with Judah has not yet taken place. This is an axiom, not a possibility to be looked into. The theorist, having picked out what he supposes to be Israel among the nations, usually tries to support his choice with arguments of absurd flimsiness. But to laugh at his scholarship or science may well be to mistake his position. Quite likely he does not feel any obligation to prove that the Lost Tribes exist. He is simply identifying Lost Tribes which *a priori* he already knows to exist. Hence he needs far fewer and less compelling facts than a sceptic might think. One striking coincidence may be enough to supply the tell-tale clue.

Granted his erroneous premiss, the rest more or less follows. The real trouble is that the tell-tale clues have pointed to half a dozen different Israels. The Afghan claim is the least improbable, and for that reason, perhaps, not widely favoured. Several authors have proposed the American Indians or some section of them; Israel (it seems) crossed the Bering Strait on the ice; and to one Indian-Israelite, Lord Kingsborough, we owe a genuinely valuable work on ancient Mexico. The Japanese candidature is based on the fact that the last King of Israel was named Hoshea. A Japanese royal genealogy begins with a similar-sounding name at about the same period. More famous, however, is the British-Israel doctrine.

British pretensions to be the Chosen People became attractive, and to many even plausible, in the decades when Britain had an empire. The idea still rather cantankerously survives. While its much touted prophetic proofs have collapsed, it has also grounded its appeal on dubious ethnology and tendentious ecclesiastical history, confirmed by measurements of the Great Pyramid. But actually it all springs from a pun. The word "British" suggests the Hebrew *b'rit ish*, meaning "Covenant Man."

What did happen beyond Euphrates, nobody can tell precisely. Most of the exiled families, lacking the system of preservation possessed by the Jews in later times, must have been gradually absorbed through intermarriage with Gentiles. In such cases their Israelite character leaked away. Some, on the other hand, may have re-entered the stream by intermarriage with southerners from Judah, after these also became dispersed through the Middle East.[6] Conceivably, too, a number of so-called Jewish communities in Kurdistan and the Caucasus are descended from northern exiles.

6

Samaria's ruin bore out the prophets. Events had shown that apostate Israelites could indeed lose the Land, that they could be disowned and banished from the divine presence. God had "rejected all the descendants of Israel, and afflicted them, and given them into the hand of spoilers, until he had cast them out of his sight" (*II Kings* xvii:20). The total Israelite Palestinian population was now reduced to far less than a million; the whittling-down dimly foreshadowed by Elijah was proceeding apace. We notice, in tracing its progress, that the confusing political use of the name "Israel" to mean a part of the whole people now disappears. The promises are inherited by the Remnant, which, for the moment, is Judah with its Benjamite annex. Henceforth the true Israel of God

6 For evidence that some sort of northern strain was later believed to have remained or reappeared in the population, see the *Letter of Aristeas* mentioned further on; also, in the New Testament, *Luke* ii:36.

always is a Remnant, namely, that portion of the whole stock which is deemed to have kept faith. Waverers and idolaters can fall away into oblivion. Their Hebrew blood will not save them. An ethical conception supplants the purely hereditary.[7]

Shortly before the northern tribes crumbled, King Ahaz of Judah had bought protection from Tiglath-pileser of Assyria with the Temple treasure. But his submission, though abject, was not irrevocable. His stronger son Hezekiah succeeded him at the age of twenty-five, and revolted. In 701 came an Assyrian invasion under Sennacherib. Hezekiah's attempt to purchase peace was a failure, and while he was contemplating an Egyptian alliance, Sennacherib's army arrived to besiege Jerusalem. A parley was held in Hebrew outside the gate. The Assyrian commander sneered at the defenders' Egyptian hopes ("Egypt, that broken reed which will pierce the hand of any man who leans on it"), and announced his intention of destroying the city. Hezekiah's envoys, acutely conscious of the crowd listening on the wall, begged him to speak in Aramaic instead. The commander took the hint gleefully. He walked forward and began shouting—still in Hebrew—advising the citizens to surrender, and pointing out justly enough that whatever the folk of Judah might think of their God, none of the other nations' gods had been of any service against Assyria. But Hezekiah had told his people not to reply, and they obeyed; there was silence on the wall. The parley ended and the King consulted Isaiah, who assured him that the Lord would rescue Jerusalem. Hezekiah prayed earnestly in the Temple . . . "and that night the angel of the Lord went forth, and slew a hundred and eighty-five thousand in the camp of the Assyrians; and when men arose early in the morning, behold, these were all dead bodies."

Sennacherib's hexagonal tablet recording the war does not mention the epidemic, bubonic perhaps, that defeated him. It makes much of his early victories. On the other hand it nowhere claims that Jerusalem was captured; all it says is that Hezekiah

7 This change in the significance of "Israel" is the real answer to the dogma about the Lost Tribes.

was "shut up in his city like a bird in a cage." Moreover it is certain that Sennacherib left Judah alone for twenty years afterwards. The outside evidence, therefore, is quite in accord with Scripture.

Another archaeological sidelight on this reign comes from the King's Siloam water-tunnel, which is still there. We are told that he "made the pool and the conduit and brought water into the city" (*II Kings* xx:20). His chief aim was probably to render enemy interference with the water-supply more difficult. Two crews dug towards each other through two thousand feet of rock, one starting from Siloam, one from the spring of Gihon. After a slightly erratic convergence they effected a junction. On the side of the tunnel a contemporary scrawl states triumphantly that "the boring is finished" and explains how the gangs found each other by listening for the sound of voices and picks.

Hezekiah gave Judah a spell of peace. Both before and after his declaration of independence he was active in religious reform. Judah still had the Ark and the Temple and the Davidic line. Pilgrims came to the Temple even from the lost territories. Impressed, no doubt, by Isaiah's teaching and by the fall of Samaria, Hezekiah set himself to focus the kingdom upon the central cult which was unique and indubitably valid. His workmen dismantled, at long last, the ambiguous hill-shrines on the high places. They broke the images and cut down the sacred groves. The Temple still cherished a bronze serpent which was supposed to have been made by Moses; Hezekiah smashed even this. By such actions he tightened up Yahweh's cult as none of his predecessors had done. The course of his reign seemed to augur well, and Isaiah gave him a special blessing.

Yet no king of Judah was fully free in such matters. Religious policy depended to a great extent on external affairs, on the kingdom's relations with the paramount power Assyria. When Jerusalem bowed to Nineveh, the pagan divinities had to be treated with respect as part of the bargain. When Jerusalem broke loose, Yahweh could recover his own. Ahaz had set the pattern when he attached himself to Tiglath-pileser, by ordering a replica of an Assyrian altar. Hezekiah could do as he pleased. But during the long reign of his son Manasseh, Assyria renewed the pressure; an Assyrian army occupied part of Egypt; and Manasseh, from expediency or conviction or both, undid his father's work. He restored the high places, revived the cultus of Baal and Asherah, worshipped the stars, burned his son as an offering, and employed magicians and mediums as advisers. Furthermore he put his altars and idols in the Temple itself, converting the Lord's house into a pantheon.

Manasseh was denounced by the *nabhi* prophets, and crushed opposition ruthlessly. In some obscure clash the Assyrians took him prisoner and held him in Babylon for a while—an occurrence mentioned in an inscription of Sennacherib's son. As a result he is alleged to have repented. Late apocryphal manuscripts give a prayer ascribed to him. But he certainly did not restore the state of affairs established by Hezekiah.

His young grandson Josiah became king in 640. By that time Assyria's bolt was shot. The empire was rapidly declining. Josiah resumed the purification of Zion. The Temple was not only polluted but dilapidated. About 622 he told the chief priest Hilkiah to allocate a large sum from the collection-box to the overseers in charge of the building. They were to buy stone and timber to repair it, and hire masons and carpenters. To quote Moffatt's touching translation: "No audit was ever taken of the money thus handed over: the men acted honestly." One hopes so. Nevertheless Hilkiah kept close to the operations.

Presently a strange thing happened. While peering into some long-forgotten niche, he spied and extracted a scroll of writing. Having glanced through, he handed it to a secretary, who read from it to the King. It concerned the Covenant and the divine penalties for its breach. Josiah was alarmed at the book's menacing tone, and sought guidance from "Huldah the prophetess." She warned Josiah of God's anger against the paganism of Judah, but promised him that his own contrition would bring him to his grave in peace. The King summoned an assembly at which the book was read through, and pledged himself to observe its teaching.

Even before the book came into his hands he had perhaps been moving in Hezekiah's direction. But under its inspiration he embarked on a programme of reform that eclipsed Hezekiah's. He disinterred all the apparatus of paganism that he could find anywhere. He collected vessels used in Baal-worship and Asherah-worship and the cult of the stars, and incinerated the whole heap. He dragged the statue of Asherah from the Temple, burned it, pulverised it, and scattered the ashes. He wrecked the sanctuary of Topheth where children were sacrificed to Moloch. He carted away some model horses and chariots which earlier kings had set up for the sun-god. He felled sacred poles and he shattered sacred obelisks. He banished wizards and mediums, tore down the houses of temple-prostitutes, and unfrocked every pagan priest he could lay his hands on. Then he held a great Passover with all his subjects, a custom which had long been neglected. "Before him there was no king like him . . . nor did any like him arise after him."

What was this tremendous book? The priest Hilkiah is represented as calling it "the book of the Law," and speaking as if he already knew of it. For various reasons there cannot be much doubt that it was an early form of *Deuteronomy* ascribed to Moses himself. Since it could be read through aloud at a public meeting, it was not the whole of the present book. Perhaps an unidentifiable nucleus of Mosaic matter had been spun out during the long interval into something like *Deuteronomy* Chapters xii to xxvi, plus a few of the threats that come later.[8]

More important even than the discovery of the book was its development. Quite soon an unknown author of genius expanded it further into the extant *Deuteronomy*, which became a manual for all reform in Judah. It was a product of repentance and an attempt at a fresh start. *Deuteronomy* to-day stands fifth in the

8 The supposition that the job had been done recently seems to involve difficulties. Hilkiah could hardly have imagined that a scroll written within his own lifetime was the work of Moses. On this showing, either he had reason to think it was a transcript of an older original, or his "find" was a fraud. But regarding the fraud theory, see Kuhl, *The Old Testament*, p. 84.

Pentateuch. Its title means Second Law, implying a re-statement of
ordinances already given in the previous books. In fact, however,
it was completed in its present form before any of them. Its composition was the beginning of the formation of a scriptural canon.
Many writings of course already existed, sacred and secular: the
old Law codes, the histories by the Yahwist and Elohist, the poems
and court annals and collections of prophets' sayings. But *Deuteronomy* is the first finished book of Scripture with an official stamp,
the first essay in systematisation, and the nucleus of the Bible.
Everything else has been added on to it and built round it.

The author has a prose style of his own, highly rhetorical and
imaginative. His work is a vivid example of Hebrew concentration
on the central idea, on what the writing is "about." His theme is
the Law; the process of its formulation is telescoped into a single
discourse by Moses in the wilderness, just before his death. Moses
is made to review the forty years' wanderings and to draw lessons
from them for the future. The literary device gives an air of
authority and passion to the entire work.

Prophetic teaching has influenced this writer, who calls Moses
himself the greatest of the prophets, and speaks cryptically of another
to come (xviii:15-19, xxxiv:10). Not that he is by any means a
codifier of prophecy; his concern is always with the Law, and the
inseparable Cult. But he has digested the prophets' case against
mechanical ceremony. He presents both Cult and Law against the
moral and theological background supplied by God's acts in
history. Moreover he is aware that the form without the spirit
is dead. His Moses not only repeats the Decalogue but goes on to
enunciate the master-commandment:

> Hear, O Israel: the Lord our God is one Lord;
> And you shall love the Lord your God with all your
> heart, and with all your soul, and with all your
> might. (vi:4-5)

These words are still the opening of the *Sh'ma*, the basic prayer of
all Jews. The first verse at least is repeated constantly through life
and at the moment of dying.

The Prophets and the Law

Like the prophets and nearly all biblical contributors, the author of *Deuteronomy* invokes the experience of Israel. In his text Moses refers many times to the historical proofs of God's power and purpose (e.g. iv:32-35). There is the same stress as in Amos on Israel's utter dependence and its nothingness apart from God's choice (vii:7-8). The divine promises involve duties as well as privileges. Israel must deserve the Land which God gives (iv:1; vi:18). If the people keep the Covenant, in spirit and in letter, they will flourish there (vi:3; vii:12 ff; viii:1). If they break it, they will lose their homes and suffer a God-forsaken exile (iv:25-28; xxviii:58-68; xxix:18-28; xxx:17-18). In prosperity, therefore, they must be on guard always against forgetfulness (viii:11-14).

The author's view of the Covenant itself is cosmic yet curiously exclusive. Yahweh is world-ruler as the prophets imply, and mankind, in all its diversity, remains under his control (xxxii:8). But he has picked out Israel from the nations, and Israel alone knows and worships him, its Father (xiv:1). For the others he has appointed false gods, and seemingly they will never learn better. There is no hint here, as there is in Micah and Isaiah, that the Gentiles' darkness may be lightened. The most that can be looked for is that they will treat Israel with respect (iv:6). Meanwhile the Covenant, as it were, sustains the world, which without Israel would be wholly alienated from its Maker.

In these and other ways, a correspondence exists between *Deuteronomy* and the rigour and centralisation of Josiah's reform. When its Moses gives instructions for public worship, he declares (as the Yahwist, the Elohist, and the prophets do not) that there is only one proper place for it. He never names the place, but he means Jerusalem.

> When you go over the Jordan, and live in the land which the Lord your God gives you to inherit, and when he gives you rest from all your enemies round about, so that you live in safety,
>
> Then to the place which the Lord your God will choose, to make his name dwell there, thither you shall bring all

that I command you: your burnt offerings, and your sacrifices . . .

Take heed that you do not offer your burnt offerings at every place that you see;

But at the place which the Lord will choose in one of your tribes, there shall you offer your burnt offerings, and there shall you do all that I am commanding you.

(xii:10-14)

The obverse of this insistence on the hard distinctions produced by divine choice—on the difference of God's people from other peoples, of God's place from other places—is a holy xenophobia. When this Deuteronomic Moses mentions the inhabitants of Canaan, and lays down the lines of Israelite policy towards them, he says nothing to endorse the accommodations which were in fact made. They will seduce Israel into false worship, therefore they must be shunned and exterminated. *Delendi sunt.*

You must utterly destroy them; you shall make no covenant with them, and show no mercy to them.

You shall not make marriages with them . . .

(vii:2-3)

In the cities of these peoples that the Lord your God gives you for an inheritance, you shall save alive nothing that breathes,

But you shall utterly destroy them . . .

That they may not teach you to do according to all their abominable practices which they have done in the service of their gods, and so to sin against the Lord your God.

(xx:16-18)

At the end of his speech and the hymn that follows it, Moses blesses the tribes individually. The author closes with a brief account of his death, and says his grave is unknown. This passage used to be a favourite piece of freethinking ammunition against the belief that Moses wrote the Pentateuch. Actually the crux was faced by believers long before any freethinkers came on the scene. Jewish tradition explicitly recognised many centuries ago that the last eight verses were by another hand . . . as a similar note is supposed to be, at the end of *All Quiet on the Western Front*.[9]

7

Equipped with its handbook of reformation, the rump kingdom of Judah laboured on. It was defended now by a form of military conscription. Josiah had the satisfaction of outliving Assyrian hegemony in Asia. Shaken by Scythian attacks from the north, Assyria crumpled in 612 when the army of a resurgent Babylon captured Nineveh.

The metropolis on Euphrates was already a giant. After the victory it became colossal. All its august inheritance revived—the royal cult of Marduk, with his annual festivals and grandiloquent liturgy; the star-lore and number-lore of the priests, who worked out their magic with a scientific skill that brought it to the verge of true science. Chaldean engineers created a city of brooding vastness, where despots rode like gods up the processional avenue from an Ishtar Gate covered with bulls and dragons to a Babel-pyramid where mankind's invisible masters hovered. Babylon was a walled city of terraces and opulent gardens, of massive brickwork and glazed tiles, blue and white and scarlet; a city drawing nourishment from a countryside watered by a web of canals.

When Nineveh fell and Assyria's empire ended, Egyptian forces pressed into the power-vacuum. Josiah, trying to do the same, was killed in a brush with them at Megiddo. His successors (like those of Jeroboam II in Samaria) were weaklings. One of Josiah's sons, Jehoahaz, ruled for a few months; then Pharaoh Necho evicted him and put another on the throne, an amenable tribute-payer called Jehoiakim. Afterwards came Jehoiachin and Zedekiah. But the sum of the four reigns was not much more than twenty years.

Meanwhile a second quartet of prophets had arisen. Zephaniah prophesied early in Josiah's time, and his ferocious verses may have

9 The excellent Remarque parallel was pointed out by the late David Philip.

affected the King's policy. Nahum, a little later, denounced Assyria
and foretold its fall. With Nahum's contemporary Habakkuk the
main point of interest is that alone among literary prophets he was a
nabhi in the old sense, and employed some sort of technique to
put himself in a receptive state. But immensely more notable than
these was Jeremiah, who witnessed the end of Judah.

Apparently a priest by profession, he was a sombre, lonely-
spirited man, devoted to his nation and saddened by its many
apostasies. He was deeply disturbed by the perversion of prophecy
itself to sedative ends, to the repetition of "peace, peace" when
there was no peace (vi:13-14; xxiii:30-32). With one false prophet,
Hananiah, he clashed in public (xxviii). His visions and symbolic
acts were usually ominous. The breadth of Jeremiah's horizon is
shown by his many oracles about Gentile countries. Politically his
main theme was the rising Chaldean power of Babylon, against
which, he declared, resistance was vain and even impious. Its
king Nebuchadnezzar was God's appointed agent and world-
conqueror. Judah was doomed by its transgressions and would be
laid waste for seventy years (xxv:8-28; xxxiv:1-3).

This condemnation of poor Judah may sound cruel, coming as
it did soon after Josiah's clean sweep. But the immediate effect of
that gesture, as distinct from its remoter effects, was disappointing.
His feeble successors, under Egyptian and Babylonian pressure,
did not hold the ground gained. The sole positive improvement
acknowledged by the prophet was a decline in star-worship . . .
but this went with the decline of Assyria. Child sacrifice had crept
back; and in Egypt Jeremiah saw expatriate fellow-countrymen
offering cakes to the "Queen of Heaven" and burning incense
in her honour, remarking that they had had nothing but bad fortune
since her cult was suspended. The same goddess was not without
her adorers in Jerusalem itself (vii:18; xliv:15-19).

But Jeremiah looked beyond the impending calamity. Babylon
would not reign for ever. After seventy years God would bring
enemies from the north, among them the Medes (xxv:12; xxix:10;
l:9; li:28). A part of Judah, faithful and penitent, would then be

restored while the rest would be permanently cast off. The survivors would include the puritanical and conservative Rechabites
(xxxv:19). In Chapter xxiv the prophet describes a vision of two
symbolic baskets of figs, good and bad. This is a *locus classicus* for
the continuing idea of the Righteous Remnant which inherits
Israel's whole legacy. With the re-established Remnant, said
Jeremiah, God would deal graciously . . .

Behold, the days are coming, says the Lord, when I will
make a new covenant with the house of Israel and the house
of Judah,

Not like the covenant which I made with their fathers
when I took them by the hand to lead them out of the land
of Egypt, my covenant which they broke, though I was their
husband, says the Lord.

But this is the covenant which I will make with the house
of Israel after those days, says the Lord: I will put my law
within them, and I will write it upon their hearts; and I will
be their God, and they shall be my people.

And no longer shall each man teach his neighbour and each
his brother, saying "Know the Lord," for they shall all know
me, from the least of them to the greatest, says the Lord; for
I will forgive their iniquity, and I will remember their sin
no more.   (xxxi:31-34)

These sayings were momentous. The exact-sounding seventy
years led later to a whole literature of ingenuity, starting in the
Bible itself. Yet it may have been a purely conventional number
applied to the desolation of a city or state. As for the pledge of the
New Covenant, its majestic phrases were destined to be construed
as foreshadowing Christianity.

Jeremiah was disliked, and thrown in jail as a traitor. When
his secretary Baruch gave public readings from a scroll of his
prophecies, King Jehoiakim sent for it and showed his opinion with
a directness which even the head of a corporation might shrink from
to-day:

Jehudi read it to the king . . .

It was the ninth month, and the king was sitting in the winter house and there was a fire burning in the brazier before him.

As Jehudi read three or four columns, the king would cut them off with a penknife and throw them into the fire in the brazier, until the entire scroll was consumed in the fire that was in the brazier. (xxxvi:21-23)

Jeremiah is said to have died abroad.

The end came quickly enough. In 605 Nebuchadnezzar had beaten Egypt and annexed all the Egyptian-held territory in Asia. About 603 he asserted his control over Judah, and King Jehoiakim became his vassal instead of the Pharaoh's. Three years later Jehoiakim rebelled; a Babylonian army occupied Jerusalem and looted the Temple. When this king died, his son and successor Jehoiachin was deported almost at once to Babylon, together with a large part of the aristocracy and the wealthier families in general. Nebuchadnezzar left a third son of Josiah, Zedekiah, to reign over Jerusalem as viceroy with the regal title. Despite Jeremiah's warnings Zedekiah also rebelled, insanely relying on the broken reed Egypt. The Babylonian troops, led by Nebuzaradan, appeared again under the walls of Jerusalem. An Egyptian counter-attack did bring a momentary respite, but that soon passed. In mid-August of 587 the Babylonians burst into the city, and on the day numbered as Ninth of Ab in the Hebrew calendar, Nebuzaradan "burned the house of the Lord, and the king's house and all the houses of Jerusalem; every great house he burned down. And all the army of the Chaldeans . . . broke down the walls around Jerusalem" (*II Kings* xxiv:9-10).

So perished the southern monarchy, and, in its ruin, Solomon's Temple. Most of the priestly treasures and golden vessels were already in Babylon. The movables of silver and brass were now carried off as well. A surprising silence or near-silence overhangs the fate of the Ark of the Covenant. The tribes' most precious possession sinks virtually without trace. A legend in the apocryphal *II Maccabees* (ii:4-8) relates how Jeremiah himself rescued it before the siege and hid it in a cave in the same mountain where Moses surveyed the Promised Land. It will never be found again till the people are re-united in their ultimate peace.

Nebuchadnezzar had no more patience with Judah. Zedekiah was blinded, and dragged to Babylon like his nephew before him. A wholesale transplantation of inhabitants followed. "Judah was taken into exile out of its land" and held in bondage in Mesopotamia. Again the victors cannot have removed the entire nation. Indeed Scripture itself says that the poor, the vinedressers and ploughmen, were left behind (*II Kings* xxv:12). Probably a quarter would be a fair numerical estimate for the deportees. But this fraction, as in the north, included all the town-dwellers and persons of consequence. Trade withered away in the absence of merchants, and only a peasantry endured. Archaeology confirms this appraisal. The break in culture is absolute. For many years afterwards the country might as well have been empty.

Nebuchadnezzar appointed a "collaborationist" as governor in an effort to hold the province together. But this official was murdered, and many of the people drifted away to Egypt. Nothing, it seemed, could arrest the disintegration of Judah. A time came when the only districts not practically deserted were small patches of territory north of Jerusalem and in the Negeb.

No more is heard of Zedekiah. The deposed Jehoiachin, however, lived on in Babylon with deposed monarchs from several other kingdoms. Nebuchadnezzar's archives contain an entry about the rations issued to "Yaukin king of Judah" and his sons. That cuneiform tablet, by every rule of human probability, ought to have marked the final ignominy of David's house, and the fading of the Chosen People toward perpetual night.

CHAPTER SEVEN

A HERALD WITHOUT A NAME

By the waters of Babylon, there we sat down
  and wept,
when we remembered Zion.
On the willows there
  we hung up our lyres.
For there our captors
  required of us songs,
And our tormentors, mirth, saying,
  "Sing us one of the songs of Zion!"
How shall we sing the Lord's song
  in a foreign land?
If I forget you, O Jerusalem,
  let my right hand wither!
Let my tongue cleave to the roof of my mouth,
  if I do not remember you,
If I do not set Jerusalem
  above my highest joy!

    Amid the terraced architecture and the maze of irrigation canals, the Hebrews tasted bondage and poverty. They were not alone in their plight. Through the four decades after Zion's fall, Babylonian policy resembled Assyrian. Uprooted nations streamed into Mesopotamia with their captive kings, and the Temple's holy furniture was joined by the images of their captive gods. The reduced Israel which clung to its dignity in the heart of Nebuchadnezzar's empire comprised the last cohesive fractions of the tribes of Judah and Benjamin, plus the Levite families that were associated with them. These exiles were not completely enslaved: they could move about, and build villages for themselves; but they were subject to forced labour and insulting treatment. Their king Jehoiachin, released from prison when his masters judged him to be harmless, assembled a shadow-court that kept hope alive. After his death the hope was transferred to his grandson Zerubbabel, the legitimate heir of David. But even if Zerubbabel had been allowed back to Palestine, he would have found no kingdom to rule. By then the Land was not merely depopulated but partially lost to others. The north belonged to a hybridised Samaria, the Edomites had occupied the south-east. Some lingering Israelite, a disciple of Jeremiah perhaps, had sung the grief of Zion in the poems now called the *Lamentations* . . .

> How lonely sits the city
>   that was full of people!
> How like a widow has she become,
>   she that was great among the nations! . . .
> The roads to Zion mourn,
>   for none come to the appointed feasts;
> All her gates are desolate,
>   her priests groan;
> Her maidens have been dragged away,
>   and she herself suffers bitterly . . .
> Jerusalem remembers
>   in the days of her affliction and bitterness
> All the precious things
>   that were hers from days of old . . .
> "Is it nothing to you, all you who pass by?
>   Look and see
> If there is any sorrow like my sorrow . . ."

But this poet was a lonely voice in an emptiness.

The city's downfall had vindicated the prophets. It was to be expected, therefore, that fresh prophets would now arise and obtain a hearing. The Exile in fact produced at least two, of whom the second was the greatest and most mysterious of all. Before him came Ezekiel. Ezekiel was one of the priests whom Nebuchadnezzar had carried off after the first capture of Jerusalem. He seems to have been in his twenties when deported. He began writing in Babylonia before Jerusalem's final fall, and continued into the 570's. Tradition asserts that he wrote two books. The biblical text may be a selection of passages from both.[1]

With Ezekiel we again find most of the prophetic phenomena, but the spirit is no longer spontaneous. He composes planned literary essays in an established style. Not that there is any loss of flamboyance or colour. He opens with an astonishing account of a vision of the Lord rushing toward him in a chariot borne on the north wind. The description is a labyrinth of symbolic details that owe something to Babylon: lights and wheels and jewels and winged creatures. One is left in doubt whether Ezekiel actually "saw," like the older prophets, or imagined himself seeing, like Dante. He does not give a picture—nobody could draw the chariot from the specifications—but an emblematic structure which is tossed at the reader without a word of commentary. The commentary, of course, has since been forthcoming from other hands. Among medieval Jews the "Work of the Chariot" was held to be a supreme secret which only a few master-initiates understood. Once, when the celebrated Rabbi Eleazer expounded a portion of it out of doors, fire came down from heaven and encircled the field, a host of angels gathered to listen, and the terebinth-trees burst into a psalm. More recent writers have pointed out that the word *hashmal* (amber), which Ezekiel uses of the Divine Glory, has been adopted in modern Hebrew to mean "electricity," and that his vision is not wholly unintelligible as a description of a dynamo.

Whatever he intended, the apparition has one striking feature that is too easily overlooked—its location. God shows himself

---

1 For some sceptical views about Ezekiel, see Eissfeldt's discussion in Rowley's *The Old Testament and Modern Study*, pp. 153-8.

outside Palestine, in the unhallowed land of the Chaldeans. No more will be heard henceforth of the belief that in a foreign country one is entirely cut off from Yahweh. God speaks to Ezekiel from his chariot by the Chebar canal, and many times more in visitations spread over twenty years. He addresses the prophet as "Son of man." The earlier messages expand Jeremiah's image of the good and bad figs. The undeported folk of Judah are rebellious, wicked, and spiritually dead. They are given over to practices like sun-worship and the cult of Tammuz. A purified Remnant of deportees has the task of atonement.

The prophet's tone is vituperative and violent, and he exploits a Hosea-like allegory of sexual vice to the limit, labouring Jerusalem's "harlotry" for pages together. But he has moments of flashing originality. For instance, he is one of the first in Israel to discriminate between a communal and an individual guilt. God says:

> The son shall not suffer for the iniquity of the father, nor the father suffer for the iniquity of the son; the righteousness of the righteous shall be upon himself, and the wickedness of the wicked shall be upon himself.
>
> But if a wicked man turns away from all his sins which he has committed and keeps all my statutes and does what is lawful and right, he shall surely live; he shall not die . . .
>
> Have I any pleasure in the death of the wicked, says the Lord God, and not rather that he should turn from his way and live? (xviii:20-23)

This is a foretaste of the enlightened rabbinic teaching of later ages which is taken up by Christianity.

Ezekiel has unflinching trust in God's promises. Given repentance, the purged Remnant in Babylonia will be re-possessed of the Land. They will live under a prince whom Ezekiel, perhaps taking a hint from Jeremiah, calls "David." Since "David" is to reign for ever, the prophet presumably has in mind not only a restored monarch of Davidic stock but a dynasty to be fathered by him. He seems not to have given up hope of the northern tribes.

In a famous vision of dry bones coming back to life, he foresees the resurrection of the supposedly dead, and the re-union of Judah with "Ephraim." Israel's ultimate peace or *shalom* is to come through the miraculous rout of one last enemy—a dreadful conqueror from the north, "Gog of the land of Magog, the chief prince of Meshech and Tubal." Gog, like the Chariot, has provoked much comment. Several of the tribes that accompany him are native to the Caucasus region and southern Russia; he even has contingents from the Ukraine represented by "Gomer," i.e. the Cimmerian. This prophecy is glanced at again in the New Testament. It has not yet been fulfilled. British-Israelites used to explain it as an invasion of Palestine by the U.S.S.R., "Meshech" being Moscow and "Tubal" Tobolsk.

Ezekiel goes beyond his forerunners by making a serious and interesting attempt to predict what the future kingdom will be like. His last section could fairly be described as a pioneer Utopia, antedating Pythagoras by forty years and Plato by much more. He deals mainly with a restored Temple in a restored Jerusalem, and his architectural minutiae become tedious. However, he also touches on frontier demarcation, land tenure, and other economic arrangements, providing at least by proxy for all twelve tribes. He envisages the Lord blessing Palestine in a practical way with a giant irrigation, causing a river to rise from the Temple precinct and run downhill eastward. This will turn the Dead Sea valley into a lake of sweet water, with trees on its shore and shoals of fish in its depths.

But until Ezekiel's dream was fulfilled, what was to keep Israel in being? The State had gone and the Cult was extinct; the king was a pitiable pretender, no priest offered the daily sacrifice. It was again a season for reflection, and in this reflection it appears that Ezekiel himself played a major part. Jewish tradition stresses some remarks of his about meetings of elders at his house. Such consultations had two important results. One was the birth of the synagogue. While we do not hear of this as a formal institution till much later, there is little doubt that Israel's soul was nourished in exile by small regular gatherings devoted to prayer and reading and the singing of psalms. The synagogue service could never take the place of the Temple service; it was a stop-gap, a make-shift; but its value was inestimable.

More influential still was the dawn of the conception of "Torah." The word means "teaching" or "direction." It is sometimes translated "law," but misleadingly, since it covers every revelation of God. Palestine for the moment being out of reach, Israel's unity demanded a temporary substitute homeland, a portable patrimony secure against theft. This could take only one form—Scripture. For the first time the sacred writings began to be assembled and edited, to be given a central position and a canonical shape.

The Yahwist and Elohist episodes of the Pentateuch (of course there was no actual Pentateuch yet) had been reverently preserved and perhaps already interwoven. The scrolls of the prophets circulated among disciples and reached a widening public. The priests treasured their handbooks of law and ceremony. Also Israel had writings of a more secular kind—the songs and warrior-sagas and royal annals. However, the cornerstone of the chief work of the Exile was *Deuteronomy*. Scholars took up its main themes and pursued them further, with the same instructive intent, in a complete history of Israel. This is known as the Deuteronomic History. In the Bible it is divided into the books of *Joshua*, *Judges*, *Samuel* and *Kings*.[2]

The History was the first thing of its kind to be undertaken in Israel. It was not totally unparalleled; its writing was part of an international trend, a widespread revival of interest in the past. At about the same period Phoenician authors were making collections of mythology, Egyptian artists were resuscitating antique styles. But the Hebrews, as always, were far more deeply and

2 It has been maintained that the History was written in Palestine. But this idea creates a difficulty about the canonical acceptance, on such a large scale, of matter issuing from the "rejected" non-deportee body.

passionately engaged than their neighbours. The problem was to understand how their kingdom could have lurched down the centuries to a double ruin in spite of God's pledges. The prophets had sketched their ethical answer, and the Deuteronomists now worked it out in detail, though not altogether in the prophets' spirit. Essentially the answer was that Israel had been disobedient. But whereas the prophets had concentrated on the theme of final overthrow after long divine forbearance, the historians tried to trace God's hand throughout, and make the extinction of each kingdom appear as the climax of a comprehensible process. In their eyes prosperity had often been a specific divine reward for right conduct, disaster a punishment for sin. God's government of the world was not simply a general Providence broken by shattering interventions at long intervals. He acted (so to speak) habitually, and history made sense in detail. This thesis was given substance by a thoughtful rehandling of the conquest traditions, the court annals, and much else.

There was scope for thought. Even at the outset, in the record of the triumphs of Joshua, the writers stumbled on a crux. The Land as promised in the Lord's oldest oracles was not the Land as actually occupied. Its ideal frontiers had never been achieved. The Sinai generation had hoped for a long strip of territory from the Red Sea to the Euphrates, including all the coastland, but nothing east of the Jordan. Israel in fact had conquered the country east of Jordan, but had never firmly dominated the whole strip. This inexact fulfilment was duly accounted for by sin, chiefly the flirtation with Canaanite baals.[3]

David and Solomon had come nearest to perfect kingship, and the History extolled them accordingly. But as the kingdom split apart after Solomon's death, it was necessary to look for a cause. This was found in his toleration of his wives' alien gods. Afterwards came the long twilight. The northern kingdom, it was explained, had failed and fallen mainly because of Jeroboam

---

3 Ezekiel, in his Utopian Israel, does not include any territory east of Jordan (xlvii:15-20).

I's calf-cult. Through all that series of memorable narratives—
the stories of Ahab and Elijah, of Jezebel and Jehu and their successors—ran a dismal refrain: each king in turn "did not depart from
all the sins of Jeroboam the son of Nebat, which he made Israel to
sin." Condemned by that test even the ablest of the northern monarchs, even Omri and Jeroboam II, shrank into minor figures who
could be dismissed in a few lines. The effect of the Deuteronomic
perspective was to reduce the truly heroic in Israel's past, and to
place nearly all statesmen and soldiers under suspicion of impiety
or at least presumption. Hence a heavy loss, in the sense that much
material did not go into the new work at all. Again and again we
are maddeningly told that the rest of the acts of King So-and-So
are in the chronicles of the kings of Israel ... which no longer exist.
But the loss due to the disappearance of matter that did not go in
is more than compensated by the noble candour of a great deal
that did. The History's portraits of faulty human beings are
far more credible and exciting than the panegyrics that encircle the
famous in other nations of the ancient Near East.

When the History reached the collapse of the northern kingdom,
it summed up the reasons in a wholesale denunciation.

They would not listen, but were stubborn, as their fathers
had been, who did not believe in the Lord their God.

They despised his statutes, and his covenant that he made
with their fathers, and the warnings which he gave them.
They went after false idols, and became false, and they
followed the nations that were round about them, concerning
whom the Lord had commanded them that they should not
do like them.

And they forsook all the commandments of the Lord
their God, and made for themselves molten images of two
calves; and they made an Asherah, and worshipped all the
host of heaven, and served Baal.

And they burned their sons and their daughters as offerings,
and used divination and sorcery, and sold themselves to do evil
in the sight of the Lord, provoking him to anger.

Therefore the Lord was very angry . . . and removed
them out of his sight.   (*II Kings* xvii:14-18)

Judah's collapse presented a more serious difficulty, since its
kings had never been guilty of the calf-cult, and Hezekiah and
Josiah had made sincere efforts to purify the realm. Hence, the
Deuteronomists' view of Judah was ambivalent. On the one hand,
baal-worship and other abominations, copied from the north and
encouraged by King Manasseh, had doomed the kingdom. But
on the other, it had inherited an inner soundness from David, and
the Lord's pledges to the righteous king meant that its doom was
not permanent. The faithful southern exiles in Babylon kept the
vital orientation toward the Land and Zion and all that these stood
for. Penitence no doubt (as Ezekiel said) would sooner or later dispel
God's anger and bring them home.

The sad lessons of the History were popularised by the exiled
priests. Having no Temple to officiate in, they became chiefly
expounders of Torah in the infant synagogues. They formed a
closely-knit educated caste. By now all priests were Levites, and
the rule henceforth was never relaxed. Besides teaching the
Deuteronomic and other Torah, this caste produced its own work
in the shape of the "Priestly" writings which were to go into the
Pentateuch—the first account of Creation, the time-scales, and
further bits of interpretive text conceived in the same spirit.[4]

Thus, while the people of the Captivity were still far from having
a Bible, a fair proportion of the laity came to know something
incipiently like one. They were learning to fathom their forefathers' experience, and go beyond the national politics which
had become suddenly meaningless. They were at last grasping
moral implications, and sensing a need for moral change. The
seventh step in the logic of Israel was taken in Babylon; Ezekiel
stated it, the Deuteronomists expanded it.

Why the Captivity, why did we lose the Land?
Because of the very apostasy which the prophets warned us about.

4 Again it is not perfectly certain that the work was done in Babylon; but
again there are obstacles to supposing that it was done anywhere else.

We, the Remnant, must repent, and then we shall be restored to Zion.

The prophets' rightness was apparent in one other respect. They had stressed the stark distinction between the Lord's people and the rest. In Palestine that distinction had not always been easy to see. Foreign visitors were not very common, apart from invaders whom one never observed under ordinary conditions, and those who came did not bring their civilisation with them. But the Babylonians obviously were different, hugely and repellently different. So were the gaudy Babylonian gods in their cyclic ballet. Exiled Israel, unable to blend into the world around, studied and accentuated its own sacred oddities to maintain its identity. With a new zeal for the diet laws and the Sabbath and circumcision, the servants of Yahweh clung to their spiritual autonomy, cherished their traditions, and waited through weary decades for deliverance.

2

Deliverance came.

Nebuchadnezzar (whose mind, according to the *Book of Daniel*, was for some years unhinged) died in 562. After two short intervening reigns, the accession of Nabu-Naid or Nabonidus placed the empire in the hands of an eccentric, more antiquarian than king, who liked to potter about unearthing ruined temples and forgotten inscriptions. He estranged several of his principal cities by carrying off their gods' images to Babylon, to join the captive religious objects already there. Assur of Nineveh, Shamash of Sippar, Shushinak of Shushan, squatted in his museum-pantheon alongside the vessels of the invisible Yahweh. Nabonidus was not on good terms even with his own court-priests. Babylon's divine patron the Lord Marduk ("Bel-Marduk") was said to resent the King's neglect. Nabonidus, however, roamed happily westward in pursuit of his hobbies. He left his son Belshazzar in Babylon as regent, virtually as sovereign, and took hardly any notice of a perilous shift in the international situation.

After Nebuchadnezzar's demise, the kingdom of Media had

gained abruptly in power under its ruler Astyages. Media was a country with Indo-European inhabitants, lying south of the Caspian. It had suzerainty over Elam, which stretched toward the lower Tigris, and over the Persians who lived both inside and outside that area, far across the wide plateau of Iran. Astyages himself was peaceable, but with his overthrow by Cyrus a political avalanche had begun to slide.

Cyrus's name in his own Persian language was *Kurash*, the Shepherd. His descent from a certain Achaemenes gave him the title of King of Elam. But his coup against Astyages counted as a vassal's rebellion, not as an external attack, and he was aided by a Median faction. According to Herodotus he was a grandson of the Median monarch himself, whom prophecies of Cyrus's greatness frightened into a vain attempt at infanticide. However that may be, Cyrus after 550 was King of the Medes and Persians, whose names became almost interchangeable; and Herodotus's romance at least reflects an aura of divine destiny which soon surrounded him.

He found himself at the head of an army which was more than equal to any enemy within range. The three topics of Persian education were riding, archery and telling the truth. The warriors' fine mounts of Nisayan breed, the armour they wore on horseback and the bows they could shoot with from the saddle, gave them a clear ascendancy over the Babylonians or anyone else. A frieze in the Louvre portrays them in colour, with green turbans, tan boots, long light robes, and girdles of green or yellow. Their bows are white and their lances silver-hilted. Cyrus, while not a military genius of the first order, was quick-moving and decisive, able to attract good advisers and keep their loyalty. War with the proverbial Croesus of Lydia ended about 547 with a crushing success which gave him control of Asia Minor. From that time forward his efficient Persian Empire overshadowed and encroached upon decadent Babylon. Its remains give an impression of openness, of extroversion, contrasted with the heavy and haunted grandeur of Mesopotamia. Persian palace halls were spacious, with slender columns lovingly carved at base and capital. The realm of Cyrus produced a fine decorative sculpture, and excellent glazed ceramic pictures of plants and animals. Its young energy burst out on all sides: a final contest with Babylon could not be long postponed.

Israel's exiles began to lift their heads. Would the world-overturner set them free? Jeremiah had forecast Babylon's defeat by Medes and bowmen from the north (l:9, li:28). Very likely some furtive Hebrew envoy at Cyrus's court sounded out the royal intentions and received assurances which he took back to his kinsfolk. At any rate, in the gathering crisis a new voice was raised among them—a strong, confident, eloquent voice proclaiming extraordinary things: the voice of the poet-prophet responsible for the section of the *Book of Isaiah* which begins at the fortieth chapter.

This is a separate work which editors attached to the true Isaiah because of affinities of thought and phrasing, to Chapter xxxv for instance, and perhaps also because of some misunderstanding. One guess—it is no more—is that the author had the same name as Hezekiah's prophet, and the two were afterwards confused. In the absence of other information about him, he is uncouthly called Deutero-Isaiah or "Second Isaiah." His share of the book extends unquestionably to Chapter lv. The rest is a mixture. Changes of tone and traces of later composition have prompted theories of a "Third Isaiah" or school of disciples adding appendices. However, the leading ideas are carried on and developed without flagging, in a similar style which would not have been easy for an imitator to manage. Even if a distinct Third Isaiah existed, rather than a series of minor interpolators, he was a faithful follower. It is safe to use the last chapters to illustrate or clarify any thought which occurs in the undoubted sixteen.

Second Isaiah is one of the most important people in history, the creator of a world-religion, and the first writer who distinctly foreshadows Christianity. He almost certainly lived in Babylon, and he prophesied during Cyrus's advance in the 540's, when the Persian was planning an assault on the metropolis but had not yet launched it. The first words of his prophecy are a call to hope:

> Comfort, comfort my people,
>> says your God.
> Speak tenderly to Jerusalem,
>> and cry to her
> That her warfare is ended,
>> that her iniquity is pardoned.

Jerusalem—the afflicted queen Zion, personified as in *Lamentations*—has expiated her sins by these desolate years. She is absolved, and so, for the same reason, are her separated children. A celestial voice rings out over the desert between Babylon and the holy city. Her God will be reunited to her, the lost citizens will come back to her, and heaven will make their journey smooth.

> "In the wilderness prepare the way of the Lord,
>> make straight in the desert a highway for our God.
> Every valley shall be lifted up,
>> and every mountain and hill be made low;
> The uneven ground shall become level,
>> and the rough places a plain.
> And the glory of the Lord shall be revealed,
>> and all flesh shall see it together."

With Jerusalem, in Chapter xlvii, the prophet contrasts Babylon personified in the same way. She is doomed to ignominy and childlessness, through her trust in false gods and wizards, and the pride which lured her into the blasphemy of saying like Yahweh, "I am, and there is no one besides me." Babylon's fall, Zion's resurrection: round these interwoven themes the prophecy grows.

Here at least in the Bible it is right to speak of great literature in a strictly literary sense. As a flight of sustained rhetorical poetry the whole performance is astounding. Yet its splendour should not be allowed to obscure its novelty. On a hasty reading it might seem to be nothing but a hymn to the salvation already promised by earlier prophets. In fact it takes a colossal step forward from any previous Israelite position.

Crucial here is the writer's view of Cyrus. Hitherto the human agent of the peace of God's people had been pictured (in so far as he had been pictured at all) as a prince from among themselves, a lineal successor of David who would be, so to speak, David revived. Jeremiah had said it, Ezekiel had said it. The role assigned to him concerned no nation but Israel; he was simply going to restore the kingdom on a permanent footing. There was, however, one special point about this leader. If he was to be a new David, he would necessarily be the Lord's "anointed," consecrated by the pouring of oil as David was (*I Samuel* xvi:13). The word is "Messiah," a generic title not originally standing for any one person. With rescue near and the longed-for reinstatement dawning, we might expect Second Isaiah to give this key-word something like the meaning of "saviour" which it now bears. So he does. But he launches the Messianic idea on its mighty course with a startling gesture. The man he hails as Israel's "Messiah," metaphorically anointed of God (xlv:1), is King Cyrus himself . . . a Gentile. This Persian, whom God has "stirred up from the east" and given "victory at every step" (xli:2), is the only individual who ever is described as "Messiah" in anything like the familiar sense throughout the Old Testament.

Cyrus, declares the prophet, is the Lord's "shepherd" (xliv:28; the verse looks like a word-play on his name). He is divinely commissioned to crush Babylon and release the captives. They will go home in triumph and rebuild the Temple, with accompanying manifestations of God's glory which are set forth in language of soaring marvellousness. Moreover the hour approaches for the new Covenant pledged by Jeremiah, which the Lord will institute through his appointed servants, of whom the prophet is one. This is glanced at several times—in Chapters xlii, xlv, xlix— and it is coupled with an unprecedented announcement. As a result of Persia's victories the Gentiles, as well as Israel, are to enjoy the fullness of divine light.

All major religions to-day make universal claims. Hence it is hard to realise what a radically new thing enters the Bible in such passages as xlix:6, where God speaks of his salvation reaching the end of the earth. No Israelite had ever clearly proposed this before. The God of Israel had created all mankind, but since Babel he had revealed himself only to the descendants of Abraham. Other nations were benighted, and humanly speaking there was nothing that could or should be done about it. Some of the prophets, as we have seen, foretold that Zion's eventual glory would awe the Gentiles at large into respect for the Lord. Isaiah, the real Isaiah, even foretold (xix:19-22) that the Egyptians would sacrifice to him. But not, one supposes, to him alone. Nobody contemplated an Israelite mission, or a universal cult, or a general destruction of idols.

With the anonymous genius in Babylon, Israel's God for the first time is the prospective Deity of a world faith. Also for the first time, he is in plain terms the only God who exists, not merely the only God who matters.[5] "I am the Lord, and there is no other, besides me there is no God . . . Turn to me and be saved, all the ends of the earth! For I am God, and there is no other." (xlv:5, 22). In this respect the implications of Moses and Amos are at last fully worked out, and "Third Isaiah," whether or not he is a different author, pursues the same theme. Heathendom's ignorance is now no longer invincible. The Holy One of Israel shall be called the God of the whole earth (liv:5). Nations shall come running because of the Lord, summoned by his servants (xlix:6, lv:5). A new Temple will be a house of prayer for all peoples (lvi:7), the Gentiles will flock out of their darkness to the radiance of Zion (lx:3). World-wide peace will prevail, apparently through Persian supremacy, and the re-enthroned Chosen will be the aristocrats of the future empire. Zion's domain will grow larger, richer, more fruitful; kings and queens will bow down to her; strangers will rebuild her walls; any nation that refuses to serve her will perish (xlix:22-23, liv:1-3, lx:5-14).

While this vision sometimes reads like a magnificent power-fantasy, it cannot be twisted into vulgar imperialism. Israel's

5 Similar texts in *Deuteronomy* xxxii:39 and *I Kings* viii:60 are doubtless a little earlier, but apparently do not mean quite the same.

grandeur is bound up with its calling, with its role in the salvation of mankind. God's anointed, Cyrus, is to usher in an age conceived in this manner. It is quite wrong to suppose that the Messiah was always imagined as an Hebraic tribal chief till Christianity gave the title a higher significance. It would be truer, however short of the full truth, to say that Christianity banished a chauvinistic perversion in the name of the original concept. Second Isaiah does not call Cyrus *the* Messiah, a unique saviour; but he makes the vital transition. "Messiah" before him means, normally, any man who is physically anointed by priests to reign. After him it tends to mean an individual, figuratively anointed by God to glorify Israel and renew the world. The hope has its roots in this prophecy. Cyrus's Messianic work in Second Isaiah is not merely conquest but exaltation, reaching to the entire human race.

3

The prophecy, however, is a riddle as well as a marvel. Its deeper strangeness becomes evident as soon as we compare it with the religion of the Persians themselves: a religion of which the true nature has been slow in coming to light through millennia of misrepresentation.

The Persians had the same ancestry as the Hindus, and down to Cyrus's lifetime their pantheon had retained some common features. As the Hindus believed in a host of *devas* (gods) and *asuras* (demons), so the Persians believed in two opposed classes of celestials called *daevas* and *ahuras*. They reversed them, however, making the *ahuras* kindly and the *daevas* sinister. Furthermore the shape of Iranian society, especially in the east, had sharpened the opposition and given it an ethical flavour. Age-old struggles of an industrious cattle-keeping peasantry against savage highland marauders were reflected in a religion of cosmic conflict. The *ahuras* were spirits of righteousness and order, perpetually menaced by the legions of chaos.

Until recently it was thought that the prophet Zoroaster, who reformed this Persian religion in the early sixth century B.C., merely simplified the conflict into a war of two opposed gods. That mistake arose from summaries of the Persians' ideas compiled long after his death, when their dualistic mental habits had corrupted his doctrine. It is now certain that he did not teach a double divinity himself. What he did teach was more interesting. He called his system the Good Religion, and its progress dated from his conversion of a local king in eastern Iran, almost simultaneously with the burning of the Jerusalem Temple. The genuine works which embody it are poems in a compressed, abstract style that demands careful reading. Zoroaster was a pioneer theologian. His intellectual gifts commended him even to the philosophers of Greece, who took him more seriously than they took most barbarian sages.

His major step was to single out one of the principal *ahuras*— a sky-god who was identical, far back, with the Greek Uranus and the Hindu Varuna—and promote him to the status of a sole, beneficent, Supreme Deity. The prophet gave him the title Ahura Mazdah, the Wise Lord. Ahura Mazdah, Zoroaster affirmed, had made the entire universe out of nothing by his own thoughts. "Through the mind he filled the blessed spaces with light." No other gods existed; the rest of the celestials were his creatures. Yet the world had a predetermined form which was still a cosmic antithesis, a polarity. Zoroaster's dualism was a dualism not of gods but of opposed principles—good and evil, light and darkness, above all "Truth" and "The Lie." Ahura Mazdah ranged himself on the side of Truth and against The Lie, which was an unexplained datum somehow inseparable from the creative act.

Despite this last anomaly, Zoroaster's system could fairly be described as ethical monotheism. A further doctrine dramatised and intensified it. Among the beings who sprang from the Wise Lord were Spenta Mainyu, the Holy Spirit, and a twin of his who chose The Lie and became evil. The latter was Angra Mainyu, the Destructive Spirit, a dark agent of lawlessness in a world which Ahura Mazdah had created good.

Human beings, the prophet maintained, could enlist under either banner. But each had his own proper vocation, and if he followed this with a strenuous endeavour, he was on the side of Truth and Ahura Mazdah. Virtue meant above all constructive social action, and it brought an earthly reward; the righteous would prosper. To the objection that this is not always so, and that the problem of unmerited suffering cannot be brushed aside, Zoroaster seemingly had no answer. However, he insisted that after death everyone went to a heaven or a hell according to his deserts. Our present dispensation (he went on) was not eternal in any case. The world was passing through a succession of epochs, like the phases of the moon, which would end with the Wise Lord's complete victory over Angra Mainyu. At length a saviour, Saoshyans, would arise to lead a united humanity. There would be a resurrection of all the dead, and a Last Judgment.

Necessarily, therefore, the Good Religion knew no tribal limitations. Zoroaster openly claimed that he had a mission to all mankind. His teaching was taken up by the Magi, an order of priest-magicians, and subsequently perverted by them. But when the Persian conquests began—about the time of the prophet's death—the reform was still in its first fiery purity. Its virile, combative, practical spirit appealed to the Persian warrior caste. One of Cyrus's few inscriptions implies that the King himself was at least well-disposed towards it, and venerated Ahura Mazdah's name. As to the Zoroastrianism of his most noted successors there is no doubt whatever.

Is it pure chance that the Hebrew who greets Zoroaster's people so joyously is also the first to preach, like him, an ethical monotheism for the whole world?

> Thus says the Lord to his anointed, to Cyrus,
>   whose right hand I have grasped,
> To subdue nations before him . . .
> "I will go before you
>   and level the mountains . . .

I will give you the treasures of darkness
  and the hoards in secret places,
That you may know that it is I, the Lord,
  the God of Israel, who call you by your name.
For the sake of my servant Jacob,
  and Israel my chosen,
I call you by your name,
  I surname you, though you do not know me.
I am the Lord, and there is no other,
  besides me there is no God;
I gird you, though you do not know me,
That men may know, from the rising of the sun
  and from the west, that there is none besides me;
  I am the Lord, and there is no other.
I form light and create darkness,
  I make weal and create woe,
  I am the Lord, who do all these things."

(xlv:1-7)

In thus urging that Cyrus will attain and propagate the knowledge of Yahweh, Second Isaiah might seem to be indulging in a wild dream of the King's conversion. Surely, however, it is more likely that his eye is on the religion which so many of the Persians already have. Cyrus or his successors will realise its wider bearings. Ahura Mazdah is Yahweh under another name, as his earthly agents will soon confess, and that is why Persian conquest will spread his glory everywhere. The antithetical phrasing of verse 7 has a Zoroastrian tone which has been observed before now, though misconstrued owing to the illusion that the Persian preached dualism. Actually Second Isaiah portrays Israel's God as saying to Cyrus in effect: "I myself am your Wise Lord, the maker of this double creation, of light and dark, of good and ill." The "I" is emphatic.

Moreover the identification cuts both ways. Perhaps the Hebrew affirms monotheism—in this very passage—because he has learnt to do so from Zoroaster. Perhaps he proclaims a world faith overleaping national bounds because Zoroaster has lately done so. Granted a belief in his mind that Zoroaster was a true prophet among the Gentiles (not an inconceivable idea to an Israelite, as the story of Balaam proves), there is no reason why he should not have drawn upon him.

Babylon fell and Israel was freed; but with an ambiguity and anti-climax that gave no room for satisfaction.

In 539 Cyrus advanced on the capital. Nabonidus's army, or rather Belshazzar's, waited a few miles outside its enormous walls. The Persian cavalry drove back the spearmen and chariots of the Babylonians, who, however, withdrew in good order into the city. Administrative forethought of the Maginot type had laid in a vast supply of food, and as there seemed to be no way of storming the moat and fortifications, the garrison saw grounds for hope that a siege would fail. But Cyrus, according to Herodotus, hit on a stratagem. The walls divided in two places, one where the Euphrates flowed in, the other where it flowed out again. Under normal conditions the rush and volume of water ruled out any idea of an entry through either gap. Cyrus, however, posted some of his best troops near both, and made the rest dig a canal from a point upstream to a basin formed by past Babylonian excavations. The diversion of water into this basin caused the level at the walls to drop, and the Persians waded in by both routes. Even so, their entrapment would have been easy for a resolute defence. But enemy strength was sapped by disaffection and over-confidence. The unrest among Bel-Marduk's priests, which Cyrus knew about and exploited, had fostered defeatism; and Herodotus records that a festival at the centre of the city distracted attention from events at the outskirts. Within a few hours Babylon was a Persian provincial town, and empire had passed from the sons of Shem to the sons of Japheth.

The biblical account of this revolution is in the *Book of Daniel*. It is a brilliantly dramatised version of the fatal festival. Belshazzar, we are told, was sitting at his wine with the nobles, when he had the notion of using the vessels of the Temple as tableware. So they were brought into the banqueting hall, and "the king and his lords, his wives and his concubines drank from them." But while they drank and praised their false gods, a man's hand appeared and wrote on the wall. Belshazzar stared in terror; the soothsayers of Babylon strove in vain to interpret the markings. Then the aged Israelite Daniel was sent for, and rich rewards were offered him if he could furnish an explanation. He could.

"This is the interpretation of the matter: MENE, God has numbered the days of your kingdom and brought it to an end;

TEKEL, you have been weighed in the balances and found wanting;

PERES, your kingdom is divided and given to the Medes and Persians." . . .

That very night Belshazzar was slain.

(*Daniel* v:26-30)

With its towering scorn and irresistible verve, the tale of the doomed pagan feast is a worthy pendant to Second Isaiah. It is true in spirit and quite possibly in substance. While the name "Darius" which it gives to Babylon's new master suggests a confusion, this may have been an alternative name for Gobryas, whom Cyrus made viceroy, or perhaps even for Cyrus himself. As for the writing, we might suspect a Hebrew patriot reaching out from behind a curtain and scribbling in his own alphabet, which was doubtless beneath the notice of Babylonian scholarship. Slogans on walls, a nuisance and no more in a free society, are unnerving in a despotism.

At all events Cyrus captured Babylon and annexed what was left of its shrunken empire. Now comes another puzzle, though this is soluble. At the opening of the biblical *Book of Ezra* stands a passage which suggests that Cyrus, as foreshadowed by Second Isaiah, did recognise Israel's God as his own and did take the Remnant under his privileged protection.

The Lord stirred up the spirit of Cyrus king of Persia so that he made a proclamation throughout all his kingdom and also put it in writing:

"Thus says Cyrus king of Persia: the Lord, the God of heaven, has given me all the kingdoms of the earth, and he has charged me to build him a house at Jerusalem, which is in Judah.

Whoever is among you of all his people, may his God be with him, and let him go up to Jerusalem, which is in Judah, and rebuild the house of the Lord, the God of Israel— he is the God who is in Jerusalem."

The edict looks fantastic. But an inscription of Cyrus's makes its essential authenticity clear, while at the same time betraying its meagre significance. That inscription is for the Babylonians, and in it the King says very much what Second Isaiah says—that the divine hand has taken hold of his, has led him to success, and so forth—only the deity he extols is Marduk. Having paid his compliment to the god of a proud nation, he goes on to speak of the other gods and nations whom misguided Babylonian rulers have made captive, and to give assurances that he will send them home and repair the damage that has been done.

Thus the permission to go back to Jerusalem, though granted, was simply part of a broader policy; and Cyrus's acknowledgment of the God of Israel, though given, was scarcely more than a political gesture, as was his sponsorship of the Temple's rebuilding. He talked of Yahweh when he was dealing with Israelites and of Marduk when he was dealing with Babylonians. To judge from inscriptions of other Persian monarchs, his claim that "the Lord, the God of heaven" (or Marduk as the case might be) had "given him all the kingdoms of the earth" was a translation into local terminology of a Persian formula, "Ahura Mazdah has bestowed the kingdom on me." Cyrus, or his vizier, did identify Yahweh with Ahura Mazdah, but he identified Marduk with him too. It was not a question of theological insight, but of a slipshod verbal syncretism that was coming into vogue elsewhere. All Supreme Gods were the same. From Herodotus onward, Greek authors writing for Greek readers treated every chief national deity as Zeus in one disguise or another.

So the liberated Israelites who turned toward Zion were not to march home in the spirit of the prophecy, with a resplendent Asiatic sunrise breaking around them. Nobody else took much notice, and the task facing them held out no near prospect of a rise to world spiritual aristocracy. Even in a mundane sense the Persian Empire proved disappointing. Cyrus was killed trying to push the frontier north-eastward. His heir Cambyses took up an easier portion of his programme and annexed Egypt. Then, after some palace upheavals, a cousin named Darius came to the throne. Though Darius was an outstanding ruler, he embroiled the Empire in European campaigns beyond its capacity. After the failure of his son Xerxes to conquer Greece, Persia sank into decline.

The words of the arch-prophet had finally to be read as looking forward to a more distant future. His vision was re-interpreted as symbolic of a coming age. The point however is that it was re-interpreted, not brushed aside as an exploded fancy and dropped from the list of inspired writings. Its impetus was too powerful. As the sequel proved, its hour was still to come.

CHAPTER EIGHT

THE SECOND ZIONISM

Within a few years of the prophet's raptures, it was quite plain that
the fulfilment of his hopes would be lame and piecemeal. In 538,
when the path home actually lay open, most of the exiles showed no
enthusiasm for taking it. None but the oldest of them had been
born in the Land. Many saw a prospect of freedom in Mesopotamia
under the more humane Persian rule. Indeed, they had managed
to make respectable progress even under the Babylonians. Israelite
villages in the Nippur district were flourishing; there were Hebrew
slave-owners and perhaps already some Hebrew bankers. Those
who preferred to remain were not strictly assimilationists in the
modern sense. As yet no distinction of Church and State had been
worked out, and the legalistic idea of setting up as "Mesopotamians
of the Hebrew religion" would not have occurred to them. They
simply believed that they would be allowed to live tolerably in
their own way, observing their own customs, worshipping their
own God. In their eyes it was an excellent and a necessary thing
that Zion should be re-peopled—so long as somebody else did it.
Some of the richer ones are said to have supplied funds for the
re-peopling, as Baron Edmond de Rothschild financed Jewish
Palestinian colonies in the nineteenth century. But they themselves
stayed in Mesopotamia; and their descendants, and the descendants
of many others who took the same decision, spread out gradually
through the Persian dominions and beyond.

What Cyrus inferred from the slight response to his edict, it
would be intriguing to know. He honoured it to the extent that
he was called upon to do so. A Hebrew aristocrat bearing the

Babylonian name of Sheshbazzar approached him as leader of a small Zionist group. Cyrus handed over the vessels of the Temple (who put them away, and where, after Belshazzar's feast ended so unceremoniously?) and made him governor of Jerusalem. The caravan set off. Its route is not stated. One could wish to imagine the repatriates passing into the Land from Jericho, winding in procession up the long track through tawny desert, and at last catching sight of their immortal ruin far off and far above against the hard blue: the city set on a hill that cannot be hid.

Sheshbazzar's settlement established a foothold, but hardly more. The walls of Jerusalem lay flat, and apart from a token clearance of the site, nothing was done to rebuild the Temple. Then a second and much larger migration took place led by Jehoiachin's grandson Zerubbabel (another Babylonian name; Israel had not withstood all Chaldee influences). Any project for a new monarchy under this descendant of David was of course ruled out, but Zerubbabel too was allowed the title of governor. According to the Bible he headed a party of fifty thousand. However, this figure must include many who came later. His territory was confined to Jerusalem and a small area round about. In this enclave a new Israelite society took shape, a poor society, yielding scarcely anything to the archaeologist apart from a few administrative buildings. Its everyday speech was not Hebrew but the Syrian Aramaic language, the common medium of communication in the Persian Empire.

Yet it started with a solid inner conviction and confidence. The term "Israel" was now entering a fresh phase of definition. The fall of the north had ended its specialised political use, and Jeremiah and Ezekiel had written off those inhabitants of Judah who had not gone to Babylon. In the books of Scripture composed after the Exile, "Israel" means the descendants of the deportees: primarily the restored southern community, and secondarily the "diaspora"—the scattered deportee families which never returned, but kept their identity, and looked toward renascent Zion with loyalty and a sort of nostalgia. Since Nebuchadnezzar had carried off, not a random sample, but the leading elements in society, this Remnant was of exceptional calibre. Loss of the Land and Temple had left fidelity to Torah as the real bond, and the deportee stock was capable of learning to live by that principle. Even after Zion's rebirth the new emphasis persisted. As the prophets had foreshadowed, the Chosen henceforth were defined more by faith than by heredity or geography, although their claim to the Land was a vital part of the faith.

Thus a somewhat high-grade selection from the tribes of Judah, Benjamin and Levi became the true Israel and succeeded to the whole heritage. These people did not deny that others of Israelite descent might exist, and might, through penitence, be re-grafted to the main stem. Indeed they actually did re-graft some of their kinsmen in Egypt, and such undeported peasants of Judah as were still there and willing to abjure heathen "pollutions" (*Ezra* vi:21). But they were absolutely clear that they themselves were the main stem. They might offer sacrifice hopefully on behalf of their lost cousins (if that is the right interpretation of *Ezra* vi:17), but the fullness of Israel could subsist, if necessary, in them alone.

And these people were THE JEWS, and their physical and spiritual progeny still are. The word is simply "Judahite." It makes its début in Scripture with that political meaning, in passages written during the sixth century. At a slightly later date, when it was manifest that the bond of Torah remained unbroken wherever the faithful might be living, it became proper to speak of them as "Judahites-by-allegiance.' From the fifth century onward they were the Chosen Israel of God, and apart from a few ambiguous phrases we find no biblical indication that anyone else was. They are so regarded even in the New Testament, much of which is hostile to them, or at least to their official spokesmen. The Jewish people were defined by the Second Zionism, as ancient Israel was defined by the First.

Devout Jews after Cyrus were convinced of three things—that their God was the only God; that they themselves were his elect, his earthly witnesses in history; and that he would make them glorious among the nations. Anti-climax or no anti-climax, the settlers who formed the new parent community in Judah were happier than their grandfathers. Unlike any Gentiles, they had mastered suffering by accepting it as expiation for themselves and their kinsfolk. With them the logic of Israel took its eighth step.

Why the recovery of Zion?

Because we, of the Remnant, have collectively repented and made atonement. We are purified by sorrow. But we have a duty to stay pure in the fullest sense. Then, at last, we shall prosper in the Land; then, at last, the Gentiles will hold us in reverence and turn toward our God.

Beliefs which Jews everywhere endorsed.

A few months after arrival Zerubbabel put up an altar on the Temple site, and the daily offerings were resumed by a corps of priests. The name of the chief priest was Jeshua, the same as "Joshua" before and "Jesus" afterwards. With a view to rebuilding, Zerubbabel hired Syrian workmen and had cedars of Lebanon imported by way of Joppa, the port subsequently called Jaffa, now a suburb of Tel-Aviv. To an accompaniment of cheering and fanfares the foundation of the Second Temple was laid. Very little is known of its plan, because of reconstruction which effaced the original. Old men who remembered the First Temple burst into tears when they saw the layout of the second; we are not told why! No attempt was made to realise the dream of Ezekiel. That stayed securely in the clouds.

Almost at once a dispute arose with Samaria. A deputation waited on Zerubbabel and his builders, urging that the mixed Yahweh-worshipping people of northern Palestine should be permitted to take part. The governor, however, sternly declined to recognise their bastard cult. His Temple was for "the Lord, the God of Israel," and the descendants of Assyria's colonists were not "Israel." (In much the same accents George Orwell's sahibs grumbled at the mission-taught natives who said "Me Christian, all same master.") As a consequence of this rebuff the Jews had to endure endless trouble from their neighbours, who kept accusing them of

seditious designs. Several Persian kings were sufficiently impressed
to forbid Jerusalem's restoration as a walled town. For some years
after the initial clash the Temple itself languished. But about 520
two prophets, Haggai and the highly visionary Zechariah, persuaded
Zerubbabel to press on with the work.

To judge from an unfortunately corrupt passage in Zechariah's
book (vi:9-14) there was talk of proclaiming a restored monarchy
in defiance of Persia. Not unnaturally Zerubbabel's superior, the
Persian Tattenai, pounced on the Jews: who had given them leave
to build? They referred him to Cyrus's edict and the arrangements
made with Sheshbazzar. Tattenai wrote to the recently crowned
Darius asking for confirmation. Darius had the archives searched,
and at Ecbatana a memorandum was found showing that Cyrus
had not only authorised the Temple but ordered its financing out
of the public funds. Darius now showed himself a willing patron
of Zerubbabel's project. About 516 the Second Temple was
dedicated, probably reproducing the salient features of the First.[1]

However, when this had happened, nothing else did. The
Gentiles persisted in paying no attention. Most of the Zionists
themselves lived meanly and with reduced zeal, half-camping in
and around a derelict citadel which they dared not improve for
fear of Samaria. Some of the mingled exaltation and gloom of
"Third Isaiah" belongs to this period. So does the prophecy of Obadiah, whose target was the Edomite nation, supposedly descended
from Esau, which had stolen Israelite territory during the Exile.
So does the prophecy of Malachi, with its curious forecast of the
return of Elijah to herald a divine judgment. Joel, and several minor
prophets whose sayings have been annexed to Zechariah's, were yet
to come; in fact they belong to the time of contact with Greeks
(*Joel* iii:6, *Zechariah* ix:13). But by the middle of the fifth century

1 See *Ezra* chapters iv to vi. Chapter iv is most confusing. It starts with
the first quarrels over the Temple; goes on, in a lengthy parenthesis, to
trace the harrying of the Jews in other respects down to the reign of
Artaxerxes, seventy years later; then springs back abruptly (verse 24)
to the original hitch.

the prophetic afflatus was almost spent. Nor did the Judah settlement grow. There was still no mass return of exiles.

2

Through three or four generations this apathy and deadlock dragged on. A fresh impulse was surprisingly given by Artaxerxes I, whose long reign over Persia began in 465. The Samarians' charges had induced him to forbid any refitting or refortifying of Jerusalem till he himself ordered otherwise (*Ezra* iv:21). But about the middle of the century he did order otherwise; and he went further. He appointed two Mesopotamian Jews to go to Judah as his accredited agents. Nehemiah was to be governor, and rebuild the capital complete with its walls. Ezra was to carry out what can only be described as an ecclesiastical reform.

We must assess again what was in the minds of these Persian kings when they concerned themselves with Israel, and issued documents acknowledging Israel's God. Cyrus we have considered. He was a practical soldier-statesman, content to speak of his vague Supreme Being in various ways, according to which nation he was trying to win over. But Darius believed firmly and explicitly in Ahura Mazdah. His inscriptions prove that while other deities might exist for him, they did not count in his eyes, and he would have been unlikely to finance any temples for them. Yet he did finance the Jerusalem Temple. Jews of the sort who compiled the *Book of Ezra* would scarcely have forged a Gentile sponsorship. Perhaps syncretism—a true and reasoned syncretism—actually was at work here, and Darius's court-theologians explained Yahweh for him as the Wise Lord under another name. If so, Artaxerxes doubtless had the same thoughts. Certainly he hoped for political results based on community of outlook. He aimed, by means of Ezra and Ezra's religion, to render his Jewish subjects more amenable to "the law of the king" (*Ezra* vii:26), as a step toward stabilising an area beset by chronic unrest. But whatever motives of policy existed, it is astonishing how much the developed Jewish religion was to owe to Persia. Cyrus ended the Captivity; Darius helped to pay for the new Temple; Artaxerxes's actions not only restored Jerusalem but, through Ezra, created the Bible as we know it and the ceremonial separatism of Jewry; and more, immensely more, was to follow. Second Isaiah had been right in pointing at Cyrus as a figure of destiny.

Ezra is represented as going to Jerusalem early in Artaxerxes's reign. However, this visit may have been only a reconnaissance. There is reason to think that he received his major commission after Nehemiah did. The crucial date is 445. Nehemiah was cupbearer in the royal palace at Susa, the Persian capital, and therefore had access to the Great King. Hearing gloomy reports of the state of Judah, he asked Artaxerxes for authority to go to Jerusalem. Artaxerxes consented. Nehemiah went there, armed with royal credentials. His first step was to ride all round the ruins, going at night so as not to arouse comment, and determine what needed to be done. Then he announced his plans to the head priest and other notables, and the restoration started. It had to face much hostile ridicule from Sanballat, the governor of Samaria. First Sanballat laughed at the idea of shoring up such a heap of rubble. Next he talked of arresting the proceedings by armed force; the Jewish labourers took to working with spears handy. But no attack came, and although Sanballat tried to revive the charge of sedition, his threats blew over. Jerusalem was walled and repopulated. Besides carrying through his main task, Nehemiah persuaded the wealthier Jews to cancel outstanding debts which had become a social burden.

He was joined by the greater Ezra, whom he willingly assisted. While there is evidence that they were both there at the same time, the overlap may have been a brief one, with Ezra's main activities going on from about 430. Ezra was roughly contemporary with Socrates: their relative importance would be a fertile theme for debate. He is referred to both as a priest and as a scribe. His priestly status would have been a matter of descent. As for the second description, he was perhaps really designated a "royal commissioner"; but the word "scribe" has been used to translate it because his function was essentially what Jewish "scribes," after his time and under his influence, began to do. They were jurists, exegetes, expounders of the divine Law—natural products of an age when inspiration was yielding to erudition, prophecy to editing and commentary. Ezra gave them the impetus.

Artaxerxes sent the commissioner on his way with lavish promises of gifts to the Temple. The authority vested in Ezra extended not only to the Jews in Judah but to all those who lived in the province or satrapy "Beyond-the-River," i.e. the Euphrates. With full royal support, backed by threats of penalties, he was to teach and enforce "the laws of his God." Artaxerxes gave leave for any Jew to accompany him who wished. He set out from Babylonia with a following of several hundred.

How did Ezra imagine Jerusalem before he came to live there himself? Possibly with a touch of the romanticism which a distant loyalty tends to inspire. When he arrived, and found many Zionist families ignorant of the Law and worse than slack in its observance, he "rent his garments and his mantle, and pulled hair from his head and beard, and sat appalled." So, *mutatis mutandis*, did many Communist sympathisers who sought Utopia in the Russia of Stalin. But the more fortunate Ezra had power to apply correctives. Setting up a wooden pulpit in the main square, he gave public readings from the Law in the presence of Nehemiah and other dignitaries. These readings were well organised. A team of translators and commentators expounded the Hebrew as he went along. Next he presided over a national ceremony of re-dedication and re-consecration. His prayers eloquently recalled the whole history of Israel, to which the depressed Remnant was heir. The Jews were still being afflicted for the transgressions of their race: "Behold, we are slaves to this day; in the land that thou gavest to our fathers to enjoy its fruit and its good gifts, behold, we are slaves. And its rich yield goes to the kings whom thou hast set over us for our sins; they have power also over our bodies and over our cattle at their pleasure, and we are in great distress." If any Persian officials heard these dangerous remarks of their Jewish colleague, they did not interfere. Henceforth, Ezra declared, Israel must truly change. A written covenant was drawn up, and sealed by Nehemiah and all the notables. The people swore to walk in the right path which Ezra was showing them and would continue to show them.

Ezra was not content with words. He took action of an audacious kind. One scandal which had shocked him as much as any was the contamination of Jewish stock and integrity through marriages with surrounding pagans. Nehemiah had already made some rather undignified attacks on the same abuse, leading to fisticuffs ill becoming a governor. But Ezra grasped the nettle. On a December day he summoned an assembly in the square in front of the Temple, and bluntly told the husbands of foreign wives to give them up. They listened submissively, shivering in a downpour of rain. Not caring to get any wetter, they agreed in principle and deputed representatives to make plans for the mass divorce. A few objected. Ezra, however, created administrative machinery which ground relentlessly through case after case, and by the following April the mixed marriages were dissolved.

With every allowance made for the potency of Persian backing, Ezra and Nehemiah showed phenomenal courage and phenomenal faith. Undaunted by all the disillusioning centuries, they set themselves to achieve what no reformer had ever achieved yet, a complete religious purification of Israel. Their campaign might have been expected to peter out like Hezekiah's or Josiah's. But the strange truth is that it succeeded. Before they came, Israel still harboured paganism in spite of everything. Some of the "Third Isaiah" fragments allude bitterly to the survival of divination, child-sacrifice, and other practices of varying hatefulness. But after Ezra and Nehemiah the Lord's battle was at last won. Paganism was dead, slain by what amounted to a renewal of the Covenant. Ethical monotheism was firmly planted, with all noxious excrescences pruned away.

Of course Israel paid a price. Because of this very cleansing, the universalism of the nobler prophets dropped for a while into abeyance. It was not suppressed or even entirely dormant. All the preconditions existed for its full re-awakening. But the bias lay temporarily on the other side; the stress was on permanent defence. Inside and outside Palestine—thanks to the scope of Ezra's commission—the Jew was now made utterly different from other men, with a systematic and standardised difference based on the six-hundred-and-thirteen commandments of the Law. That difference pervaded all life, not religious ceremonies alone. Ezra's war on mixed marriages was only a first instance of the separatist trend. He and his helpers and successors pursued it much further. They enforced a new tightening-up of the diet rules, in particular the veto on swine's flesh; and the peculiarities of the Sabbath were enhanced.

In all this the hand of the priest, rather than the lay jurist, may be pretty plainly detected. Where we can identify priestly work in the Pentateuch it betrays the same outlook. Thus Moses and Aaron are described as being carefully taught to distinguish the holy from the common, the clean from the unclean, Israel from the Gentiles. In the "P" Creation story, God himself proceeds by a series of cosmic separations. The *Book of Esther*, datable perhaps two hundred years after Ezra, still expresses a frame of mind ultimately due to him and his priestly disciples. *Esther* is a miniature novel about the supposed origin of the feast of Purim. The author's main concern is with the status of Jews as a besieged social minority. Unhistorically, he portrays them as threatened by persecution under the Persian king Xerxes, "Ahasuerus." The royal vizier Haman resents the lack of servility shown to him by the Jew Mordecai, and advises a pogrom: "There is a certain people scattered abroad and dispersed among the peoples in all the provinces of your kingdom; their laws are different from those of every other people, and they do not keep the king's laws, so that it is not for the king's profit to tolerate them. If it please the king, let it be decreed that they be destroyed." Xerxes approves. His latest wife, however, is Mordecai's foster-daughter Esther. Coached by Mordecai, she contrives Haman's disgrace and the countermanding of his orders. Instead of the Jews being destroyed they are given royal licence to kill their own enemies. They exterminate five hundred in Susa alone. Purim, the author says, commemorates and celebrates this joyous event. Throughout the book he has made no reference to God.

Jewish separatism in the Second Zionist period could be ugly. Yet it was not merely sour or negative. The motive-power which Ezra harnessed was an inviolate sense of concentration, of a terrible sanctity attaching to a small portion of earth and a small fraction of mankind. The single biblical text where the precise phrase "Holy Land" occurs is *Zechariah* ii:12, written in the post-Exile community. Most of the allusions to Jerusalem as "the holy city" and to Zion as "the holy hill" are also late rather than early. When such ideas were set in the forefront, any measures against defilement could be justified. And the God of Israel, whose choice made these places holy, was more peerlessly glorious than ever. The Temple of the reformed Jews had little to show in the way of demi-pagan pomposities. Its Lord transcended them. A tall seven-branched lamp, the Menorah, burned continually; priests offered the daily sacrifice; the shewbread was laid out; and a gradation of solemnity reserved a few ceremonies for the head or "High" Priest alone. Like his predecessors in Solomon's day, he had the sole right to go inside the Holy of Holies. But when he did, he stood in an empty room, without even an Ark. No conceivable image or token could be worthy of the Presence.

The idea of God had grown so tremendous that misgivings were astir about mentioning him; or rather, about the proper method of doing so. Not very long after Ezra the tetragrammatic Name, Yahweh, began to fall into practical disuse as being too sacred. Eventually only the High Priest ever spoke it, in an undertone on rare occasions, and its utterance by anyone else was counted as a grave sin. Already in the last centuries of the pre-Christian era, half a dozen circumlocutions and synonyms were current. A pious Jew could employ the old name "Elohim." When he met with the Tetragrammaton in Scripture while reading aloud, he was apt to say "Adonai" instead, meaning "Lord." Another substitute which advanced in favour was "the Most High," that mysterious pagan phrase found in the Melchizedek episode and in an early passage of *Deuteronomy* (xxxii:8). God was also "the Lord of Hosts" (*Sabaoth*), "the Holy One of Israel" as in *Isaiah*, and "the Ancient of Days." Each title acquired its own nuances. All this proliferation and ritualisation arose from the fact that "Yahweh," the true Name which expressed God's nature, was for that very reason too holy to enunciate.

It might seem curious that the reforms of Ezra and Nehemiah were so effective, and in Jewish communities outside Nehemiah's jurisdiction as well as in Judah where he could give orders. Persian power is, of course, the key, however puzzling a key. It could not have operated if the reformers themselves had not been men of character; but it made the difference. Under Persia, not before, Jerusalem at last became securely the headquarters of Israel's faith as prescribed in *Deuteronomy*. Indeed the vast reach of the Great King's arm enabled the reformist group to find out about anomalies which they might not otherwise have heard of at all.

There exists, for instance, a file of correspondence on the affairs of Elephantiné, an island in the Nile close to Aswan. Certain alleged Jews living there, who spoke Aramaic, were probably descended from Judahite mercenaries recruited by Egypt somewhere about 600 B.C., with an admixture of post-Captivity elements. Throughout the fifth century they still guarded the southern frontier and were called the "Jewish force." They had a miniature temple of their own. In 410 an Egyptian priest persuaded the local authorities to pull this down and forbid rebuilding. The Jews wrote to Bagoas, who was then governor of Judah, and to the High Priest Johanan, asking for help. After waiting more than two years without result they tackled Bagoas again. This time he sent a message to the Persian viceroy of Egypt, who seemingly gave permission to rebuild.

The Elephantiné papyri deal with many other matters besides this, and most of them are business letters. However, they raise

questions about the procedure for Passover and other festivals;
and they make surprising disclosures about the little temple itself.
It was dedicated to the Lord "Yaho." But the Jews paid their
respects to three other deities as well, including the lady Anath.
They had provided the Lord with a divine consort and retinue.

Two points emerge. First, these far-away Jews were unreformed
and barely conscious that reforms had occurred. Probably most of
their ancestors were the sort whom Jeremiah met in Egypt and
elsewhere—bad figs. Secondly, a certain Hananiah who figures
in these documents appears to have been a commissioner for Jewish
affairs in Persian service. In other words, the policy implied by the
appointment of Ezra was followed up. We do not know whether
Hananiah in fact drew the Jewish force into concurrence with Zion,
because it was disbanded soon afterwards and sent no more letters.
But the support given to the petitioners would suggest that they
conformed.

Others did not. The folk of Samaria, whom Zerubbabel had
snubbed, continued to resent their neighbours' monopoly. Their
chance came (according to one reading of the evidence) when
Nehemiah banished Manasseh, a High Priest's grandson. Manasseh
had married the daughter of Samaria's anti-Jewish governor
Sanballat. He fled northward to his father-in-law, who took
revenge for this and other affronts by building a rival temple on
Mount Gerizim for Manasseh to officiate in. Perhaps; perhaps not.
Certainly, during the fourth century B.C., Gerizim became the
stronghold of a northern sect perpetually at odds with the Jews.
These "Samaritans" in due course produced a version of the
Pentateuch with passages glorifying Gerizim. Noah built the Ark
there, Abraham bound Isaac there, Jacob dreamed of the ladder
there, and it stayed above water in the Flood. They also harassed
the Jews by more direct methods. Thus it was customary, for the
convenience of a nation without printed calendars, to mark special
dates by lighting beacons. The Samaritans caused confusion by
lighting beacons at the wrong times.

A few hundred of them are holding out still, mostly in Nablus.

3

An old and stubborn tradition makes Ezra responsible for the Bible itself. Not, of course, for the Christian Bible or even the Jewish in its entirety, since parts of it were written after his death. But there is every reason to think that he did make some sort of canon of the existing books; that he gave a decisive lead to the task of editing; and that he laid the basis for popular instruction by translating the Law into Aramaic. Whatever the extent of his own share, all the expansion that ensued was a continuation of his work.

The reform of Israel, in fact, was anchored on an authorised and more or less unified Holy Writ. It was due to Ezra that the collective experience was consciously organised, so that the Jews became "people of the Book," the first in the world and the spiritual progenitors of all others. They divide the Bible which he created into three sections: Law, Prophets, and Sacred Writings or Hagiographa. Under the "Law" heading come the five books associated with Moses (*Genesis, Exodus, Leviticus, Numbers, Deuteronomy*). Under the "Prophets" heading come the books of the Former Prophets—meaning, oddly, the Deuteronomic History (*Joshua, Judges, Samuel, Kings*)—and those of the Latter Prophets (*Isaiah, Jeremiah, Ezekiel*, and the short ones beginning with *Hosea*). Under the "Hagiographa" heading comes everything else. From its first construction the whole series was generally reckoned as revealed Torah, though there were dissenters from that view. But the Pentateuch of Moses was the Torah *par excellence*. Here the Lord's purpose for Israel was articulated, here he promised the Land, here his edicts were proclaimed. Precious as the lesser books were, it was an error to suppose that they could teach any essential point which was not at least implied in the books of Moses.

When Ezra came to Jerusalem the four bodies of Pentateuchal matter—the Yahwist, the Elohist, the Priestly, and the Deuteronomic—were already venerable, and had already been combined

in various unofficial ways. Ezra himself may have been the final
redactor, the editor who reviewed the texts and fitted pieces of
them together in the familiar order. Minor revisions continued
to be made for another century or more, but the main task must
have been accomplished in Ezra's time or fairly soon afterwards,
because the Samaritan schismatics were able to take the Pentateuch
with them (it remained their only Scripture). To the five fundamental books, Ezra or his disciples attached the Deuteronomic
History, and the scrolls of those favoured individuals through whom
the Holy Spirit was agreed to have spoken.

So much for "Moses and the Prophets," as the two chief divisions
of the Old Testament are called in the New. Among Sacred
Writings was the Psalter, the hymn-book of the Second Temple.
Israel's psalms were the property of a guild of singers including
both men and women. When Ezra lived, their collection was still
in process of formation. It probably reached its present form under
guild editorship a few decades afterwards. The *Book of Psalms*
contains the poetic accumulation of half a dozen centuries. Though
ascriptions to David are made too freely, some of the Psalms may
well be authentically the king's. Several are old enough to be his,
and have parallels in the Canaanite matter from Ras Shamra.

The Psalms distil the whole atmosphere of Hebrew life, in
poetry of the utmost beauty and profundity. They fall into four
or five main classes. Examples of hymns in the simple sense, praising
Yahweh and extolling his mighty deeds, are Psalms xcvi, xcviii,
c, cv, and cxlvii to cl. Their tone is jubilant.

> Let the heavens be glad, and let the earth rejoice;
>   let the sea roar, and all that fills it;
> Let the field exult, and everything in it!
>   Then shall all the trees of the wood sing for joy
> Before the Lord, for he comes, for he comes to judge the earth.
>   He will judge the world with righteousness,
>   and the peoples with his truth.

But Israel's many griefs are voiced also, in poems of national lamentation and entreaty such as Psalms xliv, lxxiv, lxxix-lxxx, lxxxiii. Several express the shock of the First Temple's fall:

> O God, why dost thou cast us off for ever? . . .
>   Remember Mount Zion, where thou hast dwelt.
> Direct thy steps to the perpetual ruins;
>   the enemy has destroyed everything in the sanctuary!
> Do not deliver the soul of thy dove to the wild beasts;
>   do not forget the life of thy poor for ever.

Such psalms are not exclusively communal. Some are cries of lonely distress. Psalms iv-vi, xxxv, lv, lxix, lxxxvi, can all be so described. Best known of these is cxxx, the *De Profundis* ("Out of the depths I cry to thee, O Lord"). Yet triumph outweighs sorrow. Royal paeans celebrate the glory of Israel's rulers, and odes of thanksgiving and rejoicing commemorate the Lord's bounties. Psalms like xviii, xxx, xxxiv, speak for individual happiness. Psalm cxxvi is a song of the resettlement after Cyrus:

> When the Lord restored the fortunes of Zion,
>   we were like those who dream.
> Then our mouth was filled with laughter,
>   and our tongue with shouts of joy;
> Then they said among the nations,
>   "The Lord has done great things for them."
> The Lord has done great things for us;
>   we are glad.
> Restore our fortunes, O Lord,
>   like the watercourses in the Negeb!

A hundred and fifty Psalms were deservedly approved. The related *Lamentations*, ascribed to Jeremiah, were admitted to the canon as an additional corpus of Sacred Writing.

The reform had Scripture of its own. An early product—though it has been revised—was the linked series of books *Chronicles-Ezra-Nehemiah*. The leading "Chronicler," responsible for the first book so named if not the second, was very likely Ezra himself, writing toward the close of his strenuous career. At any rate the Chronicler and his chief continuator are the only authors in the Old Testament who try to embody its editorial principles in a sustained composition. The result, one must admit, lacks lustre. Their Hebrew has been characterised as stilted and academic and strongly influenced by Aramaic; their work is not a fair compilation from sources, but a didactic essay which manipulates the past in the interests of the intended lesson.

After a massive genealogical preface, the two books of *Chronicles* re-tell the story of the kingdom from David to the Captivity. But the moral restrictiveness of the post-Exile age dominates the entire scheme. First, David is held up as a model God-fearing monarch, idealised as he is not idealised in the older books. Then, a sort of Davidic orthodoxy is made to decide which people shall count and which shall not. After the split, *II Chronicles* follows Judah alone, the state centred on David's city, David's dynasty, and the Temple which David at least prepared to build. The heretical north only comes in as it affects the faithful south. Moreover, the movement of events is forced into support of a naïvely moralised theory of history. We are asked to believe that devout kings flourished and idolatrous kings did not; that when the community was loyal to Yahweh he gave it well-being, and when it backslid he sent misfortune. In principle there is nothing novel here. But the authors of *Chronicles* try to correlate prosperity with piety in a far more rigid and tit-for-tat manner than their predecessors. Not satisfied with special divine judgments or acts of guidance, they want to show that all the vicissitudes of the Lord's people are a direct consequence of their ethical and cultic relationship to him. If you sin, you suffer—and if you suffer, you must have sinned.

This attitude is especially clear in the second book. Rehoboam "forsakes the law of the Lord, and all Israel with him"; thereupon the Egyptians invade the country; then the king and his princes "humble themselves" before the Lord; so the disaster is mitigated and "conditions are good" (xii:1-2, 6, 12). Hezekiah "seeks his God" and accordingly "prospers" (xxxi:21). Every defeat is a punishment for the rulers' sins (xxiv:24, xxv:20, etc.). Every success is a reward for godliness (xiii:18, xiv:11-12, etc.). Prophets are mentioned, but almost solely as giving curt warnings and exhortations to the same effect, even in such matters as shipbuilding (xx:35-37).

Here and there this moralisation of history has a slightly desperate tone. The supremely wicked Manasseh reigned for fifty-five years . . . therefore he must have repented. The supremely virtuous Josiah died young in battle . . . therefore it must have been the Lord's will that the Pharaoh whom he opposed should have gone unopposed. (xxxiii:11-13, xxxv:22.)

Yet it should not be inferred that *Chronicles* is a moral romance with no independent value as history. The authors give some proved facts which are not copied from previous biblical texts; for instance, Manasseh's capture by the Assyrians. Also the author of the second book, in spite of what modern historians might call his disingenuousness, is a shade nearer to them in one respect than any of his Israelite forerunners. He cites letters verbatim, such as Elijah's to King Jehoram of Judah (xxi:12-15). In such cases he is imitating contemporary diplomats, who made it a practice to be careful about passing on their masters' exact words. By so doing he edges toward the world of honest documentation and scholarship.

Ezra and *Nehemiah*, in which the same author has a hand, take that trend much further. These books, which were not originally separated, give an account of the repatriation and the early stages of the reform. They are compiled from authentic lists and registers, from reports and dispatches in Aramaic. The first-person narratives of the two reformers seem to be based on diary notes actually kept by them.

So within a lifetime of Ezra, the experience of Israel was gathered together into a Bible. More was to come, and as long as it continued to come there could be no finally fixed canon. However, the great step had been taken. Law and doctrine and the divine gift of Palestine were embedded for ever in historical time, codified and glossed. The Jewish philosophy of history was a fact—destined still to develop, but already a fact.

Over the whole process, as over the reform itself, there hovered a priestly spirit, true to that side of Ezra's character. This clericalism in the mind extended to clericalism in institutions. Under the House of David the priests had not formed a hierarchy or wielded any real power. They were simply royal officials. While the head priest had special functions, he was no more than an official himself, subject to the king. In the Second Zionist community the arrangements were different. The priests grouped themselves into a graded caste drawn entirely from the tribe of Levi; and without a king, without any prospect of a king, the High Priest had no superior. A hazy royalist ideal glimmered in the background, kept from extinction by the promises of the prophets. But so far as Persian authority permitted, the High Priest was *de facto* and *de jure* the sovereign of Israel.

Ezra, however, had been a "scribe" as well as a priest. From this more mentally-active side of him came another influence, tending to supplement the hierarchy and in some degree to challenge it. The Law vindicated its claim to give life—not only by the spirit, but by the letter. A static clerical Fundamentalism turned out to be impracticable. The more loftily Scripture was exalted, the more important became the scholars and teachers who drew out its meaning. And these were not necessarily priests. The office of scribe grew to be a recognised and honoured profession. Scribes abounded, and they had the immense advantage of being able to work among Jews everywhere, not merely in Jerusalem where the Temple was. To some extent the scribe embodied a protest, the democratic movement of an increasingly literate laity.

For two and a half centuries the guardians of the Faith were essentially Ezra's followers. It is said that besides his other achievements he founded a teaching synod to carry on his work Whether or not he personally did so, there was such a synod, a "Great Assembly" of scholars and jurists. Three guiding rules are attributed to them: "Be deliberate in judgment, raise up many disciples, and make a fence around the Torah." These are scarcely the maxims of revolutionaries, but they allow progress of a Fabian kind. The Assembly's main business was "Midrash" or exposition. When we are told that Ezra "sought" or "studied" the Torah (*Ezra* vii:10), the verb used is *darash*, to interpret. The corresponding noun *midrash* occurs in *II Chronicles* xxiv:27 with a notion of "commentary."

The sages of the Assembly devoted themselves to a deeper and deeper understanding of Scripture, and, on the practical side, to a more and more precise fulfilment of its injunctions in Jewish life. A body of case-law grew up. During the third century B.C. the Assembly gave place to a more formal body called the "Sanhedrin"—a Hebraised form of the Greek *sunedrion*. This was a large council of priests and laymen presided over by the High Priest, which had judicial powers. The Sanhedrin tended to be conservative. However, its lay members (as is often the case) were more ardent than the priests. It was chiefly because of this lay element—scribes and their pupils—that when another crisis confronted Israel, a fund of intelligent zeal was there to be drawn upon.

4

Jewish history between the Old Testament and the New is overshadowed by a single event. That event was at once terrific and inconclusive. It inspired, yet it divided. It rekindled, yet it disquieted. Since the books which record it are not in Jewish or Protestant Scripture, but consigned to the Apocrypha, it seldom receives all the stress it should.

Through a century of Persian decay the Zionist community was to outward appearances almost stagnant. Nobody noticed that it was producing the Bible. Its domain was far too small to enjoy the status of a distinct imperial satrapy. Jerusalem and a patch of land round about constituted the district of "Yehud" in the satrapy "Beyond-the-River." The Persians recognised this district as a local hierocracy or priestly preserve, not the only one in their huge dominions. Yehud was allowed its own treasury—the Temple's —and its own silver coinage. Despite all separatism, the Jews were not cut off from the world, even the world outside the Persian system. They traded across the Mediterranean with Greece, and their licensed coinage imitated Greek issues.

Such copying was a symptom. The future was not Persia's, the Persian realm was crumbling, and the last Great Kings at Susa were oppressors who did nothing to retain Jewish loyalty. An Egyptian revolt in 351 had Palestinian support. Its collapse was followed by punitive deportations of Jews, back to Mesopotamia and beyond. Twenty years later Persia suddenly ceased to exist. Alexander of Macedon, leading a united Greece, took possession of the whole mosaic of satrapies in a three years' campaign; Europeans replaced Asiatics as the custodians of civilisation; and for the first time, Israel faced a conquest that was also a challenge.

Alexander advanced through Palestine by the coastal route. He is alleged, however, to have gone up to Jerusalem, received the salutations of the High Priest, and caused a sacrifice to be offered on his behalf. In view of the visit which he did pay to the shrine of Ammon, and his fondness for collecting flattering oracles wherever he could, the story has something to be said for it. At all events he became aware of the Jews and showed favour to them. In the first phase of the "Hellenistic" society which his conquests created, they fared better than before. Greek policy throughout Asia was to win over and re-educate rather than subdue. Palestine's city life revived, and many citizens were Jewish. When Alexander died young, the division of his empire among his generals gave Palestine to Ptolemy, founder of the Greek dynasty in Egypt of which the best-known member is Cleopatra. As long as the Ptolemaic house held on to their country, the Jews flourished.

However, fresh dangers inexorably gathered. Alexander's real successors (in so far as he had any) were the kings descended from Seleucus, another general. These managed to assert their authority over nearly the whole Asiatic part of his empire, which was by far the largest. The Ptolemies kept their foothold for several decades, but eventually succumbed, and withdrew into the isthmus of Sinai. In 198 the Seleucid Antiochus III, called "the Great," became the Jews' new master. Personally he was no worse disposed toward them than the Ptolemies had been. He lightened Jerusalem's tax burden, and helped inhabitants displaced by his wars to return home. Nevertheless the atmosphere cooled, because he involved the Jews once again in world politics and the consequent tensions.

Here two momentous names enter the story together. Antiochus granted asylum to a distinguished refugee, Hannibal, who had left Carthage soon after his defeat at the Battle of Zama. "Hannibal" means "the grace of Baal," the same Baal combated by Elijah; Carthage began as a Phoenician colony. Baal could still make mischief for Israel. Partly through Hannibal's influence, Antiochus drifted into collision with Rome and lost much ground. To raise money for his army and the indemnity which the Romans squeezed out of him, he and his successor imposed special taxes, and tried to confiscate treasures from various temples. That of the Jews did not escape. Predictably the royal demands led to quarrels among them, to disputes over the amount of resistance that might be offered, to dreary recriminations and charges of collaboration. Two rival families fought for the High Priesthood, each with its attendant faction. The House of Onias, on the whole, attracted the nationalists, the House of Tobias the pro-Greeks.

This party squabble might have smouldered on indefinitely with no serious outcome. But it was fanned into a blaze by one of those crowned cranks, like Akhnaton and Nabonidus, whom the ancient world occasionally produced. In 175 Antiochus IV, "Epiphanes," inherited the rump Syrian kingdom which was all that the fast-declining Seleucids had left. After a fruitless march into Egypt (the Romans compelled him to retire) he gave all his energies to a policy that was then novel, religious uniformity. Though weirdly un-Greek, it was grounded on an appeal to Greek cosmopolitanism and Greek liberalism. The idols of local superstition were to be subordinated everywhere to the enlightened

Olympians, with all that their reign implied. In most places Antiochus had his way. In Jerusalem he found obstacles.

Antiochus made use of the pro-Greek faction. Its existence had been brought to his notice by the overtures of its leaders: first a certain Jason, whom he had forced on the Jews as High Priest; later Menelaus, who had supplanted Jason in the same sacred honour by giving the King a bigger bribe. These Israelites' adoption of Greek names seemed to hold out a prospect of agreement, and their conduct was indubitably progressive, in the sense which people like Antiochus tend to give to that term. Menelaus murdered Onias, the legitimate High Priest, and Menelaus's brother robbed the Temple. Under these auspices the liberalisation of Jewish worship could proceed. Antiochus ordered, and obtained, the cessation of the daily sacrifice. In December 167 he installed a statue of Zeus in Yahweh's precinct, and altars for offerings of swine's flesh—which no faithful Jew could touch. He forbade Sabbath observance and the further circumcision of children.

Some Jews were prepared to reopen the door to paganism. Jason and his friends, indeed, had been cultivating the Greek way of life ever since Antiochus's accession. They maintained a gymnasium in Jerusalem which was a cause of much scandal, and the inherent logic of the "progressive" position, the need to oppose "reactionaries" at all costs, ensured their acquiescence in the cultus of Zeus and other gods. But there were also Jews who refused; and their refusal gave birth to a new phenomenon, religious martyrdom.

Persecution as such was not new. That had happened before, and in Greece itself. Hitherto, however, religion had been on the persecuting side, attacking isolated sceptics like Socrates. Now, the victims suffered collectively for a faith instead of a doubt. They rallied to the Torah; Ezra had done his work well. Antiochus made it a capital crime to own a copy, yet copies were still owned. He tried other measures. Could he discredit the faithful by making them violate their Law? Several were arrested and told to eat pork at a pagan altar, on pain of death by torture. The story of their ordeal sets a literary pattern that has run through innumerable "Saints' Lives" and Jewish legends ever since.[2]

Here was Eleazar, one of the chief scribes, a man of great age and of noble features, being required to eat swine's flesh; but though they held his mouth open they could not force him to eat. He would rather die gloriously than live defiled; on he went, of his own accord, to the place of torture, scanning every step of the path that lay before him. He must endure all in patience, rather than taste, for love of life, the forbidden meat.

Old friends among the bystanders, out of misplaced kindness, took him aside and urged him to let meat of some other kind be brought, which he could taste without scruple; he could pretend to have obeyed the king's will by eating the sacrilegious food, and his life should no longer be forfeit. Such kind offices old friendship claimed; but he thought rather of the reverence that was due to his great age, of his venerable grey hairs, of a life blamelessly lived from childhood onwards. True to the precepts of God's holy law, he answered that they would do better to send him to his grave and have done with it. It does not suit my time of life, said he, to play a part. What of many that stand here, younger than myself, who would think that Eleazar, at the age of ninety, had turned Gentile? To gain a brief hour of this perishable life, shall I disgrace this hoary head of mine and bring down a curse on it? . . .

And so without more ado he was led away to his torturing; his executioners were in a rage, that but now had been gentle with him; pride, they would have it, spoke here. And this was the last sigh he uttered, as he lay there dying under the lash, Lord, in thy holy wisdom this thou well knowest; I might have had life if I would, yet never a cruel pang my body endures, but my soul suffers it gladly for thy reverence.

It was the most cultured and intellectual race of antiquity, the

2 I have used Knox's translation of *II Maccabees* vi:18-30.

source of nearly all that humanism holds dear, which brought this sort of thing into the world.

The persecution broadened into a political and social upheaval, which determined the history of the Jews thenceforward. Antiochus tore down Nehemiah's wall and poured troops into Jerusalem. Many of those loyal to the Torah fled into the wilderness to live like their ancestors. They were called Hasidim, meaning "pious" or "saints," willing sufferers for the cause. For a moment Israel seemed to be splitting again into time-servers and a new Remnant. But the Hasidim were not hermits or schismatics. They formed a resistance element, the main force in a popular revolt which, astonishingly, restored the monarchy.

Antiochus's officers overreached themselves at Modein, between Jerusalem and Jaffa. One of them ordered the villagers to sacrifice to pagan gods. When a Jewish collaborationist did so, a retired priest named Mattathias killed both him and the officer. Mattathias understood quite well that this was an act of rebellion. He called on "everyone loyal to the Law and the Covenant" to follow him, and took to the hills with his own sons. One of these—Judas nicknamed Maccabeus, the Hammer—assumed leadership after the priest's almost immediate death. Judah's narrow defiles and deep gorges, its eastern barrier of desert and mountain, are favourable to guerrilla war. A growing army won several victories over second-rate Greek commanders while Antiochus himself was away in Parthia. In December 164 Judas dispersed the defenders of Jerusalem and captured the Temple. After a gap of more than three years the daily sacrifice was resumed, a triumph commemorated to this day in Hanukkah, the Jewish Feast of Lights. According to legend the victors found only one day's supply of lamp-oil; nevertheless they lit the Menorah, and it burned miraculously for eight days, till a fresh supply came.

The Seleucid government tried to strike a bargain with the heroic Judas by acknowledging him as the King's local representative. Religious freedom was conceded and Menelaus was executed. Momentarily unharassed, Judas and his companions made overdue repairs to the Temple, embellished the front of it with gold crowns, and built a fort on Mount Zion. But this was not the end. The brothers, inspired to re-possess the whole Land, pressed on to reverse the verdict of half a millennium. Religion and patriotism fused; Seleucid counter-attacks provoked fresh offensives; and step by step, fidelity to the Torah revived the kingdom. Judas's death in battle transferred the command to his brother Jonathan, who became High Priest. By now Antiochus was dead too, and the patriots exploited dissensions at the Seleucid court. Their forces appeared in Galilee and across the Jordan. In 147 Jonathan seized Jaffa, securing access to the sea. Subsequently a third brother, Simon, took charge of the campaign. Rome gave a distant blessing, and in 142 the Seleucid Demetrius II recognised Jewish independence.

Simon became High Priest but not King. The first monarch of the Maccabee or "Hasmonean" dynasty (Hasmon being an ancestor of the family) was his son John Hyrcanus. John, after a stormy start, ruled over the state as combined High Priest and King *de facto*—though without using the royal style—from 128 onward. Like David, he held most of Palestine and a good deal of land beyond the Jordan: in other words, a substantial alien population. During his rise and ascendancy many inhabitants of the conquered areas embraced their overlord's religion . . . admittedly under pressure. Possibly as a gesture toward these neophytes, John made a habit of referring to God by his title of "the Most High," with its pagan echoes and antecedents. Two regions thus largely Judaised were Idumaea and Galilee. The Idumaeans or Edomites, who lived south-east of the Dead Sea and had encroached on Palestine at times of Israelite weakness, were suspect as descended from Esau. However, their rapid conversion into Jews, and ardent Jews, was more or less accepted. Galilee lay far to the north; it was an increasingly cosmopolitan area crossed by trade routes. While its old allegiance to Yahweh perhaps lingered on in a few villages, the Jews for practical purposes found it missionary territory.

John Hyrcanus further enhanced his prestige by destroying the Samaritans' rival temple. He could not destroy the Samaritans themselves, who went on loathing Jews as before, but henceforth that activity lacked a centre. Being a Levite, John had no claim to be the new David promised by the prophets. As a matter of fact he removed treasure from David's tomb to pay foreign mercenaries. Yet he had more than a touch of Davidic majesty; he was outstanding as a prince, and at least competent as a priest; while his extraordinary foresight earned him the reputation of a prophet as well.

This glory did not survive him. The kingdom petered out in another anti-climax. Politically it was a freak and anachronism, the last sovereign Semitic power. Its monarchy after John did not differ much from other monarchies, and its decadence may be skimmed over with glancing distaste, as a mere preface to the far more memorable happenings in Jewish minds under its aegis.

John Hyrcanus died in 104 and was followed by further priest-monarchs, who did call themselves "king." His son Aristobulus I gained ground in Galilee, and the next, Alexander Jannaeus, conquered Gilead and pushed the southern frontier down toward Egypt. However, the combination of gifts which had made John so successful did not recur. Alexander, a military type, performed the Temple ritual so badly that a crowd pelted him with citrons. His guards cut down the demonstrators and a rising broke out, followed by fierce repression. Alexander watched the executions from a table where he was dining with several concubines. His son Hyrcanus II was dominated in civil affairs by the queen-mother Salome; a younger brother displaced him and assumed office as Aristobulus II; Hyrcanus took refuge with Antipater, the governor of Idumaea, who marched on Jerusalem but failed to capture it . . . and then the sordid business ended in smoke.

Rome, now growing to imperial stature, stepped in. Pompey arrived with an army and tried for a while to restore order under the pretender, but gave him up and declared for Hyrcanus. He besieged Jerusalem, taking advantage of the defenders' unwillingness to fight on the Sabbath. Twelve thousand Jews were killed. In 63 the Temple fell after a gallant resistance, and the Gentile intruder drew the curtain aside and walked into the Holy of Holies, where he behaved with perfect propriety, though he was bewildered to find no image. Aristobulus was deported to Rome, Hyrcanus was left as High Priest and "ethnarch," in charge of Galilee, Idumaea, Peraea across Jordan, and Judah itself, which the Romans called Judaea.

The real ruler was the king-maker Antipater. In the Roman civil war he adroitly favoured Julius Caesar against his own patron Pompey. Advised by him, Caesar treated the Jews generously. He reduced their taxes, granted them religious autonomy, authorised the further refortification of Jerusalem, and exempted the city from billeting Roman troops in winter. His gestures had very little effect. The Hasmonean phase, with all its squalors and disappointments, had made nationalism a passion. Jews in general repaid Caesar and Antipater by hating both of them, Caesar as a Gentile, Antipater as an Edomite, whose Jewish religion did not melt them at all. In the anarchy after Caesar's murder the assassin Cassius was for a time in control of Palestine; Antipater stood by him, and then by Mark Antony. In 37 Antony appointed Antipater's son as a client king in Judaea. When Antony waned, this son went over to Octavius, and was confirmed in his position. He proved a loyal vassal, a capable tyrant, a lover of ostentatious building, and a detested man—perhaps not unlike a Latin-American dictator. His name was Herod.

5

Historically the main point of the Greek persecution is not so much that it led to a false dawn and disillusionment as that it indirectly promoted new alignments, new doctrines and modes of thought, within Jewish society. As soon as it began, the road lay tragically open to the convulsion which came in the first century A.D. From the Temple's pollution to its destruction, from the clash with Hellenistic pagans to the schism caused by St. Paul's preaching among them, Israel progressed through an inevitable and fatal growth.

After Antiochus the contrast between the unprepossessing externals and the doomed majesty of spirit within becomes more and more poignant. Political and economic events almost cease to be history. They supply no clue. They are only occasions for the unfolding of something more profound.

Before exploring the inner kingdom of matured Jewish ideas, it is as well to understand whose ideas exactly they were.

The loyalists or Hasidim whose revolt made the Maccabee state possible survived as a body after its launching. They carried weight both inside the Sanhedrin and outside. But two parties presently emerged within their own ranks, Pharisees and Sadducees. These drifted to an open split during the reign of John Hyrcanus. The Pharisees at first energetically supported him; but they protested at talk of his being called "king," on the ground that the Lord alone was King. One of them rashly hinted that John was illegitimate, whereupon he allied himself with the Sadducees. Throughout the rest of the monarchy's distracted career the two parties were, politically speaking, Ins and Outs. Salome reinstated the Pharisees, her son Aristobulus II turned to the Sadducees again. But the crucial point, once more, is that these see-sawings in public affairs have no meaning. They could have happened in reverse order without its making any real difference. The significance of the rival groups lay in their respective beliefs. To these, the only further prologue required is an indication of the groups' social character and outlook.

The Sadducees were few, but wealthy and therefore powerful, especially in the Sanhedrin. They were also highly cautious, mistrusting anything that went beyond the explicit precepts of Moses. They had close links with the Temple, and with the tiny cluster of families tracing a pedigree to Aaron, from which the High Priests were always drawn: an "establishment" so rigid that even the Romans, who had no scruples about deposing a High Priest, never ventured outside the charmed circle to enlist a replacement for him.

Against the exclusive Sadducean club, the far more interesting Pharisees were the leaders of popular ideology and the true heirs

of the Hasidim. Their own name is supposed to be a Greek derivative, through Aramaic, from the Hebrew *Perushim* meaning "the
separated." Their separation was not social. It rested on their
insistence that the distinction which the Law drew between God's
Israel and the rest of mankind was eternal, fundamental, and
hallowed—a sort of vocational nationalism, which was undoubtedly
implied in the Jewish position, but which the man-of-the-world
Sadducees toned down in practice. One outcome was a Hebrew
literary revival.

Whereas the Sadducees tended to be harsh and aloof, the Pharisees
in their prime were friendly and outgoing. Some were priests, but
the party's strength of six thousand or so included members from
all classes and most occupations, such as shepherds, butchers,
sauce-vendors, and blacksmiths. Pharisee scholars were the arch-
practitioners of Midrash, the technique of scriptural exposition.
They were also its revolutionisers, bold and brilliant in their efforts
to make the Law more comprehensive, more flexible, better
adapted to every circumstance of life. The oral tradition which
grew up among them was organic and vigorous. Their aim was
to enrich piety, not to water it down or narrow its scope. They
said "yes" more readily than "no"; they sought formulae to fit
in any idea that appealed to them as valuable.

Sadducee influence, though strong in Jerusalem, dwindled to
vanishing point as distance from the Temple increased. Pharisee
influence went wherever Jews went—in other words, through all
Hellenistic Asia, Egypt, Greece and parts of Italy including Rome
itself. A document composed not much after the Maccabee rising
asserts that Jews are already "everywhere," and the dispersal was
still extending its range during the Roman Peace. The faithful
non-Palestinian Jew always looked toward Zion. He contributed
an annual tax to the Temple's upkeep, he tried to make at least
one Passover pilgrimage there, he prayed facing in that direction.
But he claimed, and was conceded, a spiritual status in his own right.
He was not a second-class Jew.

The problem of remaining first-class without attending the

Temple had been solved long since by the invention of the synagogue. In the last pre-Christian century synagogues were numerous both outside and inside Palestine. Any Jewish community that could furnish a quorum of ten male adults could form one. A synagogue was in essence a civic centre, used as a school, a meetinghouse, and a place of prayer. At least three services were held every week. Sacrifices, of course, could not be offered anywhere but in the Temple. The synagogue service consisted mainly in a reading from the Torah in Hebrew followed by exposition in Aramaic, with the aid of a written commentary. At first only the Pentateuch was read, but toward the beginning of the Christian era the prophets were admitted as well. Any man was eligible to do the reading. The congregation joined in reciting prayers, blessings, and a short creed. Within these groups, of varying size and composition, Pharisee doctrine made its way.

Its exponents were those typical synagogue figures, the scribe and the rabbi, either of whom might be a Pharisee himself. The scribes we have noted. The rabbis, who have since become the only recognised Jewish clergy, began chiefly as organisers and gradually absorbed other functions including the scribe's—education, learning, the adjustment of religious disputes. They did not form a clerical clique apart from the populace. Most were married, and supported their families by ordinary labour in workshop or field. The more erudite rabbis were known as Tanna'im, teachers, and their schools flourished even in Judaea within range of the Temple.

Rabbis differed among themselves and so did Pharisees; but the greatest Pharisee was also the greatest rabbi—namely Hillel. Rabbi Hillel was descended from David. Born in Babylon about 60 B.C., he migrated to Palestine and became prominent in the Sanhedrin at Jerusalem. Seven rules of Midrash laid down by him did much to stabilise it, and ensure that there would always be room for humane and enlightened exegesis. Among many stories of Hillel the most famous concerns a potential convert who challenged the rabbi to sum up Jewish principles for him within the time he could stand on one leg. Hillel told him to take up his stance, and then said: "Do not unto others what you would not have others do to you. This is the whole Law; the rest, merely commentary."

Hillel was a culmination. But it was chiefly his own Pharisaic precursors who, for a full lifetime before him, had been gathering certain confused elements in Jewish thought and most daringly re-moulding them.

CHAPTER NINE

THE KINGDOM OF STONE

Around the First Zionism, bringing liberation from Egypt, the ancient faith of Israel had formed. The Second Zionism of the liberation from Babylon had been, by comparison, scrappy and sporadic, with no hero and no single dramatic action. Sheshbazzar had begun it and left hardly any mark. The chief men of the next few decades—Zerubbabel, Jeshua, Nehemiah, Ezra—had indeed rebuilt the Temple and codified the Law. But none of them had attained the stature of a new Moses.

As far as words were concerned, the Moses of the release from Babylon had been the Second Isaiah. In him the Jews were given a voice infinitely more splendid than their achievement answering to it. The cramping Neo-Temple cult absorbed his teaching only imperfectly. Yet there were always some who did breathe his ampler air; and after the Maccabee episode, with its shocks to Jewish apathy, its reminders of the ardent past, its renewal of urgency in the present, fresh streams of thought with sources among the peaks of his prophecy began to flood the devitalised lowlands.

This enlargement of spirit appears first, of course, much sooner, in the continuators of Second Isaiah himself who break in after Chapter Fifty-five. Its accents can be caught again fitfully in some of the last-written books of Scripture. Then the Tanna'im take it up. Pharisees, and rabbis of Pharisaic outlook, pursue it further. Much of their teaching is preserved in contemporary literature; much of it, revalued, is in the New Testament; much of it is in the Talmud, a later compilation which is nevertheless full of matter dating from the days of the Sanhedrin. In its exploratory stages the new thinking seems to have outdistanced the old orthodoxy so far as to threaten schism. But in the end its popularity swept even the cautious toward a synthesis.

Behind it we can detect a patient probing of fundamentals by the more active minds of Israel. From the Babylonian Exile onward they were re-examining the logic of the situation and drawing inferences.

To the logic of the Second Zionist situation as of the First, the Land was central. Because of the return to Jerusalem, however meagre its practical fruits, the axiom that history made sense in the light of divine purpose could still be sustained. There had been a frightful moment at the fall of Solomon's Temple when God had seemed to fail altogether. That ultimate nightmare was past. The Remnant had repented beside the waters of Babylon, and God's pledges to Abraham and Moses had in due course been honoured. In the eyes of his people so incredibly re-possessed of the Land, his word was kept and his providence thereby proved. The miracle of the Exodus had happened again.

That fact is one of the chief reasons why few Jews ever felt obliged to dismiss their God as outgrown or judge him inadequate, as educated Greeks did with the Olympians. He had been put to a specific test, and he had not been found wanting. The cogency of this test for the survivors of the southern captivity may serve as a last note on the victims of the northern. The tribes deported to Assyria did not go through the same spiritual crisis; they were not restored to the Land; and so they faded away, losing their faith and their identity. Except perhaps for a few scattered families they gave Yahweh up, and apostasy made them fully assimilable among pagans.

At Zion Yahweh stood vindicated. The historical axiom remained. And yet, how hard it still was to apply! The prophecies, the winnowing-out, the agonies of bondage, the dispersion, the failure of so many to come home, the dreary squabbles and frustrations of those who did come . . . all these things must mean something, they must be tending somehow toward salvation. Could human wisdom piece out the mystery?

Well, to begin with, there was Jeremiah's distinction between the good and bad figs. Many Israelites had been cast off for transgression and had forfeited their birthright. The Remnant had gone to Babylon and endured, but with bitter tribulation. As to the tribulation, God's purpose was clear. He had sent it so that the Remnant could expiate collective sin, learn penance and be purified, as Second Isaiah had declared in his very opening words. Whereas other nations put the blame for their woes on outside agencies, the Jews looked within. They had to, or else defy their own logic. If their God ruled the world, then affliction could only come upon his Chosen in one way—by his sovereign permission, because of their own disloyalty to him, their breach of the Covenant. So they confessed their faults, their idolatry and hypocrisy and injustice, and hoped for mercy.

However, it was a question not only of atonement but of the form the atonement took, and where it was supposed to lead. Israel, the reduced Jewish Israel that carried on the heritage, was still focused on Zion. But why was the restoration so feeble? Why were so may Jews spread abroad and showing no sign of coming back? As time crept on with no major change, interpretation passed into analysis, into a further quest for vocation. The position, inquirers felt, must contain some implied commandment. Some task must be left which God intended his Jews to do, and which this unsatisfactory plight of theirs was a precondition of their doing. From that statement of the issue, fresh departures were undertaken: fresh attempts to devise a picture of history, of the way the world was moving and of the way it ought to move.

Such a picture needed to be far broader and more comprehensive than the myopic notions of the *Chronicles* school, content with the insistence that if the Jews kept all the six-hundred-and-thirteen rules they would prosper in the Land, and no other nation or aim was worth bothering about. The shallow theology of "welfare as the reward of virtue" and vice versa, in a short-term automatic sense, could not convince or satisfy an honest Jew. Among Gentiles

Zoroaster too had maintained it, but the Persians, after all, actually had prospered during the heyday of the Good Religion. It was a long while before they had any reason to criticise the principle, whereas the unhappy Jews were given occasion continually to see through it. Israel had to probe deeper.

Those who made the effort in writing faced peculiar difficulties. They could safely insinuate original-sounding doctrines in books mainly concerned with other topics. Some of the insinuations found their way into Scripture. But after the last prophets were dead, a huge obstacle blocked the path of anyone wishing to affirm such doctrines outright. For as to doctrine, the Law and the Prophets were supposed to be final. To teach anything which they had not already laid down amounted to heresy. Thinkers who were original, yet faithful to orthodoxy, were therefore driven to a bizarre expedient. This was "pseudepigraphic" writing—the making of books purporting to be the work of others: of scriptural patriarchs and prophets whose names everyone revered, and who were thereby made to "reveal" more than Scripture revealed.

The technique takes a little getting used to. It sounds merely fraudulent. One recalls Samuel Ireland's forged Shakespeare play. The state of mind of the serious and devout Jewish pseudepigrapher is hard to recapture. His starting-point was pragmatic. If the inspired canon of Law and Prophets was final, then a new prophecy or principle could only be added by hitching it to the canon, in other words by fathering it on a canonical figure such as Enoch or Noah. However bogus this procedure may look, we must remember that it is warranted by Scripture itself. Thus all law, even the late matter in *Deuteronomy*, is ascribed to Moses. Many psalms which must be later than David are ascribed to David. Collections of mixed maxims in *Proverbs* and *Ecclesiastes* are ascribed to Solomon. Even Second Isaiah is blotted out as a person and made anonymous by the ascription of his work to the first and true Isaiah, an ascription which was made early. There is evidence, furthermore, that some Jewish scholars were far from naïve in their acceptance of the supposed "authors' names," and granted that convention could play a legitimate part in assigning them. Besides perceiving that Moses could scarcely have written the account of his own death, they speculated freely about the true authorship of the Psalms and other things. *Proverbs* (xxv:1) recognises the role of editorial committees.

Hence, what we should now condemn as a falsehood can be justified from biblical precedents. The substratum is the lack of rigid distinction in Hebrew minds between individual and community. In a roundabout way every Israelite was every other Israelite, because any Israelite whatever was, so to speak, Israel-manifest-at-a-given-time-and-place. The propriety of an ascription lay not so much in real authorship as in fitness. A notion of archetypes is apparent. Laws were attributed to Moses as *the* Lawgiver, psalms to David as *the* Psalmist, aphorisms to Solomon as *the* Wise Man. A Hebrew writer who saddled Moses with some unlikely precept was not necessarily faking in the style of a literary impostor. He might be saying in effect, "This is what Moses would have told you if you had questioned him on the subject, provided, of course, that you fully explained what the situation was that led you to ask." Nobody could maintain that the pseudepigraphic writings outside the canon are always so moderate in intent. But the thought is there; and it is summed up in a Jewish maxim which might seem to allow almost any essay in this vein—"Whoever says a thing in the name of the one who would have said it, brings salvation to the world."

The most important pseudepigrapha which have survived are Pharisaic in authorship. Their literary standards are on the whole rather low, but their ethical standards are often high. All profess to be vehicles of revelation, and a tendency is detectable in them to reach back behind Moses for authority, into the patriarchal world of Noah and Abraham and Jacob. They exist in various versions which are not always easily sorted out. In the pre-Christian era, four complete major pseudepigrapha of this type can be distinguished: the *Book of Jubilees*, the *Book of Enoch*, the *Testaments of the Twelve Patriarchs*, and the *Psalms of Solomon*. To some extent they are composites, in which previous productions of the same sort have been combined and re-edited.

Jubilees is transitional. As it stands it was made up in Hebrew toward the end of the second century B.C., but from older matter, some of it Hasidic. It purports to be an angelic revelation to Moses, put on record by him. Most of it is really a series of exercises in Midrash extending the Chronicler's pietism back into *Genesis*. The author or compiler is a strict Pharisee and perhaps a priest. His object is to depict the patriarchs and even God's angels as obeying the Law, which is eternal, and was not framed at Sinai but only disseminated there. He re-tells the story from Creation, showing us on the way how some of the riddles had been resolved: thus he is the source of the information that Cain's wife was his sister Awan. Some of the disclosures are curious. God, for instance, made the angels already circumcised. Israel's rights in Palestine are traced to a secret treaty among the sons of Noah. The author lays out his scheme in a chronology of "jubilees" or fifty-year periods, whence the title. His book is exclusive in the spirit of Ezra; the novelty consists in his cosmic exaggeration of the ordinary priestly claims. Yet he includes one or two odd asides, brief poetic prophecies, with hints at future events not deducible from the Torah. By admitting these he gives his readers licence to range much wider . . . as the other pseudepigraphers most zealously do.

Originality or apparent originality enters on a larger scale in the *Book of Enoch*, which is a compendium of Hasidic and Pharisaic writings composed over a fairly long stretch of time. Some are in Hebrew and some in Aramaic. It digests matter from a so-called *Book of Noah* and other pre-Maccabean sources. The bulk of it belongs to the second century B.C., but parts are as late as 64. *Enoch* is the most important of the pre-Christian pseudepigrapha, and the real prophetic majesty which it shows in places led to its being treated with high respect. As will appear, it is the closest thing to a literary bridge between the Old Testament and the New. It consists of a medley of verses, visions and parables, in which the patriarch, called "the scribe of righteousness," learns many secrets about the divine counsels and the destined course of history.

The book called *The Testaments of the Twelve Patriarchs* is doubtless the best as literature. It was written in Hebrew by a strong Pharisee during the reign of John Hyrcanus, and probably between 109 and 106 B.C. There are slightly later Jewish interpolations, and much later Christian ones, but these can be picked out. The patriarchs are Jacob's twelve sons, and the testaments are their death-bed admonitions to their families. They are made to warn against various besetting sins—Reuben against lust, Simeon against envy, Judah against the love of money, and so forth. They utter wise counsels: "love God and your neighbour," "teach your children letters." They recall their own lives and make predictions about the future of Israel. The novelties are inserted in these prophetic sections.

The *Psalms of Solomon*, eighteen in number, exist only in Greek and Syriac versions; but in view of allusions to Pompey the lost Hebrew text must have dated from the middle of the first century B.C. Most of the "psalms" are passable imitations of the canonical series. Again the author's bias is Pharisaic, and when he mentions powerful sinners in Israel he means chiefly the Sadducees.

In reviewing the doctrines which these pseudepigraphers teach or assume, we must be careful not to see them as forming a left-wing sect, combating the legalism of the Temple. They are loyal after their fashion. The author of *Jubilees* is fanatically so. If in the others' loyalty there is sometimes a perfunctory tone, there is never any sign of rebellion. Although this type of writing does at last break away into eccentric revolt, it does not do so till after its primary teachings have blended into the main stream of Jewish thought.

2

What then were the post-Exilic ideas which these books took up and enlarged upon, and which slowly re-moulded the beliefs of most Jews, making Roman Judaea into a bomb within the Imperial body?

First, in the background, there perpetually hovered that tragic dogma of the isolation and purification of God's People by suffering. But beyond this, in the eyes of the sort of Jews we are considering here, the concept of divine election was itself glorified. The Chosen People were now held to be "chosen" in a sense only vaguely glimpsed hitherto.

That their special status meant more than a crude national superiority had, of course, been grasped by the prophets before the Exile. God was not simply the divine tribal leader of a conquering host. He was a Father who loved Israel even though Israel was the least of nations, and the chief gift of his love was not greater power but greater wisdom. Moreover, that wisdom was not a treasure to be hoarded in secret. The prophecy of a golden age found in both *Isaiah* and *Micah* looked forward to a time when foreigners would flock to Jerusalem to be given laws by the Lord's spokesmen. Yet limitations remained. Though the foreigners were to come, Israel had no duty to invite or encourage or assist them; and according to Micah they would still not renounce their own false gods.

Some time after the Exile, in keeping with the vision of Second Isaiah, these limitations were overleapt. Many of the best minds now held that the Jewish people had been given the task of bringing the Torah to the nations without waiting for the nations to come to them. And the nations were not merely to be taught to treat Israel's God with honour, they were to be weaned from their idols altogether, till they served the Lord alone. For the growing number who thought thus, the Jews became a people consecrated to a world-mission. Here surely was the explanation of the promise to Abraham, "In you all the families of the earth shall be blessed." One could almost speak of a Chosen Message rather than a Chosen People. The theme runs all through the *Testaments of the Twelve Patriarchs*, where we are told repeatedly in one way or another how God, through Israel, will "visit the Gentiles in his tender mercies for ever."

The potent argument behind this belief was that an adequate clue could be found in it to the whole sequence of tribulation—the Temple's fall, the uprooting of the Remnant, and the failure of the majority to return to Zion. God had scattered the Jews precisely for the purpose of extending his kingdom among the Gentiles through their influence. The Exile, by inducing its victims to purge themselves of idolatry and repent, had made them worthy of this adventurous calling. It had also taught them to live away from Zion without disloyalty to Zion: they could now worship in synagogue as well as Temple, taking their stand on Torah as well as cult. Palestine remained essential, but strictly as the place of God's manifestation through Israel, not as Israel's divinely granted private estate. Israel continued to exist as a sort of nation, but its unity was religious according to the exact derivation of the word. Jews in every country were spiritually "bound" to the Holy Land and the physical city of Jerusalem by their common apostolate and the Torah which embodied it.

Early statements of this opinion are few but firm. One occurs in the apocryphal *Book of Tobit*. "Sons of Israel," says Tobit, "make God's name known, publish it for all the Gentiles to hear; if he has dispersed you among heathen folk who know nothing of him, it was so that you might tell them the story of his great deeds, convince them that he, and no other, is God all-powerful."[1] Again, we find a rabbinical dictum that "God exiled Israel among the nations solely so that proselytes should be added to them." However, the dawning awareness of the full potentialities of Gentile redemption is also shown, indirectly, by certain preoccupations. These affect several late contributors to the biblical canon itself.

Precedents exist even in the older portions. But the authors who set these down pass them by without special interest. David's Hittite captain Uriah would seem to have assumed his name in token of allegiance to David's God. Elisha causes the Syrian Naaman to worship the Lord. Neither of these early cases amounts to much. In the *Book of Ruth*, however, which is a romantic re-

[1] Knox's translation of *Tobit* xiii:3-4.

handling of folk-tradition executed fairly soon after the Exile, the writer depicts his heroine herself as a Moabite convert (i:16, ii:12). He stresses her equality with the most famous women of Israel (iv:11-12), and then reveals the point of his tale in a pioneer instance of the surprise ending—Ruth's son was Obed, and Obed's son was Jesse, and Jesse's son was none other than David the King. Nothing could fix the proselyte's respectable status more securely. In *Job*, composed about the same period, we have another Gentile brought face to face with the God of Israel and bowing down to adore him, after a long debate on life's gravest problems without a single Israelite present.

More notable still in this respect is the *Book of Jonah*. Jonah lived during Jeroboam II's reign in the north, and spurred on his conquests. The story told of the prophet may be contemporary in part. But the scriptural version, with its queer allegory of the "great fish," can be assigned to a date slightly after *Job*. God commands Jonah to prophesy in the Gentile metropolis of Nineveh: the city, like Sodom, is in peril on account of its sins. Frightened at the task, Jonah takes ship at Jaffa to flee to Tartessus, at the world's western limit. A storm comes on. The crew, seeing the hand of the guilty man's God, throw Jonah overboard at his own request. Calm ensues, and the awestruck sailors make appropriate sacrifice. Jonah meanwhile vanishes remorsefully into the belly of the fish, which vomits him on to a recognisable coast. When he hears the divine order again he at last goes to Nineveh. The king and citizens, stirred by his preaching, reform their conduct and pray penitently to Jonah's God. As a result God spares them—to the extreme annoyance of Jonah himself, who has to be reminded of the virtue of mercy.

It is a pity that the fish episode has overshadowed the rest of this concise fable, and diverted attention from the breadth and charity of its outlook. Yet the issue is still not quite fully faced. Jonah persuades both the seamen and the Ninevites to acknowledge the power of the true God; but he does not persuade them, or even distinctly urge them, to put away their false gods. In fact the missionary ideal of Israel, though sketched by Second and Third Isaiah, never was clearly developed by the makers of the Bible itself. Its development was the work of others, in whose hands, over the years, a fairly coherent view of the matter took shape.

These, let us recall, were mostly Pharisees and rabbis under Pharisee influence. They did not flatly reject the separatism of the Temple. They professed entire fidelity to the edicts of Ezra, and made no attempt to breach the "fence round the Torah." While some of them (casuists in the best sense, like Hillel) were skilful at easing the Law's rigidity, none ever suggested that any part of the Torah was not from God, or that even the least of its commandments could be disobeyed without sin. They did, however, begin to regard Jewish separatism in a gentler light, and to discriminate more carefully between precepts of different kinds. The greater commandments were of course ethical absolutes, arising from human nature and relevant to all men. But the lesser ones that appeared peculiarly Israelite, and lacking sometimes in moral content (the diet rules and so forth), could be viewed as more or less arbitrary badges with symbolic meanings. By these God imposed a sanctifying discipline on his own people, and that, no doubt, was their chief purpose. By these also, however, he made Israel unique, and prevented its merging into other nations. Why should he do so? Precisely because of Israel's ministry to other nations.

To set out as a lonely evangelist like St. Francis Xavier or Livingstone would not have occurred to the community-minded Jew. There had been indeed the grand succession of holy men within Israel—kings and prophets and scribes—but it was to Israel itself, not to the Gentiles, that God had sent them. Among biblical figures even Jonah is only a partial exception. *II Kings* establishes him as a prophet within Israel, and God's order to go abroad horrifies him. Advocates of the Jewish world-mission held in any case that individual prophecy of the old type was at an end, and unlikely to revive. No; the Jews were to be a prophet-*people*, the vehicle of revelation. They were collectively appointed to lead the Gentiles to truth, without losing their own strange identity as a group. They were set apart to teach by example and precept. "If ye work that which is good, my children," says Naphtali in his testament, "God shall be glorified among the Gentiles through you."

3

Set apart to teach; yet one must ask, to teach what exactly. . . .

As to the written Torah there could be no disagreement. This at least was for all mankind. If Israel refused to share the writings on which its whole claim depended, it had nothing to share. The author of the transitional *Book of Jubilees* might acquiesce in that conclusion, and urge, as he did, that God's major gifts belonged to Israel alone; but those who believed in a Jewish mission at all were bound to think more liberally. A verse in the *Testament of Levi* speaks of "the light of the Law which was given to lighten every man." According to some, God had offered his Law to all the nations, and chosen Israel solely because Israel accepted it. If the people had not assented to the message of Moses they would have died in the desert, and their children with them. Saved by the ancestral assent, the Jews could now be God's agents to give the Gentiles a second chance.

Even the sourest approved this proposition in some degree. If an outsider persisted in a wish to worship with them and learn from them, they did not drive him away. Palestinians of non-Captivity stock were admitted to the rebuilt Temple (*Ezra* vi:21); Zechariah looked forward to a time when every Jew would have ten assorted Gentile inquirers at his heels (*Zechariah* viii:23). Indeed the Jews of the Second Temple showed less religious exclusiveness than their pagan contemporaries in Greece, where the city-cults were for citizens only, and strangers were debarred.

But hospitality was one thing, evangelism another. Many issues remained. The religion which moved toward definition in the last two pre-Christian centuries, and which the Pharisees proposed to teach to all nations, was by no means simply the religion of Moses or that of Solomon. The stealthy growth which had been going on since the prophets, shaping the pseudepigraphic books and the debates of the Tanna'im, had done more than add details. It had produced something veritably fuller and richer, even among the more restrained elements. This growth was chiefly internal, a working-out of doctrine by Jews for Jews. Yet in some degree also it was a result of the need to cope with a world outside. Some of the new beliefs were common ground. Some were upheld only by the more enterprising, those for whom the outside world really mattered. All were of radical importance.

They owed their being to Israel's ethical monotheism: to the sharpening of its outline and the tragic national paradox which followed from that.

The Lord God stood more than ever alone, in unapproachable holiness and omnipotence. Not only did no other gods exist in fact; no other gods even of the religious imagination could be compared to him. That conviction was solidly based. Zoroaster's creed had sunk into dualism, while in the Hellenistic culture the name "Zeus," though allowed to several chief gods, did not suggest any vital unity, much less uniqueness. Most human beings were polytheistic.

God's existence was still treated by Jews as axiomatic. Philosophical proofs of it were simply not offered. The Hebrew mind functioned, as some might say, existentially rather than metaphysically. When the scriptural "fool" says in his heart "There is no God," he is not stating an abstract proposition—that, to a Jew, would have been meaningless—but a principle of conduct. The fool believes, or wants to believe, that life is lawless and that he will never be called to account for his actions. The only species of atheist recognised by the rabbis was the "Epicurean" to whom God is irrelevant. "Not inquiry but action is the chief thing," as one sage put it. Except for a few isolated and suspect intellectuals, the nearest the Jews came to proving God was by an appeal to experience. Long before the Pharisees, this mode of thinking had brought Israel closer to the famous "verification principle" than any other ancient people. God was held to be proved in practice and by events. When his tribes broke the Covenant he uprooted them from the Land; when they repented he put them back, in a marvellous manner which heathen wisdom had altogether failed to anticipate. Fire came upon Carmel for Elijah and not for the prophets of Baal. The verse "Taste and see how the Lord is good" points to a similar test of a more profound kind, and has in fact been cited by a writer on logical positivism.

God was absolute and ultimate, the Most High, to quote the title which the Maccabee priesthood inherited from Melchizedek and the pseudepigraphers often reverted to. There was nothing whatsoever, there had never been anything whatsoever, that was not made by him and subject to him. He had created the universe *ex nihilo*, not out of primal matter existing before him, nor in conformity to any law or pattern, other than what his own will prescribed. The Jews came to stress this doctrine as marking his difference from all other deities. Again a study of comparative religion bears them out. Yet their confidence was based more on intuition than on inquiry, more on general ideas as to the world's nature and degree of enlightenment than on knowledge of it in detail. In fact, their notions of it as a physical structure showed little advance on the old standard mythology of the Near East. They clung to that conception of a flat disc-Earth with water all round it and a dome overhead. When they did add further particulars, these took the form of picturesque fables: for instance, that the first piece of solid matter was the future site of the Temple, and that God built Palestine round it, and then the rest of the world round Palestine.

However, if the Earth of rabbinic imagination was still crude and cramped, the heavens had grown with the majesty of the Lord. The *Book of Enoch* has chapters of celestial visions which are vast and crowded in their effect. A schema of later date, inspired by the Roman army, divides the stars into twelve "constellations," each constellation having thirty "hosts," each host thirty "legions," each legion thirty "files," each file thirty "cohorts," each cohort thirty "camps," and each camp 365,000 myriads of stars. This daunting anticipation of the St. Ives riddle gives 1,064,340,000,000,000,000 stars. Here at least, the claim that biblical religion assumes a tiny pre-scientific cosmos turns out to be demonstrably false.

The universe which God had created, he also governed. Nature was orderly, but with the living orderliness of soldiers on parade obeying commands, rather than the lifeless orderliness of a clock left ticking by itself. Hence, one could find room for the miracles of Scripture. God had given his creatures general directives as to how to behave; but he had also given them special instructions to behave otherwise at certain junctures. These exceptions were woven into the world's fabric from the beginning. In the language of myth, God covenanted with the new-made sun that on a single afternoon in the remote future it should stand still for Joshua. A miracle, in Jewish thought, is not a feat of magic deliberately performed by a human being, by a wizard with a secret which he can exploit as he pleases. Miracles are worked by God only. They are divinely ordained exceptions. A man may be described loosely as performing them, but, strictly speaking, the man is merely the occasion for God's action. God may grant miracles to support him or confirm his mission, but the miracles are God's doing, not his. The intelligent person's just scepticism about magic has no bearing on them at all. Furthermore, no appeal to " what usually happens "—the province of the scientist—can, strictly speaking, rule an exception out.

Well-read Jews were aware that the sacred canon raised difficult questions. The theory of miracles was not so much an historical device as one of many attempts to think about the Lord and his ways with men. In the last centuries B.C., Jewish efforts to pierce the *mysterium tremendum* by means of language continued to be diverse and often surprising. God was transcendent, yet also immanent. He was high above us, yet intimately near. To convey his nearness, approval was given to anthropomorphic figures of speech; while because of his unmoved "otherness," it did not matter (it was even good, as ruling out naïve literalism) that these sometimes clashed or sounded incongruous. He could be suggested without being restricted. Israel was his first-born as in *Exodus* iv:22, yet also his betrothed as in *Hosea* ii:19. The *Song of Songs* carried this allusive style to extremes. To pretend that its ecstatic phrases really "mean" only some dull abstraction is mere prudishness. The speakers—Solomon and the girl and the other voices that break in—mean what they say. Yet the whole drama of earthly love echoes the heavenly. The *Song* is surely the boldest of theological works, and one of the hardest to refute. When St. Thomas Aquinas, enlightened from beyond the world, dismissed his encyclopaedic writings as so much straw, he could still find it in his heart to compose a commentary on this marvellous thing.

Love, indeed, was moving into the forefront of Jewish thought. The rabbis declared that Earth was made for Man, in spite of his smallness. They perceived that size is no measure of importance. Creation in their teaching was good, life was good; God was our heavenly Father, a title foreshadowed in the Pentateuch but not quite explicit till *Jeremiah* xxxi:9 ("I am a father to Israel"). Granted such a bond, the precept in *Deuteronomy* vi:5 to love the Lord now stood out from all others as the master-commandment. God's purpose in creation was to multiply responsible beings in this community of sonship; so with the great commandment there went another, "You shall love your neighbour as yourself," strangely buried in *Leviticus* xix:18. Its freshness under the changed circumstances lay in a widening of definition. While conservatives said that "neighbour" meant simply "fellow-Israelite," Hillel and others extended it to all mankind.

Law was therefore the ordering and systematisation of love.[2] However seemingly complex, it was rooted in that one principle. God, the Lord of history, ruled in justice and mercy over the destinies of all peoples, and all could be his friends through that Torah which one people had accepted.

2 St. Augustine's maxims "Love and do what you will," and "Virtue is the ordering of love," are entirely in keeping with the best of Jewish teaching.

Plainly the doctrine of God's world-rule was, so to say, a gigantic pearl which had grown gradually round the Israelite claim to Palestine. It contrasted starkly with the impersonality of Greece. The Jewish scheme of things allowed movement and progress. God was not confined, nor was Man condemned, to self-cancelling ups and downs such as Herodotus pictured, or the cosmic rotation of the Stoics. Though God's will might really be fixed in an unchangeable eternity, the unfolding of that will in time could be viewed from any human standpoint as an intelligible series of fiats. It was "as if" God were an infinitely wise, powerful sovereign. His acts made sense . . . if you could see deep enough.

But perceptive Jews had learnt all too painfully that you had to see very deep. He did not respond at all promptly to compliance with his will. In the lives of individuals, the good palpably did suffer and the wicked flourish. In the lives of nations, God could not be relied on to show his favour by giving the most prosperity to pious and law-abiding states. The riddle of evil was baffling, and on the whole the Jews were too honest to pretend that they had fully solved it. Their stress on the community helped them a little. The innocent sufferer might be undergoing punishment for an ancestor's wickedness; in other words the community, through its present representatives, might be making amends for sins committed through its past representatives. Again, some tended to insist that we can never see far enough, and, above all, to invoke time. God spared the wicked because he was patient. Their impunity was a revelation of his mercy. It was not, however, a denial of his justice. When the whole tale of the world was complete, it would be apparent that every man had received his deserts. One day God's goodness would be patent to all. Israel would emerge into the sunshine and prove to have been right all along.

The question was, how and when. Fundamentally the Jews' answer to every discouragement was "faith." God moved in a mysterious way, and, somehow, he would save his own if they were worthy. But still . . . when? Four centuries had crawled by since the rescue from Babylon. By comparison with the times of Ahab and Ahaz, Israel was pure, idolatry was negligible—yet was the golden age any closer? How to account for the bitter contrast between the Jews' tremendous theology and their national ignominy?

More and more it came to be felt that the course of history as known hitherto could never bring things out to a fair issue. Some factor or factors which would revalue the past, and give reason for expecting a future unlike it, had still to be found. With that belief a new preoccupation grew up, which affected not only the non-biblical literature but the last additions to the Jewish Bible itself, and, through both, the spirit of Israel's nationalism. This was an interest in the Unseen: in the affairs of a realm of superhuman forces, a mighty context encompassing the visible world. As above, so below. Events in various heavens and hells were invoked to supply the key to history which history itself withheld, to put disaster finally in its place and give substance to the hopes of Israel. In the attempts to delineate this Over-World, some of the imagery of anathematised myth began most curiously to creep back.

4

There arose, mainly after the stimulus of the Maccabee outbreak, a species of writing known as Apocalyptic. The word implies a revelation of secrets, the hidden counsels of the Lord. This literature was unofficial, but not disloyal to orthodoxy, which it professed to extend, not to undermine or supplant. It was much read and much discussed. We find that modified versions of the authors' concepts, and of the doctrines which they present, begin after a while to appear in more reputable quarters. Many (though not all) of the teachers of Israel begin to talk in similar language.

Outside Scripture, most of the pseudepigraphic works contain sections which belong to this genre. The *Book of Jubilees* has a trace only. The *Book of Enoch* and the *Testaments of the Twelve Patriarchs* are the chief early instances. Afterwards come wilder and weaker fantasies, in books fathered on Baruch, Ezra, even Adam. The standard apocalyptic programme is that the pseudo-author describes a series of visions of supernal realities, which enable him to foretell events after his own time, in a mixture of plain statement, symbol and rhetoric. The climax is a world-transformation and final triumph of Israel through special and violent divine action. Much of this writing is marred by an inherent lack of integrity. The "prediction" is largely bogus, because, at the true date of composition, most of the events have already happened. Similarly the faked medieval prophecies of Mother Shipton, concocted in the middle of the nineteenth century, foretell such phenomena as railways—and then, unfortunately, fix the year 1881 for the end of the world.

Apocalypse is a growth out of canonical prophecy; as witness the hints and foretastes in the later portions of Scripture itself. The sombre threatenings of Joel, and his sketch (iii:18-19) of topographical changes like Ezekiel's, are essays in this manner. So are some of the appendices to *Zechariah*. Chapters xxiv-xxvii of *Isaiah* seem to be a kindred interpolation dating from the third century B.C. But the outstanding case is the *Book of Daniel*, which is the prototype, and largely the source, of other apocalypses.

Daniel is not classed as prophecy by Jews. Its place is among the mixed Sacred Writings. The main apocalyptic parts, here as hereafter, are pseudepigraphic and illusorily predictive. Cast into its present form under Antiochus Epiphanes, the book tells the story of one of the captives in Babylon, giving long dream-interpretations and "visions" which he is made to recount in the first person. Daniel himself is puzzling. The Ras Shamra tablets mention "Danel," a Canaanite sage or demigod. Ezekiel names "Daniel" with Job and Noah—both non-Israelites—as proverbial for righteousness, and "Daniel" by himself as proverbial for wisdom (xiv:14, xxviii:3). *Jubilees* introduces him as the father-in-law of Enoch. But while this Daniel may be the same as Danel, he is not the same as the hero of the book. Perhaps the captive was a person named after the sage, and famous in folk-tradition.

Daniel's flair for scholarship wins him a post at Babylon as a royal seer. Nebuchadnezzar has a dream which Daniel expounds when the Babylonian soothsayers cannot: a dream about a tall image with a head of gold, a body silver above and brass below, legs of iron, and feet of iron mingled with clay. A stone strikes its feet overthrowing it, and grows to a huge size. The head, Daniel explains, is the King of Babylon himself; the other parts of the image are three other political powers which will come after him; the stone is a divine kingdom which will replace and outlast the rest.

Nebuchadnezzar's four dream-kingdoms are the Babylonian, the Median, the Persian, and the Greek. The distinction between the second and third of these is historically awkward, but a careful reading of ii:39-40 shows that it is more or less acceptable. After Nebuchadnezzar's death attention shifts to the "inferior" but briefly dominant realm of the Mede Astyages; then to Cyrus's Persia which "rules over all the earth," absorbing both Media and Babylonia; then to the conquests of Alexander, "breaking all to pieces" like iron, and creating an empire of mixed races that never fuse. The stone, of course, is the ideal Israelite kingdom which God will found on the ruins of the others.

Further on Daniel records visions of his own, confirming and expanding Nebuchadnezzar's. He sees the Greek realm as a dreadful monster with ten horns. Among these a little horn sprouts up, and plucks out three of them. This is Antiochus, whose early successes against various enemies the plucking-out seems to signify. He will "speak words against the Most High, and wear out the saints of the Most High, and think to change the times and the law." He will set up an "abomination that makes desolate"—i.e. an idol in the Temple. But the Lord will interpose, Antiochus's power will collapse, and dominion will be given in perpetuity to "the people of the saints of the Most High." The Jews' trials and their promised salvation are placed against a cosmic background. Kingdoms have guardian angels, and a resurrection of the dead is foretold (xii:1-2).

It is clear from *Daniel*, and from the uncanonical writings related to it, that Greek persecution and the Maccabee revolt played the largest part in inspiring such thrilling dreams. *Daniel* itself was undoubtedly the chief manifesto of the Hasidim. There was indeed a continuing correlation. As long as the Hasmoneans flourished, the apocalypses preserved a certain balance, and had literary and ethical value. When the dynasty declined and the alien Herod came on the scene, all touch with reality was lost, and they grew more fantastic at the same time as they grew more numerous.

Daniel supplied most of the essential themes. Jewish imagination re-applied it, and the events of B.C. 167-164 were seen as archetypal. Antiochus became, in a sense, all persecutors. The horned beast, the phase of ascendant evil, the abomination defiling the sanctuary, were taken up and given fresh meanings. Exegesis of this kind is known as typology. Its practice sheds light on the last creative crises of Jewish religion. An historical person or event in inspired Scripture may be construed as symbolic of another person or event yet to come. Antiochus prefigures a supreme Enemy of God, an Antichrist; but the Antichrist will be more than Antiochus. The old Jerusalem prefigures a new Jerusalem; but the new Jerusalem will be more splendid. The past rescues of Israel by Cyrus and the Maccabees prefigure a final rescue; but the final rescue will be . . . final.

This new scheme of ideas implied a definite mechanism in the movement of history toward a climax. The apocalyptists peered into the Unseen, and detected a more dramatic pattern than the lawgivers or the prophets had ever spoken of. They were not escapists. They never fancied that the justification of God's ways could be entirely transferred to some spiritual Cockaigne outside this world. They placed history's fruition within history, in the shape of a sublime destiny for Israel: a golden age not in a lost past, as with other nations, but in an attainable future. It was the mode of attainment that concerned them, and the belief that liberation could only dawn through a divine intervention, bringing, in effect, the end of the present world and a transformation of all life. Israel could and should work towards its deliverance, could grow to deserve it better and better, but could never actually set it in motion. Several times in the *Testaments* the motif of a theophany occurs. In *Naphtali* viii:3 we are told that "God shall appear on earth to save the race of Israel, and to gather the righteous from among the Gentiles."

That blessing, alas, could not be expected to come painlessly. The last prophets, and those others who took up the theme, projected the cataclysmic doings of Yahweh from the past to the future. Reviving the notion of a Day of the Lord, they approved both the old popular optimism and the contrary warning of Amos. The Day would indeed be terrible, but it would lead to peace. As the Lord had drowned Pharaoh's host and crushed Babylon in her pride, so he would do again, with all Israel's foes, for ever. *Isaiah* xxiv was interpolated in that spirit. Thus likewise Joel and Malachi, and, in post-Maccabean chorus, the apocalyptists, the latter so horrifically that the word "apocalypse" at length came to suggest chiefly doom.

For the assumed hopelessness of the course of history in itself, the apocalyptists gave reasons of a grandiose sort. Endless talk of the Jews' own unworthiness had become a platitude which, by itself, shed no light. Attempts to blame everything on mere mortal failings rang sadly hollow. Hence the discovery of a conflict at the cosmic level, and of superhuman powers ranged against each other, with the darker ones active—by God's forbearance—in thwarting human aspirations.

Angels had been acknowledged for centuries; but now they were given names and relationships and political roles, with Michael as protector of Israel. More important, devils appeared too. The petty demons of immemorial folklore were promoted to the rank of seditious angels, and credited (or rather debited) with a boundless and deliberate malice. At their head stood Satan. His name was a common noun meaning "adversary," and satans were spirits of testing and accusation authorised to make men uneasy. However, once Jewish thought had arrived at Satan with a capital S, the Adversary of God, he began to drop what were assumed to be his disguises and emerge in fearful majesty. With the advent of Satan, and of an evil dragon-monster called Beliar, the ancient War in Heaven found its way into sacred literature after all. The fallen angels were charged with corrupting humanity at or near its source. While no dogma of original sin was fully worked out, a belief grew that Satan and his followers had injected a moral poison into mankind and brought death into the world; that among Adam's descendants the evil tendency is prior, and will prevail unless the good is consciously cultivated—as it usually is not.

When the Lord did act, he would rout the demonic hosts. But Israel's glory would have an additional feature. The victory would be won through a special divine champion, hitherto unrevealed.

This idea took two forms. The first went back to a hint in *Daniel*. Besides the august figure of the Lord himself, the author refers to another character (vii:13-14), "one like a son of man" in the clouds of heaven, to whom an everlasting dominion is given. The Son of Man, human yet more than human, may here be a personification of Israel. But before *Daniel*, Ezekiel had applied the phrase to an individual, namely himself; and in *Enoch* the Son of Man is again a distinct person. He is the Righteous Elect One, a celestial viceroy who will sit enthroned ruling all, judging all, and enlightening the Gentiles.

The Son of Man belongs to supernal regions. But Jewish thought in the Hasmonean era became more deeply engrossed with another being who swam gradually into view through its reveries: the Messiah. We have already glanced at the antecedents of this most potent hero. "Messiah" (in Greek, "Christos") means an anointed person. The rite implied sanctification and consecration, as in *Numbers* vii:1, where Moses pours oil over the Tabernacle and its contents. Saul was anointed as the Israelites' captain and as their monarch. So were all his successors. In the Second Zionist community the High Priest was anointed. Messiahship, however, came to be seen in terms of divine choice rather than ephemeral office-holding, and of religious metaphor rather than the physical pouring of oil. Patriarchs and prophets were said to have been "anointed" figuratively. In Second Isaiah's address to Cyrus, a Messiah for the first time was a designated man with a special commission from the Lord of Hosts, likewise anointed figuratively and not literally.

The struggle against Antiochus and its sequels compelled the Jews to seek once again for secular leadership. Toward 100 B.C.—that is, in the same period as the *Enoch* prophecies of the Son of Man—the Messianic title acquired, under Pharisee influence, a fresh and radical meaning. Israel (it was now proclaimed) could expect *the* Messiah, the Christ, a man anointed of God as none had ever been before. He would be a national leader and deliverer chosen by heaven to bring history out to a just issue. A blend of king, priest and prophet, he would crush Israel's oppressors and place her first among nations. The peace and plenty of his reign, the supersession of the old world and its sorrows, would justify all the agonies that had paved the way there. They would be seen in retrospect as necessary for the moulding of Israel, for its education in worthiness to preside over mankind.

The Messiah, presumably, would be a prince of David's line in the tribe of Judah. That belief had its origins in the blessing of Jacob (*Genesis* xlix:8-12), and in the Lord's message to David by Nathan (*II Samuel* vii:8-17), which pledged that David's house would never be deprived of its sovereignty. So also two of the Psalms. Jeremiah had foretold that Israel would one day find peace under a Davidic ruler, and Ezekiel had also. If God's word were not to fail, David's house must sooner or later be restored for an everlasting future. Its eclipse, however long, could only be an interregnum.

Re-establishment of a local Davidic kingdom was all that the older generations had looked for. But the Messiahship of Cyrus as Israel's liberator had given the first impulse to a more daring trend in speculation, and the Messiahship foretold for the Coming One went further again. In the *Testaments* (Judah xxiv:1) he is "a star arising from Jacob," "a man who shall arise like the sun of righteousness," with a universal reign ardently portrayed. In the *Psalms of Solomon*, where the explicit title of "Anointed" occurs first (xvii:23-36, xviii:6-8), he is to be "girded with strength" to "shatter unrighteous rulers."

With such a secret in their pockets, Jews inevitably tried to improve on it, and spell out the divine programme. Many asked when the Messiah would arrive. On this point commentators exerted their ingenuity with enthusiasm. Calculation of the type they indulged in, which is by no means extinct, mostly goes back to Jeremiah's prophecy of the seventy years. In the ninth chapter of *Daniel* the seventy years are re-interpreted as seventy "weeks of years," that is, 490 in all. This long period is connected in some obscure way with the vicissitudes of the High Priesthood. At the end—whenever it does end—an upheaval is to follow. Pseudo-Daniel's re-working of Jeremiah was anxiously discussed, and his own list of empires was scrutinised in its turn. After Rome's entry the fourth empire was sometimes asserted to be the Roman instead of the Greek. Those of a less conjectural temper inclined to the theory that no Messianic day had been set, and that the advent could be advanced or retarded by the conduct of Israel. It would come as the reward of piety.

Besides the guessing about dates, there was guessing about the Messiah himself. The author of the *Testaments* imagined that John Hyrcanus actually was the Anointed One, although, being of the tribe of Levi, John was not a descendant of David. But the author was a Pharisee, and Hyrcanus's quarrel with the Pharisees dispelled his delusion. Another theory was that the Messiah would be King Hezekiah returned, like King Arthur. Another was that he had been born already, on the day when the Babylonians burned the Temple, and that God chose to wait before revealing him openly. This curiously haunting myth has been resurrected by a number of modern rabbis as the true doctrine, in the sense that the scattering of the Jews launched their mission among the nations, the Messiah being a personification of it. Such a notion, however, could not commend itself to many when it was possible to hope for a spectacular saviour yet to be born. Catastrophe might follow catastrophe without quenching that hope: the sufferings of the Jews and of mankind at large could be regarded as the "birth-pangs of the Messiah," the darkest hour before sunrise; and then there was only a step to a kind of *politique du pire*, a conviction that the Messiah never would come till the last limit of horror had been reached.³ But further disappointments were to be undergone before that step was taken. In the days of the Hasmoneans and Herod, the triumph of Israel could be dreamed of as something close.

At the heart of the excitement lurked a flaw, an incoherence. All Jews under these influences foresaw a world-revolution ordained by God, but they did not all distribute the emphasis in the same way. The vision of the hundred-per-cent apocalyptists was an inflated fantasy about the Lord's mighty deeds, with antecedents in *Exodus* and *Isaiah*. The Messianic hope, rooted in other portions of Israel's experience, was more welcome in responsible circles and also more mundane. As a rule the Messiah was not pictured in an apocalyptic setting. Nor was he pictured as a wonder-worker or divine being, transcending humanity and acting independently of the efforts of Israel.

The founding of the earthly Kingdom of God might indeed be the Messiah's work. But then again it might be the work of the celestial Son of Man. Strangely enough there is no certain evidence that any Jewish mind, down to the last years of Herod, ever identified them. In *Enoch* xlviii:10 the Son of Man is "the Lord's Anointed," and it may well be that the two figures did coalesce, but proof is lacking. One school of thought tried to fit everything in by elaborating the programme, and treating the Messiah's reign as a phase rather than a completion. According to this view (not found among the earlier rabbis) a temporary Davidic commonwealth would come first and an apocalyptic End afterwards. Further complications were prompted by *Deuteronomy* xviii:15-19 and *Malachi* iv:5. Besides the Messiah, God might send a new prophet after all as herald and forerunner, or he might summon the immortal Elijah from his haven of concealment.

But all these eager anticipations looked toward a World to Come, whether conceived as the Messianic Age or as a subsequent glory for which that age would prepare. The World to Come was an immense iridescent daydream in which everyone saw what he

3 See André Schwarz-Bart's novel *The Last of the Just*, p. 49.

wished to see: peace and plenty, or national freedom, or military success, or a reign of righteousness. Poetic yearning embroidered the fabric of the vision with gorgeous images. The whole community of Israel—even perhaps the lost tribes, cleansed of apostasy and regrafted to the stock of the faithful—would be assembled in its own Land. Jerusalem, rebuilt and bejewelled, would be the world capital. The sun would shine brighter; a stream of lustral water would flow from Zion; waste places would blossom, and ruined cities be restored; living creatures would cease to harm each other; Satan would be vanquished. At some stage in this universal healing, God would pronounce judgment on mankind, awarding each his deserts. Israel and the Gentiles, the righteous and the wicked, would thus be put in their true relationship.

Thence a problem arose about the millions who had already expired, the saints unrewarded and the sinners unpunished. It was no longer possible (especially in Hellenistic society) to rest content with an immortal collective body in which the individual life did not count. Jewish logic pressed forward relentlessly. The death of these millions was incompatible with divine justice, therefore they had not died. Or at least, their death was not permanent. Dead men would live again in the World to Come, and the second life would redress the inequities of the first. This doctrine was not pure salvationism. It promised no discarnate spiritual destiny in heaven or hell. The un-dualistic Hebrew mind moved only slowly toward belief in a soul able to exist apart from the body. "Living again" meant bodily resurrection. This had been hinted at by a few before the apocalyptic era, but now it grew popular. It was a daring deduction not approved by the Sadducees, who denied that the Torah gave any warrant for it. However, the Pharisees upheld it, and from them the Resurrection of the Dead passed into the teaching of most rabbis.

Who exactly would rise, they did not agree. The tendency over the years was to broaden scope. At first it was predicted that the righteous of Israel would be restored to life and enjoy their reward in an almost empty world; Gentiles would remain in the dust, and so would Jews if they were unworthy. Later the Resurrection was extended to bad Jews as well as good, and began to include punishment as well as reward, as in *Daniel* xii:2. Later still it was extended again, to human beings in general. This final step, taken in the *Testaments* (Benjamin x:8), was never unanimous.

As to the mechanics of the Resurrection, and of the Judgment ensuing, various theories were entertained. It would happen when the Messiah came, but the dead would be raised by Elijah, in Palestine. God would transport them all to the Holy Land by miraculous means. So some said; others demurred. Speculation as to who would have the best chance of happiness, and which Gentiles would qualify, led to debates without resolution. Nor was real agreement reached as to the ultimate destiny and abode of mankind. Jewish thought evolved the concepts of a heaven for human beings, Gan Eden, and a hell, Gehinnom; but not in the ethereal sense familiar among Christians. Both were geographical regions, either existing or in preparation. Gan Eden lay eastward, Gehinnom westward, and pre-eminent saints and sinners would go off accordingly. However, only in late and decadent literature do we find these places depicted with the sort of gaudy description that repels and makes ridiculous. In their more creative days the Jews felt no need for such fairy-tales. Their best minds cherished a faith summed up for all time in a great rabbinic saying: "The Holy One gave three gifts to Israel—Torah, the Land of Israel, and the World to Come; and all of them through suffering."

5

We can now formulate the ninth step in the logic running through the Jewish experience.

The questions posed by the situation were:

Why this anti-climax? Why are so many of us still scattered abroad? And why hasn't everything come right in the Land itself, in spite of all our penitence and purification?

The answers arrived at were:

As to the scattering: To make our people missionaries among the Gentiles. We are called to play an active part in guiding them to the true God.

As to the Land: Our disappointments are partly the work of strong forces of demonic evil, hitherto hardly suspected and not yet beaten; partly a lesson that the Lord's ways are not ours. We can't set the world to rights—or compel him to do so—entirely by our own actions. In his own good time he will establish justice and bring us out in triumph, but through a special intervention, a consummation of history transcending the normal course of events. Then the dead will rise and the world will be transformed.

Out of these meditations, prolonged through four or five centuries, "Judaism" emerged as a world faith. In its full credo we are on familiar ground. Judaism in the last pre-Christian century is recognisable. It is the noble but incomplete religion which Jesus is held by Christians to have completed. To sum up, it affirms a single righteous God, creator of all things; a fallen and hostile spiritual power, Satan, with demonic helpers; the perversity of mankind due to sin at its origin; the immortality of the individual, with a happy or unhappy fate according to his relationship with God; an eventual divine triumph through the historical agency of a Saviour, and an end of the present state of the world; bodily resurrection and a last judgment, with a new universe; moral law in the context of these beliefs; and a duty incumbent on the faithful to spread God's earthly reign.

All of which was far more novel then than it looks in retrospect. Christians who set forth their own Jewish-derived orthodoxy on more or less the foregoing lines are apt to assume that it is simply "the religion of the Bible," Old Testament as well as New. Impartial study of the Old Testament is fatal to that assumption. The tenets listed are scarcely traceable there at all, and not one of them appears indisputably in a passage earlier than Second Isaiah. The sages of Judaism inherited the Law and the Prophets, but this doctrinal system to which they accommodated the text is not explicit in either. It is at most latent in the form of symbols and types, a cryptogram to be deciphered. The decipherment may be said to have begun with Second Isaiah's exhortation to Cyrus . . . and to have continued, startlingly enough, along the same quasi-Zoroastrian path.

Consider the articles of the creed item by item.

The categorical statement that no other gods exist but Yahweh occurs for the first time in the Cyrus text. Zoroaster's assertion of the solitary Wise Lord who thinks all beings into existence, even saying (very nearly) "Let there be light," antedates the Hebrew prophet.

The Old Testament mentions Satan in only three passages (*I Chronicles* xxi:1, *Zechariah* iii:1-2, and the *Job* prologue). All are post-Exilic. Even these do not quite stand up under scrutiny. Direct diabolism is hard to establish. The Prince of Darkness is so meagre a character in canonical Jewish Scripture that his niche in Judaism has never been secure. But in Zoroaster's teaching, there is no doubt whatever about Angra Mainyu, the mighty spirit who chose The Lie and became evil.

The Adamic dogma of original sin corresponds to no plain statement in the Old Testament. There are many expressions of human wickedness and abasement, as in other ancient literatures, but nothing links depravity firmly with the Fall. Again, however, something akin to the doctrine is to be found in Zoroastrianism.

Then, as to death itself. To anyone with a grounding in real or nominal Christianity, one of the most surprising discoveries to be made in the Old Testament is that it has no message about immortality. Nor, except in a few late passages, does it envisage an end to the present state of the world, or a radical transformation of earthly life, or a Messiah. Indeed the word "Messiah" is never employed in it at all with the familiar sense. Prophecies of the Last Judgment are post-Exilic. The Resurrection is mentioned once unambiguously in the late book *Daniel*. *Isaiah* xxvi:19 is an interpolation, also late. *Job* xix:26 is obscure and also late. Much earlier, however, Zoroastrianism had its heaven and hell, its coming saviour Saoshyans, its general resurrection, its Last Judgment, its end of the world, its new creation.

Lastly, the idea of a mission to convert all mankind originates for Israel with Second Isaiah. It is not discoverable in older layers of Scripture. But it does appear earlier in Zoroaster's hymns.

Thus the shapers of Judaism, striving to come to terms with the sombre facts of history, waded out into deep waters. They professed to be elaborating a cosmic religion in fidelity to Zion; and it turned out, when elaborated, to bear an uncanny likeness to the Good Religion of Iran. Their Judaism, for the moment at least, was almost a sect of Zoroastrianism.

The most obvious question is how these foreign beliefs—if they were foreign—could have been learnt. One would suspect Mesopotamia, the preaching of wandering Magi during the captivity, the digestion of Persian doctrines afterwards by Jews who remained there, and transmission by the companions of Nehemiah and Ezra. Second Isaiah, prophesying in Babylon under Cyrus's shadow, is the first Hebrew to talk Zoroastrian language; Daniel, when portrayed as receiving revelations about angels and the Resurrection and the Last Judgment, is also portrayed as still in Babylon serving the Persian rulers. A single recorded rabbinic saying—that "the names of the angels were brought by the Jews from Babylonia"—shows that the rabbis did admit acquisitions in this area.

But in any case the oddity is that this Jewish "Zoroastrianism" should only have emerged centuries later, after the Persian civilisation had dissolved and the Good Religion itself had become corrupted. It is a tempting guess that a "Zoroastrian" school had existed among the Jews from the Captivity onward. This remained subdued and ineffectual, until the drawn-out disappointment of the return, and the crises consequent on Antiochus, led to so much drastic re-thinking. Then it came into its own, drawing fresh energy perhaps from Hellenistic ideas about immortality, but impelled

chiefly, like so much else, by the course of events in the Land of
Israel.

On this showing the apocalyptists were not innovators. The
ground had been prepared for them. And that is why apocalyptic
motifs do enter the main public stream of Judaism, despite their
lurid presentation and shabby credentials. They had been current
quietly for hundreds of years, and when a changed situation made
them attractive, any of them could be supported with a tradition
that the respected scribe So-and-So had taught something of the
kind.

Such a conjecture fits in with the attitude taken by the rabbis
themselves, which is most intriguing, and depends on a certain
view of the Torah.

Axiomatically the Torah was God's word, perfect and sufficient
if properly understood. No scholar ever maintained that it could be
tampered with; that any part of it was not inspired; or that any
doctrine could be held binding which was not in it. As we observed,
however, the Great Assembly and the Tanna'im always acknowledged that the Torah needed interpretation. Hence the activity of
Midrash—elucidation by way of comment and case-law—which
was going on, mainly orally, all through the generations after
Ezra. Nobody offered the fruits of Midrash as total novelties. The
claim was not that something had been invented, but that something
(buried treasure, so to speak) had been lifted to the surface. The
seven rules of Hillel all had this intention. Oral tradition accumulated into a bulky mass, and one major split between Pharisee and
Sadducee was over the status that ought to be given to it. The
Pharisees—popular, forward-looking, lofty in their conception of
what Judaism should mean—argued that the oral tradition had
authority in itself. The Sadducees—rich, close to the Temple,
minimisers—did not. For them, only the Pentateuch, the Torah
par excellence, was God's word. Anything not explicit in the writings
ascribed to Moses himself was a matter of opinion, not doctrine.

Now it was within this doubtful zone of interpretation and oral
authority that quasi-Zoroastrian teaching finally took root. The

best known of several instances is the Resurrection. The Sadducee minority made a stand against it, and so did the Samaritan heretics, who lived in their own backwater away from the currents of active Jewish thought. Between these incongruous groups the one link was their common allegiance to the Pentateuch alone. Such Fundamentalism presented the Pharisees with a problem. They could scarcely pretend that the Resurrection was affirmed in the five books of Moses. Yet if a dogma so important were true, it ought surely to be there. They and their disciples accordingly tried to prove that it was there by implication. It was a truth which Moses knew, and though he preferred not to commit it to writing, his choice of words sometimes presupposed it: as Midrash could demonstrate. Thus, in *Numbers* xviii:28, a law intended to be perpetual enjoined that an offering be given to "Aaron the priest." How could that be done after Aaron's death if there was no prospect of his ever coming back to claim it? Again in *Deuteronomy* xxxii:39, the Lord said "I kill and I make alive, I wound and I heal." Was not that a hint that he would restore the dead to life free from blemish?

Reasoning of this kind could detect other controversial matters in the Mosaic text. The four senses of Scripture were now beginning to be distinguished: the literal, the allegorical, the didactic or moral, and the esoteric or mystical. Yet however fair this drawing-out of the latent might be, it remained debatable. A doctrine like the Resurrection could not be insisted on if the process of inference and interpretation—the oral tradition—were merely human. It could not claim a firm basis unless the oral tradition itself were inspired and divinely guaranteed like the sacred text.

So it was declared to be. At some uncertain stage, the theory of an Oral Torah took shape. Pharisaic scholars said tradition had equal weight with Scripture. The Oral Torah, moreover, was not actually recent at all. God had communicated it to Moses at Sinai, and Moses had passed it on to Joshua.

This teaching was subtle and elusive. The Oral Torah could not mean the entire body of Midrash, which manifestly had grown up over the years, and was full of discrepancies. It meant, rather, a system of ideas and rules by which the growth could be safely guided. What these were, the historian can never be sure, because one of the rules was that the Oral Torah must not be written down. Codified, it would become rigid, and then the life and adaptability would leak out. This mystique of the Oral Torah was invoked to justify apparently new teachings, and, by implication at least, the technique that saddled Enoch and others with strange things which they "would have" said. It was, and is, inseparable from Judaism. For three hundred years it waxed steadily in importance. Some at last maintained that the Oral was superior to the Written Torah. Some maintained that the eternal uniqueness of Israel lay in possessing it. Even when the Gentiles had the Written Torah, the Jews would still have the Oral as their secret wisdom, and share it with nobody.

The Sadducees of course had no use for it, and the Pharisees were its custodians. Hillel proved its necessity to a sceptical student by telling him to read letters written on a strip of papyrus, and then asking how he knew which was which; the unavoidable answer being that his teachers had told him, by word of mouth. Certainly the simplest solution of the Zoroastrian puzzle is that the Pharisees were right, at least in part. The Resurrection, the Last Judgment, and so on, were contained in—or assimilable to—a long-standing oral tradition commanding high respect. One noteworthy suggestion is that the name "Pharisee" itself has nothing to do with separation, being cognate with the Zoroastrian sect-name "Parsee" and meaning "Persian." But the origins are lost in mist. Second Isaiah may be the key figure or he may not. Again, conceivably Zoroaster himself was taught by some genius from the deported northern tribes, and the Zoroastrian tenets were Israelite tenets after all, coming home by a circuitous route.

Whatever it borrowed, whatever it rediscovered, the Jewish world-religion was an extraordinary birth. It was continuous with the old religion of Israel, but not the same. To construe it as a monstrosity spawned by rationalisation and wishful thinking is plausible up to a point . . . but up to a point only. Leopold von Ranke remarked that we often encounter something evasive in history, an unexplained residuum, an impression of hidden forces at work. Judaism, whether divine or not, is a supreme instance. *Omnia abeunt in mysterium.*

Unless Zoroaster was a crypto-Israelite, the Jews' adoption of his ideas raised a profound question. If these teachings were mere speculation, what value had they? If they were truths revealed by God, then God had revealed them to a Gentile in Persia—and what became of Israel's exclusive status, and the unique presence of God in Palestine? Little remains to show directly how that issue was faced, beyond a bare rabbinic admission of the existence of Gentile prophets, Balaam and Job being the leading names. The logic of the situation, however, plainly called for a theory of fulfilment or endorsement. Jews were bound to confess that the Gentiles were not entirely benighted. Among many superstitions they harboured some truths. These, when they were paralleled in the Written Torah, received a stamp of approval disentangling them from the surrounding error. Even when they were not, they could be singled out and corrected and adapted to the Lord's service by applying the Oral Torah. Judaism transcended Gentile wisdom indeed, but also perfected it.

When we turn to the Jews of the diaspora, who lived in everyday contact with the Gentile world, we do find that such reflections were entertained.

CHAPTER TEN

WISDOM AND HER PEOPLE

Pharisees on Mount Zion could exchange generalities as they pleased about the Gentiles' conversion; but the actual process, if any, depended on Jewish-Gentile relationships in other countries. To the Jews of the diaspora, Jerusalem remained the world's spiritual capital. The question was whether they could persuade those around them to view the Holy City in the same manner, and accept the implications.

As Persia declined, the thinking pagan came more and more to mean the Greek, or ar any rate the pagan under Greek influence. By the close of the fourth century B.C. Alexander's victories had planted Hellenic civilisation throughout most of the known world, and thereafter the Jews met it everywhere. In northern Palestine there was now a growing overspill of Greeks and Greek-speaking Syrians from the flourishing borderlands. A brisk movement of traders furnished abundant contacts with Greece itself, Asia Minor and Mesopotamia. Cities that became prominent hereabouts during the next centuries, such as Antioch, were meeting-places of Jew and Gentile. Beyond, in Mesopotamia itself, large communities descended from the unreturned exiles mingled freely with the merchants and civil servants of the Seleucid empire. Along all the routes opened up by Alexander, Jews were gradually spreading farther and farther as opportunity offered, often migrating in groups that kept their identity.

Antiochus IV notwithstanding, the Greek dynasties that succeeded to Alexander's domains were on the whole friendly to them. That was particularly true of Egypt. Under the auspices of Ptolemy

Lagi (who had ideas about holding the Egyptians down) a big Jewish population was allotted a district in Alexandria. Here Jews could live in their own fashion and enjoy an equal status with Greeks. Another Ptolemy granted asylum to Onias, son of the murdered High Priest of the same name, and let him build a rival temple at Leontopolis, invoking *Isaiah* xix:19 in justification. But most of the Seleucids were also kindly disposed. Antiochus III, "the Great," transplanted two thousand Jewish families from Babylonia to western Asia Minor to join others already there, and gave them favoured treatment in their new and more agreeable home. These Hellenistic kings rather liked Jews, who made good soldiers, and they employed them for garrison duty in well-endowed military colonies.

As civilians too the Jews were above average. Their chief occupations were socially useful ones such as agriculture. They were not then noted at all for financial or huckstering activities. Through each working week they applied themselves diligently, and on the Sabbath they assembled for prayer in their synagogues.

Their pagan neighbours had certain reasons for sympathy. Hellenistic society was groping toward a world religion as the tiny Greek city-states had never done. A civilisation uniting many peoples had inspired the vision of a Cosmopolis, a world order. Stoic philosophers were talking of cosmic law—of *Nous*, of the *Logos*, of the Divine Reason. Theological syncretists were blending all chief gods into a single infinitely magnificent Zeus, all chief goddesses into a single Mighty Mother. Alexander's brief empire never actually was reassembled; but when Rome acquired most of it, and combined that portion with western provinces into a realm that almost was a Cosmopolis (at least in extent), the same spirit of religion or religiosity continued to flourish. Romans like Cicero were attracted to Greek Stoicism, which harmonised with the patrician virtues of *gravitas* and *pietas*. Stoics like Posidonius, for their part, cemented the alliance by ascribing the Romans' victory to their special reverence for the gods. The Roman Empire was not, as is sometimes imagined, a purely secular creation. It was religious from its inception, and the later attempts to hold it together by a universal cult of the Emperor or the Sun were not aberrations but logical developments.[1]

Thus, both in the Hellenistic culture and in the Hellenistic-plus-Roman culture that succeeded it, the Jews had at least the potentiality of a hearing. They had long been saying things which were not unlike what Athenians and Egyptians and Syrians were learning to say. Greece indeed meant an inheritance of scepticism. But it also meant Plato, it also meant the Divine Reason of the Stoics, it also meant a Father Zeus of increasing grandeur and comprehensiveness. The atmosphere—for a time—was good. In some places it was very good. The Phrygian Jews of Asia Minor were admitted to high office, including even the local priesthood; while the pagans of those parts adopted biblical stories into their own mythology, and struck coins with pictures of Noah's Ark. A few Greek authors frankly attest a fascination which the Jews had for them. Respect might not lead to understanding, but respect existed.

These authors were not impartial investigators. All of them influenced by Plato and Aristotle, they were searching in the opened-up East for a social order that would bear out the philosophers' theories. What they wanted to find was an aristocracy of wisdom and virtue. Hence they became interested in the Magi, and in the Brahmins. They also became interested in the Jews, whose theocracy they interpreted somewhat freely to suit their own wishes. It heartened them to discover a whole people who rejected divine images and worshipped a solitary "God of Heaven." That title does occur in a few late biblical texts such as *Ezra* i:2 and *Daniel* ii:44. It fitted into the Greek inquirers' vocabulary, and they picked it up.

In the hopeful mood thus induced, Aristotle's literary executor Theophrastus writes of the Jews as a "philosophical race," and says they spend their festival nights contemplating the stars. Clearchus asserts that they are descended from the wise men of India,

[1] On the Cosmopolis and the Graeco-Roman ideology, see Sir Ernest Barker, *From Alexander to Constantine.*

and portrays a Jew arguing for the soul's immortality in the style of Plato. Hermippus, another Aristotelian, also alleges a Jewish belief in immortality, and maintains that Pythagoras learned the doctrine partly from that source. (These allusions, at a date before any known Jewish writings on the subject, would seem to support the claims about an oral tradition.)

Hecataeus of Abdera regards the Law as a constitution for an ideal state governed by priest-sages. Moses, he explains, based his system on courage, discipline and endurance. He organised the conquest of Palestine in order to plant a commonwealth there—not a bad summary, in humanised terms, of what we met with on page [129] as the fourth step in Israel's logic. Hecataeus discerns Jewish perfectionism in the decree restraining the sale of land (*Leviticus* xxv:23), which he construes as aimed against concentration of wealth; also in the Jews' abhorrence of pagan altars on their holy soil, and in the contempt shown for pagan superstition by those in diaspora.

But the conspicuous point about all these passages is that they are early in date. They were written before the Jews formed a large element of the population outside a few restricted areas. When they spread abroad in serious numbers, pagan feelings toward them tended to cool. Educated men were less inclined to praise them as philosophic Utopians. Among the masses, and despite the royal patronage, popular anti-Semitism was born. Alexandria witnessed outbreaks of violence; the Egyptian priest Manetho, retorting perhaps to the annual affront of Passover, composed his scandalous version of the Exodus; a long ridicule of the Sabbath began; and a certain Mnaseas launched the famous rumour that the Holy of Holies contained an image of a donkey adored by the priests with degraded rites.

Pagans, in short, were prepared to treat Jews with respect just so long as this respect could stay passive and academic. Where weight of numbers made Israel a public challenge and censure rather than a mere curiosity, attitudes hardened and ranks closed. To most people aware of it at all, the Jewish religion was either a theme for dilettante discussion or a nasty superstition. It was not in either case a source of ideas.

The scattered Jews could never hope to convert others unless they could breach this barrier and effect contact with Gentile minds. In their efforts to come to terms with the civilisation round them, they struck against problems which the Greeks, looking at them from outside, did not. They believed in their own rightness and vocation with a seriousness which ruled out dilettantism. But precisely because of this belief, they could not simply leave paganism alone. They had a duty to understand it, to make sense of it, to fit it into their scheme. Nor could it be dealt with summarily by anathemas, like the corruptions of Canaan. These Gentiles at least were not crude idolaters, expendable victims of the Day of the Lord. The thoughtful Jew in diaspora confronted what was plainly a higher culture than his, a literature of equal excellence and wider horizons, a body of philosophic teaching with affinities to the inspired wisdom of Israel's own teachers. He confronted Plato and Aristotle and Homer and Herodotus and Euripides. In what his ancestors had supposed to be outer darkness, away from the Land and the Lord's presence, he found not darkness at all but light; and beside it the light of Zion itself might sometimes look paler. The Israelite ideological map, already damaged, was in danger of being turned inside out. This then was a crisis, and he had to decide what to do about it.

He might do a great deal . . . too much, indeed. He might desert or play down his own heritage and ape the Greeks. In Palestine itself, which was not untouched by the crisis, the "Hellenisers" were often wealthy men of the type who eventually took the name of Sadducees. It sounds paradoxical in view of their close links with the Temple. But the insistence of such people on the literal sense of the written Pentateuch, and nothing but that, left them free in all matters which it did not cover. Hence they could mingle at will with congenial pagan gentlemen, and let the disreputable Pharisees go their own way with their vulgar improvements.

Outside the Holy Land, some Jews Hellenised completely like the collaborationists described in *Maccabees*, dropping the ritual and ceremonial altogether. However, this tendency died out leaving only the faintest traces. A far more powerful growth was Hellenistic Judaism: that is, Judaism which enriched and strengthened itself from foreign sources without making any vital surrender. Ultimately, throughout the East, Jewish culture alone proved able to meet classical culture head-on and keep its own character.

It did not do so without heart-searching and adaptation. To a people whose sole achievement lay in the realm of ideas, Greek philosophy in particular was disturbing to face. It contrasted violently with the beliefs of Israel, yet neither its critical scepticism nor its poetic creativity could be ignored. Some tried doggedly to argue that everything of value in Greek thought had been copied from Moses. Others were more receptive and more constructive. Jews of this latter sort evolved their own variety of Judaism, which finally combined with that of the Pharisees, but only after a brilliant separate development; and Hellenistic Judaism was this movement in its later stages.

At first it was not specifically Greek in spirit. The influence showed itself merely in a certain detachment, a certain questioning, a certain disengagement from Law and Prophets. Its earliest literary products were not composed in the diaspora but in Palestine—in a Palestinian milieu opened up, however, to the unsettling impressions from beyond.

2

Out of this reflective, rational Judaism came, in the first place, the "Wisdom" books. These had mixed antecedents. In ancient Egypt, in Babylon and in Canaan, there had been sages who uttered maxims and parables. A few persons resembling them appear far back in the Bible: Jotham, for instance, with his fable of the trees (*Judges* ix : 7-15). Solomon of course was pre-eminently and proverbially " wise." Hellenism turned the attention of several Jewish writers to this neglected strand of Israel's tradition.

Through them the abstract Wise Man took substance as a moral model. He was akin to the perfect scribe in that he knew much, and thought much about what he knew. But his concentration was less intense. He strove, by the use of reason, to order his life in keeping with the cardinal virtues, prudence, justice, temperance, and fortitude. Authors who upheld this ideal enjoyed drawing instructive contrasts between the Wise Man and his counterpart the Fool. It should not be fancied that they were trying to arrive at a purely humanist ethic. Atheism was out of the question for them. They traced their spiritual ancestry to Solomon, and their wise men and fools were very like the righteous and evil-doers of the older terminology. It was chiefly the point of view that differed. The wise man was righteous because he discerned the right way and chose correctly. He was a Jewish embodiment of the moral teaching of Socrates. But he was still Jewish.

Wisdom went with knowledge, and the original notion was one of enlightenment or elucidation. The oldest specimen of Wisdom literature is the *Book of Job*. Here Israelite beliefs are analysed by Edomite characters, in a long dialogue-plus-theophany probably indebted to Greek drama. *Job*, in other words, is a work of synthesis and a work of transition. Written towards 400 B.C. by a Jew who had travelled, it draws in several of the themes which were beginning to disturb his compatriots' minds at that time, and poses more queries than it answers.

Egyptian texts mention a Job in Canaan about 2000 B.C., and another in the fourteenth century. Ezekiel's allusion (xiv : 14) implies that the biblical Job was proverbial for righteousness. He is presented as a very rich Edomite. The prologue to his story is the only Old Testament passage where a being called " Satan " enters without disguise as a speaking character. He is not so much an Anti-God as an angelic troubler of Man, whom he tests and accuses by divine leave. Satan tells the Lord that Job is righteous merely because he is well off. The Lord allows Satan to sweep away

Job's wealth, and his family too, in a series of disasters, and then to cover Job himself with revolting boils. Job refuses to complain. At the end of the story, God restores everything—sons and daughters to the same number, and double the number of animals, " fourteen thousand sheep and six thousand camels." Summed up like this, the fable belongs to the Zoroastrian world of thought, or to the Israelite in its more naïve moods. God rewards the righteous; Job being patient in misfortune, God " blessed his latter days more than his beginning." But the prologue and epilogue are bracketed round a conversation which stands between them, and this forms the bulk of the text. When Job is at the nadir of woe, three friends come to condole with him. They find him altered by his disease almost beyond recognition. Days pass in silent grief. Then Job opens his mouth, and at this point it seems as if the burden has at last broken him. He curses the day he was born. His shocked friends remonstrate, and the debate goes on through many chapters to a startling conclusion. Only after this comes the epilogue with virtue rewarded.

The resultant book is a masterpiece of the highest order, even though, in places, it is confused and confusing. Textual upsets and difficulties of translation have made it harder than it need be for modern readers, but at best it remains hard, and extremely mature.[2] Job's pseudo-comforters are mouthpieces of simple faith in the bad sense, cliché-ridden and smug. Job himself speaks with the awful voice of one who has really suffered, and who sees through the hollow consolations of commonplace piety.

The friends argue that Job's afflictions are sent for his good, that he must have sinned to deserve them, and that if he turns humbly to the Lord all will be well. Job retorts that such platitudes are of no use to the worn-out victim. He is not conscious of any proportionate sin, and what is the point if God never shows him?

2 I recall a most intelligent English Honours student, who, a few months after taking a first-class B.A., read *Job* in the King James Bible and complained that he "couldn't see which side Job was on." The Knox translation of this book reads well.

He introduces a theme that becomes a preoccupation in Wisdom literature—the cosmic gap, God's remoteness. Israel, confined to the intimacy of its small sacred Land, had never deeply felt this. Israel forced into consciousness of the huge alien world could feel it most poignantly. Job does not deny that God is glorious and great and just. But how can human beings approach him, what dialogue can there be? "Where shall wisdom be found, and where is the place of understanding?" By what flight of spirit or intellect can a man soar to his Maker and wrest any reply from him?

After long discussion, and totally without warning, comes a terrific reversal. The Lord does reply. He swoops down in a desert whirlwind, as when he carried off Elijah, and as when he appeared to Ezekiel. His answer is . . . to echo the cries of Job himself, but with an inverted implication. Yes, Job *is* insignificant. Yes, Job *is* incapable of piercing the secrets of heaven. And therefore, who is he to protest, to ask all these questions, to demand a hearing in open court? Now it is the Lord's turn.

I will question you, and you shall declare to me.

Where were you when I laid the foundation of the earth?
Tell me, if you have understanding . . .
On what were its bases sunk, or who laid its cornerstone,
When the morning stars sang together, and all the sons of
God shouted for joy?

He goes on to enumerate other works, in a passage mingling sublimity with colourful antique science and natural history. Presently incomprehension is transcended by a sort of higher incomprehension, a "deep but dazzling darkness." God comes as close as he ever does come in the Bible to being an inscrutable power like Fate. Yet he talks and teaches as Fate does not. Hitherto Job has been saying, "I don't *understand*! How can this happen to me?" Afterwards he says quietly, "So be it. I *don't* understand. I acknowledge it. You know best." He achieves resignation, but by this indirect route. Thereupon God reproves the friends for misrepresenting him (an interesting touch), and commends Job. The ensuing happy ending, with Job made rich again, may be a relic of some primitive version of the legend which the author used. In conjunction with the rest it now mars the effect.

Job with all its perplexities stands on a peak by itself in the Old Testament, and is several centuries ahead of its time. However, it has a kinship with other books of the period. It shows one reaction of Jewish minds to a bigger, more complex world. Contact with the swarming nations accentuated the gulf between Man and God. There were no easy answers any more. To many the Law and cultus of Israel seemed less adequate, the focusing of divine majesty on Zion less meaningful. *Job* indeed hardly mentions the Law. Subsequent books betray the same consciousness of the gulf, and offer or reject methods of bridging it.

3

Wisdom's later exponents deal with the same topics in cooler and less exalted language.

Ecclesiastes, assigned to the early third century B.C., is a strange little work. It is the *Rubaiyat* of the Bible. The speaker or "preacher" is supposed to be Solomon, "the son of David, king in Jerusalem." His sceptical sermon is broken up by pious interpolations or after-thoughts, and by maxims which editors appear to have jumbled. However, one mood prevails, and in a restrained way the speaker's remarks unmistakably anticipate Omar. Only as a personal record of his impressions of life—sometimes correct, sometimes erring through emotion—can *Ecclesiastes* be defended fairly in orthodox terms.

Vanity of vanity, he says, all is vanity! Without citing *Job* directly, he comments on it by implication. He agrees as to God's ways being beyond us. The gap yawns. But his conclusion is almost Epicurean. The issues which human beings regard as great are scarcely real issues at all, because the world has no logic within which they can be defined or valued. We should simply and unin-quiringly make the best of things, eat and drink and work at the task in hand. God doubtless knows what he is about, but he does not tell us. The speaker glances at the hope of immortality which other Jews are beginning to cherish. His verdict is negative. Man perishes like the beasts. Then how to govern conduct? He recurs to the one theme: do what you can with the ordinary things of life, there is nothing else; don't expect much; don't try to unravel God's mysteries; at the same time don't forget him, because, in their incomprehensible way, his mills do keep grinding. The true Wisdom is a reverent Unwisdom.

Such is *Ecclesiastes*. Together with *Job*, it strikes discords which other authors try to resolve.

A note at the end of it refers to Solomon's proverbs, three thousand in number, according to *I Kings* iv : 32. At the date of the book's appearing, a collection of the sayings ascribed to him had lately become current—so lately that the arrangement was still in flux. Such compilations had long been popular in the East. One version of the Solomon collection, with a prologue and additional matter from other sources, forms the biblical *Book of Proverbs*, our last piece of canonical Wisdom literature.

Most of the aphorisms are short, pithy, and not closely bound up with any special religion, though the God of Israel is assumed and often invoked. The commonest form is a pointed illustration of good or bad conduct, or both contrasted. Wisdom is set against Folly. The model Proverb-man is kind, thoughtful, soberly cheerful; humble and hard-working and temperate; respectful to his betters, strict but affectionate to his children. There is also a model Proverb-woman. We catch glimpses of her occasionally throughout, and see her at more length in a charming description at the end of the book. One defect of the Proverbs is an old-fashioned insistence (despite *Job*) that the righteous prosper and the wicked do not. But some sound thinking has been done as to what prosperity means. It need not mean fourteen thousand sheep and six thousand camels. Peace of mind is a truer wealth, virtue brings its own solid recompense.

The prologue is a remarkable document mainly on the theme of Wisdom, which it pursues beyond *Job*. Wisdom is portrayed fortifying the reader against the blandishments of a temptress, a faithless wife, who may stand for Folly seducing the unwise. Personified Wisdom is given three speeches. In the second and most interesting (Chapter viii) she takes up the Lord's ironic question to Job, "Where were you when I laid the foundation of the earth?"

"The Lord created me at the beginning of his work, the first of his acts of old.

Ages ago I was set up, at the first, before the beginning of the earth . . .

When he established the heavens, I was there . . .

When he marked out the foundations of the earth,

Then I was beside him, like a master workman; and I was daily his delight, rejoicing before him always,

Rejoicing in his inhabited world, and delighting in the sons of men . . ."

Job was not there, but Wisdom was. She does know the divine secrets, and God sends her down to instruct those who revere him. Here is the beginning of a hint as to how the gulf can be bridged. Wisdom is at the Lord's side, an intermediary between himself and his world. She lightens our darkness . . . and she is the source of all the wise sayings in the book.

Yet however serviceable, she is a lady of baffling antecedents. To this day no one knows where she came from. Is she a Platonic Idea? a disguise of the *Nous* or *Logos* of Stoicism? an emanation of Ahura Mazdah? a Canaanite-Aramaean celestial power? or an independent invention of the Jews themselves? On the whole it seems more judicious to look for her in Semitic myth than to suppose any borrowing from further afield.

Whoever she is, she reappears with still greater splendours in *Ecclesiasticus*, which forms part of the Old Testament Apocrypha. *Ecclesiasticus* is a Greek version of a Hebrew treatise which survives only in fragments. The translator tells us that he worked in Egypt in 132 B.C., and that the author was his grandfather, Jesus (i.e. Jeshua), who was the son of Sirach and lived in Jerusalem. Ben-Sira, as this writer is often called, seems to have been a traveller, though he never states where he went. In his book a response to the external challenge can be seen taking shape. Wisdom in the fullest sense, the goal of every philosopher's quest, is said to belong specially to Israel. She bestows her best gifts on the worshippers of Israel's God, and imparts her highest truths in the Torah. Plato and Aristotle, in other words, were only expressing imperfect insights which the study of Moses could have perfected.

Wisdom, Ben-Sira says, is to be attained through fear of the Lord and diligent searching. He makes her speak for herself in the twenty-fourth chapter, most eloquently, "in the midst of her people."

"I came forth from the mouth of the Most High, and covered the earth like a mist.

I dwelt in high places, and my throne was a pillar of cloud . . .

In the waves of the sea, in the whole earth, and in every people and nation I have gotten a possession.

Among all these I sought a resting place, I sought in whose territory I might lodge.

Then the Creator of all things gave me a commandment . . . and he said, 'Make your dwelling in Jacob, and in Israel receive your inheritance.'

From eternity, in the beginning, he created me, and for eternity I shall not cease to exist.

In the holy tabernacle I ministered before him, and so I was established in Zion.

In the beloved city likewise he gave me a resting place, and in Jerusalem was my dominion.

So I took root in an honoured people, in the portion of the Lord, who is their inheritance.

I grew tall like a cedar in Lebanon . . ."

And so on with a wealth of gorgeous imagery drawn from trees and fruitage. Then Ben-Sira injects his key idea. "All this is the book of the covenant of the Most High God, the law which Moses commanded us."

Thus the link is forged. Moses, as Wisdom's own voice, is the master of all philosophers, and no other teacher can take his place.

Ben-Sira clinches the implication of *Proverbs*. Wisdom is more than an allegory, more than a personified attribute of wise people or of God. When God called her into being before Creation, there were no wise people; nor could he be said to create his own qualities, or make a beginning of something he already possessed. Judaism at this point is straining and creaking in the direction of polytheism, and Wisdom is a goddess, or nearly so. Her author's language precludes any term less catastrophic. She even bears a likeness to other goddesses. Her poetic description recalls the Syrian Astarte; her birth and function, the Greek wisdom-goddess Athene. As Athene sprang from the head of Zeus, Wisdom blossoms from the mind of the Lord. She is the true armed virgin as opposed to the false.

If we turn from this apparition to the homilies within which she stands, we find that they carry on the tradition of the Wisdom literature, but in a broader, less depressing spirit. The gap between Man and God remains indeed. God knows what he is doing, but in its fullness it is beyond us. However, the emphasis is now on the conviction that he knows best. The act of submission is more cheerful. " Trust in him and he will help you." Man is an exalted being, made in the divine image for lofty purposes. The world is a good place, where the righteous can be happy. No matter how wide the cosmic gulf, Wisdom is at God's hand, and our piety and learning can draw her into our lives to enlighten us.

Where Ben-Sira diverges sharply from his sceptical predecessors is in his noble reaffirmation of the idea of Israel, which for them was in abeyance. Israel is the unique nation, the undying entity cherished by God and linked to him by Wisdom. Other nations have their appointed rulers, Israel is the Lord's own. Its life is continuous, renewed endlessly in the shining succession of patriarchs and princes and prophets. Its past history determines the present and guarantees the future. The wise and the just have immortality in their perpetual renown among their people. Several chapters are devoted to the great litany beginning "Let us now praise famous men," the best-known passage in the Apocrypha. Ben-Sira's list includes Adam, lord of all living creatures; Enoch who was taken away to heaven; Abraham, Isaac, Jacob, with whom God made his first covenants; Moses, faithful and humble; Aaron the pattern of all priests, Joshua the pattern of all warriors; Samuel the incorruptible, David the royal, Solomon the wise; Elijah and Hezekiah; Isaiah who foresaw things far distant, Zerubbabel and the good High Priest Simon II. "Their posterity will continue for ever, and their glory will not be blotted out."

It may be doubted whether Ben-Sira's philosophy, as such, has much to commend it to a Gentile. It offers him what might be described as a "package deal." He cannot simply read it as he reads Plato. He is faced with a choice. You are either Inside or Outside, and if the latter, you are expected to come Inside before Wisdom has anything vital to say to you. She dwells in Zion —quite literally in the Holy Land—and even a pilgrimage will probably not take you much nearer to her. You must study the Law and the Prophets, you must practise Jewish piety, you must (there is no getting away from it) become a Jew. At the same time, the religion which the Gentile would thus embrace is larger and more philosophic, better interwoven with the common experience of mankind, than earlier Judaism.

Last of this group of books is the *Wisdom of Solomon*, written in Greek by an Alexandrian Jew within a few decades of the Christian era. It shows acquaintance with Plato, Xenophon, Herodotus, Epicureanism and Stoicism. Again Wisdom enters, now rather abstract. She is "a reflection of eternal light, a spotless mirror of the working of God, and an image of his goodness." If we attend to her we shall not be led astray by the pagans and scoffers, and in the end they will be confounded, while we live eternally in the World to Come.

Here the idea of "wisdom" is sliding towards the connotation which it acquires later in Gnostic cults and the Kabbala. It is narrowing into a notion of *secret* wisdom, a monopoly of initiates.

Ecclesiasticus itself contains the germ of this. We might ask whether the two apocryphal books already show traces of an undivulged secret doctrine.

There may be a hint in *Ecclesiasticus* xxiv, where Wisdom comes from the mouth of God. A possible implication is that she is his speech, his language, which he had to enunciate before he could frame the sentences for creating other things, and which he then used to define all the rest. It is a fact that Jewish speculation pursues a mystical theory of language to surprising lengths. Hebrew is said to be the speech of God. His Name is a Hebrew formula devoid of meaning in any foreign vocabulary. The creative fiats in *Genesis* are Hebrew sentences actually uttered by him: if he had spoken another language the world would be other than it is. Furthermore, the letters of its alphabet—the twenty-two basic sounds by which it is articulated—are the matrices of Creation. They contain all beings, somewhat as a complete fount of type contains all books. That idea has left its mark on the *Book of Jubilees*, where God's creative activity is subdivided into twenty-two steps. In the Christian era it inspires a cryptographic approach to Scripture, and a series of semi-alchemical theories which raise curious questions. A legend credits Ben-Sira himself with super-human feats performed by combining letters. It adds that he was rebuked by the Holy Spirit for giving away its secrets.[3]

The likelihood that the two apocryphal authors had such thoughts in their heads, at least in embryonic form, is far short of proof. But whether they did or not, the doctrine of divine speech and self-expression, of the word proceeding from God's mouth, was destined to go far. And the belief that the Jews' domicile and language placed them in occult contact with the divine counsels was destined to spur them into actions that nearly took away both.

3 On the other hand a dictum of his about not seeking to know what is above you (*Ecclesiasticus* iii:22) has been construed as a warning against such studies. Even so, it implies that they already existed.

4

Long before it did, that age produced its one major Jewish philosopher, in anything like the pagan sense. Philo of Alexandria, called Philo Judaeus, grew up during the reign of Herod and the apogee of Hillel. His family was rich and his education excellent. He learned all he could from the surging Jewish life of his city, and from the Pharisaic teaching which by then was thoroughly at home there. He had a profound respect for Plato and the Platonic school. Yet he was also a faithful Jew. On the one hand, he wanted to acclimatise the best of Greek thought in Judaism. On the other, he wanted to preserve Judaism intact, and restate it so that pagans would see it as Ben-Sira did, and adopt it as the highest philosophy. This mutual accommodation was the main theme of his voluminous work. It involved him with the problem posed by the Wisdom books, of the gap between Man and God; and also with the problem posed by Apocalypse, of humanity's future.

Philo's chief difficulty was to show how the Torah could be said to teach philosophy at all, as Greeks understood the term. He founded his solution on the doctrine of the different senses of Scripture. To be more precise, he founded it on a special exploitation of one of them, the allegorical. He construed Scripture as an allegory of ideas, something like *The Faerie Queene*. While he never presumed to call it fictitious, he took the line that in most cases its historic truth was of little moment. In effect you could take anything in Scripture as meaning anything, so long as you kept to the rules of allegory; and these involved arithmetical and other techniques which are not normally concerned with the sense of words.

Philo succeeded in giving philosophical dignity to whatever he cared about: to all the biblical stories, all the laws and rituals. His greatest achievement was in his theory of Creation. Plato had spoken of an eternal realm of forms or patterns, which were God's models in his creative work. Philo assented, but subordinated the

Platonic " ideas " to God. In his scheme they are no longer eternal. God projects his own thoughts to make an upper Creation or " intelligible world." This world contains the blueprints for every being in ours. It occupies the gap between him and us.

The realm of divine ideas is harmonious and alive, a kingdom of ministering angels. Its indwelling spirit is God's " Logos " or Word. The Logos is like the Divine Mind of the Stoics. Though they themselves occasionally used the same term, Philo did not borrow it from them. His own derives from the Hebrew *dabhar*, the spoken word as inseparable from the fact. It is another version of Wisdom, and in some sense a personal being. Philo allows himself such figures of speech as " the Son of God." (Not " Daughter ": Hebrew masculinity has reasserted itself.) We must beware of shifting the Logos either upward or downward. It, or he, is not the soul of our world, or otherwise embedded in Nature. Nor is it God or an aspect of him. God is cause, Logos is effect, the prism of living thought in which the will of the One becomes the complexity of the Many.

Like the Stoics, Philo dreams of an earthly Cosmopolis. For him this is an ideal which mere expansion of empire by Rome cannot realise. What he foresees (again as some Stoics did, in their own way) is the Messianic Age. There is no clear evidence that he expected a personal Messiah. His hope, as it emerges from his various writings, is not focused on a man but on a state of affairs. In his Messianic Age, the scattered Jews will return to the Holy Land. Nothing can replace that, and they will still have only the one Temple, at Jerusalem. Palestine will become a model commonwealth, prosperous and wisely ordered. Wars will cease everywhere, as foretold by Isaiah. The Lord will subdue such enemies of Israel as remain stubborn. All nations will look to Zion and become proselytes. A democratic world state will bring perpetual peace.

Such in outline was Philo's synthesis. Though heroic, it fell flat. In a way it was a *reductio ad absurdum* of the whole attempt to make Judaism a philosophy, which went no further. His methods were so foreign to Jewish mental habits that they tended toward a new religion rather than a new presentation of the old. Once he had expounded Scripture as allegory, it was hard to see why Scripture was necessary. The unique idea of Israel-in-history had largely evaporated.[4] As for bridging the gap between Man and God, his effort to do this intellectually was not so satisfying in its results as the myth of the Lady Wisdom. Putting in the Logos between had merely created two gaps instead of one, since the Logos was neither identical with God nor given in the experience of Man. It hovered in metaphysical interspace, with a gulf above and a gulf below.

Actually Philo's work was not stillborn by any means. His theories and his terminology were to play a major, even a sensational role in human thought. But not during his life, and not in the way intended. The Jews were to follow other paths. His immediate importance is as a symptom of the recovered confidence which Ben-Sira also reflects. The shock of Hellenic contact had died away. Judaism could stand up against the world. To assess, at last, its net impact in the diaspora and its missionary achievement, with the implications for Jewish morale and nationalism, we must retrace our steps a little from Philo himself to happenings before his time.

5

Neither Philo nor Ben-Sira had lost sight of the fact that Judaism was more than a quarry of ideas to be ranged over freely like the

---

4 Comparative religion shows how close Philo came to selling the pass. It is the whole point and distinctiveness of the biblical scheme that it does matter whether the history actually happened. Attempts to present Krishna, for example, as an Indian Messiah break down for this reason among several—that while there may have been such a man, it makes no difference to Hinduism whether there was or not. Similarly Buddhism, at all events the greater Mahayana Buddhism, would be unaffected by a proof that Buddha never existed. With Judaism (and the Christianity that came out of Judaism) it is otherwise.

philosophy of Aristotle. Jewish wisdom was only fully attainable by becoming a Jew. Before either of them, a group of Jews in Philo's own city had supplied the ammunition for an offensive. They had translated the Scriptures into Greek—not merely the edifying parts that had an obvious Hellenic appeal, but, with splendid effrontery, the entire collection as it then stood.

There was no " Bible-designed-to-be-read-as-literature " evasion about this. The Alexandrian translators faced the glory of Hellas undazzled, and spread out all they had : the Lord commanding the light and the Lord scuffling with Moses, the trumpet of Sinai and the tambour of Miriam, the Sabbath and the Song of Songs, Abraham sacrificing Isaac and the firmament displaying God's handiwork, the talking snake and the talking donkey and the morning stars singing together. All these were Israel's, and not even Greece had the right to pick and choose among the gifts of the Holy One.

The standard legend about the Greek Bible is given in a pseud-epigraphic work called the *Letter of Aristeas*. The real author of the " letter " was a zealous and highly literate Alexandrian Jew, but it purports to be written by a Greek officer at the court of Ptolemy Philadelphus. Aristeas is made to tell how, toward the year 270, the King urged his librarian that " the Jewish laws " should be translated. Ptolemy himself applied to the High Priest asking for scholars to be sent from Jerusalem. Seventy-two were chosen. Aristeas went to escort them to Egypt. On arrival in Alexandria the seventy-two learned Jews were entertained at court, where their sagacious answers to deep questions enthralled the audience. Then they went to quarters prepared for them on the island of Pharos, and completed their task in seventy-two days. The number of translators being about seventy, like the number of Israelites who first went into Egypt, their translation came to be called the Septuagint.

It was, of course, a boon to Greek-speaking Jews, and it may in reality have been undertaken with them chiefly in mind. However, Pseudo-Aristeas is right to assume that Gentile readers were always envisaged. Indeed his own story is a sustained attempt to impress such readers. No other Asiatic people ever translated their sacred books in this wholesale manner. A little Egyptian history leaked through via Manetho, a little Babylonian mythology leaked through via Berossus. But other peoples in general hugged their mysteries to themselves . . . and the mysteries perished of suffocation. Judaism alone braved the foreigner, and Judaism alone kept its vitality. The Alexandrian religion which produced the Septuagint had nothing of the ghetto about it, and came under Pharisee influence as soon as there was a Pharisee influence to come under.

One sign of the translators' intentions is the care they took to adapt their vocabulary to Greek minds. In rendering key words they clearly asked themselves how a Greek reader would react. To represent Yahweh's names and titles they employed the terms *kyrios* (lord) and *theos* (god), which had weaker and vaguer connotations, rather than seek fidelity in the unfamiliar. The teaching of Moses was reduced to the narrower *nomos* (law). The gods of biblical paganism became *daimonia* (unseen agencies in a very general sense).

So the version of the Seventy made its way through the world. Jewish congregations not only read it but allowed Gentiles to read it. Little by little the mission did start to take effect. Clusters of converts and " fellow-travellers" grew up round the synagogues, and studied a more or less Pharisaic Judaism. In spite of all hostility the enlightenment of the Gentiles had at long last begun. *Tobit*, with its forthright assertion of the evangelic diaspora, was most probably written in Egypt about this time. The post-Exilic eagerness to exalt the Lord above all the earth made him acceptable now to pagans who would have had no use for a Semitic tribal deity. Yet however universalised, Israel's God never ceased to be himself. The unwavering stress on Israel's special relationship with him meant that those who did accept him could not escape a touch of the Israelite spirit. Judaism, as it spread, was in no danger of dissolving into abstractions and platitudes.

Nevertheless a problem arose as to how much of it a proselyte should be expected to embrace. Was he bound to adopt the whole scheme of life and ceremonial, including circumcision—a cruel requirement for an adult, in the existing state of surgery?

Subsequent rabbinic sayings shed a backward light over this period, and show that opinion was elastic. As a rule, when a recorded pronouncement is harsh and implies a wish to make things tough for the would-be convert, it is a late one and a result of provocation. In the golden age of the Alexandrians and Pharisees the tendency was to make things easy. A Gentile could "Judaise" if he wanted, but he would never be forced to. If the ceremonial was a symbolic hallmark to distinguish the teacher-nation, there was a certain logic in the pupil's *not* adopting it. A popular compromise laid down seven commandments, ascribed to the sons of Noah, through which Gentiles might qualify. These covered abstention from theft, bloodshed, and other specified sins. In the same vein was Hillel's willingness to give a convert his welcome after a few seconds' instruction in the Golden Rule. One rabbi is even quoted as saying that "whoever repudiates idolatry is accounted a Jew." Bold thinkers maintained that these makeshifts would pass away, and that Judaism was groping toward its own supersession by something larger.

If Jews disagreed a little as to how much they should demand of a convert, they disagreed more as to what attitude they should take to him. However, those of the Pharisee cast of mind were prepared to go far on his behalf, and to make him thoroughly at home if they judged him sincere. Such statements are preserved as that " a Gentile who obeys the Law is equal to the High Priest." A consequence of this trend was that the strictly hereditary conception of Israel passed into even deeper eclipse. It became necessary to treat newcomers as Israelites, when by birth they were nothing of the kind. Passages in the last part of *Isaiah*, such as lvi : 3–8, had already referred to the Lord's adoption of aliens into his family. Gradually many Jews learned to accept this principle. In the New Testament a born Jew addresses born Jews and proselytes, without distinction, as " men of Israel " (*Acts* ii : 10, 22).

Through such tactful concessions the Chosen People began to be reinforced by an appreciable influx of men and women without Israelite blood. The city of Antioch was one notable recruiting ground. Asia Minor was another. The " devout persons " mentioned in the New Testament's account of St. Paul (*Acts* xiii : 50, xvii : 4) are certainly proselytes. Judaism attracted not only the poor and unhappy, but also some of the wealthy who had grown dissatisfied with official cults. By the first century of the Christian era the gifts of such patrons had lavishly enriched the Temple. Gentile eyes actually did turn toward the Holy Land, willingly or reluctantly, as a centre of prestige and power. According to Suetonius, when Nero had to face giving up Rome, several advisers urged him to make Jerusalem his capital.

Before passing on we might wonder whether, after Judaism came to such close quarters with paganism, an overlap occurred; whether pagan myth was ever annexed and Judaised, or Judaism itself was in any degree paganised, so as to reawaken the spectre of ancient Canaan.

Evidence is scanty, and its bias nearly all one way. Judaism was not paganised. It kept its integrity. Hellenistic culture had given Palestine itself a fresh numinousness: Pan was said to dwell near the source of the Jordan, and the rock from which Perseus detached Andromeda was located at Jaffa; yet neither Pan nor Perseus forced an entry into the court of the Lord God. Pagan symbols in the Temple and other Jewish houses of worship—zodiacs and vines for example—were, precisely, symbols. No more.

Judaism among the Gentiles did not suffer any contamination. None of its literary borrowings, none of the questionings of the Wisdom writers, amounted to a clear-cut retreat or compromise. But conversely, it did assimilate scraps of paganism to its own ends. It used without being used, or ceasing to be itself. One curious *tour de force* was the reconstruction of the Sibylline Books.

The background of these famous oracles is obscure. There are Greek references to a prophetess called the Sibyl, whom Plato speaks of with respect. In Rome, collections of verses ascribed to a Sibyl at Erythrae, and supposedly bought by King Tarquin, were stored in the Capitol to be consulted in times of crisis. These were burnt in 82 B.C., whereupon a delegation went to Erythrae to collect more. But the search inspired the production of many spurious verses as well as genuine. Soon " Sibylline verses " by the thousand were in circulation, some dating from before the fire, some not. Augustus had most of them suppressed. As a result of all these vicissitudes no true Sibylline canon survives. For two centuries, however, from about 160 onward, the most accomplished of the Neo-Sibylline authors were Jews, who thereby extended the pseudepigraphic technique into a pagan field. Whether their work ought to be viewed chiefly as a pious fraud, or as a species of joke, or as an effort to restore what the Sibyl " would have said " in a sincere belief that pagen wisdom derived from Israel, it is hard to decide. At any rate they mingled secular predictions quite cunningly with Jewish matter condemning idolatry and urging the unity of God. The Sibyl was made to foretell the Messiah, and a future age of peace and abundance, with Jerusalem as capital of the renewed world. These prophecies were never very popular with the Jews themselves, but they enjoyed a vogue among Gentiles. In due course they were cited and improved by Christians who fancied them authentic.

More important than Pseudo-Sibyl's vaticinations (perhaps, in view of later events, enormously more important) was the Jewish-inspired worship of Israel's God as " the Most High." That non-Hebraic title—originating in *Genesis* xiv as an equivalent of the Canaanite El Elyon; associated with the pagan Melchizedek, and through him, in Psalm cx, with a Messianic hint; and repeated in *Daniel*—had since acquired, thanks to the Maccabean priesthood, a mystical aura. The author of the *Testaments* (Levi viii : 14) had taken it as a sign of the glory of Israel dawning over the Gentile world. Meanwhile, however, outside Palestine and outside Judaism, the same title was coincidentally being heard again among pagans. It was heard because it filled a need created by the emergence of Zeus as a world-deity, as a Heavenly Father for whom "Jupiter" and "Ammon" and so forth were simply local epithets. Thus *Aristeas*. The Zeus of common worship was still not God in anything like the Jewish sense. He was simply the President of the Immortals. But it was proper and natural to speak of him as " Theos Hypsistos," the Most High God, and many did. That verbal agreement or ambiguity was a temptation too powerful to resist. In Asia Minor, where Antiochus the Great had planted so many Babylonian Jews, there arose during the second century B.C. a cult of " God Most High "—the Hypsistarian cult, it has been called—which was in essence Basic Judaism. It was Judaism with the path made smooth for newcomers accustomed to Zeus and other chief gods. The Gentile could turn into a Hypsistarian Jew by an almost painless transition.

Inscriptions, not only in Asia Minor but in the Balkans and Rome, attest the spread of monotheism in this form under Jewish aegis. All too little is known about it. But, in keeping with Hellenistic tastes, there seems to have been more stress than in ordinary Judaism on a future life for the individual.

CHAPTER ELEVEN

A RACE HATEFUL TO THE GODS

Herod's kingdom, on the brink of the Christian era, was affluent and tense. It held four or five million people, rather more than half of them Jewish.[1] Palestine at last had an appreciable external trade. Oil and honey, figs and balsam, linen and wool, went out as exports, and the goods of the larger world flowed in. To the north of the rocky heartland lay Galilee, with its gentler hills, its recently Judaised peasantry, and its sudden eastward plunge to the blue-green Lake of Tiberias and the fields and fishing ports lining the shore. In that pleasant country the highways crossed and the caravans met. Aliens wandered in from the "ring," the *galil*, of Gentiles, and Jewish ideas crept outward to regions beyond Palestine. The conversion of Idumaea had been imposed, but other such extensions of Judaism were not. Its seeds were borne to the little Mesopotamian state of Adiabene; Mesopotamian Jews aided its growth there; and within a few decades of Herod's time Adiabene was a Jewish enclave in the Imperial borderlands.

Herod himself reigned for more than thirty years, successful and hated. His subservience to Rome was unswerving, because he had grasped from the outset that Roman power was the only adequate prop for his own. At first he tried to rally local support by marrying Mariamne, Hyrcanus II's granddaughter, and giving the High Priesthood to her popular brother Aristobulus. But in due course Aristobulus was drowned in an alleged accident, Mariamne was executed on a charge of adultery, and the surviving

---

1 The essential Palestine west of Jordan never supported so many, but the Romans had given Herod a good deal more than that.

Hasmonean pretender was put to death for "conspiring with the Arabs." Herod went on to wipe out the rest of the family and confiscate its wealth. He persuaded Augustus to enlarge his kingdom and governed it through Greek ministers, crushing various plots with efficiency and dispatch. After marrying nine more wives, he fell sick, attempted suicide in delirium, and died revoltingly. But his demise was not the end for his astute family. Several more Herods reigned after him, so that he came to be posthumously distinguished as "the Great."

He left his marks on the country. These offended pious Jews because they presupposed pagan civilisation and followed pagan models, yet were too glorious to condemn. Judaea, under Herod, sprouted impressive fortresses. He remedied Palestine's lack of natural harbours by supplying an artificial one, complete with a new port-city provocatively named Caesarea. The population of Caesarea was never more than forty per cent Jewish, and control of its council slipped out of Jewish hands. In Jerusalem itself he built a palace, a theatre, an amphitheatre and a hippodrome. Also he strengthened the city walls, and added a fort on the north-west side near the Gate of Jaffa, and a citadel which was called the Antonia.

A more grandiose project still was the reconstruction of the small Second Temple. This was launched in 20 B.C. and took more than eighty years, though the main part of it was finished in eight. To ensure a supply of workmen who could go anywhere in the sacred fabric without impiety, Herod reinforced his thousands of labourers with a body of priests who were given special training as builders. The ponderous blocks in the shattered remnant known as the Wailing Wall testify to the scope of his operations and the skill of his engineers. Terraces and colonnades, cliffs of white marble plated with gold, soared up to a roof a hundred and seventy feet above the pavement, bristling with golden needles designed to prevent birds from settling. Around was a court a quarter of a mile long.

By this work Herod hoped to placate his Jewish subjects, whose religion he nominally shared. However, his attitude was far too equivocal; he also restored heretical Samaria (giving it the Greek name of Sebaste) and financed, at Rhodes, another temple . . . of Apollo. Hence the Jerusalem project failed to disarm the resentment of the devout. He set up a golden eagle above the sanctuary, and two rabbis pardonably denounced it as an Imperial rather than a Jewish emblem. While Herod was sick a small party of climbers, incited by the rabbis, scrambled over the roof and removed the idol. They fully expected martyrdom, and Herod, on recovering slightly, did not disappoint them. Climbers and rabbis were impartially burnt alive.

Yet nothing like a boycott ensued. Herod won to this extent, that the Jews not only went on practising their religion in his capital, but used his facilities to do it. The Temple ritual rose to a peak of splendour. Awestruck visitors streamed in through a spacious " Court of the Gentiles," beyond which only Jews could go. This led into two inner courts, one containing the altar of burnt offering where the priests officiated. Over the porch of the sanctuary hung a vine of golden grapes, in dazzling clusters six feet long. The sanctuary itself was shielded against the outer world by double doors, also golden, and a veil of blue and purple. Inside stood the seven-branched Menorah, and the altar of incense, and the table for shewbread. Beyond again was the sacred emptiness of the Holy of Holies, entered once a year by the High Priest alone. He made that solemn visit on the " Day of Atonement " in October, and then only he saluted the Lord by his true Name.

In the ordinary way the main feature of public ceremony was the daily morning sacrifice at the outdoor altar, which was performed when the sun appeared over the Mount of Olives. But many other offerings were made, and the aesthetic adjuncts of worship were highly developed. A choir sang psalms accompanied by an orchestra—horns, cymbals, pipes, tambourines, harps and other stringed instruments, together with an organ, the personal contribution of Herod. It was all very fine, and very practical. In the principal court there were thirteen chests, called "trumpets" because of their shape, for receiving gifts. Traders were permitted to set up stalls where they sold animals for sacrifice and exchanged currency—a paying business during the major festivals which drew pilgrims from all over the Empire.

Outside the precinct, meanwhile, there had been no breakdown of institutions. Rome had suppressed the august national Sanhedrin, but local Sanhedrins were allowed to take its place. To judge from certain debatable hints Jerusalem had two, one for religious matters and one for matters of secular administration. If so, the Jews had taken a pioneer step toward the momentous distinction of Church and State.

2

Thus Judaism was full of vigour at the centre, Herod or no Herod. Yet very largely because of that vigour, it was generating fresh forces adverse to its own mission. Anti-Semitism had so far been sporadic, formless, a warning rather than a peril. Roman rule in Palestine built up a far graver confrontation of enmities.

Rome was resented, and bitterly. Pompey's correctness toward the Temple had been nullified shortly after by Crassus, who looted its treasury; Julius Caesar's generosity, never appreciated, had been forgotten in the imposition of Herod. Furthermore the latter's megalomania overburdened the economy and ended by weakening it. His death in 4 B.C. was followed by a reorganisation of the territory. First Augustus divided it among Herod's three sons. But Archelaus, who got Judaea, ruled with such combined cruelty and ineptitude that in A.D. 6 the Emperor banished him and made Judaea a garrisoned province, under a procurator responsible to himself. Such autonomy as remained was vested in the High Priest.

Judaea sank into a morass of grudging semi-tolerance, administered with virtues that seemed like insults. Roman benefits earned no thanks; Roman tax-collection bred a detested class of Jewish collaborationists; and a hundred Roman gestures of amity could all be cancelled by one gaffe like that of the procurator Pontius Pilate, who, on entering Jerusalem in 26, marched his guards into the Temple area, although the effigies on their standards, being graven images, were a flagrant affront. Pilate found that his subjects would actually die rather than tolerate the standards, so he gave way, but he did not learn. He tried subsequently to apply some of the Temple treasure to the financing of an aqueduct. That an idle public fund should be put to such beneficent work was only rational. But Roman logic collided with a logic that functioned differently. Jerusalem exploded with rage at the sacrilege, and to suppress the riots Pilate was driven to sending soldiers among the mob in disguise with concealed weapons. Another mob (Samaritans this time, treasure-hunting on Mount Gerizim) provoked another massacre. In 36 Pilate was recalled. One can easily imagine him in old age, as Anatole France did, grumbling about the people he had been sent to govern and had never understood. What could a sane Roman make of such lunatics?

The Jew of Judaea now had no means of escape from this inflaming presence of foreign troops and officials. Nor did he get much sympathy from his neighbours, many of whom were Arabs, grown implacably hostile. He felt hemmed in, trampled, exasperated. His sense of possessing unique light was as strong as ever, and justifiable: no other nation of the Empire or the known world had arrived at an ethical monotheism like his. That made the collapse of the Hasmonean realm, and the second apparent failure of God's promises, all the more dreadful. Somehow it *must* all come out right. But the logic of the situation was now poignant and pressing. Since the Land remained central, the Land's visible sufferings engendered a crisis. To the question " How long? " it became unbearable to admit any answer but " Soon."

In that Judaean hothouse a passionate expectation boiled up. Apocalyptic fancy grew madder. The figure of the Messiah, the Christ, expanded. The populace looked simply for a hero who would throw off the Roman yoke. But students of the literature were tending, like some of the *Enoch* contributors, to fuse the Messiah's role with God's direct action, and foresee a more than human manifestation. Prophecies were reconsidered. The brutal

Fourth Empire of *Daniel* vii, destined to a divine overthrow, was now accepted to be the Roman. The "seventy weeks" of the same book (ix : 24–27) were reckoned from Nehemiah and made to end in the imminent future. The last ominous chapter of *Malachi*, with its pledge of an august herald, echoed fearfully:

You shall tread down the wicked, for they will be ashes under the soles of your feet, on the day when I act, says the Lord of hosts . . .

Behold, I will send you Elijah the prophet before the great and terrible day of the Lord comes.

And around, creeping in and intensifying all, was a spirit which strife and disillusionment had lately been fostering among the pagans themselves—a blind sense of terror, of evil demonic powers enthroned, of the need for some divine advent to break the spell and establish the true City of Mankind.

But the Jews could not agree as to what stand to take or what goals to strive for. Pressure was producing not unity but flaws and factions.

Close to the Temple and its staff sat, as ever, the clique of Sadducees, wealthy, narrow, and unpopular. Their dead hand lay heavy on the Sanhedrin. About them no more need be said, except that their inability to adapt was growing plainer. The skull (to borrow a telling phrase) was showing plainer in their faces. The literal sense of the Pentateuch could not supply all the answers, or even the answers that were really wanted, and it was no use to pretend it could.

More genuinely effective—immensely more, outside Judaea— were the Pharisees. But even they were losing momentum and gradually declining from what they had been. Despite the talents of Hillel's grandson Gamaliel, a rival school inspired by Shammai, distrustful of Gentiles and hostile to all things foreign, was gaining ground. There was a drift toward oppressive formalism and decadent pride. The once-fruitful stress on tradition now favoured the sort of tradition that is merely cramping. Pharisees could be seen ostentatiously pattering prayers in the street, wearing special caps to shut out undesirable sights, walking bent to symbolise the burden of God's commandments, making their almsgiving a public ceremony accompanied by fanfares, haggling and quibbling over details of exegesis and minutiae of conduct. Those who did so were not necessarily neglecting the " weightier matters," yet they laid themselves open to suspicion and invited cynicism. Also, while Gentile converts might be excused full submission to the Law, this pedantic emphasis on the Law was a psychological repellent.

Pharisees had written the chief apocalypses, and promoted the Messianic hope. But Pharisee political caution no longer satisfied Israel's more active spirits. The yearning for the Day of the Lord and the grand showdown (our language supplies no better word than Dr. Gray's) had led to a fresh insistence on the Jews' share in their own salvation, hence on nationalism and revolt, on the maxim that God helps those who help themselves. At the same time, many were also conscious as never before of the practical handicaps. Pacifists drew a disturbing argument from a bizarre source—the inviolable Sabbath. They urged that a Jewish holy war was a contradiction in terms. If Jewish warriors kept the Law, they would stay inactive on the Sabbath, or at most fight in self-defence. Then their opponents would make use of the respite to outmanoeuvre them, and they could not win. If, on the other hand, they treated the Sabbath like any other day, they would be flouting one of the major divine ordinances, and then the war would not be holy. This argument was much more than a debating point. Pompey actually had captured Jerusalem by raising earthworks with towers and siege-engines while the defenders were keeping their day of rest. In the light of such experiences, and common sense, thoughtful Jews were beginning to ask whether the entire notion of military and political glory might be misconceived; whether the primacy of the spiritual side of Israel's mission, to which nearly all paid lip-service, might be such as to demand that its other aspects should be reduced to a footnote, and left in the hands of God.

The ardent reacted to such doubts and warnings in two ways.

One was secession in the form of monasticism. Societies of "Essenes"—ascetic, celibate, vegetarian, communist—seem to have come into being almost as early as the Pharisees and Sadducees; but under Rome Jewish monks grew more numerous, whether they took the Essene name or not. Going out into the fearful wilderness that stretches toward the Dead Sea, they lived in forbidding cells, pored over the Torah on a meagre diet, and admitted recruits to their intensely disciplined life only after a strict probation. It was a community of this type at Qumran which produced and stored the Dead Sea Scriptures. Far from everyday concerns, under a harsh uncompromising light that seemed to burn away almost everything but Man and God, they studied and laboured and waited for the hour of deliverance.

Some of the monks drifted in despair toward an un-Jewish doctrine of salvation as simply the escape of the immortal soul to some distant heaven. But others took up the theme of the Faithful Remnant, and pursued it further. They condemned most of their fellow-countrymen as tepid and backsliding; they themselves were the true Israel, God's earthly agents and representatives. The Pharisees too, of course, were a minority, but whereas the Pharisees lived among the people and worked for them, these ascetics generally cut themselves off. Their purification was meant to prepare them for the great change and the coming Kingdom. Their world-picture was dramatic and dualistic even beyond the Zoroastrian. One of the Dead Sea documents horrifyingly speaks of God as creating two spirits to influence Man, a good spirit and an evil spirit; and the evil one is made evil in essence, he does not merely go astray. From premises of this kind the monks deduced a rigid division of all sentient beings into "sons of light and sons of darkness," a motif in keeping with the fierce glare and shadow of their desert. They even drew up plans for a sacred army, which owed an unacknowledged debt to the hated legions. As for difficulties like the Sabbath, God would resolve those when the time came.

This mode of living depended on the hope of the Messianic advent. It does not appear that any actual monk was ever looked to for the fulfilment of the hope. An unidentified " Teacher of Righteousness "—or rather " Right Teacher "—in the Dead Sea Scriptures is not a Messiah. The Jewish historian Josephus, however, does note a man who seems to have belonged very much to the ascetics' world, though as a loosely affiliated hermit rather than a member of any community, and who grew to be famous for his words about the imminence of the Saviour and the Kingdom of God. He was " John, called the Baptist." Josephus pays tribute to his moral character, and speaks of him as preaching to large audiences; also as baptising with water to cleanse the body and wash away " some sins "—a rite which the Essenes certainly practised. John's outspokenness, and the strength of his following, finally scared one of the junior Herods (Antipas, tetrarch of Galilee) into imprisoning him in the fortress of Machaerus. There he was put to death. John's activities may be dated about A.D. 28 to 30. He was regarded by some as the forerunning " Elijah " promised in *Malachi*.

The other type of Jewish extremist was the political, the apostle of sanctified chauvinism and armed force. This programme agreed better than most with the revolutionary dreams of the masses. Its adherents therefore had wide support, even though vocal opinion declared almost solidly against them. It was, of course, inconsistent. To justify his claim that the Lord would aid Israel in an otherwise mad rebellion, the chauvinist had to appeal to the apocalyptic tradition; and this presupposed the prophets, and endorsed their more enlightened teachings. Its faked early origins and dating confused the issues but could not expunge the texts, which gave no warrant at all for assassination or xenophobia. However, its lurid imagery unfortunately did favour the acceptance of violence as part of God's purpose. The chauvinists picked on that and neglected the rest. One result of their efforts was a form of Messianic prophecy in which God's anointed ruler had the specific task of humbling " King Armilus "—Romulus, a symbol of Rome.

This heady nationalism began with the agitator Judas of Galilee, who went about upbraiding his contemporaries as cowards. It is conveniently described as the "Zealot" movement, although the Zealots were not constituted as a party till 66. The nationalists conspired and agitated and prepared for a rising, confident that when the day dawned the Messiah would come to take command. Despite their Pharisaic theology the Pharisees disowned them. As tempers rose, some of them resorted to the filthier tricks of terrorism. Professional killers called *sicarii* prowled through the cities; they knifed opponents invisibly in the crowd, and avoided detection by joining the shocked circle round the corpse instead of running away.

Desert ascetics and town fanatics had much in common. Both groups were apocalypse-intoxicated. Both saw everything in a crude black and white. Both expected a Messianic triumph, and saw themselves as belonging to dedicated bands set apart from the duller multitude. Indeed the two types of extremism were not mutually exclusive. A certain "John the Essene" figures among the champions of armed revolt. Psychological kinship is suggested perhaps by evidences of sexual oddness. The rules of the desert communities betray a prudish morbidity which oriental and Christian monasticism either avoided or outgrew. The Zealots, if a hostile witness is to be trusted, found time and heart for homosexual amusements even in the grimmest of crises.

Such were the currents running in Palestine, and the logic of Israel channelled them toward rocks and rapids. Jewish claims had grown so towering that acquiescence in a debased provincial status could not go on much longer. Something tremendous had to happen—a mighty birth, or an appalling death.

The Romans, for their part, were slow to recognise the Jews as even a special problem. No Roman writer gives a detailed account of them till somewhat later, after further embitterment and a further convulsion. But the first who does is one of the greatest, namely Tacitus. His statements may be taken as reflecting most educated pagans' ideas at any time from Herod onwards. They may be somewhat darkened, but brief earlier observations by (for example) Seneca show that there has been no abrupt change of outlook.

The most significant feature is the Roman's ignorance. With the Septuagint to consult, and rabbis in the capital to interrogate, he has simply not bothered. His sources are almost pure hearsay. Two further points are also worth making. First, that the contrast with the former friendliness of a number of Greeks carries a sad implication as to the strength of the forces of estrangement. Secondly, that in reviewing Tacitus's objections one notices what he does not complain of, as well as what he does. The stereotype is different, the human target of anti-Semitism in that age is not the same as in this. Tacitus's Jews are not usurers or backstairs power-seekers. They are a kind of colossal Mau Mau, guiltily knit together by a comradeship of perversion. The ideal of uniqueness marked by ritual has made an impression, but a bad impression. Here the historian is undoubtedly typical of Gentiles in general, and especially in some unkind remarks which he makes about the Sabbath. A weekly holiday is one of the Jews' gifts to the world. Pagan nations had nothing like it. But whereas, for the Jews themselves, the Sabbath was a day of devotion and recollection, most Gentiles saw only idleness. Tacitus's contempt echoes a similar contempt displayed by several other Romans.

Yet the Jews do interest him; he goes on about them for pages. After sketching various theories of their origin, he gives a version of the Exodus which is like the Egyptian Manetho's. They were expelled from Egypt during a plague, as a race " hateful to the gods "; Moses led them through the desert, finding water by following a herd of wild asses; they marched on, conquered Palestine, and put up a temple with a statue of an ass in it (that persistent rumour). Moses confirmed his power over them in perpetuity by introducing religious practices " quite opposed to those of all other religions." Nevertheless these " base and abominable " customs attract converts, " the worst rascals among other peoples," who renounce their ancestral cults and send tribute to Jerusalem.

With all his errors and prejudices Tacitus is sometimes right. He more or less grasps the ideas of monotheism and martyrdom, and he alludes to the " ancient priestly writings " which indicated that in the first century A.D. " men starting from Judaea should possess the world." He has, heard in fact, of the Messianic hope. The Romans did take note of the Messiah, however little they understood him. They even carried the prophecy on to a grotesque pseudo-fulfilment, which, by Tacitus's time, had become orthodox political doctrine for them. But in the days of Herod and Herod's sons, no one could have foreseen that ultimate irony.

3

We are getting ahead of events. During the last phase of the Second Temple's existence, in spite of all constriction, the Jews were closer to being what their leaders thought they should be—a world-wide apostolic nation based on Jerusalem—than at any period before, or since. Strengthened by proselytes and descendants of proselytes, they had multiplied vastly. They were four million strong at the very least and perhaps almost double that, forming a large part of the Roman Empire's inhabitants: fully seven per cent, more than in the United States to-day. They were an energetic, clearly-distinguished element throughout the Levant, and they lived and worshipped as far west as Rome and beyond. Because they talked freely of their promised kingdom, a Gentile's submission to their creed was a semi-political act. In pagan eyes it looked like disloyalty to the State as well as the gods. Yet many saw that the Jew's outrageous difference was the difference of a man who had something worth differing about. Despite every social deterrent, the converts did come in. When a lady of noble family embraced Judaism in Rome itself, an attempt was made to expel Jews from the capital; and a few years later we find Seneca grumbling about the universal influence of " that most criminal nation " over its own conquerors. When Tacitus refers to " tribute drawn from the worst rascals," etcetera, he is thinking of the proselytes' gifts to the

Temple. The loathing felt by the cultured classes, unable to kill this idiocy with silence or scorn, acquired a touch of shuddering fascination. Obviously more was at work than plain silliness.

Around the Jew's head there shone what has been felicitously called (though in another connection) a halo of hatred. That, in itself, was no fatal obstacle to his making further progress, and winning the mass of Gentiles away from paganism. It was a sect characterised by such a halo that eventually did. But in order to decide where the Jew really stood in relation to the larger world, where he might have gone from there and with what consequences, a final effort must be made to evaluate his religion in fact and in prospect. Judaism claimed a divine origin. The question here is not whether it actually was divine, but whether belief in its divinity was so absurd that its practitioners must be treated as obsessed and corrupted, as the slaves of a lie. That affects the issue. In modern terms, to discuss the Nazi movement as if it were a phenomenon of the same kind as British Labour or the Republican Party would be to falsify the whole case. Burning faith in palpable nonsense calls for a psychological type of inquiry which is far less to the point in cases where the nonsense, if perhaps present, is at least not manifest on the surface.

Was Judaism nonsensical, and had the Jews argued themselves into a kind of mania?

Little can be said for the construction placed on Scripture by Fundamentalists. However, this goes against not only the main tradition of Christianity but Judaism itself. Indeed, when Herod reigned, the rabbis had still not altogether settled what was Scripture and what was not. No rigidly defined Bible in the Fundamentalist's sense even existed. This recent aberration therefore need not be reckoned with. Whatever the implications, it is certain that Judaism had evolved. It had not been handed down from heaven in a homogeneous text-book. Nor did even the champions of the Oral Torah pretend that it had, unless in some disguise without relevance to the visible career of Israel. The web of post-Exilic doctrine was linked to the older literature only by the flimsiest-looking threads. It was not so much a sequel as a huge marginal commentary within which that older literature was supposed to become intelligible—a key to Scriptures which the faithful now had to read partly as a cryptogram, because of proven insufficiency at face value.

In this enlargement of Israel's religion, a sceptic might discern only the frantic improvisations of diehards trying to rationalise its failures. He might urge that despair would have ended the agony long before, but for a few accidents like the edict of Cyrus which kept hope alive. I do not see how this view could be directly refuted, at least by historical arguments. But the facts do admit other interpretations. Life is growth; and it can fairly be argued that the Living God, in ordaining a living human community, *ipso facto* ordained a growing one, not static in Egyptian stagnation but advancing in wisdom through a series of individual lives. As perhaps with biological evolution, God wills the process, as well as the products along the way. Development is a good in itself, creation is continuous and organic. That principle, if it applied anywhere, would apply pre-eminently to the community shaped by God to unfold his purposes and provide a model. Jewish progress in charity, in wisdom, in breadth of vision, would thus be the hallowing and the pledge of progress in general.

Not, of course, the smooth automatic progress which is now harder to credit than the dogmas its prophets used to sneer at; rather the sort of zigzag trial-and-error advance which has so far been the rule, and which the story of Israel does exemplify. The very failures which the religion seems to rationalise could have been divinely ordained to save the Chosen People from a narrow complacency. God could have willed to shock them into asking such questions as would lead them on to new insights—to insights discovered for themselves under human conditions, and therefore inscribed upon their hearts as mere dictation could never be. Even a rationalisation may be right. Nor should it be forgotten that the Israel which the Covenant formed was, in a sense, a single immortal person. The whole record can be read as a supreme *Bildungsroman* or education-story with Israel as hero, teaching its readers through life rather than static precepts.

From these abstractions, we may turn to more pragmatic issues. The unbeliever who derides Jewish doctrines has the task of accounting, without their aid, for the Jewish fact in history, and explaining it all by an ordinary sequence of cause and effect: the origins, the ideas, the long survival in dispersion, the flouting of all normal " trends." Here the difficulties are many. Whatever the reason for Israel's uniqueness, Israel indubitably was, and remains, unique. There is at least no obvious way of brushing the divine claims aside, and there never was.

The openness of the other alternative, the believer's, also depends to some extent on the character of the phenomenon in practice. If Judaism, by the first century A.D., had dwindled into an ineffectual myth which mature minds always outgrew, its divine origin might still be very hard to refute, but it would also be very hard to assert. We would have to regard Jewish belief henceforth as an obscurantist bondage, and make whatever we could of later events in the light of that judgment. It is a mistake to suppose that reason and psychological rightness have nothing to do with the staying-power of a religion, or that religions normally linger on in defiance of both. Most of the ancient cults did expire through their own proved inadequacy; most of the gods of Egypt and Babylon simply faded away. But the God of Israel, for whatever reasons, did not. His worshippers, the wise as well as the thoughtless, never sank into a disenchantment deep enough to allow him to die. Therefore he kept, and still keeps, a claim to be taken seriously which Marduk and Ammon have forfeited for ever. The history of Judaism continues to be the history of a creative and vital movement, not a fossil.

One potent factor in the faith of a Jew was the conviction that Judaism, in the hands of its teachers since the Exile, had become what it was meant to become: the great religion foreshadowed by Second Isaiah, satisfying the needs of all mankind. Not that the

Greeks and Romans could be expected to adopt the complex of ceremonies that set Israel apart, but simply that Judaism could provide everything essential. For the Jew himself there was nothing to be gained by apostasy, no excuse for turning away. Future spiritual progress for anyone anywhere could only be a movement toward his own God. The Gentiles were not an argument against God's justice, because there was no longer any question of his having left them in darkness. By listening to the Jews they could all find their way to him. The Messianic Age, it was proper to think, would give substance to the highest dreams they cherished themselves. When God somehow broke down the barriers, the healing waters could immediately flow.

The value of this further belief must also be carefully assessed. The tragedy which left Zion desolate again arose, in part, from a fatal failure to work it out in practice.

Judaism's hope of capturing decisive numbers of pagans lay in whatever power it had to fulfil their own aspirations. It could hardly do so unless it embodied something answering to their ideas, as it embodied the best features of Zoroaster's system. This latter act of digestion had been so successful that Judaism, and religions deriving from it, were to supersede Zoroastrianism itself. However, the issues raised by classical paganism were more complex. Its two chief trends matched the two trends in Judaism; but not so closely as to allow any simple assimilation.

The first corresponded—and indeed, as we have seen, was related—to the religion of Jewish ideologues like Philo. Well-read pagans who were not purely sceptical commonly followed the Hellenistic lead by acknowledging a single Supreme God, called Zeus in Greek, Jupiter in Latin. For them as for their Stoic masters, Supreme Gods in general were all aspects of the same one. He remained ill-defined, an indwelling spirit rather than a personal being. The lesser recipients of popular worship were still conceded a sort of reality. But this was growing steadily more tenuous: even Olympus's shining deities were already flimsier than mere angels were in Judaism. The extension of Plato's thought along allegorical and theological lines, in which Philo had assisted, still had an active future before it. Politics added another factor, the deification of the Emperor. After Augustus the Roman world was drifting toward a state religion based on one God with the Emperor as his viceroy, and a medley of traditional rites in support of the Empire, viewed as the Stoic Cosmopolis under another name. Within that gradually clarifying scheme it was granted that everyone might construe his local gods as he pleased—the illiterate masses naïvely, the literate few symbolically.

Pagan religion, however, had others ways of flourishing. Judaism's Messianic-apocalyptic strand also had its counterpart, though this was more remote, and without traceable connection. The same motif of triumphant and transforming change inspired a whole group of special cults, each with a Messiah or saviour of its own. These saviours were not human beings, past or prospective, but gods taken from ancient myth. Their gift was not welfare in time, but salvation in eternity. Their function was not to free nations from oppression, but to free individuals from the fetters of bodily existence.

All these cults had their roots in the seasonal fertility-ritual of the Near East—the Tammuz pattern which Israel had met in Canaan, centred on a young god or demigod who annually died and rose, and a goddess of Nature. Adonis and Osiris, Attis and Orpheus, each had his devotees. The more sophisticated versions supplied the themes of the Mysteries, Eleusinian for example, and later Mithraic. In these the god's myth became a passionate drama of suffering and death and revival, not of course in historical time, but in " dream time." Through ecstatic rituals the worshipper shared in these events and established a rapport with the god. Thereby he ensured his own release from the dark prison of mortality. The Mysteries were refined esoteric systems. They made moral demands which the cults usually did not, and connected the unregenerate flesh with ideas of sin and evil.

Of what went on at Eleusis hardly anything is reliably known. Its drama seems to have involved the earth-goddess Demeter, and (at least by allusion) Zeus the Father and Dionysus his Saviour-Son, who was the divine patron of all drama. Mithraism, a species of solar worship based on a Zoroastrian heresy, was in some respects a departure, since its god was the slayer and not the victim; but it spread through the Empire organised in Mystery form, with seven grades of initiation. This restrictive aspect is most important. Contrary to a common delusion, the saviour-cults never aspired to be universal. The more advanced were expensive to join and highly discriminating. Mithraism, for instance, excluded women. But they bred a spiritual élite: almost the only non-Jewish subjects of the Empire, at least above the level of superstition, for whom any deity was a matter of deep conviction and personal concern.

In the time of the Herods, pagan religion of this type was still largely at a formative stage. As it developed, it could certainly have been combined with pagan monotheism. Indeed, it was. The Empire itself had a Messianic aura, reflected in Virgil's Fourth Eclogue; the One God came to be symbolised as *Sol Invictus*, the Unconquered Sun; Caesar-worship and sun-worship and Mithraism slowly converged, and the Emperor Julian at last fused them, though he came too late. In this movement toward a world religion, Judaism was to have hardly any direct share. Its exponents were pagans, its unexpected heirs were not Jews. But the Jewish community of the early Empire could not foresee that future. To grasp the nature of the crisis that crippled it and the wound it sustained, we must understand what the chance was that it missed; how it might have guided mankind toward the spiritual coherence which so many desired; how the hopes of the last prophets and Philo might have borne fruit, with the Land made holy for all the world. What-might-have-been is the preface to What-was.

To fill such a role and achieve such ends, Judaism would have had to resolve its own inner conflicts, or at least reduce their acrimony. With that proviso, its ability to speak to the pagan condition was clearly not to be despised. As the only developed ethical monotheism, it was well qualified to put the groping monotheism of pagans on a firm basis. The God of the Jews could be placed without dishonour at the apex of Gentile theology. Philo, moreover, had accomplished a feat which few Gentiles had then so much as attempted, the blending of metaphysical theory with everyday cultus. For in that broader sense the God of classical thinkers had not hitherto been truly comparable to the Lord God of Hosts. A philosophical deity was always the deity of a school, a small circle of exceptional men. Such men seldom evinced the slightest interest in evangelising the masses, who worshipped an Apollo, an Aphrodite, a Hermes, quite differently conceived; and the more exalted the philosophers' god became, the more remote he grew, despite all syncretism, from these gods of the people. Both parties indeed might speak of Zeus or Jupiter, but even then they did not really mean the same thing. No Gentile had yet clearly envisaged a single theology embracing scholar and peasant, noble and commoner, slave-owner and slave. Thus the Jewish God in his complete majesty more than fulfilled classical aspiration. He was immanent and transcendent. He was the object of popular devotion, yet he was also abstract enough to be approved by philosophers.

But to become a faith for Gentile mankind, Judaism would have had to offer more than its perfected vision of One God. It would have had to plant itself in the realm of the cults and Mysteries. It would have had to satisfy the hunger for cosmic drama, for personal salvation, for a key to life and death. A couple of centuries before, its incapacity to do so would have been obvious. Israel's own concept of deliverance had nothing to do with the soul's immortality, or salvation from an imprisoning flesh. It meant the earthly welfare of the community and the downfall of enemies. But Judaism in the Empire, without giving up the older position, had carried its debates on the World to Come to a point where individual souls with immortal destinies were at least admissible. A chance did exist that the tragic yearnings to which the saviour-gods appealed might find their true goal in the God of Israel, if he could be regarded as " saving " his worshipper by some divine action analogous to theirs. In that case, Jewish egalitarianism would certainly give his cult an advantage. His saviourship would not be confined to a club of leisured insiders.

Did any Jews actually see their Lord in that light, or endow him with a new mode or emanation as Saviour? We have indications. They are slight and tantalising enough. Hasty claims about the Dead Sea Scrolls have collapsed. Philo's reference to his Logos as the "Son of God" is only a metaphor, with no hint of a real procession of persons within Divinity. But far away from Jerusalem, Jews explored more hazardous paths, and had been doing so for some time. In one form of the Hypsistarian cult in Phrygia, the Lord God seems to have been equated with an odd deity called Sabazius, a composite of Zeus and Dionysus (that is, Father and Son), who had Mysteries and was a sort of saviour.

Under the circumstances, however, this could scarcely aspire to be much more than a local eccentricity. Whatever the Jews of the diaspora might do, the official Judaism of Zion and the Temple could not sanction experiments. Above all else, while it might tolerate some of the Mysteries' intentions, it could not tolerate anything too much like them. Its integrity prevailed here against a temptation. The last step toward satisfying the Gentiles' needs might have been taken by an apt theological manoeuvre, without bringing in Sabazius or any other alien. Let the God of Israel, or his Messiah, be portrayed as fulfilling the saviour-myths of suffering and recovery—as triumphing through some paradox of mortal defeat—and the gap would close. Judaism would have equipped itself to do all that the Mysteries could do, while going far beyond.

But to that potentiality Judaism turned a blind eye. Israel's faith had purified and defined itself, negatively at least, through its wars against Baal and Tammuz and the other villainous guises of the Nature-god. The prophets had at last managed to negate that god with a theology excluding him. How could the prophets' heirs commit the frightful betrayal of reinstating him, even symbolically? God simply could not become Baal again. The Messiah could not be a new Tammuz. He had to be splendid and victorious. It was rash even to contemplate his death. While that might occur in some remote future, it could not conceivably be part of his mission.

The difficulty was not that Judaism had shirked any issue. Israel's collective memory made it impossible to ignore tribulation, or pretend that there were easy ways to get rid of it. Like so much else, it was an historical datum which had to make historical sense; and it was faced, for instance, in the doctrine of martyrdom. Suffering and death were part of the system as burdens proper to Man, the creature. But to match the cults and Mysteries, Jewish thought would have had to extend them somehow to God the Creator, or to his Messiah, giving them a cosmic value. Here it confronted the hateful spectre of Tammuz, and halted. The urgency of the time clamoured for a major triumph, either political or spiritual. Judaism, seemingly, could not achieve the latter, because of its refusal to talk the same language as the pagan mysticism which alone possessed a vitality like its own.

4

Yet there was one chink in the armour, one gap in the wall that partitioned Judaism off. Embedded in the poetry of Second Isaiah, the herald of Israel's mission to the Gentiles, were four songs about a " Servant of the Lord " who was to figure in it. The last and longest of these, in chapters lii–liii, was most disquieting.

> Behold, my servant shall prosper,
> > he shall be exalted and lifted up,
> > and shall be very high.
> As many were astonished at him—
> > his appearance was so marred, beyond human semblance,
> > and his form beyond that of the sons of men—
> So shall he startle many nations;
> > kings shall shut their mouths because of him . . .

He was despised and rejected by men;
    a man of sorrows, and acquainted with grief;
    and as one from whom men hide their faces
    he was despised, and we esteemed him not.
Surely he has borne our griefs
    and carried our sorrows;
    yet we esteemed him stricken,
    smitten by God, and afflicted.
But he was wounded for our transgressions,
    he was bruised for our iniquities;
    upon him was the chastisement that made us whole,
    and with his stripes we are healed.
All we like sheep have gone astray;
    we have turned every one to his own way;
    and the Lord has laid on him
    the iniquity of us all . . .
By oppression and judgment he was taken away;
    and as for his generation, who considered
    that he was cut off out of the land of the living,
    stricken for the transgression of my people?
And they made his grave with the wicked,
    and with a rich man in his death,
    although he had done no violence,
    and there was no deceit in his mouth.
Yet it was the will of the Lord to bruise him . . .
    he shall see his offspring, he shall prolong his days;
    the will of the Lord shall prosper in his hand;
He shall see the fruit of the travail of his soul and be satisfied;
    by his knowledge shall the righteous one, my servant,
    make many to be accounted righteous;
    and he shall bear their iniquities.

    What had been in the prophet's mind when he composed that haunting passage? How had he dared to speak of vicarious suffering and resurrection, so bluntly recalling Tammuz, without a word of explanation? And who was he talking about—the Messiah? This last question at least was causing perplexity in the days of the Herods, and the New Testament preserves a curious answer to it (*Acts* viii : 34). The answer which the rabbis gave then is not recorded. Later, while unable wholly to dismiss the Messianic view, they argued that the Servant was an ideal Israel.

But whatever one made of him, the breach was there. Through it the light of a fresh vision might at any moment stream in—the awful, blasphemous, yet inevitably conquering vision of a Messiah for Gentile as well as Jew: a Messiah who should appear in history, suffer and die, and return to life.

5

In the summer of A.D. 64, during the reign of Nero, Rome was devastated by a great fire.

Nothing (says Tacitus) could remove the sinister suspicion that the fire had been brought about by Nero's orders. To put an end to this rumour, he shifted the charge on to others, and inflicted the most cruel tortures upon a body of men detested for their abominations, and popularly known by the name of Christians. This name came from one Christus, who was put to death in the reign of Tiberius by the procurator Pontius Pilate; but though checked for the time, the detestable superstition broke out again, not in Judaea only, where the mischief began, but even in Rome, where every horrible and shameful iniquity, from every quarter of the world, pours in and finds a welcome.

First whose who acknowledged themselves of this persuasion were arrested; and upon their testimony a vast number were condemned, not so much on the charge of incendiarism as for their hatred of the human race.

Christianity was born as a Jewish sect. It came into the world with a challenge which the main body of Israel refused. Not very long after that refusal, Israel was stung to challenge the world in its own way, and collapsed in ruins. The Christians spoke of cause and effect. It could be argued, even on agnostic assumptions, that they were right.

Tacitus witnesses to the hatred felt for Christians, which enabled Nero to fix the blame on them. Most of Israel came to share this hatred. To-day, after two embittered millennia, passions have subsided a little. But the spokesmen of Judaism still attribute the split to a fundamental and impious mistake. Christians, they say, chose to worship somebody who was no more than human. A popular teacher or late-coming minor prophet was turned into God. If the issue were really thus, the record of the downfall of Zion might be simpler. It is not thus. In briefly examining Christian origins I have no wish to introduce Christian apologetic. My sole aim is to elucidate the issue.

We should beware of loose assumptions about a "gradual growth of legend." The main Christian assertions were certainly being made while many witnesses of the Church's alleged foundation were still living. Theories shifting the bulk of the New Testament to a much later date will not hold water; literary faking on the scale required would have been far beyond the resources of the age, in several respects. The Christian assertions were made in the first century A.D. by Jews who accepted Jesus as the Christ and by Gentile converts of theirs. They were made publicly, in the teeth of contempt and persecution. But they were made effectually, partly for reasons which will already have begun to emerge, and partly for others which elude ordinary inquiry.

Christian faith was grounded on the Incarnation of God. Jesus was the Son of the Eternal Father and mysteriously one with him. God, therefore, had lived on earth as Man, entering into the role of Jewish Messiah, but investing it with a higher meaning. The Lord of History had stepped into history himself. He had taught a lesson of love and righteousness, worked miracles, undergone crucifixion by his own consent, risen from the grave, and departed Elsewhere. His sufferings as Man mystically expiated the sins of mankind. He gave believers eternal life with him, to which his

resurrection pointed the way. Christians predicted a Second
Coming when he would judge the world. They summoned all to
repent, to put away their sins and idols, and to become united with
Christ through participation in the life of the Church he had
founded, under the wings of the Holy Spirit.

There are likenesses here to the Gentile saviour-myths, and hence
partly the strength of the appeal. But it must not be supposed that
Christianity could have been produced by grafting such myths on
to Judaism. The story of the Incarnation remains unique. God
(not *a* god) becomes Man, once, in history (not in dream time).
He meets well-known figures like Pilate (not unverifiable heroes of
legend). He suffers death voluntarily (not because of Fate or the
Nature of Things). He physically returns to life. According to the
Christians the Incarnation *happened*, closing the gap between
human and divine. Because it did, all the world was changed.
Some expressed it in terminology borrowed from Philo, speaking
of the Son as the Word. But their crucial declarations, "The
Word was God" and "The Word was made flesh and dwelt
among us," were wholly unprecedented. As for the myths of
Attis and Dionysus and the rest—and such parallels in general—they
may be regarded from the believer's point of view as hints, dreams,
anticipations, converging on a Christ who fulfils and transcends
them; in fact as a species of Gentile prophesying.[2] If not so
regarded, they have less historical bearing than is often supposed.
One can never reach the heart of Christian theology simply by
exploring the labyrinth of the Mysteries. The Church's main
theme cannot be shown evolving from them. Nor can it be found
in the Dead Sea Scrolls. The last Servant Song in *Isaiah* opened a

2 Sir James Frazer, whose research supplied so much ammunition for those
who have attacked Christian doctrine by stressing such parallels, himself
realised that the parallels were two-edged. See Victor White, *God and the
Unconscious*, p. 236. Incidentally the divine unity of Father and Son was
anticipated in the Sabazius cult. But this derived partly from Judaism.
It is an interesting speculation—it cannot, at present, be more—that the
Phrygian Jews carried on some lost strand of Messianic prophecy, and that
Jesus used its metaphors.

door, but Jesus Christ could never have been deduced from it.

So the Church gave this narrative of its birth. It was extraordinary, but a Christian could urge (and still can) the extraordinariness of the Church itself. To attempt to cover the facts in any other way is to become conscious of peculiar difficulties. The hostile leaders of Judaism had to face a question which still faces the non-Christian historian: If the Church's own account of its origins is false, then what is the truth, how did it originate? Their answer seems to have been the one usually given to-day—that a perfectly natural series of events had been misconstrued, mythologised, falsified, perhaps even by outright trickery as hinted in *Matthew* xxviii : 11–15. But there is no evidence that they, or the Roman persecutors, ever arrived at a clear alternative version of what actually had happened; and their problem remains unsolved. Apparently the Christians' enemies never did what would have been easy to do if they were lying—refuted them by producing eye-witnesses and publicising a true account, an exposé, to destroy their claims. The numerous modern efforts to reconstruct a "Christ Myth" or a non-divine, non-miraculous "Historical Jesus" have thus far led only to paradoxes and contradictions.[3]

What we confront is a kind of rift in history. Either the thing happened essentially as the Church maintains . . . or something else happened which is totally unparalleled and unfathomed. On either showing, however, the challenge to the Jews of the first century was much the same. A concept of the Messiah was put to them which was primarily spiritual. The divine deliverance was preached

3 Much Christian apologetic is dismissed by sceptics with a deserved contempt. Yet the question "If not this, then what?" seems as disconcerting to them as ever. Scrutiny of the long lists of conflicting theories compiled by a Protestant writer, Albert Schweitzer, and a Jewish one, Joseph Klausner, confirms the impression suggested here: that the reality must have been more mysterious and (so to speak) richer than any critics have imagined, and that the strength of Christianity, while comparative religion can rationalise it to some extent, was bewildering because it lay so largely in the mysterious element—whether this was what the Church said it was or not.

as salvation from sin and death rather than from oppression. The majority opposed or ignored this doctrine and preferred nationalism, thereby courting a catastrophe which soon overtook them. But the challenge turned out to be more than a mere sermon. The insignificant-looking Church embodied *something* unsuspected and beyond human normality. *Something* not bargained for gave it power to surmount disaster, to annex the Jewish world-mission, and to break free in triumph, doing among the Gentiles what Judaism had vainly tried to do, while leaving Judaism itself bewildered and crippled.

As for the relation of Christian teaching to prior Jewish thought, all that need be added is that its antecedents in this respect are Pharisaic. Jesus expounds more or less the ethics of Hillel, but in a more memorable and positive tone: his Golden Rule says " Do unto others." Also he uses the language of apocalypse, a Pharisee creation. But the apocalyptic violence, the insistence on complete transformation, the vision of the divine reign, are all raised to another level. Men are to be transformed by a rebirth in spirit, and the kingdom is within. Three Gospels give a discourse in which he takes up a prophecy about another fall of the Temple, already made in the *Testament of Levi*. His hints at ruinous warfare, his association of the fall with his own rejection, mark the same antithesis between a Messianism of conversion and a chauvinistic will-o'-the-wisp.

After his execution for sedition and blasphemy, the Church existed for a few years as a small group of Jewish Christians, in bad odour because of his reputed crimes. Then it passed into a phase of readjustment. Its members in Jerusalem continued throughout to live as Jews. They kept the Law, and hoped for their Lord's return to complete his work. The death of Judas had reduced the apostolic leadership to eleven, but another had been recruited to make it up to twelve, Christ's number. That number was related to the tribes of Israel, and probably implied that the Church was the new Faithful Remnant from which a reborn Israel would spring. The Christian body, under the presidency of Peter, organised itself on

similar lines to the Essene and kindred groups which saw their
vocation in the same light.

Jerusalem, however, was gradually overshadowed by the missions. In that field the most vocal figure was the tent-maker Paul,
formerly Saul. A Pharisee, and a pupil of Hillel's grandson Gamaliel,
he had been converted by an apparition of Christ and accepted as
an extra apostle. It became evident early that Christian preaching
was making more headway in the mixed population of northern
Palestine than it was in Judaea. Paul threw himself into missions in
Asia Minor. He applied himself to two main problems: the right
method of reaching pagan minds, and the full unravelling of the
riddle of Christ's death. He solved both at once by developing the
doctrine of divine saviourship and atonement. This gave him the
missionary key which had eluded Judaism. His experience among
Gentiles led him to the conviction that the Jewish Law was now
transcended in a higher fulfilment, and was not binding on the
converts. He, or someone under his influence, wrote of Christ as
" a priest after the order of Melchizedek "—outside the Jewish
system.

The tone taken by Paul, who had never known Jesus, offended
the veterans who had. Peter himself clashed with the tireless
theologian. But Peter's own travels helped him to fuller comprehension, and both were comrades in martyrdom under Nero. The
triumph of the Pauline spirit undoubtedly saved all that was vital.
It enabled the Church to spread without limit. However, it also
entailed a selectiveness in the presentation of Christ which postponed
any wide acceptance of him by Jews, and condemned the Church
in Jerusalem to nullity.

There was a clear immediate reason for this estrangement. Few
Jews would admit a Messiah whose words and acts were of no
direct help to the earthly community in its urgent straits. The
Pharisees had put the moral and spiritual side of Judaism above the
political, but as a matter of emphasis, not in an otherworldly sense.
Israel as a living body of people, with its Land and its holy institutions, had to be maintained at all costs. Under Roman pressure

the need was more desperate than ever. But as the Gospels show, the Church preserved very little indeed of anything said by Jesus with a bearing on that issue. Certainly he did not endorse the more gloomy Mystery-cults, by teaching that earthly life was irredeemably evil and that salvation lay in escape. He did, however, put the inward transformation first. Other kinds of welfare, by Divine Providence, would follow on that. "Seek ye first the Kingdom of God, and all these things shall be added to you." How he enlarged on such sayings in the political context, or whether he did, we do not know. But Christianity in its actual development laid so much stress on individual salvation and the Hereafter that it seemed to offer nothing to Israel as such, nothing to the Jewish social order in its struggles and agonies. It seemed, in fact, a public peril. The rejoinder that Christ could nevertheless be safely followed because he was God, and knew best, and would come back to put the world to rights, was no answer for most Jews. It was an outrage. The Holy One could not become Man, except by an unthinkable degradation.

So hesitation ceased, and they turned away from the Church. Paul lived long enough to see that they were doing so, and he responded nobly. His chief pronouncement on their alienation is in the eleventh chapter of his *Epistle to the Romans*. God, Paul declares, has not rejected his people. Defections from truth have occurred before, yet there has always been a Remnant, a faithful Israel which inherits the promises and the burden. That role is now filled by the humble band who have faith in Jesus. As for the rest, their "blindness" is providential and sent by God. The handful who accept the true Christ have been driven out among the Gentiles; and that very separation is God's device to enrol the Gentiles into his Church. Yet the Jews of the blind majority are not cut off for ever. The Church as Paul is learning to see it is an inspired expedient, a divine makeshift. When it has done its work among the Gentiles, the veil will drop. Then all will be reunited, and the Jew will still be what he has always been, the senior partner, the Lord's own.

With that last glance of beatitude the apostle went his way, and the Jews went theirs. On the one hand, personal salvation; on the other, the vision of the earthly community as inseparable from the World to Come. To this day the conflict is unresolved, the Pauline prophecy unfulfilled.

6

In spite of the momentum toward a split, Christianity was slow to become a distinct religion. Suetonius, drawing on records of the Emperor Claudius's reign, writes confusedly and confusingly of the Jews in Rome who " made disturbances at the instigation of Chrestus." Among the Jews in Palestine, disturbances took a different form. Their dilemma gathered to a head in a series of Messianic blazes. About 44 an agitator named Theudas attracted a following and briefly rebelled. So in due course did an Egyptian, whose desperadoes, more than four thousand strong, marched round to the rear of the Mount of Olives and tried to surprise Jerusalem by pouring suddenly over the top. They were dispersed by the procurator Felix with heavy infantry. This Egyptian achieved a curious immortality in *Acts* xxi : 38. A graver menace came from the apocalyptic terrorism, which reached its climax with the Zealots' organisation as a party by John of Gischala in 66. Zealotry in alliance with banditry had already produced a sinister " underground."

Roman rule, meanwhile, was a chronic provocation. The Emperor Caligula demanded that his own statue should be set up in the Temple. A similar demand made on the Jews of Alexandria brought Philo himself to the capital in their defence. The mad emperor's murder gave a respite, but it did not last. His successor Claudius, though of sound mind, first experimented with a Judaean monarchy under Herod Agrippa, then made the country into a province again; in 49 he expelled many Jews from Rome. The climax came with the governorship of the corrupt and cruel Florus, who took office in 64. Far from pacifying Judaea he let the bandits go free—in return for a percentage. Next he seized treasure from the Temple, ostensibly " for Caesar," an interpretation of its character as a public fund which Pilate's discomfiture should have warned him against. The Jews made savage fun of him by pretending to take up collections in aid of their poverty-stricken governor.

Plainly an explosion was imminent. The Zealot cry for blood was heard everywhere. Against it rose the voices of the more cautious, and of all who, like the Christians, took a spiritual rather than a political view of their faith. Peace was the policy of the Pharisees, and also the majority of the priests, who struggled to mediate. Apart from anything else their Temple was at long last finished, and they shuddered at exposing its beauty to the huge Roman catapults.

Josephus, the main authority for the history of this crisis, was of priestly family and Pharisaic leanings himself. His book *The Jewish War* is not wholly to be relied on, partly because of his obvious mistakes and illusions, partly because he was a rich intellectual out of sympathy with the crowd, and partly because he wrote after he had gone over to the Romans. However, in spite of all these drawbacks, there is no reason to doubt that his account of the peace movement gives a fair picture of the mode of thinking which was actually current. In two long discourses, one attributed to Herod Agrippa II, the other to himself, Josephus enlarges on such doctrines as that the Chosen People were never meant to bear arms; that the Sabbath laws made a holy war impossible for them; that as guardians of consecrated gifts from all nations, they had a duty not to put these in danger; and that earthly sovereignty was manifestly God's will for the Romans, not the Jews, whose calling was of another order.

Josephus also takes up the theme of the doom hanging over Jerusalem, and over the Temple in particular. He speaks of "an age-old saying of inspired men that the City would be taken and the most holy Temple burnt to the ground by right of war, if ever the citizens strove with each other and Jewish hands were the first to pollute the house of God." And again, of " the writings of the old prophets and the oracle pronounced against this unhappy city," which would fall when " some man began the slaughter of his fellow-countrymen." Neither of Josephus's allusions is easy to document. He may be recalling the verse in the *Testament of Levi*, supposing it to be a genuine prophecy by the patriarch. He may also be recalling the Christians' reaffirmation of this. At any rate the defilement of the Temple, to him, means its exploitation as a mere military base, by Jewish fanatics at odds with the true genius of Israel. Doubtless he is indulging a touch of hindsight, in view of the actual turn of events. But here and elsewhere he testifies plausibly to the spread of forebodings.

They were ineffectual. Neither Pharisees nor priests could arrest the landslide. Clashes occurred in Jerusalem; and it was Eleazer the Temple Captain, son of the High Priest Ananias, who took the fatal step. He announced that no more gifts would be accepted from foreigners, and no more sacrifices would be offered for Rome or the Emperor—an overt act of sedition. In Caesarea, a town of uneasy civic politics, the indignant Gentiles expressed their feelings by a pogrom. This was answered by Jewish counter-violence throughout Palestine, whereupon the administration crumbled. The year was 66, towards the end of the reign of Nero.

A first Roman attempt at suppression clarified the nature of what was happening. The legionaries approached Jerusalem on a Sabbath, at the Feast of Tabernacles. Devout Jews were bound twice over to inaction. Yet when the Romans faltered before the gate, the rebels fought and won. Nationalism was already in the saddle. Its most active support came from the downtrodden masses —peasants and craftsmen, slaves and proselytes—whose Messianic belief was not a tepid theory but a fiery vision. The odds were gigantic: three million people at most (since the Jews outside Palestine gave no tangible aid) against well over fifty million. But as matters stood, counsels of prudence could not be expected to carry weight. Nor were the rebel leaders *ipso facto* irreligious. The faith of some, on the contrary, erred by excess. It amounted to a conviction that an absolutely reckless reliance on God would force his hand. He would be compelled to rescue his people. And the odds had been no less daunting of old when he smote Sennacherib.

For some time the Jews had the advantage. Their country was a long way from Italy and hard to invade. A provisional government, nominally headed by Ananias and a certain Joseph ben Gorion, was set up in Jerusalem. Coins were struck with "Liberation of Zion" on them. But while the centre held firm, the outposts weakened. The Jewish commander in Galilee was no other than Josephus himself. At first he defended his stronghold of Jotapata with some gallantry. But when the veteran Vespasian, one of the conquerors of Britain, arrived in 67 to take charge of operations, Josephus decided that the cause was lost. He surrendered; and he went far beyond surrendering. Apparently he supposed himself to be a seer. Persuaded that the Empire was divinely ordained, he had the brilliant notion of applying the Messianic prophecy itself (in a vague form) to Vespasian. "A man coming from Judaea" was destined to rule the world . . . and where, after all, was Vespasian at that moment? The Imperial general had already heard hints of the same sort from an oracle at Mount Carmel, and was impressed as well as flattered. In the ensuing three years, the course of politics bore Josephus out. Nero committed suicide; his successor Galba reigned into 69 but was assassinated; two further pretenders lasted only a few months; and then—first in Egypt, a few days later in Judaea itself—the army declared for Vespasian. Leaving his son Titus in command, he returned to Rome as emperor. Thus, by a supreme irony, the prediction seemed to be fulfilled in the person of the enemy it had raised against Israel.

One might feel more secure in trusting Josephus's narrative if he were less conceited. He says he was conscious, during his Galilean heart-searchings, that once the Romans had captured him "the war would be virtually over." In a sense this was true, but in virtue of the position he held rather than his own indispensability. Anybody with such a warped idea of his importance is likely to have warped ideas of human relations in general. While *The*

Jewish War is correct in outline, its account of the leaders and factions in the last campaign is almost certainly partial and quite certainly repellent. We see, or half-see, a tragedy of hopeless courage through a fog of abuse; an epic of unflinching fidelity through the eyes of a traitor. But there is nowhere else to look.

When Galilee had gone the free territory dwindled. Scattered pockets of resistance remained, but before very long the Jewish area was reduced for practical purposes to Jerusalem itself. Here John's Zealots had risen to supremacy. They fortified the Temple for their own use. The pacifists were now not merely pacific but horrified. The Zealots, however, silenced all talk of seeking terms, and consolidated their grip with the help of an Idumaean corps. Then the bandit element in Zealotry got out of hand. Its looting ignited a small war inside the big one. The Idumaeans became restless, and a rival nationalist named Simon seized control of most of Jerusalem and blockaded John in the Temple. But the Romans, distracted by the crisis following Nero's death, failed to profit by Jewish dissension. When Titus at length advanced to besiege the city there was no one ready to betray it.

Titus established his headquarters on Mount Scopus. Here, and behind, he laid out camps for his legions, while posting other troops eastward on the Mount of Olives. At the sight of Romans along the skyline, all fighting inside Jerusalem died away instantly. The defenders made a sortie which threw the forces on Scopus into disorder; Titus had hard work rallying them. But having stabilised the position he began to press closer. All the way down the hillside his soldiers systematically demolished walls, cut down fruit-trees, and filled up gullies, till the ground between crest and city was a smooth expanse without cover. The Jewish retort was to lay a trap. As if the struggle of factions had been resumed, an armed party pretended to drive another out of the gates. Romans approached to take the expellees prisoner and were promptly captured themselves.

Realising that the siege would be formidable, Titus next put up three eighty-foot towers from which missiles could be discharged to drive the defenders off the walls. The legionaries managed to swarm over into the north quarter of the city. Here, however, they were checked in street battles. Another wall was taken, but lost again; one of the towers collapsed.

Titus tried diplomacy. He sent Josephus, now an amenable puppet, to appeal to his fellow-countrymen to give up. Josephus mounted a Roman horse, rode with a Roman escort toward the walls, and . . . appealed. According to himself, he talked for a long time and most eloquently about the Jews' sacred duty to be submissive. But the spectacle of the wealthy collaborator, with his classical education and his sanctimonious distortions of history, was not mollifying in its effect; and the siege went on.

Its horror increased. As famine set in, fresh waves of looting swept through Jerusalem. Anybody suspected of hoarding a scrap of food was in danger of being tortured till he revealed its where-abouts. Accusations of treachery poisoned the air, yet still there was no surrender. The Romans drew their net tighter. Their siege-works crept toward the walls under a hail of arrows. A real detestation of the enemy had grown among them. Jewish foragers who slipped out into the valleys were ambushed and cruci-fied by dozens. Arab auxiliaries, filled with ancestral hate, were unleashed to commit atrocities. At last the whole city was ringed by a Roman wall, and it was no longer safe to take a step outside anywhere. The shortage became worse. Entire families died together, roving gangs robbed the corpses, and cannibalism began to be heard of, all under a constant shower of boulders from a battery of siege-engines. The defence finally cracked at the Tower of Antonia, and a path lay open to the barricaded Temple. Roman troops poured along to the gate and assailed it with battering-rams. When it held, they set fire to it and streamed through as the timbers fell.

Jerusalem had its second death in an atmosphere of the monstrous and terrible. Prophets shrieked of doom in the streets, omens were recalled, rumours flew round—how a star shaped like a sword had glared balefully in the sky, how a heifer had given birth to a lamb, how supernatural lights had flashed on the buildings, how chariots and armed men had been seen careering over the clouds. And now, in this fatal year 70, the calendar had come round to the same August day on which Nebuzaradan had sacked the Temple of Solomon. Fire broke out in the sanctuary. The glorious fabric was wrapped in smoke and flame; yet the survivors still fought frantically, choked and scorched and bloodstained, not despairing that even in this final extremity God would intervene and send his Anointed to scatter the impious intruders. Around the altar, where daily sacrifices had never ceased throughout all the siege, bodies were piled and blood ran down. As the Jews perished one after another, the noise of war sank toward an exterminatory hush. But the holocaust raged on; the holy veil disintegrated; un-hallowed spoilers snatched God's Menorah; and still the Anointed did not come.

CHAPTER TWELVE

THE PROLONGATION OF DAYS

Apart from the crushing of a few suicide groups and outlying fortresses, the war was finished. Titus's soldiers took possession of the holy precinct. They propped up their idolatrous eagles facing the east gate, and—abomination of abominations—sacrificed to them. Further use of the wrecked building was forbidden. So lately completed, it slid now into dereliction. Jews, for the present, were permitted to go on living in their own capital, though many were sold as slaves. But all Jewish organisations had perished, and a strong garrison ensured that they should never revive. Order reigned and a grim quiet fell. In Rome Titus held a triumphal procession, and erected an arch (which is still there) portraying the captive Menorah and other booty.

That, like the previous disaster, ought by every rule to have been the end. In a way it was, at least for many heart-breaking centuries. However, the nature of the wound was slow to become clear, because of immediate activities that covered it up. Manifestly the life of Israel was again hanging by a thread; but again the thread held.

It held, in the person of Rabbi Johanan ben Zakkai. Johanan is said to have been a pupil of Hillel, the youngest and the most learned. This is just barely possible. A strict traditionalist with little use for Messianic excitements, he had opposed the rising. The death-agonies of Jerusalem convinced him that independence was a mirage, and he resolved to save whatever could be saved. According to tradition he slipped away during the siege by a reversal of the stratagem of the wooden horse. He hid in a coffin which three other rabbis carried out of the city, obtaining permission to pass the Roman lines with their supposed corpse. They left the coffin in a cave, and after they had had time to get safely home, Johanan climbed out. However that may be, we find him soon afterwards at Jabneh near Jaffa, setting up a small unofficial Sanhedrin and a rabbinic academy called " The Vineyard."

Almost imperceptibly a faint pulse began to beat again. The shattered Jews of the dispersion discovered that they still had a leader, and a centre of sorts. When the venerable Johanan died he was succeeded in The Vineyard by Gamaliel, grandson of the Gamaliel mentioned in *Acts*, who was himself the grandson of Hillel. Gamaliel II was a hard-working and intelligent man. A restraining presence at his elbow was the moderate Joshua ben Hananiah, ugly, threadbare, but very sane, who lived by making nails. These two rabbis maintained the continuity of the Tanna'im, and kept Judaism afloat while it reappraised itself. A third appeared alongside, the more original Rabbi Akiba, with whom the true recovery, to the extent that there was any, may be said to have started.

Akiba ben Joseph was born somewhat before A.D. 50 in humble circumstances. For many years he was a shepherd. He married a wife named Rachel, of whom nothing remains to us but an endearing impression of loyalty. They had raised a considerable family when, at the age of forty, Akiba underwent a conversion. A spell of study under Joshua ben Hananiah and another notable rabbi, Eliezer, made him famous as a scholar, but he reached his fifties before he presumed to teach students himself. After that he acquired many pupils and much influence. In the years 95 and 96 he was travelling overseas, visiting Jewish communities as far off as Rome. His popularity surrounded him afterwards with a cloud of amiable legends; but there is no reason to doubt the traditions which show him as conspicuously modest and kind, an unwearying benefactor of the sick and the needy.

Akiba and his colleagues faced a daunting task of reconstitution. Titus's victory had confirmed the schism of the Christians, and strengthened their hand. Those in Jerusalem had managed to escape to Pella, on the east side of the central Jordan valley. They and their brethren said the siege was not only a judgment on the Jews for rejecting Christ, but a sign of the dawning of his new dispensation. Some added that their Lord's return would soon follow. So the rabbis drew the line at last. The Christians, they ruled, were no longer a sect within Israel but *minim*, heretics. Towards the end of the first century A.D. Gamaliel II inserted an anti-Christian prayer in the synagogue service. St. Justin Martyr refers to hostile emissaries whom the rabbis sent round. The Pella group expired; Jewish Christianity petered out in a last series of ephemeral phantoms calling themselves " bishops of Jerusalem," and in a fading breakaway sect of Ebionites (" the poor ") who honoured Jesus but denied his divinity. The extinction of Jerusalem as a vocal Jewish-Christian headquarters meant that the Gentile Christianity of Paul's converts, with Jesus reverenced as Saviour rather than King, reigned almost unchallenged. Before long the bishops of Jerusalem were Gentiles themselves.

As a result the two societies fell apart. Both lost by the split. The Jews, in spite of all their defeats, retained the sense of historic community and the ideal of an earthly commonwealth of God. But while continuing their old stress on Man as a social being, they shut their eyes to the fresh vision of Man as a person, freed by God for an eternal destiny as such. Christians, for their part, had the latter but tended to lose sight of the former. Cut off from the wisdom of that Israel of which they professed themselves the heirs; living chiefly away from Judaea, in the Samaritan country, in cosmopolitan cities like Caesarea and Antioch, and in Asia Minor —they felt their way very uncertainly, sure of nothing except that tremendous Intrusion.

It is necessary to grasp how they diverged, in order to see how Judaism developed into what was partly a mere reaction against them. Except in principle, the Church was still an improvisation. As a human structure it still owed most to Jewish models such as the Essene brotherhoods. There was a growing consciousness, however, that although one could make out prophetic hints at a suffering Messiah, the life of Jesus did not fit easily into Jewish patterns. He had not complied with popular hopes by founding a kingdom, nor had he given substance to Apocalypse by revolutionising the world; and to promise a Second Coming remedying all the omissions was no real solution. The treasure which the Christians possessed and the Jews did not was a new experience growing out of the basic Jewish experience, yet not to be stated entirely in its language. The task of finding how to explain this, to convey it, to inspire others with it, still called for much prayer and meditation. A full terminology was not ready.

One handicap for many Christians was their delusion that the Second Coming would occur soon, in terms of earthly time as conceived by them. Nowadays, it is obvious that the event might be deferred for ten thousand years and the interval would still be tiny, compared with the countless millennia B.C. But the early Christians had no palaeontology or archaeology, and no intuitive sense of cosmic duration such as the Hindus had. History was more or less over, was it not? The only object of studying pre-Christian Scripture was to prove to doubters that Jesus had fulfilled all the hopes expressed in it. The Church was the new Israel. In the hands of people who thought so, the story of the old Israel ceased to be primarily a story. It became a sequence of types and symbols, sometimes rather jejune and unconvincing. When Christian philosophy did take shape, it had lost organic connection with Israel's past. For many years Christian historical thinking consisted merely of adjustments to the delay in the divine advent, a delay which had given the Church itself a history, and confronted it with practical problems. The Mystical Body of Christ long seemed unable to come to terms with time. It remained salvationist and otherworldly, tempted toward rejection of life.

Christianity continued to have a far greater share than Judaism of the world-mission, and the largeness of spirit that went with it. As the years passed, it went on gaining in this respect, while its rival declined. It was not burdened with the Jewish Law. Also, it eventually proved able to adopt and baptise Gentile philosophy, whereas the rabbis (despite Philo) grew so distrustful of this that some of them became reluctant to proselytise at all, for fear the proselytes would corrupt Judaism.

But the spirit of Christianity was not quite universal. After the split it had a blind spot, or worse, toward its matrix. The received texts of the Gospels are all affected by the quarrel with Judaism at one stage or another. They all select data in such a manner as to impress readers with Jewish corruption and Jewish guilt in the Crucifixion. The authors or editors record Jesus' rebukes of Pharisee decadence; they do not mention his Pharisee forerunners, or the fact that so much of the Jewish teaching which he endorsed was Pharisaic. To heighten the effect of iniquity and imminent judgment, three Gospels enlarge on his prophecy of the Temple's fall, and mix it up in a most disturbing way with his sayings about the end of the world.

The first "New Testament" was compiled by the wealthy convert Marcion, not as a supplement to Jewish Scripture, but as a substitute for it. Marcion regarded everything from *Genesis* to the last prophets as satanic deceit. The Church disavowed that extreme view. But elsewhere in Christian literature we come across attacks on the Law, abuse of Judaism in general, biblical misinterpretation, and a good deal of sheer libel. One Jewish retort was an Anti-Gospel, a kind of debunking historical novel about Jesus which became steadily more detailed. This charged him with black magic and other crimes inviting his punishment. It would be unfair, however, to imply that the rabbis made much use of the Anti-Gospel. They preferred to freeze Christianity with silence, and steer the minds of the faithful away from it. Away . . . into a style of life studiously different.

2

After 70 the Temple was gone. The priests and Sadducees were gone. The Essenes, if not quite gone yet, were rapidly going. But the synagogues and rabbis survived, Johanan's Vineyard survived, and, with them, a largely Pharisaic corpus of thought that could nourish Israel after the Pharisees too dissolved as a group. Hillel's descendants and their followers created Rabbinic Judaism, the faith of the second and longer Exile.

This was marked by a sharp trend toward total separatism, a recoil from the embittered and embittering world into cliquish introversion. The leaders were jurists, who expounded the Torah and seldom looked far beyond it. Rabbis of this type tended to close ranks as a would-be authoritative caste. Soon after Titus's triumph some of them began trying to impose fresh regulations such as Ezra at his worst might have applauded: vetoes on theatre-going, on celebrating the Emperor's birthday, on exercising at a Gentile gymnasium, on shaving. Jewish doctors were urged not to treat Gentile mothers in childbirth. The rampart of ceremony was reared higher, and even more stress was laid on the Jew's incompatibility with those outside it.

Judaism narrowed down because it could do nothing else. The stately evolution toward a faith transcending the Temple suddenly had to produce, instead, a faith without the Temple. Growth had to turn itself into concentration, into the undistracted centring of all Israel on something strong enough to endure when the Holy City lay trampled. Ezekiel and the elders had faced that problem in Babylon, and the solution now could only be the same as theirs. The unshaken " something " was the Torah, Israel's portable homeland, augmented with the additions of a further six and a half centuries.

Accordingly the rabbis made it a point of urgency to wind up the debate as to what was Scripture and what was not, and define the canon of the Bible—or, as Christians called it, the Old Testament. This they more or less succeeded in doing about A.D. 90 at a council at Jamnia dominated by Pharisees. Hesitations persisted over *Ecclesiastes*, because of its scepticism, over *Esther*, because of its failure to mention God, and over the *Song of Songs*, because of considerations even more palpable. Akiba's endorsement, however, brought the *Song* safely into harbour, and scruples about the others died gradually away. There was never any suggestion of a special divine guidance in choosing whether to approve or exclude. Each book was submitted to the pooled judgment of scholars as to its worth, and the criteria were far from exact. But the Pentateuch, the Torah *par excellence*, passed as a matter of course; and the men of Jamnia overruled the defunct Sadducees by passing also the Prophets and Sacred Writings. A major absentee from their list was *Enoch*, which, as appears from the Christian *Epistle of Jude* (verses 14–15), had been accepted in some circles as authentic. *Enoch* and other pseudepigrapha may indeed have been set aside partly as seeming too helpful to Christianity. It was at this time also that various writings which had found their way into the Greek Bible were dropped as doctrinally unsound, or as doubtful in their authority, or as too recent to be truly inspired: thereby becoming "apocryphal," i.e. hidden, for private study only. *Ecclesiasticus* and the first two books of *Maccabees* were the chief casualties. (The Christians, who used the Septuagint, went on reading them without any restriction.)

Thus the Jewish people were given the Torah in a definitive form. They also had the developed Oral Torah, the mass of related tradition and interpretation, with the doctrines embedded in it. But they had nothing else. The rabbis therefore reiterated more firmly than ever that everything needful was in Scripture; their own function was simply to apply the words of God's universal guide. "Greater is study of the Torah," a new saying ran, "than the rebuilding of the Temple." In a sense, one must repeat, the process was impoverishing. Yet it also bred a new flexibility. If everything necessary was in Scripture, then Scripture must contain something to fit any occasion. But as its literal sense did not, Sadducee Fundamentalism was clearly nonsense and dead for ever. There was no evading the case for interpretation—and more imaginative interpretation. Midrash again was the order of the day.

Here Akiba took up the task from his Pharisee forerunners. Not enough is known about the real oral tradition to settle how much of an innovator he was; though it is likely that he adapted theories already existing, and hinted at in the Wisdom books. What he at least brought into favour, if he did not invent it, was exegesis via cryptography. It was, after a fashion, logical. If the Torah was inspired, then everything in it could be significant, even single letters. God might have planted secrets in it to be unearthed by a species of code-breaking when the time was ripe. Akiba and his disciples set out to discover truth by symbolism, analogy, numerology, word-plays, anagrams. A classic example of the last is the proof that the world was created on the first day of the month Tisri. "The first of Tisri," in Hebrew, is an anagram of "In the beginning."

Akiba's technique extended the potentialities of the sacred text. It also opened the door to irresponsible fancies. Indeed, its workings in the brain of the founder himself could hardly have been more ruinous. The good Akiba was lured by a pun to abet a final throw for national freedom.

The only reason for glancing at this mournful affair is its role in the further delimitation of Judaism. It was a mad attempt to upset the verdict of A.D. 70. After the shock of that year had worn off a trifle, Jewish communities all over the Empire had begun to simmer again. Parallels were drawn with the triumph of Nebuchadnezzar and its reversal within a lifetime. The Jews of the diaspora, who had done almost nothing in the war, made up for their desertion by massacring Gentiles in Egypt and Cyprus during the reign of Trajan. They in their turn got no support from the motherland; yet there too nationalism was recovering. Akiba favoured it, Joshua ben Hananiah the nail-maker did not. When the Emperor Hadrian, while resident in the east, considered allowing the Temple to be rebuilt, his fear of trouble caused him to require changes in its site and design. Jewish spokesmen protested, and the more excitable talked of rebellion. Joshua ben Hananiah opposed them, but died shortly after, leaving Akiba paramount.

A fresh underground movement had already come into being. It was armed most ingeniously with Roman rejects. Jewish smiths working on army contracts made a proportion of the weapons so faulty that the legions sent them back, and the smiths then repaired them and passed them to the resistance. Hadrian pursued his provocative schemes for Jerusalem, planning a pagan temple instead of a Jewish one; Rufus, his governor, forbade access to the site; and when an edict was issued throughout the Empire against ritual mutilation, no exception was made for the Jews, who were thus prevented from circumcising. Hadrian left in 132 and attacks on garrisons inaugurated the last revolt.

Akiba furnished what the other Jewish War had lacked—the Messiah. His eye fell on Simeon ben Koseba, a commander of the irregulars. Simeon was brave, popular, and perhaps descended from David. But his main qualification was the fact that "Koseba" sounded like "*kochba*," a star, so that he could be regarded as the Star out of Jacob foretold in *Numbers* xxiv : 17. Akiba summoned a conference and addressed it in Hebrew and Aramaic. At the climax he anointed the Son of of a Star, " Bar-Kochba," as king.

His audience had misgivings which were well founded. Hadrian moved relentlessly to restore order. No serious aid came from the diaspora; for the third time the Jews were out of step. Simeon, moreover, was too deficient in holiness for his claim to be convincing. He quarrelled with the rabbis, and his last stronghold, Sepphoris in Galilee, was taken in 135 on the fatal Ninth of Ab. The Messiah himself perished heroically and earned Hadrian's respect. Aged Akiba had already more than atoned for his blunder by martyrdom. He was put to the torture (skinned alive, some say) and died crying out " the Lord is one," prolonging the word " one " till he expired. The sequel for Jerusalem was annihilating. Jews were excluded from the city, which Hadrian rebuilt as a pagan town under the name Aelia Capitolina. A further scattering of exiles from Palestine nearly effaced its Jewish character. The religion itself was persecuted.

Nationalism followed priests and Sadducees into eclipse. The apocalyptic school was still not quite dead. Readers and copyists were found for a composite pseudo-Ezra, who spoke darkly of a

Messiah Son of God and otherwise echoed Christianity, and for a composite pseudo-Baruch, who mingled optimism and pessimism in poetry of some distinction. But both these books appear to have been actually written before Bar-Kochba. When they had made whatever slight mark they could in his aftermath, a gloomy silence fell. Bar-Kochba himself was posthumously cursed as the "Son of Deceit." The rabbis held the field unchallenged, and, with what was at least an acute practical insight, they preserved Akiba's techniques in the shipwreck of his policies. Cryptography flourished. A legend or parable told how Moses had beheld God fashioning little crowns for the twenty-two Hebrew letters. These were the mystical meanings, and even Moses had not comprehended them, but Akiba—in this respect more blessed than Moses—had discovered the key. By accepting his method in principle, defined so as to curb extreme vagaries, Judaism acquired elasticity. The meaning of the Torah, no longer restricted to what its sentences actually said, became multiple and unbounded. Scripture was no longer a fixed book but a living source of light. Rabbinic teaching blossomed into an art, infinitely resourceful, and able to evolve. The masters of this art, the "sages," were creative enough to be revered like the prophets or like Moses himself. There was no sense of total bondage to a sacrosanct past.

Meeting secretly at Lydda, the leading rabbis discussed how to withstand Roman persecution. Lacking power to command, they had to find means of keeping Israel in being by persuasion. They agreed to revise various rules so as to make the faithful less conspicuous, and less open to discrimination. They agreed also that the teaching of the truth must go on at whatever risk. Usha in Galilee became, for a time, the sages' headquarters. Meanwhile a new figure arose, Rabbi Judah the Prince, who was a grandson of the second Gamaliel and therefore belonged to the house of Hillel. A man of high social standing as well as erudition, he persuaded the Emperor to ease some of the anti-Jewish ordinances. He also took up a project of Akiba's and set himself to collect and write down the immense medley of legal tradition derived from over a hundred Tanna'im, which had hitherto remained oral. This was not the esoteric Oral Torah, it was that portion of its elaborated form which concerned law rather than doctrine. The result of Judah's labours during a long life, which ended about 219, was the Mishnah. Many of the laws which he compiled were obsolete, because no Temple or Jewish Palestine existed to apply them in. Still it was judged right to preserve them against the day when they would be needed again.

Judah himself worked in Palestine, but the centre of gravity was shifting eastward. Jews in large numbers had fled from the stricken Land to Mesopotamia, joining the descendants of the unreturned Babylonian captives, those who had not responded to Cyrus. Here, in a border zone where Roman power was ineffective, an interim revival took place. Jewish academies grew up. Their heads came to be known as Gaonim, and the Gaonate became a temporary informal papacy or supreme court. The trend toward Mesopotamia was in some degree checked during the reigns of the Christian emperors after Constantine, but not enough to restore Palestine's primacy.

The rabbis who succeeded the princely Judah pressed on with the labour of codifying and systematising. They laid a heavier emphasis on the synagogue's function as a school. They declared study to be a religious obligation; their insistence on the value of scholarship raised yet another barrier between the Jew and the Gentile, who was, by comparison, a Philistine—in the modern sense as well as the sense of biblical metaphor. To be a Jew one had to perform the Lord's precepts, and to perform the Lord's precepts one had to learn what they were, no easy matter in such a maze of detail as the Law had become. Jewish survival without the Land or the Temple depended on an unbroken human succession, an unimpaired transmission from father to son. The rabbis' patriarchal outlook deterred them from adding "mother to daughter," but some of their classrooms admitted girls as well as boys.

Judaism in this phase was marked by a more and more intensive

363

and supple mental activity, within a shrinking range. Pagan classical learning was virtually banned. Rabbi Judah had of course written the Mishnah in Hebrew, a terse vernacular, yet he had acclimatised some Latin and Greek words. Most of his heirs did not approve of such heathenism, and even when they allowed Greek words, they shuttered their minds against Greek thoughts. Japheth's " dwelling in the tents of Shem " (*Genesis* ix : 27) was construed as referring only to the Greek language, nothing else. When a certain rabbi who had mastered the Torah debated whether he might now study Greek philosophy, another quoted *Joshua* i : 8 —" you shall meditate on the Law day and night "—and advised him that he would have to do his studying when it was neither day nor night. While the rabbis' knowledge of natural sciences was not beneath contempt (they had, for instance, a good grasp of the calendar), there was no scientific instruction. Science was held to be a trap, an allurement to risky speculation, a distraction from the pursuits that really mattered.

One curious outcome was that the suspect Lady Wisdom, who could not be ignored because she was scriptural, came to be expounded as the Torah personified. *Ecclesiasticus* xxiv : 23, however uncanonical, may have offered the hint. An old fancy that God had composed the Torah before making the world was given a new precision. It was equated with the statement in *Proverbs* viii : 22 that Wisdom came into being before all other creatures. Everything asserted of her was applied to the Torah, which thus became the divine blueprint or programme: " God looked into Torah and created the universe." Therefore science was not a matter of observation or experiment, but of proper exegesis. All the answers were in the sacred text if you knew how to decipher them.

However, scientific stagnation was the rule in that age. Bibliolatry fortified Judaism for Jews and did not destroy whatever charms it possessed for Gentiles. It still aspired, if with ebbing enthusiasm, to be a world faith. Proselytism was made difficult and dangerous, first by pagan rulers and later by Christian ones.

But while severe penalties for teacher and convert practically stopped it within the Empire, it occurred here and there outside.

3

This phase was consummated in the Talmud, which was a culmination, but also an end. Fresh edicts against Palestinian Jewry in the fifth century at last made it plain that there was no prospect, humanly speaking, of another Cyrus. Israel's wound now stood manifest in its delayed effects. Without the Land, and without a hope of recovering it, the mechanism failed and the divine unfolding came to a halt. Judaism had neither a home nor a specific goal. It could only sum itself up and cease growing, with its heart in suspended animation. Provisionally, but for how long no one could tell, the God of History became a God of Non-History; the religion of progress became a religion of fixity; Israel the striver became a monstrosity of arrested dynamism. Jews in various places were to go on doing memorable things, enriching mankind out of proportion to their numbers. But Israel as a whole, uprooted and fragmented, could advance no further. Its doom was to wait, till the Lord himself restored its losses. When we contemplate that waiting, and the tortured heroism that went with it, fourteen dreadful centuries collapse like a telescope.

The Talmud itself gave Rabbinic Judaism an authoritative form, timeless in its complete lack of sequence, instead of being chronological like the Bible. Its title means " Study " or " Instruction." It exists in two versions, one issued from Palestine and one from Babylon. The Babylonian is much more important, and references always apply to this unless otherwise stated. Both were compiled by rabbinic Amora'im (expounders) in the fifth century, from matter accumulated over the past seven hundred years. The Talmud consists of the Mishnah written by Judah the Prince, plus Gemara. Gemara is " completion " or commentary, a collection of rabbinic opinions and sayings. The rabbis' debates are presented vividly as discussion interwoven with Judah's text. In the upshot, everything in the Talmud may be classified as either Halachah or Haggadah. Halachah, " rule," means the strictly legal material: that is, Mishnah itself plus the case-law part of Gemara dealing with the conduct of life in the minutest detail. Haggadah, " narrative," means all the residual Gemara: biblical legend, historical tradition, prayer, speculation, science or pseudo-science, occultism. The Talmud is a rabbinic encyclopaedia.

It lacks, however, the kind of tidiness which that word suggests. It is a huge work filling several shelves, a stupendous and gorgeous muddle, where even to know how to look things up requires years of training. The alphabetical index is a modern appendage, and each tractate or volume is designated simply by the first word. A staggering absence of system is combined with an equally staggering ingenuity and sheer energy of mind. Within its limitations the Talmud is thoroughly alive, unpredictable, spontaneous. Moreover it is popular, a giant masterpiece of folk art produced by men who were in no sense a hierarchy above the masses. Its contents are not a compendium of the " religious " literature of fifth-century Jews but of their whole literature. They did not draw any hard line between sacred and secular, and the day of pagan survivals in their folk-lore was long past. Everything could go in without reservations.

The resultant communication of greatness by grotesquerie must have shocked any classical scholar who ever bothered to glance through. Imitating this from the prophets, the Talmud carries it into wider fields. Its legends contain such notions as that Melchizedek was Shem under another name. It interprets history with such " inside information " as that the Romans really besieged Jerusalem because of the vindictiveness of a socially snubbed citizen, who tricked the priests into insulting the Emperor. It forsakes the stand of most earlier rabbis against magic, and pours out all manner of lore about astrology, dream-divination, and feats of wizardry performed by the rabbis themselves. It gives advice on demons and how to thwart them. And yet, with all this, the Talmud is an immensely wise book. Its superstitions and eccentricities are the quirks of minds which are over-active rather than dull, over-full rather than empty. The rabbis have something to say, however bizarre their methods of saying it.

Many of their remarks on health, for instance, are very sound. The rulings on family life, on education, on employment, are intelligently argued. Noble morality finds expression in maxims and parables. The notes on Scripture are acute, thought-provoking, and seldom platitudinous. Why did God appear to Moses in a bush? Well, to show that he was present even in so lowly a place . . . but that is only the beginning of exegesis, not the end; a page of additional symbolism follows. Or why did God demand sacrifices? Because the Hebrews had got into the habit of sacrificing to idols. They could not be induced to stop sacrificing altogether —the break would have been too radical—but they could be induced to sacrifice to the true God, and to him alone.

The religion of the Talmud is Judaism intensified. Despite all humiliations it teaches that Israel is still God's Chosen. Jewish difference from the Gentiles is not played down but stressed. The Christians, though seldom mentioned, present a difficulty, since they too have the Bible. Where then lies Israel's uniqueness? It lies in the tradition from Sinai. Others have appropriated the Written Torah, but Israel alone has the Oral Torah. It is Israel's monopoly, without which the Written Torah cannot be understood. The Talmud enforces this lesson with the story of Hillel and the alphabet.

Israel's God in the Talmud is still our heavenly Father, infinitely holy and righteous, and Deuteronomic love prevails. The spirit of the case-law is lenient. The eye-for-eye *lex talionis*, for example, is construed as merely asserting the right to compensation in principle. Accounts of procedure in Jewish courts emphasise their merciful aspects, and the safeguards against harsh sentences. Christian judicial practice took much more than a thousand years to attain the Talmud's level. Yet outside the realm of ethics there is sometimes a peculiar coarsening and shrinkage of concept, where the quest for flawless coherence takes the rabbis too far. Thus the scepticism of *Ecclesiastes* is not fairly faced, but watered down by placing the sentences in contrived contexts which alter their meaning. The point of *Job* is partially nullified by making its hero's miseries a punishment for sin after all (the sin of counselling the first Pharaoh of *Exodus* to massacre the Israelites!). And according to another legend, the Jews' subjection to Rome was a direct if tardy result of Solomon's foreign marriages.

The yearning for intelligibility and perfect justice sometimes expresses itself—as here—in the tracing of fantastic connections. Elsewhere the rabbis may appeal to the World to Come to redress all wrongs and resolve all riddles. Their tone savours a little more of "pie in the sky" than hitherto. They are more willing to admit an immortal soul, and the possibility of a heaven on Christian lines, as well as a Resurrection. But they never lapse into otherworldliness or contempt for the body. Most of them still expect an earthly Messiah, and they discuss prophecies of his advent about A.D. 500—prophecies destined to sow a fresh crop of crazy pretenders. However, theirs is an indistinct, muted hope, academic except as to the main point, and with few traces of apocalyptic. Johanan ben Zakkai is quoted as having said: "If you are engaged in planting and are suddenly informed that the Messiah has arrived, finish with your planting first, and then go to greet him." The step from caution to near-despair is not long. We are told also that when Akiba proclaimed his protégé Bar-Kochba, Rabbi Johanan ben Torta said: "Akiba, grass will grow on your cheeks and still the Son of David will not have come." The recording of these traditions is symptomatic.

In fact Jewish inadequacy and disappointment have opened the way to the *politique du pire*. Nothing more can really happen till the Messiah does arrive. Israel's woes are the protracted pangs of his birth, and he may not come till these woes reach the limit of endurance, the darkest hour before dawn. Partly as a result, the Talmud detects a hitherto unstressed holiness in suffering itself. The Jews have sinned; they have "loved mammon and hated one another," thereby losing their home; and now they have a duty of limitless atonement. Their sorrows are still a sign of election and not dismissal. There are even hints, in the Christian spirit, that they can offer up their pain on behalf of others, and that the good can die on behalf of the wicked. Several rabbis extol the Akedah, the sacrifice (or rather the alleged consent to be sacrificed) of Isaac. One or two astonishing passages speak without explanation of a " Messiah son of Joseph," who, like Jesus the son of Joseph, is slain.[1]

In whatever griefs—usually borne patiently, though we find a few flashes of excusable anger—the Talmudic Jew keeps his faith. It is the priceless treasure which he shares with all other Jews and nobody else. He never relinquishes his trust that God will restore Israel to the Land. Zion is not forgotten, or in the remotest danger of being forgotten. In the compensatory splendours of the World to Come, if not before, the exiles will be reassembled and the Temple rebuilt. Even the Lost Ten Tribes may be disentangled from heathendom to rejoin their cousins in Palestine—a hope already given expression in the late pseudepigraphic book *II Esdras* (xiii : 39–48).

Behind the grave mask meanwhile there is a quiet zest, even merriment. Somehow or other life is good, and will always be good. Numerous formulae of blessing, to be pronounced on everyday occasions, remind the Jew of God's nearness. Legend humorously suggests that all the foes and persecutors, or their descendants, ended by seeing the light: Nebuzaradan, who burned the Temple of Solomon, became a righteous convert; descendants of Haman, of Sisera, of Sennacherib, could be found lecturing on the Torah or humbly schoolmastering in Jerusalem. A typical fable recalls how Akiba was once travelling on his donkey, with a cock and a lamp. Turned away from a village inn, he went off into the woods

---

1 The Talmud, in its tractate entitled *Sanhedrin*, also contains the germ of the legend of the Thirty-Six Just Men. Replenished from generation to generation, this precise number bears the whole evil of the world, which would perish if even one of the thirty-six were to fail. The legend is the theme of Schwarz-Bart's novel, already cited.

to sleep. The wind put out his lamp, the cock and the donkey were killed by wild beasts. Yet at each blow Akiba repeated, " All that God does is done well." Next morning he heard that marauding soldiers had passed close by. If the donkey had brayed, if the cock had crowed, if the lamp had been alight, they would assuredly have found him. . . .

The Jew, in short, is irrepressible.

Rabbinic Judaism embodied the tenth step in Israel's logic, and the last, at least until recently. The question faced was:

Why this apparently final ruin? Why did the divine intervention not come, when the need for it was so desperate?

The answer was:

Doubtless Israel was still unfit for that. Too many of us thought first of our glory and prosperity, rather than the greater things from which alone our glory and prosperity could rightly proceed. With the Temple gone, we still have the Law; and our task now is to order our whole lives by it, at whatever cost in Gentile contempt. Everything we have learnt to believe about the Messiah and the World to Come is true, but we must free those beliefs from presumptuous programme-making and speculation, and leave the future to God. We must again practise penitence and atonement, humility and patience and faith. Faith above all. At his own chosen time, not ours, God will lead us home.

With such meditations at its heart, the Talmud went forth. It succeeded in its two main objects. It settled that the end of the Temple was not the end of Judaism; and it supplied Jews with a continuing bond of unity. The Talmud helped to hold them together in the chaos which followed Rome's collapse. Together with the Bible it became the basis of all later orthodoxy, a sea-deep treasure and a common inheritance. Jews on the move took it with them as they drifted apart.

They also enlarged on it, even after its text had been fixed by a generation of editors. Halachah, the defining of law, slackened off for a while. But Haggadah, the talking-around, went on. Each major synagogue kept records of its favourite stories and sermons.

These anthologies, called Midrashim because they counted as interpretation, were not incorporated in the Talmud itself, and naturally
they differed. But however much they did, and however much
local jurists exercised the right to emend or have second thoughts,
the root-loyalty everywhere endured. Even the most fanciful
Haggadah never broke away from either Talmud or Bible. Even
the lightest folk-lore—songs, tales and so forth—never ceased to
be monotheistic and ethical in spirit. The same was true of the
culturally sterile Jewish communities as of the culturally creative.
They might trudge through ages of utter dullness, yet they still
cherished the ordinances of Sinai and the fabric spun from them.
The written word was hoarded in the synagogue archives. Experience was fused, focused, co-ordinated. All life was attached to the
ever-lengthening thread of instruction and memory, that thread
which no other people on earth possessed. With their huge capital
to live on, the Jews wandered over the world affirming the Lord
and his justice.

4

They wandered far, driven on in the first instance by the
behaviour of Christian authorities. They spread across Arabia,
North Africa, Russia (where they converted the rulers of the
Khazars); and after the Arab conquests, more widely still—to
Spain, France, Germany, Poland on the one side, to China and
India on the other. As traders and specialists in various fields, they
became intermediaries between Christendom and the world of
Islam. Those who penetrated Europe split into two streams, the
southern Sephardi, the northern Ashkenazi: Spain being identified
with the Sepharad of *Obadiah* verse 20, and Germany with the
Ashkenaz of *Genesis* x : 3 and *Jeremiah* li : 27. Those who strayed
into other quarters were sometimes lost to sight altogether, till their
descendants, or their proselytes' descendants, perplexed European
travellers a millennium later. Such were the black Jews or Falasha
of Abyssinia, the Cochin Jews of Malabar, the Kai-Feng-Fu of

Hunan, though the two former colonies may well have been superimposed on Jewish groups of still earlier origin.

Our aim has been to define what Israel took out of Palestine which remained and was crucial in the reassembly. Therefore we need not follow these scattered Israelites here, except in terms of the widest and swiftest generalisations. They had no bond of unity beyond what has been delineated, and therefore they have no history as a whole, only separate histories of the fragments—sometimes magnificent, sometimes almost blank. Temporary papacies like the Babylonian Gaonate never extended very far. Nor, even in any single country, did the Jewish community amount to an *imperium in imperio*. The rabbis enjoined a dignified obedience to the law of the land, and the laymen who governed community affairs generally observed that precept. Jewish continuance was recognised as depending, under God, not on corporate structure but on the constant flow of principles from the old to the young; on training and education. Hence a dual stress on the excellence of family life and the high status of the teacher. This was most effective in ensuring further continuance.

And the results were much the same whether the Jews were tolerated or oppressed. In Islamic lands they were usually tolerated, even favoured. Under the Moslem rulers of Spain they could have "assimilated" in the modern sense, yet they chose not to . . . a strong argument against the notion that Jewish identity is due merely to pressure from outside. Where that pressure did exist, it simply reinforced the same ingrained tendencies. Christian cruelty in medieval Europe drove the Jews in upon themselves. For some time a fairly gentle policy, laid down by Pope Gregory the Great, held off the worst. Persecution came chiefly as a by-product of the Crusades. The laity and lower clergy indulged in it with horrible zeal, and the higher clergy failed to control it. Jews were charged with diabolism, plundered and massacred. They were debarred from land ownership and most occupations. They had long since diverted their energies from farming and manual crafts into commerce, as being more mobile and adaptable, while the rabbis lived more exclusively on teaching and alms. Now the rise of a Christian merchant class pushed them further, into the uncongenial trade of money-lending. This, as non-Christians, they could ply openly and straightforwardly, whereas ecclesiastical rules against interest made Christian money-lenders so furtive and devious that a borrower never knew where he stood with them.[2]

Efforts were made to force Jews into the Church; and whenever one of them was converted sincerely, he was apt to become an inquisitor of the worst type himself, and burn the books of his own former religion. Jews were banished altogether from several countries—from England in 1290, from France in 1394, from Spain and Portugal in the last decades of the fifteenth century—with varying degrees of thoroughness and permanence. The popes, after some piecemeal attempts at protective segregation, now declared outright for the ghetto. Here Jews lived huddled together in a fellowship of affliction, dreary, inbred, unhealthy.

Judaism did not exactly cease to develop, but it developed within a fixed space, like a brain growing more convoluted inside the skull. It took no new step forward. Eleventh-century France produced the arch-commentator Rashi, "light of the Exile," whose work is still used in teaching. He was the first to determine the sense of biblical texts by sound linguistic and historical scholarship. Twelfth-century Moorish Spain produced Maimonides, who went to Egypt and became Saladin's doctor. Applying Greek rational method and Roman orderliness, Maimonides made Judaism a system, and proposed a theory of religious evolution. Fifteenth-century Christian Spain produced Joseph Caro, who composed a text-book of law which is central in rabbinic training to this day. Spiritual offspring of Akiba built up the esoteric empire of the Kabbala, with its occultism, its orientalism, its strange foretastes of later science. Not only in Hebrew but in Yiddish, the semi-German dialect of the Ashkenazi, European Jewry

---

2 In view of the Marxist claim that sects and religions express economic interests, it is noteworthy that while the economic basis of Jewry has gone through radical changes, the religion has not.

continued to speak. In due course a Yiddish literature, some biblical and some secular, formed a popular adjunct to the Hebrew. The latter tended more to be a preserve of scholars. But scholarship was not rare.

Alongside the families of Israel, not one successor-religion but two had now matured. The Arabs (Abraham's descendants by Hagar) had discovered the Bible and brought forth a prophet of their own, Mohammed, who proclaimed a new revelation from the Archangel Gabriel. His Koran, the charter of Islamic society from Spain to China, owed a debt to the Talmud. As for the Christians, their relationship with Christ's kinsmen grew more and more tragic and involved. They might detest, but they could not exorcise. Several Fathers of the Church had made respectful use of Jewish advisers. Origen had rescued Philo from the neglect of his own people; Athanasius had spoken of the Jews as constituting " the great school of the knowledge of God "; Jerome had declared that they were being divinely preserved for a purpose worthy of the Almighty. Many biblical expositors of the Middle Ages relied on their erudition. During an era of anti-Semitic outrage St. Thomas Aquinas drew calmly and gratefully on Maimonides to shape a philosophy for his Church. Christians, while reviling the alleged murderers of Jesus, were sometimes haunted by a suspicion that they themselves were missing something of value which the murderers still had. They might distil their feelings imaginatively, as in the legend of the Wandering Jew, who spurned Christ yet by that very act became deathless and all-knowing. Or they might grope for a Secret Wisdom among the diagrams of the Kabbala, a process which led, through however twisted a tunnel, toward the light of the Renaissance.

The Jew, extracting wisdom of a more stable kind from his sufferings, could look out from the ghetto and regard even Christians charitably. From Maimonides he could learn the indulgent notion that Christianity, despite its falsehoods, was really a divine compromise. God was employing the Church—and Islam too—to prepare superstitious Gentiles for the Messiah, and guide them toward a truth which they were not ready to grasp in its purity. The Jews already possessed that truth, and most painfully witnessed to it. The corporate vocation which alone justified their resistance was not, in the vulgar sense, a privilege. Maimonides said that when the Messianic Age did come, it would not be an era of Jewish domination but an era of peace, in which Jews would be sages benevolently instructing mankind. At all events, however, they could cherish a hope of change, a trust in the divine purpose. That, which was so deeply inherent in Judaism, nurtured its inner calm and even happiness. Some day all the nations would see. Some day the new Messianic Law would embrace all men, reconcile all disputes, and plant justice throughout the earth.

But meanwhile the ghetto made the pattern of Jewish life perpetually more rigid and more pervasive. In the many places where it existed, Jews were set apart from their neighbours not only by the walls but by their whole appearance and mode of life: by clothing, by diet, by circumcision; sometimes by the wearing of a compulsory yellow star; and also by the minutely regulated Saturday Sabbath, a day of rest and worship that clashed most awkwardly with everyone else's. Even in countries without ghettoes, the difference in the Jews' condition was a matter of degree rather than kind. Everywhere the annual festivals (ironic word) reminded them poignantly from childhood of their calling as the Lord's witnesses and the events which had made them so: Passover recalling the flight from Egypt, Pentecost the giving out of the Law, Tabernacles the sojourn in the desert, Purim the deliverance from Haman, Hanukkah the deliverance from Antiochus. Also they had their days of mourning and fasting. The Ninth of Ab marked the double tragedy of the Temple, and the Day of Atonement the greater tragedy of Israel's backsliding. Collective memory was made dramatic and personal. " In every generation," the rabbis taught, " it is the duty of a man to imagine that *he himself* has come forth out of Egypt." To remember these things meant, as always, to " be mindful " of them in one's own conduct.

It was characteristic that there was no festival for any event in the more glorious period, such as David's anointing or Solomon's dedication. Memory dwelt on days of trial, not on days of fruition. Even musical instruments were banned in the synagogue, because of the loss of the Temple's music. As a result the custom of singing in liturgical chorus forged another link between Jew and Jew.

Zion, the literal mystic soil, inexorably remained. Just as it had entered into the earliest rituals (the one preserved in *Deuteronomy* xxvi, for instance), so it persisted when the bodily presence which they reflected was no longer a fact. Every Jew learned the fundamental Sh'ma or creed, and this conducted him through a series of Pentateuchal texts interweaving the love of God with the promise of the Land. His synagogue was normally oriented toward Jerusalem, and its chief prayers were recited facing that way. The most solemn part of the service opened with the Sh'ma itself. After it came the Benedictions, nineteen being prescribed, which were spoken silently by the people and then aloud by a reader. Not all were used at every service; but the liturgical year provided for many repetitions of those which concerned the restoration of Israel.

The tenth benediction was a prayer for the ingathering:

Blow the great trumpet for our liberation, and lift a banner to gather our exiles, and gather us into one body from the four corners of the earth.

Blessed be thou, O Lord, who gatherest the dispersed of thy people Israel.

The fourteenth was a prayer for Jerusalem.

To Jerusalem thy city return thou in mercy and dwell in her midst as thou hast spoken, and build her speedily in our days as an everlasting structure and soon establish there the throne of David.

Blessed be thou, O Lord, the builder of Jerusalem.

The fifteenth was a prayer for the coming of the Messiah.

The sprout of David they servant speedily cause thou to sprout up; and his horn do thou uplift through thy victorious salvation; for thy salvation we are hoping every day.

Blessed be thou, O Lord, who causest the horn of salvation to sprout forth.

The seventeenth was a prayer for a renewed Temple, where the Lord's " Shekinah " or glory could abide again.

Be pleased, O Lord our God, with thy people Israel and their prayer, and return the sacrificial service to the altar of thy House, and the fire-offerings of Israel and their prayer offered in love accept thou with favour, and may the sacrificial service of Israel thy people be ever acceptable to thee. And may our eyes behold thy merciful return to Zion.

Blessed be thou who restorest thy Shekinah to Zion.

This theme of the Shekinah had grown precious to Jewish mysticism. Its biblical basis was in *Exodus* xl : 34–8, describing the cloud and fire of the desert Tabernacle. God of course was everywhere, yet in another sense he had dwelt specially in the Temple. While the glow of his presence brooded no longer over that ravaged spot, it had not left the world entirely. Israel in exile could still catch gleams of it. But there could be no true dawn till it returned to its place. As long as Jerusalem had no home for its Lord or his people, the Jew was a mourner. When he married, a drinking vessel was broken, for grief at the city's desolation. When he moved into a new house, he kept a patch of wall unpainted for the same reason. When he was buried, a bag of Palestinian earth, if his family could get it, was tossed into his grave. The Passover ceremony always included the wish, " Next year in Jerusalem."

CHAPTER THIRTEEN

THE THIRD ZIONISM

As Dr. Parkes observes, the Jews as a people " had never left Palestine either physically or spiritually. The remnant actually dwelling in it might be very small, but it was always thought of as an earnest of the people as a whole, and it was always entitled to be supported by the people as a whole." How could they have taken up any other position? Their struggle to survive in a tortured stance of dissent could only be justified by their vocation. Without the Land, around which Israel's experience had grown and toward which it looked, they could have found no coherent purpose at all and no reason to hold out. " Scripture," to quote Rabbi David Polish, " makes no dichotomies between Israel's spiritual character and its territorial status." People for whom the content of Scripture constituted their claim to exist could not tear the one from the other without rendering Scripture false, and their own endurance meaningless.

From the eleventh century onward, their grief was making the dream of Zion ever more intense. It expressed itself outside the synagogue as well as inside, and in other forms besides ritual. Jews not only repeated their prayers and commemorations, they studied Palestine itself. Little groups pored over topographical writings and listened to the accounts brought back by travellers. They gathered awestruck round the most trivial souvenirs—dates and olives, for example. They comforted their hearts with songs of homesick devotion called " Zionides "; such songs were composed by many of their best medieval poets, and some were inserted in the liturgy. Many Jews came to know the Land of their yearning in minute detail without ever having seen it. When some favoured brother went to visit the few who still lived there, or even to settle there himself, he " went up " (the word for such pilgrimage was Aliyah) to a place that was already home.

An appreciable number did go up. In 1121 a party of three hundred emigrated from England and France. At that time the poet Judah Ha-Levi had perhaps begun meditating the same step. Born in Spain, where he practised medicine, Judah poured out Hebrew love-odes and elegies and impassioned hymns, but always he longed for the ruined homeland, for Jerusalem. . . .

> O city of the world, most chastely fair,
> In the far west behold I sigh for thee.

He wrote on the repatriation of Israel: " Can we hope for any other refuge? " One of his poems was taken into the synagogue service for the terrible Ninth of Ab:

> Zion, wilt thou not send a greeting to thy captives? . . .
> A greeting sends the captive of desire, who sheds his tears
> Like dew on Hermon; would they might fall on thy hills!

In a romance about a Khazar chieftain's conversion, Judah portrays a rabbi patiently enlightening the fierce Russian on the sacredness of far-away Palestine. That country, says the rabbi, is the centre of the inhabited earth; there the true God has revealed himself; only within it, or in relation to it, has the voice of inspired prophecy ever been heard.

At last Judah journeyed east himself. Towards 1145 we have glimpses of him at Tyre and Damascus, white-haired and sad. It is said that he arrived within a few yards of the gate of Jerusalem, then in Crusader hands, only to be ridden down and killed by an Arab.

The later Crusades were accompanied by a renewed trickle of Jewish migrants, some of whom bought plots of ground and farmed them. Famous names are recorded alongside the anonymous. Maimonides the philosopher, though he died in Cairo, was buried in Galilee. A Jewish guard of honour carried his body to Tiberias, where tourists to-day still pause at his tomb, a plain white structure with an enclosing wall. Then came a living scholar: Rabbi Jehiel, head of the Talmudic school in Paris. Jehiel had been in favour with Louis IX, who invited him to debate with a Jewish convert to Christianity. Jehiel defended the Talmud against attacks on its alleged contents. But the accusations alone were enough to unleash anti-Semitic violence. Though not in evident personal danger, the Rabbi left France for Palestine. So did another, Nachmanides of Gerona, who had gone through trials of the same sort. Nachmanides visited Jerusalem about 1266 and then settled in Acre. He did not settle alone; a group of disciples joined him, and revived a glimmer of Jewish erudition. Besides leading their conferences, Nachmanides reported to Spanish friends about the state of the Land. In Jerusalem, he said, he had met with only two Jews—and they were brothers.

However, his own presence was bringing a quiet change. He died in 1270 and was buried at Haifa, where Jehiel too was buried, beside his colleague; but afterwards Jewish scholarship was never again wholly extinct in Palestine. Other rabbis made their way there (Obadiah of Bertinoro, for instance, in 1488), and teachers and students who could not go themselves gave unselfish support to those who could. A fund in aid of the Palestinian schools, the Halukkah, drew alms from several countries, and went on doing so till superseded by events in the twentieth century.

By the 1480's we find that one Palestinian city, Gaza, had sixty Jewish families. The expulsion from Spain and Portugal slightly accelerated the drift. Palestine was now securely in the grip of the Turks, but Turks could sometimes be preferable to Christians. In Upper Galilee is the hillside town of Safed, to-day a haunt of artists. During the reign of Ferdinand and Isabella a small Jewish population already lived there, though their rabbi was so poorly provided for that he had to run a grocery. The fateful year 1492 witnessed a descent on Safed by Sephardic refugees from the peninsula. One of them became virtually mayor of the Jewish body. Under his administration the community began to prosper and attract able men, as the steady rooting-out in Spain sent over more fugitives. In the 1530's the Chief Rabbi of Safed was Jacob Berab, who had no need for the grocery; and with Berab came the whisper of a renewed Messianic hope, from which a devious, blurred, but unbroken line can be traced to modern Zionism.

Ever since Bar-Kochba, a very proper scepticism had generally protected the Jews against their would-be kings. One curious uprising in medieval Kurdistan had died away without spreading. European oppression fitted in all too well with the doctrine of the travail which must attain its crescendo before the Anointed could appear. Up to a point, therefore, agony discouraged action instead of provoking it. But by the sixteenth century the travail seemed hideously prolonged. The Christian blow at the Jewish culture of Spain led some to believe, innocently enough, that the limit of affliction had almost been reached. Without committing himself to any rash forecasts, Jacob Berab of Safed proposed a preparatory step: the restoration of a Palestinian centre for Jews everywhere, on the lines of Johanan's Vineyard. Rabbis, he suggested, should come to Safed to be ordained, and hard questions should be referred to its college as a supreme court of appeal.

In 1538 Berab's plan was awakening some interest, and candidates for the rabbinate actually were coming to him. However, the project of unity was premature. Fragmentation and persecution had gone too far for it to have any present chance of success. Moreover there was Jerusalem to contend with. The city now had a fair-sized Jewish population again, and a Chief Rabbi who disliked the whole scheme. When this dignitary denounced Berab to the Turks as seditious, he had no defence; he fled to Damascus.

Yet Jerusalem had not crushed Safed after all. Berab left behind him a helper superior to himself. This was the jurist Joseph Caro, who had come from Spain to Turkey. Caro, noting Isaiah's prophecy that " the Law shall go forth from Zion," took it literally and went to Palestine to work. From 1536 till his death at eighty-seven he was at Safed. He made no progress with a loyal attempt to carry on Berab's programme. However, the labours culminating in his handbook of law—still a living force in Judaism—gave Safed prestige of another kind. It became the goal of a fresh migration of scholars, assisted from the coffers of the Halukkah. The most distinguished was Isaac Luria, born of German parentage in Jerusalem, around whom a cluster of disciples assembled. Luria died young, but his academy survived him.

At about the same time as this gathering of rabbis in Galilee, a strange anticipation of later politics installed a lay colony not far off. It owed its formation to the fact that one of the Sultan's advisers was a Jew. Joseph Nasi, forbidden to practise his religion in his native Portugal, had given up trying to avert exile by concealing it, and moved to Antwerp. There he had made a fortune in banking. After various adventures Nasi arrived at Constantinople under the patronage of Suleiman the Magnificent. In the Ottoman Empire he could worship openly. He acquired influence at court, and Suleiman presented him with Tiberias and seven neighbouring hamlets, to be used for Jewish resettlement. In 1565 Nasi managed to get the town walls rebuilt, despite the sullenness of his Arab workmen, and organised the planting of mulberry trees with a view to silk production. He offered refuge to Jews on condition that they would make their own living as artisans or farmers. Two hundred did sail in from Italy, where the Pope was heaping restrictions on them. The following year, however, a new Sultan promoted Nasi and diverted his energies to affairs of state. The experiment advanced no further.

At about the same time lived Rabbi Liva ben Bezalel, a political theorist far ahead of his age. In an essay called *The Eternity of Israel*, he asserted the concept of nationality in terms that foreshadowed the nineteenth century. Every nation, he said, has its own nature and rights, and a proper habitat. Israel is distinguished by the holiness of its character and calling; the Holy Land can never cease to be the birthright of the Holy Nation. Rabbi Liva's teaching might have prompted a political movement, and, when revived and stated by others, it eventually did so. But in his own day the conditions forbade anything so practical. With European Jewry cowed, and sinking toward a nadir, nothing could shake the ghetto out of resistance to action but a visible Messianic advent.

The Messiah whom Berab and Caro had not provided, their successors at Safed—indirectly—did.

2

The school of Isaac Luria had novel ideas. While the Renaissance had affected Jews less than Christians, it had bred a mental restlessness, a disquieted boredom with rabbinic orthodoxy. In that frame of mind the group at Safed turned toward spiritual and metaphysical realms. Luria saw visions and had conversations with Elijah. He put the Kabbala (itself a factor in the Renaissance) on a broader basis, fostering a cerebral mysticism which was alleged to tend toward moral regeneration. On the Sabbath he dressed in white, with a fourfold garment symbolising the Name of God. He wrote nothing, only talked; his disciples, who were classified into novices and initiates, made notes of his lectures and passed them on to an eager public. Luria discoursed about divine emanations distantly recalling Philo, and said that all souls were doomed to transmigrate till the Messiah came.

Kabbalistic philosophy was far from absurd. But the discussion of even its most profound tenets in such an atmosphere led to mischievous daydreaming. One book that became popular was the Zohar, a medieval treatise on the Unseen, which professed to be older than it was. Among many other mysteries it contained the heady doctrine of a double Jerusalem. The earthly Jerusalem was the starting-point of creation, and had its heavenly counterpart in an "upper" Jerusalem with which it was somehow identical. From this binary heart flowed the whole strength of the world, whether the world's inhabitants knew it or not. Thus the Zohar could evoke the image of a man placing himself at the secret centre of power and transforming the earth. Such a man presumably would be the Messiah, or, at the least, a forerunner or helper of his.

Some members of the circle founded by Luria did claim to fulfil Messianic prophecies. It will be remembered that these had grown complicated, and spoke of more than one person in connection with Israel's redemption, so that there was room for several pretenders. Many tried to ascertain, by calculation or occult techniques, when precisely the great Messiah himself might be looked for. In due course their ingenuities, like Akiba's long before, contributed to the rise of a supposed King of the Jews: a tawdry, serio-comic figure, yet in the upshot not an entirely futile one.

Sabbatai or Shabbetai Zevi was born at Smyrna in 1626, on the Ninth of Ab, the designated birthday of the deliverer. His father, a Sephardi of Spanish descent, was of modest means, but made a fortune a few years later by becoming the local agent of an English commercial house. As a boy—a rather spoilt boy, one gathers— Sabbatai studied both the Talmud and the Kabbala. He preferred the Kabbala, which he had a flair for, to the Talmud, in which he showed no marked proficiency. Learning from Luria's disciples that superhuman powers could be gained by ascetic discipline, he undertook a course of cold baths; and although he was married twice at an early age, both marriages were dissolved owing to wilful refusal to consummate. The term " manic depressive " has been applied to his personality.

Partly because of his own birthday, Sabbatai was fascinated by matters Messianic. He read the Zohar. A sentence of doubtful authenticity, in that already dubious context, was widely taken to imply that the Messiah would be revealed to the world in 1648. By then, Sabbatai's odd charm and eccentric holiness had made him the idol of an adoring group. A massacre of Jews in Poland gave him occasion to speak, and he informed his friends that he was the Lord's Anointed. He would confound the Gentile rulers and restore the Kingdom of Israel in Palestine. As a token of his mission he did what none dared. He uttered the Name of God.

For three years more he stayed in Smyrna, while the rabbis watched him with suspicion. In the end they had him banished with his clique of admirers. He went to Constantinople and made more converts, one of whom forged a prophecy for him, a belated piece of pseudepigraphic literature. His next port of call was

Salonika, where he went through a ritual "wedding" to the Torah, and was again expelled by the rabbis. Events, however, were working for him. It happened that certain Christians, notably the Fifth Monarchy Men in England, were also anticipating a new era. This was due to begin in 1666. Sabbatai had already heard of them through his father's business contacts, and he adopted their date. He was not the only Jew to be seduced by the coincidence. A petition to Cromwell in 1655, asking his toleration for Jews in England, refers to a widespread belief that their situation will soon be changed by the recovery of Palestine.

Sabbatai moved on to Cairo. His proselytes in Egypt were people of wealth and standing, whose support bolstered him considerably. In 1663 he at last reached Jerusalem. He impressed himself on its Jews by self-mortification and distributions of sweets to children. He also used his voice, which was tuneful, singing psalms for hours on end, and improper Spanish ballads to which he attached esoteric meanings. When the Turkish civic administration tried to extort money from the Jews by a special levy, he went back to Cairo on their behalf.

His movement was developing a character of its own. While he was in Cairo, Sarah came on the scene. A Jewish orphan from Poland, she had broken out of a convent and spent some time in prostitution. Suitably inspired, she announced herself as the Messiah's bride. Sabbatai (with enviable aplomb) brought her over to Cairo and married her, quoting Hosea as a precedent. Her presence gave the cult an air of romantic joy, of festivity and abandon, destined to have lasting effects. Jews under Sabbatai's spell dropped some of the solemn fasts and held parties instead—logically, since the age of waiting and wailing was over. It was understood that more of the observances would shortly be done away with as out of date.

The Messiah returned to Jerusalem a popular hero. Next a visionary named Nathan arrived from Gaza and made exciting promises. Sabbatai, Nathan assured the citizens, would go off to collect the Lost Ten Tribes, and lead them to Palestine riding on a lion. When the rabbis threatened the entire sect with excommunication, Nathan proclaimed that henceforth Gaza instead of Jerusalem would be the holy city; but Sabbatai withdrew to his native Smyrna. Here at least was a prophet with honour in his own country. When he made a Messianic speech in the synagogue, he was greeted with acclamations. This time it was the turn of the Chief Rabbi to flee.

The promised year of glory was imminent. Sabbatai's envoys proclaimed his title and summons in Italy, Germany, Holland. Many Christians besides prophecy-mongers assumed that the Kingdom of Israel really was on the brink of reinstatement; Pepys noted the report in his diary. Rabbis were distrustful and could not agree, but enough of them declared in the Messiah's favour to raise the prospect of an upheaval. In Avignon the whole Jewish community began packing its bags.

How Sabbatai planned to make good his pledges, nobody knows. The fixing of a deadline virtually forced him to do something. Early in 1666 he went to Constantinople, perhaps with an idea of trying to deal with the Sultan in Nasi's style. The Turks arrested him. At first they treated him politely, and his imprisonment was hardly more than preventive detention. He was housed in comfort and allowed visitors. Rumours of miracles confirmed his supporters' faith, preparations for the Exodus were pushed on in various parts of Europe. Finding that Sabbatai was still capable of causing them trouble, the Turks took alarm and transferred him to another prison. Here his doom came to him in the person of the palace doctor, a Jew turned Mohammedan, who warned Sabbatai that he would soon be condemned to death unless he took the same step. And Sabbatai did. Admitted to an audience with the Sultan, the saviour of Israel removed his Jewish cap, put on a turban, and acknowledged that Mohammed was the prophet of God.

The Sultan was pleased and gave him a post at court. For a while he lived on at Constantinople, accompanied by a faithful few who had embraced Islam with him. He still mixed with his former co-religionists, telling them that he was secretly trying to convert the Mohammedans. He told Mohammedans that he was trying to convert the Jews. Finally his employers decided he was a nuisance and sent him off, unsalaried, to Albania, where he died poor in 1676.

Sabbatai's conduct had thrown his devotees into confusion. Throughout most of Christendom and the Ottoman Empire, a gale of laughter blew away their belief in him. Yet a handful, in the midst of disenchantment and ridicule, refused to give up. Even after his death, they fancied he would return or be re-incarnated, and enter into his kingdom in Zion. Meanwhile they faced a crisis. As the first Christians had had to explain the Messiah's execution, the Sabbatians had to explain the Messiah's apostasy; and although their quest never brought them, as the Christians' did, to an acceptable illumination, it was not altogether barren.

The legacy of Sabbatai's tortuous decline was a hybrid sect, the Dönmeh, in Macedonia. It was chiefly in this Judaeo-Turkish conventicle (which still exists) that Sabbatianism struggled on. Sabbatai's conversion was made out to have been part of his programme. He had fulfilled a text in the Zohar which said that the Messiah would be " good within and evil without." He had placed himself in the realm of darkness to rescue the sparks of light entrapped in it. The underlying theme of these subtleties was a notion of liberation, of growing bigger than the Law, of moral triumph through involvement with sin rather than separation from it. There is no doubt that Sabbatai did prepare the way for this. In pitting the speculative Kabbala against the legalistic Talmud, he was perhaps only obeying his own bent; but he certainly did it, thereby starting a trend that did not die with him. He pronounced the Name. He cancelled the fasts. In the crowning blasphemy of conversion, it might be argued, he committed almost the worst sin possible for anyone subject to the Law, precisely to show that the Law must be outgrown. With considerations like these in mind, the Sabbatians taught that their Messiah's behaviour pointed the way to a more adventurous, less guilt-ridden mode of life.

Others have had glimpses of the same hazardous path. It can

lead to the ethics of Nietzsche . . . or to those of Rasputin. Among
Jews, while the Sabbatian cult itself did not spread widely, its
vague subversiveness did, mainly through the Balkans into the
lands of the Ashkenazi. One product was a sect in Poland which
opposed Judaism. Its head was Jacob Frank. After picking up
Sabbatian theories at Salonika, he preached redemption through
impurity (i.e. sex) and the abolition of the Talmud in favour of the
Zohar. From this he proceeded to out-Sabbatai Sabbatai. He said
Christianity was a transition stage to the Messianic faith of the
future, and advised his disciples to accept baptism. A bishop
offered protection, but soon realised that the conversions were
insincere. Frank was playing some obscure game of his own. It
has been suggested that he was forcing God's hand, like the Zealots,
but more subtly. If all Israel renounced its identity and betrayed
its trust, God would be bound to send his Anointed before the
process was complete, because otherwise there would be no Israel
left to save. For such apparent impiety—the compulsion of
Creator by creature—the Kabbala gives a kind of warrant. Whatever the truth, Frankism died and decomposed.

Yet alongside these vagaries, the spirit of Judaism in eastern
Europe grew genuinely freer and more audacious. Nothing could
be quite the same after the Sabbatian shaking. Static legalism could
never quite re-establish its reign. Some cobwebs had been blown
away. The hopes of Israel began slowly to recover and to take
more kinetic forms. Though the Messiah from Smyrna was a
failure, he was not a total failure.

Nor, even in the seventeenth century, did his way of thinking
appeal only to people of his own disposition. The reactivated
awareness of Israel as a body, and its bond with the Land as a
political concept to be reckoned with, was by no means confined
to occultists and fanatics. At the opposite pole of Judaism from
Sabbatai stood his towering contemporary Spinoza. A Portuguese
Jew domiciled in Holland, Spinoza mastered the Talmud, but
veered away into scientific and sceptical pursuits for which he was
excommunicated. His philosophy had an influence extending to

Einstein; his study of Scripture launched the Higher Criticism long before any Christians were inclined in that direction. If we look for Spinoza's views on his own people—the views of the greatest Jewish mind of that age—we find him contending that they were called God's Chosen solely because God picked them out to live in "a certain strip of territory" by a Law he revealed to them. Without that territory, Spinoza says, their Law is irrelevant and void. As long as they are scattered and have no state to apply it in, they have no special status. The arch-rationalist is more Zionist than the Zionists. He adds in a memorable aside that the end may not be yet. "I would go so far as to believe that if the foundations of their religion have not emasculated their minds, they may even raise up their empire afresh; and that God may a second time elect them."[1]

3

At length the ghetto erupted. As in the 1660's, the impulse to change was external and spectacular. This time it was not a Jewish impulse. It was the French Revolution, with its Napoleonic sequel.

By now the laws which excluded Jews from various countries had been repealed or evaded, as in England by Cromwell. Intellectual leaders like Moses Mendelssohn were commanding respect. The semi-emancipation which the French armies brought gave Napoleon a Jewish problem to cope with. He seems to have considered two methods. First (and one should note that they came in this order) he apparently thought of reconstituting a Jewish Palestine.[2] For him as for Israel—despite the enhanced caution in western Europe due to Sabbatai—this would still have been the normal solution. Jewish assimilation as a set policy has its origins in the line he pursued instead. Restoration to Zion, despite certain

---

1 I have slightly compressed an unwieldy sentence.
2 The evidence for the seriousness of his scheme is open to question, but he did raise the topic in the *Moniteur*.

partisan delusions, was not invented as an alternative to assimilation; assimilation was invented as an alternative to Zion.

What Napoleon did was to convene a so-called Sanhedrin. This met in Paris in 1807. Taking a hint from Mendelssohn in Germany, the Emperor offered Jews full citizenship in return for an admission that they were set apart only by religion in a narrowly confessional sense, and were not a " people " or " nation." Hence the emergence of " Frenchmen practising the Jewish religion." The Reform Judaism which arose in educated circles during the nineteenth century was disposed to accept this principle. Its leaders sponsored resolutions declaring that Palestine was not essential, and dropped three of the Benedictions, so that prayers should no longer be offered for Jerusalem or the Messiah or the Temple's rebuilding. They reduced the distinctiveness of the religion itself, paying less respect to the Talmud.

The Reform spokesmen made their points so forcefully that Macaulay wrote of the difference between Jews and Christians as a matter of " eating pork and wearing beards." In some countries they did much to secure Jewish civil rights. In others, where the reaction of the Holy Alliance blocked the path to equality, many Jews were led to feel that their religion now meant too little to be worth the trouble, and became nominal Christians. For some, like Karl Marx's father, baptism was the passport to a job. For some, like Heine, it was simply the means to a less harassed life. In either case it was a sign of a loss of nerve, following on the partial repudiation of Israel's heritage.

Judaism of the unyielding kind still meant chiefly Orthodoxy with a capital O, based on the Talmud as well as Scripture. But this had failed to meet the challenge. When Revolution flung open the ghetto doors, the rabbis' main response was panic. They tried to condemn all non-Jewish studies and make Orthodoxy self-sufficient. The attempt was hopeless. Judaism in their hands had become inert, timeless, ghetto-bound and powerless to move; obsessed with regulations, and, what was worse, with devices for getting round them. A Jew, for example, was forbidden to strike a light on Friday evening after the Sabbath had begun, or tell anyone in his household to do so. But if he could afford a Gentile servant, a Sabbath Goy, he would remark: "How nice it would be if we had some light!" and the Goy was expected to act accordingly.

In such a setting the vigorous minds and ardent spirits could not be satisfied. Many Jews therefore looked for a third way. And their quest had already been prepared for. Out of that loosening of the framework in eastern Europe caused by Sabbatianism, another movement had sprung up. It had revived the name of the Hasidim. Its founder was a kindly wonder-worker in Poland known as the Baal Shem Tov. Aided by the Kabbala, the new Hasidim escaped from the tyranny of texts into a realm of lyrical symbol and communion with the divine. They were cheerful folk, who sang and danced and irritated the rabbis. Their leaders were popular mystics and faith-healers rather than scholars. Nevertheless they composed poems and books—mostly in Yiddish. They also resumed the Aliyah or "going up," making it more an Ashkenazi thau a Sephardic practice. Already in 1700, before Hasidism emerged from the preliminary stirrings, a rabbi had conducted over a thousand Ashkenazi settlers to Palestine. The Baal Shem Tov wanted to make the journey himself. This he was unable to do, but his great-grandson, Nachman of Bratzlav, managed after many delays and discouragements to reach Haifa. Nachman was soon proclaiming that mere contact with the holy soil, in the right spirit, conferred inspiration and a redemptive gift. Bands of Hasidim in accumulating strength had already taken the same road. Links with their forerunners were maintained. Safed had become derelict; but at the same time as the American War of Independence, Jewish newcomers from Russia were busily rebuilding the hallowed ghost-town of Caro and Luria.

After Napoleon, Ashkenazi Judaism remained largely Orthodox. The yeast of Hasidism in and around Poland, however, prevented it from settling back into unreflective dullness. It was in countries thus affected that the striving for reappraisal produced its boldest results. The inquirers accepted the enormous treasure which the rabbis had so bravely preserved; but they gazed deeper and saw more . . . saw in fact a glory and marvel which the rabbis were too near to notice. If one looked round and took stock, one immediately asked how it was that the Jews had come through at all. Surely their mere survival, after so many centuries of division and dispersal and torment, hinted at a special divine purpose for them? They ought to have been absorbed long ago, or whittled down to insignificant groups with nothing in common. Yet here they were, still recognisable, still handing on their faith and culture. They were the only people in Europe with a continuous tradition stretching back from the age of steam to the days of Egypt and Babylon. Once again, how had it happened?

That realisation pointed toward the third way which the inquirers sought, a way of wonder and pride. A series of new phenomena followed. One was a rebirth of Hebrew. Another was a literature of " Haskalah " or enlightenment. This explored the Jewish heritage with a reverent freedom, placing it in the context of general history. The apostles of Haskalah often regarded Hasidism as superstitious, yet they owed a debt to its reawakening of the Jewish imagination and sense of possibilities. Haskalah led back to the Bible; but not quite as expounded by Orthodoxy. The more sophisticated (Heine was an associate of theirs) spoke of a Science of Judaism, and surveyed their collective past in that spirit. Appreciating the ingrown effects of tradition and education, they investigated the actual process, and tried to guide it toward an ampler future through the acclimatisation of Gentile culture. In all cases the motive was the same—to find better answers to the Jewish people's perennial and ritualised questions: " What are we? how have we come to be so? and where are we meant to go from here? "

The outcome was a sanctified nationalism which, despite its unique features, could take its place with other national movements. One of its chief inspirers was the Haskalah philosopher Nachman Krochmal, who came from Galicia. His analysis of Israel's history seemed for a while to be favouring the Reform position, and the reduction of Jewishness to religion alone; but another Haskalah figure, the Russian Hebraist and musician Perez Smolenskin, drew the line firmly. The Jews, he insisted, were not a sect. They must develop their character as a people, which the study of their past proved to be valid and authentic. Privileged westerners might talk of assimilation and emancipation, but Jews in eastern Europe were wiser. There, persecution had been an abiding fact for centuries, and almost everybody agreed that it was vain to hope for peace without some vast change. As the era of chauvinism and racialism wore on, Smolenskin's view was confirmed by an anti-Semitic rekindling in Germany and France.

Inevitably the Jewish unrest and upsurge turned eyes toward Palestine again. Inevitably nationalists tended to become Zionists. The final step was neither immediate nor universal, but it was taken: by Smolenskin himself, for instance. Scrutiny of Israel's fantastic survival suggested that the firm faith in a return had been an indispensable factor. At this juncture, however, religious guidance broke down. Either way, it was too timid. Reform Judaism was working toward a general assimilation which looked like a betrayal; an aim which was probably unattainable, and, to the nationalists, not worth attaining. Rabbinic Orthodoxy, while it kept the prime loyalties, did not know what to do with them. It had nothing to offer but the ghetto, whether visible or invisible. The people must remain passive and carry on as usual, till their Messiah arrived to take them home.

The campaign which grew into an effective Third Zionism was not an expression of official Judaism in either form, but a leap beyond. That is why accounts of Jewish religion, as such, sometimes play down the Palestinian element as not wholly respectable. Zionism spread through eastern and central Europe, the Hasid-influenced area, as a quasi-religion in itself. While it could find room for the practising Jew, it could find room for others also. Jews might discard their ancestral forms of faith, as many Christians were doing; they might transform religion into patriotism or ideology, as Christians were also doing; but because of the nature of their inheritance, patriotism itself could only mean recovering Palestine, and ideology could only mean a Jewish vocation. If these things were rejected, Israel's history was a living lie and its cherished identity was bogus. There was no real Israel to be patriotic about. Conditioned as he was, a Jew who asserted his Jewishness at all could seldom think himself out of that proposition. But if he embraced it with its positive consequences, all the ardour of the frustrated generations could flood into him, whether he was religious or not.

The new Back-to-Palestine movement was kept in a state of precarious truce with Orthodoxy by two highly exceptional rabbis. Judah ben Alkalai of Zemun, near Belgrade, devised a formula overcoming the difficulty about the Messiah. The perfection of the Kingdom, he said, must indeed await God's Anointed. But human agency, in other words colonisation, could and should prepare the way. From 1840 onward he was teaching this doctrine. In 1857 he proposed forming a sort of Development Corporation, and persuading the Sultan to cede Palestine to the Jews as a tributary state, in return for their economic services. He went over to live in Jerusalem himself. Meanwhile human agency had been set to work in earnest by a group of societies which the other rabbi, Zvi Hirsch Kalischer of Thorn, founded during the 1860's after thirty years of advocacy. These were the societies of " Lovers of Zion," Hovevei Zion. They laid plans for Palestinian agricultural settlements to receive homeless Jews from eastern Europe. Kalischer believed the recovery of the Land to be the reality symbolised by the Messianic promise. His use of the name " Zion " led to the coining of the familiar title for the wider movement and tendency.

In spite of the two rabbis, it was plain that this Zionism would have to fight its way forward as a minority programme against a stiff opposition. Quite apart from its impatience with the synagogues, it was a restatement of Jewish aims through the medium of Gentile social dynamics—patriotism, progress, and so forth—and therefore suspect. While practising Jews frequently disliked it for that reason, Jews anxious to blend into their surroundings

disliked it for another. Until a much later date its exponents in
the more civilised parts of Europe could expect more sympathy
among Christians, real or nominal. These could look at it from
a political or mystical angle, without being involved in Jewish
feuds. Before it even began, no less a person than Immanuel Kant
had referred to the Jews as " Palestinians who sojourn among us."
In 1838 the reformer Lord Shaftesbury put on record his hope that
they would soon win their way back to the Holy Land. George
Eliot wrote on similar lines in *Daniel Deronda*. Laurence Oliphant,
diplomat, author and M.P., went to Palestine in 1879 and proposed
a Jewish reserve in Gilead; he consulted Perez Smolenskin, and
lived for several years at Haifa, mixing with Jewish patriots who
had made their homes there. Besides individual gestures of goodwill,
there were discussions in terms of governmental policy on a high
level. Not only Napoleon I for a time, but men close to Napoleon
III, canvassed the return as a practical project. An Italian, Benedetto
Musolino, approached eminent politicians in 1870 with a complete
and elaborate plan for a Jewish State.

Understandably then, as nineteenth-century Zionism matured,
Israel's vocation was moulded into something like the pattern of
nationalism currently fashionable among Christians. A few Jews
had early noticed this kinship of ideas and its potentialities. As
far back as 1830, Joseph Salvador had suggested that the European
Powers might re-Judaise Palestine by treaty. Nationalism was a
force which many Gentiles (especially Italians and Germans) cared
about and understood. Jews, as has been well said, are " like other
people only more so." Yet the " more so " must not be brushed
aside. Most observers define it as a quality of intensity and concentration, the result of the conditioning which we have surveyed.
While the " likeness," in the nineteenth century, produced simply
another nationalism, the " more so " gave this a moral fervour
and purposive dignity unapproached by the racial follies of Gentiles.
It was natural that Zionism should keep hold of the belief in earthly
progress, which Jews had had before Christians did. But it soon
showed signs of going further. Israel's true destiny, some declared,

was not to look for a personal Messiah, but to become, through
national rebirth, the world's Messiah itself. Israel should lead the
way toward justice for all mankind and freedom for the oppressed
everywhere. That was what the prophecies pointed to.

Zionist philosophy reached a first climax in Moses Hess. Born
in 1812, descended from rabbis, the son of an Orthodox manufacturer in Bonn, he revolted against the synagogue and the social
order. His first book, which came out in 1837, was an essay in the
philosophy of history. Four years later he produced *The European
Triarchy*, suggesting a United States of Europe controlled by
England, France and Germany, but arguing that this could never
succeed till competitive commercialism was abolished. Then he
joined Marx in radical journalism. His influence on the formation
of the German Left was exceedingly important. He introduced his
friends to the Socialist theories which had arisen in France, and
he converted Engels. However, his leaning toward the anarchist
wing estranged the others. From 1852 to 1860 he was in Paris,
where he studied anthropology and biology. The " Science of
Judaism " had revived his interest in Jewish matters. A nationalistic
historian, Heinrich Graetz, gave him a new conception of Israel's
destiny and a distrust for the nostrum of emancipation. Then Hess
and Graetz were both captivated by Rabbi Kalischer's colonial
projects; and in 1862 Hess published his chief work, *Rome and
Jerusalem*.

The title alludes to a parallel which he draws between Jewish
nationalism aimed at Jerusalem and the Risorgimento aimed at
Rome. Anticipating Bernard Shaw, he addresses himself to an
intelligent woman. She is supposed to be grief-stricken at a death.
By debating the problem of immortality, Hess introduces the
corporate immortality of the Jews. The " infinite mystery " of
Israel's survival and indestructible character is proof of a supreme
purpose. This purpose is to demonstrate moral and social progress,
the perfectibility of life. The step-by-step Creation story in *Genesis*,
the step-by-step evolution of Israel, teach the immanent dynamism
of the world in conformity with science. History is moving

toward its Sabbath, the Messianic Age. The Jewish people should be leading mankind. But they cannot do so in dispersal. They will always be strangers among the nations. They will never command respect till they can unite in their own Palestine at the meeting-place of the continents, build their own model institutions, and communicate their wisdom through their own media. The relationship between this proposed mission and their actual religion is not made very clear. Hess uses respectful language about the Orthodox (not the Reformed), but his own Judaism, if it can be called so, is an ideology derived from Spinoza. He contrasts Spinoza with Sabbatai, the true herald of dawn with the false. As to practical plans, he hopes, like the patriots in Italy, for French support.

At the time, the book seemed to fall flat. Hess returned to his science. But Graetz read him, and presently caused a controversy by maintaining that Israel should begin its Messianic task by saving itself, without waiting for any sign from God. Hess never got to Palestine; Graetz went there in 1872, and Hess died soon after. *Rome and Jerusalem* continued to make its way gradually. The later prophets of Zionism all drew on it.

One could wish parenthetically to know how much Hess there is in another, more famous corpus of thought. His contribution to the Marx-Engels partnership cannot now be precisely assessed. Yet Marxian doctrine did develop (as has often been pointed out) on pervertedly Judaic lines, in spite of its founder's contempt for the faith of his rabbinic ancestors. Marx's Revolution is an apocalypse, which the dialectics and economics merely rationalise.[3] The workers in their wage-slavery correspond to Israel in bondage. The overthrow of the capitalists corresponds to divine judgment. The future classless society corresponds to the Messianic Age, with Marx as Messiah. History—or all of history that matters—is construed as pressing on to this culmination; its inner logic replaces God. Communists have always opposed Zionism, yet if we had

---

3 Cp. Bertrand Russell, *History of Western Philosophy*, p. 383. The thesis that Marx's system is largely the attempted rationalisation of a sort of "picture" is documented by Leopold Schwarzschild in *The Red Prussian*.

a fuller record of the collaboration of Marx with Moses Hess, we might well find a backstairs kinship.

Nor was Marx the last to construct a philosophy of history. His attempt to extrapolate a Judaic mode of thought led to other attempts by Spengler, Toynbee, and several of less repute. But the Jews themselves had been pondering history for a great deal longer, and, one may believe, with advantages denied to their Gentile imitators. In the upshot, their inferences have been far more vividly borne out, and their applications far more success-ful.

4

Zionism in the "do-it-yourself" sense, the practical Zionism of Kalischer, was given immediacy a few years after his death by Russian pogroms. In 1882 a pamphlet by Leo Pinsker supplied Zionists with a manifesto and programme. Its title was *Auto-Emancipation*, its sub-title *An Appeal to his People by a Russian Jew*. Analysing anti-Semitism, Pinsker declared that the evil could not be ended till Jews had the standing of a nation again. Legal emancipation might be achieved, but social emancipation was an illusion. The Jew was an alien everywhere, so that when he did manage to better himself he only stirred up resentment and further Judeophobia. Hitherto, said Pinsker, the insistence on waiting for the Messiah had paralysed action. Most Jews did not yet feel a need to be national, and this apathy was a bad symptom, like loss of appetite in a very sick patient—Pinsker was a doctor. As for Jewry's religious mission, it was meaningless under present conditions. The solution was to organise a resettlement society on a large scale, and acquire a large piece of land where the agonised surplus could go at once. If this land could be in Palestine, that would certainly be best. The crisis, however, was too acute for rigidity. If relief could be found in some other area, Jewish territorial aspirations must be diverted. In any case, the Jews could take their idea of God and their Bible with them wherever they went; and these could hallow a secondary fatherland as they had once hallowed Palestine.

Pinsker became chairman of Kalischer's federation of Lovers of Zion, and pushed ahead with the late rabbi's projects. The pressure in Russia having relaxed a little, no need was felt to look for his alternative refuge, which few were interested in. Only Palestine was seriously considered. As Zionism in the Tsarist Empire grew stronger it approximated to Hess's position, becoming a left-wing underground movement with popular roots, in quest of Utopia. Its chief literary voice was Asher Ginzberg, whose pseudonym was Ahad Ha-am, One of the People. Born near Kiev in a Hasid family, he was the author of many vigorous essays, and emphatically not the author of one document ascribed to him, the *Protocols of the Elders of Zion*. Ahad Ha-am, who knew his Talmud better than most rabbis, taught Zionism as a mystique of moral and spiritual resurrection. It meant a Jewish Culture, an earthly embodiment of divine justice. He denied that Jewish religion could truly exist without a national basis. Israel required Palestine, not merely as a remote dream, but as its concrete goal and headquarters: Law, Land, People, God, together constituted the essence of Jewish history and could never be separated. On the other hand Ahad Ha-am was in no hurry to see Palestine converted into a Jewish republic. Moral regeneration and gradual settlement should come first, politics later.

With the colonising efforts fostered by Pinsker, a miscellaneous independent tradition of Jewish land schemes began to be channelled into nationalism. Oliphant's Gilead project, already mentioned, was far from being alone. Cranks and reformers had been talking for a long time of planting minuscule Jewish peasantries in various parts of the world. In 1825 Mordecai M. Noah, a Philadelphian diplomat and author, had opened an Israelite reservation called Ararat on Grand Island, N.Y., inviting not only Jews but American Indians, as being the Lost Tribes. No one responded, and similar undertakings elsewhere seldom reached even an opening day. Such eccentricities had little to do with Zionism. Yet they developed a bias in that direction. Mordecai M. Noah himself, after the Ararat fiasco, spent the rest of his life agitating for a return to Palestine in much the same style as Judah ben Alkalai; and several thousand Jews actually did find their way there, in a piecemeal fashion, between 1850 and 1880. A French " Israelite Alliance " founded a farm-school near Jaffa in 1870 on a site given by the Turkish Government.

The new wave of 1882 swept most of these tendencies together. Its initial creation Rishon-le-Zion, " First in Zion," originated with a party of six from Russia, who planted themselves on inland ground south of Jaffa. Meanwhile ninety students, also from Russia, went to work in Palestine as labourers till they could buy land and start their own settlement. Two years later they did, close to Ekron, and cultivated vines and wheat. Before then some Rumanian Jews had founded Zikron Ya'akob ten miles from Haifa; and more Rumanians had founded Rosh Pineh, just north of Safed. In 1883 a small team of Poles arrived. In 1884 a fresh Russian group came to Ekron.

With all their valour and energy, the pioneers could not have carried on by themselves. They faced Arab resentment and Turkish apathy, in a country crippled by rapacious neglect. For years they owed such solvency as they had to funds from the Jewish world outside. The difference between toiling upward and sliding downward was made for them by a single patron, one of a family better known in other fields. Baron Edmond de Rothschild was a millionaire of broad culture and humanitarian outlook. He took Rishon-le-Zion in charge; its population increased to several hundred, with a school, a library and a synagogue, and a wine and brandy industry. He assisted the growth of Zikron Ya'akob, where a thousand Jews raised vegetables and kept silkworms and bees. He sponsored the Ekron venture of 1884, which concentrated on fruit, and he launched or aided several others. His money saved practical Zionism from an early disaster. By 1898 Palestine had twenty-five agricultural settlements with about five thousand Jewish inhabitants. These groups were all supposed to be on the way to self-support, and a few had succeeded in paying off their principal debts and more or less managing without Rothschild. But the Baron was a philanthropist with a philanthropist's shortcomings. His charity was a private Halukkah, with the same risk of pauperisation which attended that old subsidy to scholars. He did not live on the spot himself, and his agents caused trouble. Toward the close of the century Rothschild's readiness to sign cheques was sapping morale. Some of his protégés were merely drifting. Others, with superior but deplorable enterprise, had hired Arab labour and reverted to trade and similar unproductive activities, the Jewish norm in dispersal.

The threat of patronage was raised in a different shape by the policies of Theodor Herzl. This Viennese newspaperman and playwright was so brilliant a publicist that he made the movement an international issue, and is still widely imagined to have started it. He, more than anyone, inspired the common false conception of Zionism as political salvage, intended solely to rescue such Jews as were oppressed and unassimilable. Herzl himself was very assimilated indeed. Despite a boyhood dream in which the Messiah and Moses appointed him as their earthly envoy, he grew up with no conscious notion of vocation, either for himself or for Israel. The prompting was given, not by anything within the Jewish community, but by an assault from outside—the trial of Dreyfus in 1894. French anti-Semitism drew his attention to the "misery of Jewry" as a problem clamorous for solution. He now grasped that Jews could not all be assimilated; he was slower to grasp that hopeful myriads in Russia and Poland, however brutal their present burden, might not want to be. Jews, Herzl considered, had become abnormal and bore the stamp of the ghetto, because of external pressure. They could be set free and humanised by another pressure, toward a home of their own.

Before the Dreyfus trial Herzl had been vaguely aware that this idea was current, but it had no charms for him. During the year or two after his conversion he still read neither Hess nor Pinsker, and knew nothing about organised Zionism. Indeed, the Russian

Ussishkin was to express the opinion that he knew nothing about Jews. But in both respects, ignorance was strength. If Herzl had come across *Auto-Emancipation* he would (on his own admission) have done less himself, and his influence would have been far slighter. If he had known more about his fellow-Jews, he would have appreciated the difficulties, and perhaps been discouraged. As it was he thought everything could be straightened out by social engineering. The ideal was that all Jews should be assimilated, but action was required on a large scale to look after those less fortunate than himself, and transfer them to a single place where they could live in peace. At first Herzl did not care much where the place was to be. He met Baron de Rothschild, and expressed something less than sympathy for Palestinian colonies. The Baron retorted by rejecting his schemes as too ambitious. Despairing of private charity, Herzl decided for political action and a Jewish State.

In 1896 he brought out a book with that title. *The Jewish State* (the phrase had been used by Hess) is a masterly piece of journalism, completely outshining, or at least outglittering, its precursors. It is also short. One of the virtues of modern Zionism is that its classics are all short, and can be read quickly. Herzl's main argument is Pinsker's over again, but in more concrete terms and a more political tone. He stresses that anti-Semitism exists everywhere. In some cases it can be lulled. Assimilated Jews in France " are Jewish Frenchmen, well and good! " But there are others, in varying proportions from country to country, and these are condemned to live in a vicious circle. Discrimination makes them hostile to Gentiles, and then their hostility makes the Gentiles harden. The cure is to draw off the " poor " unassimilable surplus —a change by which the assimilated themselves will gain.

The propellant, one notices, is not to be Jewish patriotism or religion or culture, but misery. If governments are roused, Herzl argues, they will help. The Jews' task is to set up not simply a colonial association but a company, a giant business concern, to negotiate and build and promote industry somewhere or other under international guarantee. Sporadic settlement, in Palestine or anywhere else, is futile. Jewish infiltration will sooner or later provoke reaction and counter-measures. As for geography, Herzl has one eye on Argentina. However, he does have the other on Palestine. In view of the sequel I do not think the implied physical image is unapt. A reader feels that he is not exactly warm toward the ancient idea, but recognises its value as a rallying-cry: " the very name of Palestine would attract our people with a force of marvellous potency " . . . however irrational. Wherever the Jewish State is, the company will sponsor emigration in groups, and build up an economy flourishing enough to supply positive allurements. Herzl is derisive at Baron de Rothschild's conduct in virtually " paying people to go." The Jewish State must start off multilingual like Switzerland—no nonsense about Hebrew here—though perhaps one language will come out on top as a lingua franca. The State, Herzl maintains, must not be theocratic, and indeed it is hard to see anything at all in his picture of it that is specially Jewish. If in Palestine, it is to be, in essence, an outpost of western civilisation. He proposes a flag for it, a white flag with seven golden stars; emblems which a Jew, recalling the yellow star of the Middle Ages, might contemplate with mixed feelings.

In the autumn of 1897 Herzl risked a prophecy which was to become memorable: that the Jewish State would be founded in fifty years. Meanwhile he had learnt more about the movement which already existed, and encountered some of its officers. They told him that no ultimate target but Palestine would do. Herzl went far to meet them, later even writing a novel, *Altneuland*, describing a future Jewish commonwealth in the correct setting. Yet he never quite—as the phrase goes—got on the wavelength. He appreciated that the vision of Zion was a datum he had to work with. He came to terms with it, however, simply because there was no other way of enlisting enough support.

What he inaugurated, in that spirit, was " political " as distinct from " practical " Zionism. Thereby he exposed himself to fire from both sides. To the well-off assimilationists round him he was a lunatic trouble-maker; this, at first, was the judgment of nearly all for whom Jewishness meant religion alone. To the mystical patriots he was a westernised hybrid, a wire-puller, a paternalist. Ahad Ha-am saw Herzl's Zionism for what it was: a politico-philanthropic relief device, aimed at getting rid of a specific evil. The rich Jews were to take action—largely through Gentile associates—to save the poor ones. The whole programme was abstract, contrived, without roots in folk-experience, unrelated to what was already being done in the Land itself. Also it had no spiritual dimension. Ahad Ha-am objected to *Altneuland* as portraying a liberal, technological Palestine, scarcely touched by the Hebraic rebirth. To become a " puny State," he protested, would solve nothing in itself. " The salvation of Israel will be achieved by prophets, not diplomats."

Nevertheless, Herzl was a born leader whom the rest could not do without. His gifts as a speaker, his reputation as a writer, his social connections, even his big beard and commanding presence, made the cause impressive throughout Europe and beyond. In 1897 he summoned the First World Zionist Congress at Basle. According to anti-Semites, it was at a secret session of this Congress that the plot of cosmopolitan Jewry for world dominion was launched. Since the only evidence that has ever been produced is a forgery, the absence of any real ground for the tale is fairly obvious. The aim of the Congress was exactly what it professed to be. Soon after it, Herzl began trying to open the door to Palestine by exerting his powers of persuasion on the great.

He asked for a national home, not for full independence. Palestine could hardly be prised loose from Turkey without war. There might, however, be room for a bargain. Joseph Nasi and Judah ben Alkalai had both glimpsed potentialities of that sort. The weakness of the Ottoman Empire lay in the chaos of its finances. Herzl hoped that the Sultan could be induced to favour Jewish land purchase and local autonomy, in exchange for a loan from some other power or powers. He went to Jerusalem—where he read Hess for the first time—and had an interview with Kaiser Wilhelm II. The Kaiser gave him some cloudy encouragement, but was too palpably interested in making Palestine a German protectorate. Herzl approached the court of Constantinople with the best proposals he could submit. The Sultan listened, and in due course conveyed that if sufficient financial aid was given, Turkey would approve a charter for Jewish settlement, under strict control, in certain parts of the Empire . . . but not Palestine.

Herzl had already complained in the privacy of his diary about the Jews' ingratitude for the " gigantic work " he was doing for them. The result in Turkey might have excused a degree of doubt. However, a frightful outburst of pogroms gave fresh urgency to his arguments. Again, as when Pinsker wrote, the situation did seem to call for instant rescue rather than gradual development. Suddenly Herzl scored a kind of success. In 1903 Joseph Chamberlain agreed to sponsor a Zionist colony under the British Crown. If the Jews wanted, they could migrate to East Africa—say Uganda.

This offer at last brought a long-hovering issue to earth, putting the question squarely and not hypothetically. The need for a haven was acute. A haven was now available, and could be used to ease the pressure without giving up Palestine. But could Israel, even in extremity, even as a partial makeshift, accept anything at all but the Promised Land ?

Chamberlain probably supposed that Zionism was aimed simply at finding a home somewhere. That delusion has been to blame for much wasted ink and wasted effort. (Even after the Herzl era, G. K. Chesterton weakened a perceptive discussion by arguing for Jewish cantons dispersed through the world; and the Soviet régime attempted an anti-Zionist counterblast by establishing a Jewish commune at Birobidjan.) By 1903 Herzl knew better than to put forward Uganda as an outright alternative. When he laid Chamberlain's offer before the Sixth Zionist Congress, he urged only that a commission be formed to study the territory as an interim goal. But delegates observed with alarm that above the platform, where a map of Palestine had always hung in the past, there was now a map of Uganda. The motion was officially carried by 295 votes to 178, with 99 abstentions. However, Herzl had won only on paper, because the "noes" came largely from the Russians who were intended to do the actual settling, and without whom the scheme was pointless. One of these climbed on to the platform and tore the map down, putting back Palestine as before.

If ever an occasion deserved that hackneyed description "the moment of truth," this was it. The very Jews who formed the Zionist backbone, and whom Herzl supposed himself to be saving, had chosen to go on in misery rather than envisage any other haven than the Land which God gave. Their votes affirmed the unbreakable continuity of Israel.

Annoyed and bewildered, Herzl reproached them with sabotaging his political dealings. He could not grasp that they had no faith in his political dealings. He angrily rebutted the charge that he had betrayed the movement, but failed to carry conviction. Visits to the King of Italy and the Pope, as being perhaps able to persuade the Sultan into a friendlier mood, were fruitless: the King was courteous but unhelpful, the Pope declined to intervene in a Jewish concern. Ussishkin led a revolt against Herzl, and he died prematurely soon afterwards. The Seventh Congress finally turned Uganda down. A splinter group pursued other African mirages, and ended in dissolution.

But in spite of all disputes the prospects were brightening. With Palestine fixed as the sole objective, the two sorts of Zionism could coalesce. On the whole it was the good which Herzl did that lived after him. Effective leadership of the movement he had so greatly strengthened passed to Chaim Weizmann, with whom we reach the last link in the historical chain. An eastern Jew with a western scientific training, he was able to combine political influence with the furtherance of physical settlement. It was in 1906 that he expounded Zionism to Balfour as "a deep religious conviction expressed in modern political terms." During the next few years a stream of pioneers of first-class ability made their way to Palestine, mostly from Russia. By 1914 the total of immigrants was well past fifty thousand, and the later arrivals proved much more capable of standing on their own feet, without sinking into dependence on Arab labour. Weizmann himself realised (as not all Zionists did) that Palestine required a new sort of Jewish society, not merely the old transplanted. There could be no solid foundation without a major revival of something resembling the rural life of ancient Israel. "It is in the village," he wrote as an elder statesman, "that the real soul of a people—its language, its poetry, its literature, its traditions—springs up from the intimate contact between man and soil. The towns do no more than ' process ' the fruits of the villages."

When his war work as a chemist gave him access to high levels in British politics, Weizmann found a well-known phenomenon recurring. In that sort of sphere the Gentiles, such as Balfour and Lloyd George, were more sympathetic than the Jews. They might be sceptical (Allenby, for instance, wondered what anybody could do with such a " sandy, marshy, derelict country "), but they gave Weizmann a hearing. The intermediary in his eventual triumph was Sir Mark Sykes, a devout Catholic. On the other hand, several eminent British Jews fought him savagely and laboured to turn the Government against him. These despised their brethren in eastern Europe, seeing them as objects for pity and charity, not political co-operation; they dismissed Zionism as " the empty dream of a few misguided idealists"; they thought Weizmann mad, just as others had thought Herzl mad; and they did not understand that the Prime Minister and his colleagues felt far more respect for nationalists than for assimilationists.

In 1917, with a British conquest of Palestine imminent, Weizmann obtained the Balfour Declaration. Here was the political bargain which had eluded Herzl. Admittedly it failed to meet the full Zionist demand. Ahad Ha-am pointed out that the British Government did not offer to reconstitute Palestine as the national home of the Jewish people, but to facilitate the establishment *in* Palestine of a national home *for* the Jewish people. The Declaration recognised no historic right to the Land. Yet it was something to work on, and it would mean whatever the colonists and their supporters could make it mean. Without the heroism of that practical element, before and after, it would assuredly have been a dead letter.

5

The progress of Jewish Palestine toward independence, with Weizmann as president, need not be traced here. Others have told the story, and it raises controversies which would obscure the larger theme. However, the main trend in Jewish affairs during this time was steadily and tragically toward confirmation of the Zionist case. Without political status and territory, even bare survival became uncertain. In the 1920's American assimilationists poured out huge sums for relief in Europe, trying to stabilise the position. Their equivalents in Germany denounced Zionists as imperilling the social acceptance which they, the " Germans of the Mosaic persuasion," had fought to attain. Hitler's Final Solution buried their thesis under six million corpses. The nationalistic vanguard stood vindicated; and most of the Jewish people caught up and acquiesced, if with widely varying degrees of enthusiasm.

In spite of Arab enmity and British ambiguities, the settlement of the Land had gone forward. As for the exact morality of the process, I am here no more concerned with that than with the political details. I am concerned with objective data, and the dynamics of the Republic. The point which matters is the uniqueness of a phenomenon and the nature of that uniqueness; the anatomy, in fact, of what Koestler comes perilously near to calling a miracle.[4]

Israel, the Republic of that name, is the only state created by international resolution. The U.N. vote which supplied its charter in 1947 occurred fifty years, almost to the day, after Herzl's prophecy, although the circumstances were such as he could not

---

4 In declining to debate "exact morality" I have no wish to give the impression of shirking major issues. I am well aware, for instance, of the squalid tragedy of the refugees; I have seen something of it for myself; and I think the Israeli case is much more convincing than the Arab.

have foreseen. The internationally-sponsored Republic attracted, and absorbed, an international population. Jews of weirdly various backgrounds and degrees of culture, after two millennia of separation, all turned out to be responsive to Palestine. The immigration workers received some of the ablest products of western civilisation; they also received a pathetic medley of displaced persons, including strange figures from Arabia who were unexpectedly content to travel by air, because the Bible had promised that they would ride on the wings of eagles, but were frightened to step into motor vehicles, because the Bible did not mention them. In its first days, the Republic had to contend with assailants in overmastering force —fifty million people against less than two million. Nevertheless it held its own. The impossible State kept itself in being by impossible victories. In so doing it rallied Jewish support which it might not otherwise have had, and secured enough aid to give its economy, for the moment at least, an impossible viability.

These are some of the externals. If one looks for the psychological basis of Israel's achievement, one soon grasps that religion, in the formal sense, is no more than a secondary feature. It is not a downright discordant feature. Apart from a small "ultra" sect, Orthodoxy has swung over to approval. Most rabbis concur with the formula recognising a role for human action in the divine purpose for the Land. Israeli synagogues are usually Orthodox, and the rabbinical party carries weight in politics, enforcing, for instance, a rigid Sabbath. But the majority are not assiduous in religious observance. Further, while a theocracy of some kind may yet arise, a theocracy grounded on Orthodoxy as it now stands would be a contradiction in terms. Orthodoxy is, precisely, Judaism without Palestine; it began as a provisional system for Jews in exile; it depends on the axiom that Jews live among strangers, so that in order to maintain their sacred identity, they must govern their entire lives by the Law which is their sole possession. In Israel, where the axiom is untrue, the relevance of the system would appear to be doubtful, and its future far from clear. The society formed by Zionism is religious in shape, rather than creed or practice. It may evolve its own version of Judaism, or it may not.

Yet despite many cleavages of opinion and clashes of interest, Israel has fused its varied components into a purposeful whole. Its non-Jewish elements add problem to problem (the Republic has harboured six associations of Boy Scouts at the same time), but most of the Christians manage to fit in, and even the Arabs are no longer wholly intransigent. The cohesion and infectious vigour of the main body may be put down partly to the sheer necessity of succeeding, with hostile armies in front and the sea behind. Still, one positive factor occurs again and again. This—as we might expect—is a genius for revivifying the past as an active ingredient of the present.

It showed itself at the outset, in the policy of uniting Jews and making Israelis of them by employing Hebrew as a language for all. Such conduct seemed the height of romanticism. Hebrew was a literary and liturgical tongue which no nation actually spoke, with a forbidding special alphabet. Yet the plan worked. A vernacular form of it, taught in a hurry to swarms of immigrants, remained with them and carried them far toward integration. While the obvious medium, English, was and is widely used in Israel, Hebrew is unshakably Israel's language. The reason why such diverse groups could be blended, and by such means, lay in the fact which our inquiry has brought out: that they all shared the Hebrew sacred literature, and, as a corollary, the idea of reunion in Palestine. Given the Zionist antecedents, it is natural that a city built by Jews should have been named Tel-Aviv after a place mentioned in *Ezekiel* iii : 15; that the port of Eilat should have been founded as a reincarnation of Solomon's Ezion-geber; that biblical archaeology should have become a national sport, with a marked patriotic tinge; and that significance should have been seen in the coincidence of the U.N. passing its resolution on the same day in which the Hebrew University in Jerusalem acquired three Dead Sea Scrolls.

None of this love-affair with history is mere antiquarianism. In the speeches of Abba Eban, the Israeli Minister of Education, one notices the official stress on practical synthesis. The argument is that Israel has three cultural possessions—the ancient Hebraic inheritance, the Jewish wisdom acquired in exile, and the civilisation learnt from others. Its national culture must keep the Jewish links, and establish, partly through language, a sense of lineal descent from the older Israel. But the science and politics of the modern world must be combined with these things. The culture must look ahead, not backward. Jerusalem's University and Haifa's Technological Institute are complementary.

Thus Mr. Eban. The "Jewish consciousness" taught in many Israeli schools includes scriptural and historical studies, and some religion, with emphasis on Judaism's prophetic strain. However, the Sabra or born Israelis are notoriously losing their Jewishness, or at least transmuting it. They tend to find the Bible engrossing . . . as family history. To many of them Israel itself is a mystique, patriotism a kind of religion; meaning not narrow chauvinism, but fulfilment of the prophets. Since the ghetto is outside their experience, Orthodoxy is losing its hold among them. Their motto might be a saying of the French Socialist Jaurès: "Take from the altars of the past the fire, not the ashes." And after all, there is nothing novel in this. The Sabra are becoming Israelites as well as Israelis. They are renewing that historically-formed purposiveness on the human level which faltered after Bar-Kochba.

They have ample justification. Zionism has proved that the long conditioning produced not merely a passive imprint, but an inward chemistry which could ignite a blaze as soon as air was admitted. No other explanation exists for what is perhaps the most crushing fact of all: the swift conversion of landless and urban Jews to an utterly different mode of life. Weizmann and his disciples were not alone in insisting on the need for this change. There were Gentile observers who said the same: notably G. K. Chesterton. Chesterton has been called anti-Semitic, but he saluted Zionism as a constructive policy, and saw its implications better than some Zionists did. When misguided partisans promised that civilisation would come to the Near East through Jewish enterprise and technical skill, he rejoined that this was exactly what the Near East was afraid of. The test of the movement, he said, was whether Jews in Palestine could be weaned away from the ideal of managing others or shining in a profession, and become ordinary farmers, labourers, builders themselves. Weizmann and Chesterton were right, and the weaning-away has taken place. After eighty deracinated generations, Jewish settlers by the hundred thousand have reverted to the ways of their Israelite forebears. They live off the soil directly and frugally—and efficiently. Under their charge the waste acres have grown green again.

Attention is due not only to the phenomenon but to the method. As is well known, a large share in the new Jewish agriculture has been taken by kibbutzim or communal settlements. These were among the firstfruits of the unified Zionism which formed after Herzl's death. They do not count for as much in the economy as they did once, but they are still functioning. Since the kibbutz, whatever its future prospects, is the most illuminating of Zionist institutions, a glance at it may close the story.

At Deganya, near the Lake of Tiberias, the farm-workers show visitors a stranded army tank with a fence round it, and a museum with specimens of every living thing in the area. In any country but Israel, one would say that the settlement was a product of crankish mysticism which could not hold together for six months. Yet it has been running for well over half a century, not only in its own right but as a training centre for the personnel of similar places.

A kibbutz (says Dr. Darin-Drabkin in *The Other Society*) is " a voluntary society based on communal property, production and labour, and communal consumption and living arrangements. . . . No private property or private economic activity is allowed." Besides the kibbutzim there are also many co-operative smallholder settlements to which much the same observations apply, if less forcefully. In the early stages of their growth these colonies were traduced as hotbeds of atheism and free love. But the ordeal blew over. Weizmann, whose dearest hopes they gave substance to, wrote during his last years: " The settlements are firmly rooted, conveniently as well as pleasantly designed; the settlers are robust. cheerful, keen on their jobs. They love the country, and are bringing up a young generation proud of their agricultural skill, eager, upstanding, independent—young men and women who have shed all the attributes of the ghetto and acquired those of a normal, healthy, self-respecting peasant class."

Israel has more than two hundred kibbutzim, with a total population of eighty thousand. Apart from incidental adjustments, they have lasted now for several decades without altering their nature or giving up their unique voluntary communism. Repeated claims that the kibbutz policy was no more than a passing expedient have been refuted by events. Even if they all vanished to-morrow, their record up to the present would stand, intact and unalterable. How, then, have they managed to persist in their defiance of everyday economic mores?

If one asks that question perseveringly, one is offered at least five answers. With five in the field it becomes manifest that the problem is not easily dismissed. Few people realise how extraordinary the kibbutz is, not as an idea, but as a durable reality. It is a freak of nature—of human nature. It is not original; it has been thought of and tried elsewhere, over and over again. The mystery is that in Israel it has succeeded two hundred times, whereas outside, chiefly in America, it has failed two hundred times.

Through most of the nineteenth century, bands of idealists kept founding similar colonies in various parts of the United States. Robert Owen led the way with New Harmony, Indiana. Within three years it had collapsed. His admirers tried again in at least a dozen places, and so did followers of the French Socialist Fourier. During the middle part of the century almost every imaginable kind of community was set up. Some were self-supporting, some were in touch with civilisation. Some were religious, some secular. (One figure in this Utopian ferment was Laurence Oliphant of the Gilead project.) They virtually all dwindled away, usually in less than ten years. Those that survived did so by changing their character.

For the glaringly contrasted success of the kibbutzim, there are three alleged explanations of an economic or semi-political kind. The first is simply that they have had money pumped into them from abroad. But money alone cannot make a community prosper. Many in America had rich backers: Owen, for example. The "Icarian" colony in Illinois, perhaps the most important, was subsidised from France on a large scale, just as the kibbutzim have been subsidised from the United States. Yet it shrank steadily to nothing.

The second explanation is crude necessity. The kibbutzim must be made to work, it is urged, if Israel is to survive at all. This again cannot be more than a part-truth. Israeli agriculture must be kept going somehow. But there is no compulsion to do so by such an unorthodox method. Mere economic pressure, if it were the only consideration, would probably have dictated an Israeli agriculture based entirely (as it actually is in part) on smallholdings.

The third explanation is that the Israeli communities are not comparable to the American because they have never attempted to be self-sufficient. But not all the American ones did, either.

Granted that some weight must be given to all these causes, it is hard to believe that they could account for the difference. On the spot another explanation is current, which boils down to a single word: leadership. Mr. Ian Mikardo has put much the same view with an altered emphasis. He argues that the kibbutz has worked because, here alone, the ideology of the founders has been passed on to a new generation born and reared in the communal context. The kibbutz is self-perpetuating.

With the stress on human factors, especially qualities of leadership, we are evidently getting nearer the truth. One of the rare stalwarts among the U.S. communities was Oneida, N.Y., which lasted after a fashion from 1847 to 1879—not as long as Deganya, but a respectable time. Its head was John Humphrey Noyes, a competent business man. Noyes made a study of the other communities and discussed what was wrong with them. Such an experiment, he decided, has certain essential needs. The leader must choose suitable companions who know and trust each other. He must preserve contact with centres of population. He must stay with his followers, share the burdens, and guide the institution himself. Noyes added that the spirit is ultimate. Socialism alone or religion alone will not sustain a community; the members need both. Lastly, the ruling doctrine must be such that the founder can hand it on to worthy successors.

Zionist history bears Noyes out. The kibbutzim have, in the main, met his requirements. But we must still ask: Why were the requirements not met in America, even in Noyes's own Oneida, which, after his death, turned itself into a factory? There can in fact be no doubt that these American kibbutzim came to grief simply as collections of human beings. Even the best leadership faltered in the abnormal surroundings. Owen, as a manufacturer in Scotland, had proved himself a leader of the highest order; at New Harmony he completely lost his grip. In other settlements, working-class members did not care enough for the theories, and leisure-class members did not pull their weight. Bigotry, dissension and litigation were rife. The wrong members had the money. If a community did crawl into its second decade, the children were liable to grow up with no respect for its ideals, and desert to the cities.

Owen and most of the other founders failed to see that their theories could do nothing without corresponding qualities both in the leaders and in the led. A venture of so novel a kind called for new abilities, for new ways of thinking and behaving, above all for a sense of vocation such as few people have. In America the right qualities were not often forthcoming. Among the Jews of the Zionist emigration, they were. Indeed the secret is to be looked for, not in the kibbutz as it exists now, but in its earlier role as a pioneering body. To-day, Mr. Mikardo's claim that the system is self-perpetuating has ceased to be entirely valid. Many of the junior kibbutz-dwellers have rejected the ideology and are drifting away. Losses can be made up, but the situation is more fluid than in the past, and more controversial. The movement acquired its impetus in the first place as the vanguard of a sacred purpose in a perilous country, and has undergone its loss of importance in a stabilised Republic.

It is misleading to look for parallels among Christian monks or Jewish Essenes. The life of the kibbutzim was never religious as Jews understand the term. But it did spring from the ancestral sense of vocation. This was shared by a far larger number than the American Utopias ever contrived to attract, and was not divorced, as theirs generally was, from practical wisdom. The Jewish conditioning had implanted ideas, not only about the Promised Land, but about the duty to live there in a certain way, distinct from the nations, affirming justice and truth.

" Kibbutz " itself means " in-gathering," and is the word traditionally used for the in-gathering of exiles, the Kibbutz Galuyot, prayed for through the centuries in the tenth Benediction. For many Zionists this exalted democracy expressed the spirit of the return, the ideal of the reborn commonwealth. Aaron David Gordon, Deganya's founder, preached the collective cultivation of Palestine as the Jews' way back to their lost harmony with Creation. It was not enough simply to set up farms. He had been a farm overseer himself in Russia, and he knew. Zionists had to " restore the wholeness of human nature " through working the soil as free, equal and reflective beings. Only in Israel's own Land, and in philosophic peasant communes, could " David's harp regain its power."

Gordon had affinities with Thoreau, Whitman, William Morris. He wrote: " When you perform your labour, the entire world shall seem to be your workshop—and you and nature the workers therein—and you shall have both a single heart and a single purpose . . . and you shall hear a heavenly voice saying, ' Work, children of man, work.' And you shall know that there exists in labour a treasure of the spirit. . . ." Noble words, yet others had said very much the same with little to show for it. Only the context of

Jewish vocation and the Zionist struggle could make such ideas into a force moulding society. Because of the qualities of the led as well as the leaders, the experiment flourished, and successors continued to come forward till the Republic was established. The momentum which they gave it assures that there will at least be no collapse in the foreseeable future.

Collapse may come in the end or it may not. But clearly this voluntary communism is not a thing arbitrarily put together by social engineers despising the past. Its continuity with the whole Jewish conditioning, with the whole millennial shaping of the Jewish mission, is the key to its nature and the main reason for its long success.

6

Conditioning . . . that persistent word. Through the shared experience and its carefully-fostered presence in Jewish minds, the Bible and the Republic are linked. It was in a religion, from the earliest days, that the mystique of Land and Vocation formed and expressed itself. To-day, however, the mystique can no longer be confined in any existing statement of the religion. We may regard this entire Judaic growth as divinely ordained, a disclosure of God through human causality. Or we may prefer to try deciphering it by human causality alone. But on any reading of the Jewish experience, the Land is central. It cannot be taken out, either in theory or in practice. A Jew may feel no personal interest in Palestine. He may condemn the actual Republic as a mistake. But Palestine's exclusion in principle would cancel Jewish identity altogether. In that respect, Spinoza was right. There would still be a religion hanging over a void, its historical foundations gone, its traditions disavowed, its scriptures deprived of credit. One may doubt, however, whether that religion could fairly be called Judaism.

To say so is not to fly to extremes and imagine that every Jew, logically, should either emigrate to Israel or stop going through the motions of being different. That would be to reduce Jewishness to a pure matter of nationhood, and encourage the anti-Semite's gibe " Why don't you go back to your own country ? " In an outsider it is presumptuous to dogmatise. But clearly one may approve of the Jewish State without denying assimilation a proper and honourable place in the Jewish scheme of things. Ever since the disappointing return from Babylon, it has been understood that the Chosen People must go on living both at home and among the nations. If they have a mission at all, it demands this double life till their Lord acts to make all things new. To dwell in Zion spiritually or by proxy may be enough. The point (and an outsider, simply on the evidence, has a right to say this much) is that Zion must be there. When its sons do momentarily forget it, the Psalmist's words are fulfilled and the right hand withers.

But can a non-Jew believe in the mission—whether as taught by the religious, or as taught, say, by Moses Hess? Has the Republic in particular any message for him? Some would argue that every good gift which the Jewish world of thought ever offered has long since passed into other systems, Christian, Moslem, Marxist or liberal-humanist according to taste. Yet perhaps the last word has not been said. Even if that digestion has occurred, we have no guarantee against the future appearance of something more to digest. The collective unfolding of ideas, the hallowed step-by-step logic, did cease after Palestine was lost. With Palestine recovered, could it be about to resume?

Speculation here is deterred in one way, encouraged in another. Israel's political future remains uncertain. But beneath the anxiety on the surface runs a deeper groundswell of striving restlessness, an awareness of matters unconcluded and unresolved. Many thoughtful Jews do see the Republic as Messianic. They say, however, that its Messianism is partial and potential, straining toward a definition which phases yet to come must perfect. With echoes of Hess, they emphasise the Jewish conviction of " order and progress in the universal design," of a cosmic law which enables Man, through knowledge of his own condition, to work towards a better state of society in this world. The Republic will lead mankind by aid and example toward the Messianic Age which Hebrew prophets were the first to foreshadow. It will do so, not only through the object-lesson of its own birth and continuance, but through special achievements such as the kibbutzim which others will learn to reproduce or adapt.[5] Not itself the divine sunrise, it is nevertheless an anticipatory glow.

In the phrases of Herman Wouk, although Zionism is not religious it is an outgrowth of religion; and although the Republic is not a final fulfilment, it is the place where " as we believe, the light of the Lord will some day blaze forth to fill not only the little land but the whole earth." Or Dr. Norman Bentwich: "Jewish nationalism in Israel is not a mere reproduction of European nationalism, but is enriched from its prophetic and Messianic root. It is a movement of redemption, with a message of universality. It has as its aim to further the establishment of a just and peaceful international society. Its ultimate object, it has been said, is to transcend itself and to involve the redemption of the world. The striving for a good social order for humanity, which is manifest in Israel, is an expression of the Messianic hope, and may give a fresh significance to Judaism outside Israel." In the atmosphere of such beliefs, the career of the Chosen may indeed press forward again.

The non-Jew—at least if he has read history, or observed the habitual conduct of public men—may be more impressed by the cardinal portent of Israel's coming into being at all, than by any aspect of its society in detail. If he goes no further, he may still be stimulated to ask how it was that the incredible happened, where this energy came from, what the implications are. As to the process, I have gathered some of the facts in this book, though acknowledging subtler riddles that slip away from analysis. As to implications . . . the outlook of many Sabra will acquit me of special pleading if I suggest that the Republic has proved the necessity of taking the

---

5 Cp. the treatment of the kibbutz and its implications by a non-religious Jew, Mr. Ian Mikardo, in *Tribune*, 7th September, 1962.

Bible seriously. It has vindicated the Zionist dreamers who did. Also, it has confounded the intelligentsia who do not.

Several years ago Mr. Fred Hoyle (Professor Hoyle as he now is) dismissed the Bible in a broadcast. " Is it in any way reasonable," he said, " to suppose that it was given to the Hebrews to understand mysteries far deeper than anything I can comprehend, when it is quite clear that they were completely ignorant of many matters that seem commonplace to me?" What he meant was not that the idea was strictly against reason, i.e. excluded by logic. He meant that it was against expectation. You would not look for any unique wisdom, or be inclined to trust pretensions to it, among such insignificant, backward, and palpably uninformed folk. No, I agree; you wouldn't. However, the question is not " What is likely?" but " What are the facts?" The entire record of Israel, ancient and modern, is itself a wild exception that makes nonsense of this appeal to probability.

Herzl forecast in 1897 that the Jewish State would be founded in fifty years. He was exactly right. It is doubtful whether any political prophecy made by " reasonable " men like Professor Hoyle has ever come within miles of such a perfect fulfilment. Yet Herzl's " reasonable " contemporaries thought he was mad, as, a little later, they thought Weizmann was mad. They laughed at the Jewish State itself, let alone the fifty years. Even "reasonable" Zionists did not see, and would have denied, that the forecast could be fulfilled as it actually was. Professor Hoyle's argument is more forceful against " reasonable " minds than it is against Scripture. As they have been so monumentally wrong about an Israel side by side with themselves, why should they be right about an Israel ages removed from them and much harder to get at? Humanly speaking we simply do not know. An inquirer can only preserve due care and humility, shutting no doors, doing his best to seek out truth. To jib at the procedure as not "reasonable" would be high-handed, ungracious, and anti-scientific.

Israel's miracle does hint that the humanist who shies away from the Bible is missing what he can ill afford to miss. It suggests hidden reserves of strength and judgment, with value for mankind at large. But there can be no point in trying to sum its lesson up in some naïve programme or set of rules; and an especially bad blunder of this type would be to concoct a facile religious formula, a pseudo-ecumenical H.C.F. supposedly applying outside Judaism. Between religions the gaps are wide, and platitudes cannot bridge them. Even the assumption of some Christians that " we both have the Bible " invites the Jewish comment that the Bibles of the two faiths are no longer the same. The Jew's is the Old Testament, read as a sacred history in its own right, and supplemented by a tradition which no one else shares. The Christian's not only adds the New Testament but imposes a layer of symbolism on the Old.

That Judaism and Christianity should never have split apart, and were not bound to do so, is doubtless a just conclusion from the nature of both. Alas, they did split apart. The Christian may ponder *Romans* xi, and such glosses as Monsignor Franceschi's to the effect that " modern Israel is linked to our own salvation." He may abjure his fathers' anti-Semitism and do his utmost to atone. He may try to silence that loathsome accusation " You killed Christ" which Jewish children still hear at school. However, as to his gaining a positive enrichment, there may indeed be a way but there is no simple or obvious way. In any case the majority of mankind are no more Christians than they are Jews. If, as various rabbis tell us, Judaism is destined to grow with Messianic maturity into something greater, we have no means of determining what the " something greater " is likely to be, or what part the Republic will play in forming it. For Jew or Christian or any other religious believer, the watchwords at the moment must be charity, clarification, reverent suspension of judgment . . . and genuine study of the Bible.

Jewish spokesmen who maintain the Republic's apostolate of progress may be supplying a hint for a quest of another sort. Israel, with its psychological mainspring of ideas and events, may hold the clues sought by the philosophers of history—the Marxes, Spenglers and so forth—with at best only fractional success. To master the present by unlocking the secret of the past; to find practical answers for those questions which are so far from being solely Jewish in their applicability—" What are we? how have we come to be so? and where are we meant to go from here?" . . . these challenges, which the philosophers have faced, the men of Zion (within their own limits) have triumphantly met. They are the arch-practitioners of history in depth. By concentrated insight into the Jewish past as a whole, with its traditions and legends, its tendencies and hopes, they have discovered a meaning and a conquering purpose, and attained an end against all odds.

There is no reason why other groups of human beings should not grow toward that fullness of memory, that inner coherence, that lucidity of aim, which projected the Jewish State on the world. Those who are not Jews may still absorb habits of thought enabling them to revalue their own history, and to assess more truly what the present requires. It is not so much a question of progress as of a temper of mind which can give to progress a crystalline authenticity. To enter into the Zionist spirit is to sense possibilities which Gentiles rarely perceive. Even the identification of Gentile Zions.

CHAPTER BIBLIOGRAPHIES

Short headings only are given here. The full title of each work will be found in the General Bibliography.

Where so much of the subject-matter has figured in one's education and general reading, it would be impossible to recall every source which one may have drawn upon. I have certainly not read everything relevant; nobody has. On the other hand, where a book of recognised value fails to appear among my references, it should not be absolutely assumed that I have never seen it.

Certain histories, like those of GRAETZ and ROTH, are not included in the chapter bibliographies. Detailed references would be hard to give when a book is present (so to speak) nearly all the time. The same is true of the chronological chart of MONTJUVIN.

Biblical quotations are from the Revised Standard Version unless otherwise stated. The Bible is listed in the chapter bibliographies only in a few cases where a translator's note is cited.

The works listed under their editors (BEVAN and SINGER; FINKELSTEIN; HOOKE (2), (3); ROWLEY; THOMAS) contain contributions by several hands. Hence, a reader looking up a reference in one of these should be careful to find out who the actual author is.

Chapter One: The Roots of Israel

BELLOC; BENTWICH, 7, 9, 29, 126, 132–40, 160; BEVAN and SINGER, 102, 407–8; BRASCH, 147–8, 154, 265–84; BUBER, *xi*, *xiii*; BUTTERFIELD, 73; CHADWICK; COHEN, A., *xxxvi*; EBAN, 54, 66–8, 115, 121–2, 155; FINKELSTEIN, *xviii*, 784–9, 1489–1509; HOOKE (1), 154–5, (3), 158, and (4), 224; JOSEPH, 15–16, 20–3, 194–8; KOESTLER (1), Part Two, and (2), 4–5; NEIL, 23, 27, 44–9; PARKES (1), 243, and (2), 237–8; POLISH, 22–7, 32, 97, 145, 193–4; ROWLEY, 25, 74–6, 351; SCHOFIELD, 27; SPINOZA, 33–5, 92–5; SYKES; VAWTER, 27, 35–6; WEIZMANN, 108, 143, 200, 436; WILLIAMS, 51–61, 70; WOUK, 30–1, 186.

Chapter Bibliographies

Chapter Two: The First Zionism

ALBRIGHT (2), 13–16, 170–1, 175, 200–3, 213–23, 239–41, 254–72; ANDERSON, 22–7, 31–6, 39, 41, 45–9, 67; BEVAN and SINGER, 10–11; COHEN, A., 29; COLLINGWOOD and MYRES, 262; COTTRELL, 143–4; DANIÉLOU, 1–2, 19, 109–11, 205–6; DANIEL-ROPS, 35, 55, 75–9, 113, 243; ELDER, 45–50, 57–9; *Encyclopaedia Britannica*, arts. "Dittany," "Jehovah"; FINKELSTEIN, 5–18, 76–7, 100–1, 792–3, 1749; GRAY, 90–2; HOOKE (3), 19–20, 162, and (4), 131–2, 147–52, 224; JAMES, 36–8, 69–70, 148–50, 201–3; *Jewish Encyclopaedia*, art. "Moses"; JOIN-LAMBERT, 15; JOSEPH, 222; KAUFMANN, 21–77, 116–17, 217–18, 228, 235, 242–4, 298–9; KELLER, chapters 9–11; KENYON, 34, 182–4, 207–8; KUHL, 37–8, 47, 312–14; MANETHO; NEIL, 46, 91, 136–40; NOTH, 3, 24, 83, 111–12; OESTERLEY and ROBINSON, vol. I, 39, 70–1, 87; PEDERSEN, vols. III–IV, 401–10 and appendix; POLISH, 22, 54, 59; PRITCHARD, 231; ROWLEY, 11, 74–6, 283–91, 351; SCHOFIELD, 78–83, 110 (plate), 157; SPINOZA, 30; VAUX, 224, 493; VAWTER, 21–8; WOUK, 68, 70, 312–20; ZAEHNER, 43, 50–5, 60.

Chapter Three: Covenant and Conquest

ALBRIGHT (1), 96–106, 113, 119, and (2), 13–15, 75–6, 205–8, 262–81; ANDERSON, 55–7, 65, 82, 87, 162; BENTWICH, 122; BORCHSENIUS, 59; BUBER, 3–10; COHEN, A., 146; DANIEL-ROPS, 81, 84, 92–3, 98–104, 115–17; ELDER, 49–59; FINKELSTEIN, 5–18, 1743; GRAY, 10, 24, 85; HOOKE (1), *vii*, 62, (3), 21, and (4), 148, 152, 250–1, 255; JAMES, 34, 272; JOIN-LAMBERT, 16; KAUFMANN, 18, 53–4, 61–2, 87–8, 102, 111–12, 128, 170–1, 201–2, 212, 223–56; KENYON, 39 ff., 58, 102–6, 135–6, 159–62, 184, 195–8, 206–15, 236–7; KUHL, 38–9, 62, 312; NEIL, 33, 59–65, 135–6, 141–2; NOTH, 8–17, 27, 66–9, 127–35; OESTERLEY and ROBINSON, vol. I, 121; PARMITER, 23–8; PEDERSEN, vols. I–II, 2–8, 18, 24, 41, 36–7, 54–6, 110, 279 ff., 356, 392–3, 428, 475–6, 485–6, and vols. III–IV, 198–200, 234, 353, 409, 434–5, 612, 619, 625–7; POLISH, 66–7, 79, 97, 192; ROWLEY, *xx–xxi*, 289–90, 307–8; SCHOFIELD, 12, 26, 49, 80, 91–2, 102–4; VAUX, 7, 47–8, 99, 143–8, 217, 236, 247, 272, 296, 333–4, 345, 352, 361–2, 417–18, 451–4; WOUK, 34, 61–2, 118, 126, 140–1, 186, 308.

Chapter Four: The Book of Beginnings

ALBRIGHT (1), 207–8, 235, and (2), 9, 64–5, 75–80, 148–55, 165–71, 193–6, 200–3,

230–50; ANDERSON, 13–23, 164–6; BENTWICH, 124; BEVAN and SINGER, I, 440–1; BRANDON, 65–72, 83, 93–4; BRASCH, 261; BREWER, art. "Iapetus"; BUBER, 10–18; BUTTERFIELD, 78; COTTRELL, 81–7; DANIÉLOU, 109–10; DANIEL-ROPS, 30, 36, 63–4, 87, 98; ELDER, 27–45, 92–4; FINKELSTEIN, 4–8; GASTER, 3–4; GRAY, 33–7, 61, 110; HERODOTUS, bk. I, sections 181–2; HOOKE(I), 1–8, 12, 18–23, 62, 70–4, 114, 118, 135, 146, (3), passim and N.B. 14–15, 21, 164–5, (4), 41–2, 104, 147–8, 256; JAMES, 20–3, 32–6, 64–70, 221–2; JOIN-LAMBERT, 13; KAUFMANN, 61–8, 73, 93–4, 123, 218–23; KELLER, chapters 1–8; KENYON, 194; KOESTLER (I), 282–5; KUHL, 18, 35–64, 72, 77, 92–5; LEWIS, 127–8; NEIL, 46, 106, 123–35; NOTH, 40–7, 111, 137; PARKES (2), 9; PARMITER, 18–19; PEDERSEN, vols. I–II, 13–15, 21, 29, 54–7, 453–4, and vols. III–IV, 505, 665; POLISH, 23–8, 33–40, 49; PRITCHARD, 28–39, 66–71, fig. 189; RASHI, 14–15; ROWLEY, *xx–xxi*, 5–7, 74–82, 286–7; RUSSELL, 373–4; SCHOFIELD, 36–52, 100, 157; SMALLEY, 132–3; VAUX, 6, 13, 49, 99, 272, 279–94, 310, 345, 374; VAWTER; VON RAD, 13–18, 23–6, 32, 44–65, 79, 124, 135–48, 171–6, 184, 200, 264–5, 291–2, 317, 362–3, 394, 428; WOUK, 31, 56, 184, 334.

Chapter Five: A World by Itself

ALBRIGHT (I), 109, 113–17, 230–3, and (2), 14–15, 47, 75–6, 169, 175, 230–5, 241, 249–50, 273, 278–94, 299–305; ANDERSON, 62, 97–8, 102–7, 115, 123–4, 134, 139, 146–51, 186, 195, 225; ASHE; BEVAN and SINGER, I, 3, 10–18; BRANDON, 53, 65–74, 83, 93–8, 134–8, 150–5; BRASCH, 8–66; BUBER, 10–18, 27, 31; BUTTERFIELD, I; COHEN, A., 17, 45–6, 51, 142–3, 268; DANIÉLOU, 19, 109–10, 117, 205–6; DANIEL-ROPS, 67, 86–7, 151–2, 168; DIRINGER, 112–22; ELDER, 60–6; *Encyclopaedia Britannica*, art. "Zion"; FINKELSTEIN, 18, 24–8, 31, 38; GRAY, 18–19, 24–5, 36, 75, 79–80, 87–8, 103–20, 124, 127, 133–9, 143; GURNEY, 35–40, 59–62, 134; HOOKE (I), 3–4, 8, 146, (3), 14–15, 31–2, 148, 155–6, 167, 176–7, 196, 200–7, 213, 233–4, 239, 250, and (4), 104–6; JAMES, 79–80, 92, 124–6, 149–50, 189–90, 233, 252–4, 309–10; *Jewish Encyclopaedia*, art. "Solomon"; JOIN-LAMBERT, 9–16, 34–43; KAUFMANN, 7–20, 87, 99, 108–17, 122–49, 215, 227, 241, 246–76, 311–6; KENYON, 221–5, 237–59; KUHL, 35–40, 72, 77, 146–8, 155–6, 231; NEIL, 33, 45, 78, 86, 125–6, 152–3; NOTH, 35–41, 66–9, 88, 93–5, 129, 142–4, 150, 166–7, 177–9, 188, 196–8, 219–20, 226–7; OESTERLEY and ROBINSON, vol. I, 168, 179, 192; PARKES (I), 8–9, 33; PARMITER, 23–9, 34, 38, 45, 53–4, 93–115, 122–3, 131, 136, 170–1; PEDERSEN, vols. I–II, 22–4, 29–40, 48–57, 99–127, 132, 157–62, 168–71, 179–82, 188–93, 205–6, 231–3, 245, 263–4 279 ff., 318–19, 356, 411, 428, 434–42, 451–82, 491–6, and vols. III–IV, 8, 12–13,

27, 40, 45–6, 61–9, 77–8, 86, 97, 107–20, 125, 130, 151–9, 201–2, 214–29, 234, 256, 265, 272, 317–20, 401, 430–5, 441–3, 467–9, 482, 507–10, 515, 524, 529–30, 573–4, 612, 633–5; POLISH, 12, 20, 49, 54–9, 145; ROBINSON; ROWLEY, 12–14, 33–4, 115–64, 295–300, 307–8, 333, 363–4; SCHOFIELD, 107–12, 142; VAUX,, 7–14, 25, 34–5, 49, 56–7, 66, 72–3, 78–82, 89, 96, 102–7, 113, 127, 142, 214–22, 229, 258–60, 272–4, 284–8, 301–11, 317, 329–34, 345–6, 352, 361–2, 374, 395, 410–1, 417–18, 451–4, 493–6; VON RAD, 291–2; WOUK, 67–75, 334.

Chapter Six: The Prophets and the Law

ALBRIGHT (1), 109, 210–12, 225, and (2), 18, 301–2, 307–15, 320–7; ANDERSON, 198–9, 204, 213, 221, 226, 231, 251, 253, 282, 308–11, 331, 375; BENTWICH, 124; BEVAN and SINGER, 17–18, 29; *Bible*, Moffatt, xv; BORCHSENIUS, 62; BRANDON, 95–8; BRASCH, 243–52; BUTTERFIELD, 1, 57–9, 68–75; COHEN, A., xv, 349–55; COTTRELL, 165–9; DANIÉLOU, 60, 162–3, 215, 260–1; DANIEL-ROPS, 63; ELDER, 66–84; FINKELSTEIN, 35–45; GRAY, 133–4, 145–50, 158, 168, 174–81; HOOKE (3), 19, 21, 176–7, 196, 226–50, and (4), 91, 104–8, 123, 180–3, 194–5; JAMES, 90–2, 256, 274–5; JOIN-LAMBERT, 43–6; JOSEPHUS (1), XI. *v.* 2; KAUF-MANN, 81–3, 98–9, 132–48, 157–66, 172–4, 200, 211–13, 281, 298–9, 343–7, 357–8, 375, 403–4; KENYON, 33, 260–7, 275–91; KUHL, 18, 27, 47, 81–6, 146–7, 157–77, 183–92, 202–7, 212–21, 309–10; NEIL, 44, 95–6, 167, 191–2; NORTH (1), 14; NOTH, 216, 257, 266, 272–3, 285; OESTERLEY and ROBINSON, vol. I, 308–21; PARKES (2), 11; PEDERSEN, vols. I–II, 29, 318–25, 334, 434–5, 478, 491, and vols. III–IV, 27, 68–9, 112–19, 125, 130–7, 250, 319–20, 347–8, 546, 569, 580, 611; POLISH, 20, 41, 100, 111, 192; ROWLEY, xxiii, 16, 19, 115–61, 183–4, 333; SCHOFIELD, 90–1, 155, 170, 175–8, 194, 230; SNAITH, 62–3, 89; VAUX, 14–15, 72–7, 225, 241–9, 288, 323, 333, 337, 384–6; WARMINGTON, 67; WHITE, chapter vii; WOUK, 116, 153, 302–7, 312–20.

Chapter Seven: A Herald without a Name

ALBRIGHT (2), 315–17, 323–7; ANDERSON, 364, 379, 383, 397–9, 431; COHEN, A., xv–xvi, 28; DANIÉLOU, 62; DANIEL-ROPS, 226–7; DUCHESNE-GUILLEMIN, 1–2, 7–8, 109, 111; ELDER, 86–9; FINKELSTEIN, 45, 49, 71, 77; GRAVES, 411–13; GRAY, 183–4; HERODOTUS, bk. I; JAMES, 75, 280–3; *Jewish Encyclopaedia*, art. "Merkabah"; KAUFMANN, 162, 201–2, 255, 447–8; KENT, 116 ff.; KUHL, 35 ff., 64, 86, 145–54, 178–83, 193–5, 268; LAMB, 15, 49, 143, 154–8, 167, 201–2; LEWIS, 139; NEIL, 95–6, 169–75; NORTH, 14–18, 23–4, 87–8; NOTH. 289–97;

PARKES (1), *xv*, 5–6, 130, and (2), 12; PARMITER, 29; PEDERSEN, vols. III–IV, 147–8, 656; ROWLEY, 153–8; SCHOFIELD, 175–6, 210; SCHOLEM, 40–79; SNAITH, 14, 145; *Talmud*, as cited in COHEN, A.; THOMAS, 83; VAUX, 99, 105, 323, 343, 362, 482; ZAEHNER, 33, 40–57, 60, 66, 74, 79–96, 150–6, 168, 182, 199, 296, 316–17.

Chapter Eight: The Second Zionism

ALBRIGHT (1), 156, 225–6, and (2), 273–4, 296, 323–5, 345–8, 353, 356; ANDERSON, 358, 377, 383, 439–44; BENTWICH, 12–13, 124; BEVAN and SINGER, 20–1; *Bible*, Moffatt, *xxi*; BORCHSENIUS, 42–3; BRANDON, 107–8; BRASCH, 250–62; BUTTER-FIELD, 78; COHEN, A., *xvi–xxiii*, 25, 141; DANIEL-ROPS, 213, 244–53, 259–63, 270–3; *Encyclopaedia Britannica*, art. "Jehovah"; FINKELSTEIN, 51, 55, 70–81, 86–8, 96–7, 197–8; GASTER, 11; GRAY, 185–91, 197, 206–7; HOOKE (1), 1, 12, (3), 178, and (4), 51; JAMES, 275–6; *Jewish Encyclopaedia*, arts. "Hillel," "Rabbi," "Synagogue"; JOIN-LAMBERT, 47; JOSEPH, 14–16; JOSEPHUS (1), XI. *viii*. 2–7, and (2), 27–31, 36, 40–1, 371–5; KAUFMANN, 148–9, 450; KENT, 116 ff.; KENYON, 297–302; KLAUSNER, 223–5; KUHL, 17, 79, 182, 206, 209, 221–38, 269–71, 287–97; LAMB, 105, 186; NEIL, 175–85; NORTH, 23–4, 29; NOTH, 293–4, 308–17, 324, 329–31, 337, 342, 348, 360–2, 382, 401–11; OESTERLEY and ROBINSON, vol. II, 159–65; PARKES (1), 17, 36, 43–8, 60–8, 95, 140, and (2), 14–27; PEDERSEN, vols. III–IV, 275–7, 464, 606–7, 656; POLANO, 221; POLISH, 91–2; ROWLEY, 33, 76–82, 105–7, 112–13, 162–209; SCHOFIELD, 100, 226; SNAITH, 19, 20, 25–57, 62, 91, 179, 190–201; SPINOZA, 128–30; VAUX, 324–5, 340–2, 378, 390, 401–3, 510, 516–17; WEIZMANN, 162–3; WOUK, 49–50, 63–4, 105; ZAEHNER, 155–6.

Chapter Nine: The Kingdom of Stone

ALBRIGHT (2), 20, 331, 347, 356, 361, 380; ANDERSON, 515; BEVAN and SINGER, 9, 436, 464; BORCHSENIUS, 65–6; BRANDON, 109–10; BRASCH, 3; BUTTERFIELD, 2, 58–9, 94; CHARLES, vol. II, *vii–xi*, 1–82, 163–367, 625–52; COHEN, A., *xxi–xxiii*, *xxxvi*, 1–4, 11, 18, 20, 27–68, 79, 81, 88–96, 114–19, 125 ff., 136, 142–8, 178, 211–13, 260 ff., 346–72; DANIÉLOU, 1–2, 6, 62, 109–10, 120–1, 141, 161, 172, 186–8, 215; DANIEL-ROPS, 160–1, 285–95; *Encyclopaedia Britannica*, art. "Apocalyptic Literature"; FINKELSTEIN, 76–7, 79, 148–9, 1432; HOOKE (3), 176, and (4), 115–16, 130–9, 224; JAMES, 187–91, 275–8, 314–15; *Jewish Encyclopaedia*, art. "Antichrist"; JOSEPH, 58, 62–7, 87–90, 150–1, 156–72; KAUFMANN,

Chapter Bibliographies

214, 281–4, 297, 311 ff., 334, 346, 357–9, 449–51; KUHL, 174–8, 212, 260, 263; NEIL, 182–3, 191–5, 210; NORTH (1), 13, 87; NOTH, 382; PARKES (1), 17, 33, 36, 43, 48, 66–8, 85–7, 91–4, 145–7; PARMITER, 131; POLISH, 61, 111; ROWLEY, 347–8; SCHOFIELD, 101; SCHWARZ-BART, 49; SMALLEY, 163; SNAITH, 74–6, 85–105, 110–41, 147, 155–6, 198–200; SPENGLER, bk. II, 206–8; *Talmud* as cited in COHEN, A.; VAUX, 57, 105; WOLFSON, vol. I, 183, 349; WOUK, 31–3, 126, 140–1, 308–9; ZAEHNER, 40, 57–8, 131, 134, 182, 296, 309.

Chapter Ten: Wisdom and Her People

ALBRIGHT (1), 226, and (2), 20, 195–6, 328–31, 340–3, 348–9, 354–5, 368–9; ANDERSON, 470; BARKER; BENTWICH, 124; BEVAN and SINGER, 29–67, 300; BORCHSENIUS, 45, 72–4, 123–8; CABROL and LECLERCQ, art. "Hypsistariens"; CHARLES, vol. II, 83–122, 368–406; COHEN, A., 6, 29, 62–6; DANIÉLOU, 117, 140–4; DANIEL-ROPS, 249, 275; FINKELSTEIN, 76–7, 82, 88–95, 100–1, 109, 229, 959–61; GINSBURG; GINZBERG, vol. VI, 402; GRAVES, 257, 338; HOOKE (1), 154–5, and (2), 125–8, 148; JAMES, 249, 296–300, 314–18; *Jewish Encyclopaedia*, arts. "Cabala," "Philo"; JOSEPH, 65, 90; JOSEPHUS (2), 27, 158–9, 289, 342, 401; KUHL, 24, 38, 60–1, 241–3, 249–50, 258, 265–6, 302–5; NOTH, 348; PARKES (1), 43–8, 55, 118–19, and (2), 32, 68; PEDERSEN, vols. I–II, 168, and vols. III–IV, 668–9; PHILO; POLISH, 128–9; ROWLEY, 215–16; SCHOLEM, 75–6, 133, 143–6; SMALLEY, 3–7; SNAITH, 30–3, 86–7, 163–76, 190–4; *Talmud* as cited in COHEN, A.; VAUX, 341; WILLIAMSON, 68–9; WOLFSON; WOUK, 34, 39–40.

Chapter Eleven: A Race Hateful to the Gods

ALBRIGHT (2), 22–3, 304–5, 373–4, 380–95; BENTWICH, 14–15, 51, 63; BEVAN and SINGER, 9, 29, 101, 436; *Bible*, Knox, note on Daniel's prophecy of the "weeks"; BORCHSENIUS, 16–19, 21, 26, 33, 42–7, 53, 59, 64, 66, 72–3, 116–17, 123–30; BRANDON, 111–13, 159–70; BRASCH, 204–6; BREWER, art. "Pharisees"; BRUCE; BUTTERFIELD, 83–4; CHESTERTON (1), part II, chapters 2, 3; COHEN, A., *xxiv*, 14, 118–19, 151–5, 299–302, 347–8; COULTON and LUNN, 130–2; DANIEL-ROPS, 264–5, 292–7; DANIÉLOU, 2–3, 274; FINKELSTEIN, 105, 129–30, 141; GASTER, 3–4, 12–20, 39 ff., 43–6, 53–4, 281–306; GRANT, 77–8; GRAY, 112–212; HOOKE (2), 115–58, (3), 279–84, and (4), 78, 91, 93, 118–22, 142–3; JAMES, 281–3, 319; *Jewish Encyclopaedia*, arts. "Antichrist," "Herod"; JOIN-LAMBERT, 11, 70–2, 79–80, 97; JOSEPH, 61, 161; JOSEPHUS (1), XVIII. *v.* 2, XX. *ix.* 1, and (2), 40, 75–9, 109–10, 126–42, 149–61, 177, 198–9, 225–328, 371–5, 390–4;

Chapter Bibliographies

KLAUSNER, passim and N.B. 20, 47, 53, 71–124, 190, 224, 376, 384; MORIARTY; NEIL, 89, 112–13, 210, 248–9; NORTH (2); NOTH, 413–14, 421, 426; OESTERLEY and ROBINSON, vol. II, 307; PARKES (1), 46, 98–102, 133, 135, 140, 145–8, 158, 163, 180, 188–9, 213, 217, 235–40, and (2), 33–7; PEDERSEN, vols. I–II, 334; PLINY, X, 96–7; POLISH, 55, 127; RENAN, especially Introduction; ROWLEY. 347–8; SCHWEITZER, passim and N.B. *viii–xvi*, 23, 154, 311; SNAITH, 57–9, 98–105, 127, 179–90, 195, 201–3; SUETONIUS, "Claudius," "Vespasian"; TACITUS, *Annals* XV, section 44, and *Histories* V, sections 1–5 and 13; VAUX, 66–7, 267; WHITE, 236; WOLFSON, vol. I, 43–5; WOUK, 61, 64, 89–95, 186–7; ZAEHNER, 52.

Chapter Twelve: The Prolongation of Days

ALBRIGHT (2), 390–1; ANDERSON, 2, 6; BENTWICH, 17–27, 75–6, 127, 145; BEVAN and SINGER, 77, 85, 89–92, 101–23, 129–71, 192–202, 240, 267 ff., 283–332, 433–4, 469, 497; BORCHSENIUS, 32, 41–2, 47–56, 68, 94–103, 116–17, 138–42, 160, 165–209; BRANDON, 164, 172–3; BRASCH, 3–7, 76–7, 141–91, 209, 227, 265–76; BUBER, 3–10, 51; CHARLES, vol. II, 163, 470–526, 542–624; COHEN, A., *xxiii–xxxvi*, 9, 20, 29, 51, 57–60, 69, 74–81, 105, 116–19, 125 ff., 135–6, 141–54, 167–9, 178, 184, 190, 236, 260–91; COHEN, Israel, 56; DANIÉLOU, 2–5, 10–11, 20, 270–7; EBAN, 133–4; 157; FINKELSTEIN, 141–9, 155–64, 170–2, 180–2, 190–5, 217–29, 394 ff., 784–5, 932–57, 1191–1239, 1381–2, 1759–60, 1776 ff.; GASTER, 17–18; GINZBERG; HESS, 63; HOOKE (3), 280–4, and (4), 199; *Jewish Encyclopaedia*, arts. "Akiba," "Shemoneh Esreh," "Talmud"; JOIN-LAMBERT, 76, 104; JOSEPH, 17–18, 34–5, 150–1, 156, 165, 214, 222, 304–6; JOSEPHUS (2), 329; KLAUSNER, 18–54; KUHL, 4, 32–3; NEIL, 48; PARKES (1), *xiii, xv*, 33, 70, 131, 145–51, 191–9, 213, 224–7, 243–4, 252–65, 274–85, 291–300, 306–11, 317–20, 328–32, and (2), 34–44, 50–1, 68, 76–80, 107; POLANO, 7–8, 122, 125, 144, 197–200, 245, 254, 267, 275, 278, 286 ff., 322–31; POLISH, 33–40, 61, 80, 115, 120–7, 133, 143, 145, 185; RAPPOPORT; SCHOLEM; SCHWARZ-BART, 4–5, 49; SMALLEY, 6–7, 13, 21, 150; *Talmud*, Introduction *xv–xxv*, and as cited in COHEN, A.; WOUK, 31, 49–50, 63–105, 116–19, 126–55, 194–203, 209–21, 241, 258–9, 302–7.

Chapter Thirteen: The Third Zionism

ANDERSON, 2; BENTWICH, 7–11, 40–2, 103–8, 127, 133, 139–45, 167, 171; BEVAN and SINGER, 115–21, 440–1, 464; BRASCH, 7, 40–1, 102–7, 182, 231, 245; BUBER, 61–161; CHESTERTON (2), chapter xiii; COHEN, Israel, passim and N.B. 56, 67,

77, 90, 100–4, 117, 127, 140, 160–1, 190–1, 238, 241, 261–2, 331, 345–6, 354; DANIEL-ROPS, 297; EBAN, 35, 54, 65–8, 121–3, 128, 131, 138, 148–9, 157, 169, 187; FINKELSTEIN, 250–1, 273 ff., 593–8, 893–906, 1201–2, 1236; HA-AM, passim and N.B. *ix, xv–xvi,* 3–4, 31, 46; HERZL; HESS, passim and N.B. 17–35, 51, 60, 63, 75, 83, 97, 106–7, 116, 132, 149–56, 175, 252; HOYLE, 115; *Jewish Encyclopaedia,* arts. " Agricultural Colonies," " Alkalai," " Alroy," " Berab," " Cabala," " Caro," " Frankism," " Ginzberg (Asher,)" " Hasidism," " Haskalah," " Hess," " Jehiel," " Judah Ha-Levi," " Kalischer," " Krochmal," " Luria," " Maimonides," " Nachmanides," " Nasi," " Noah (Mordecai M.)," " Oliphant," " Pinsker," " Pseudo-Messiahs," " Sabbath," " Safed," " Shabbethai Zebi," " Shemoneh Esreh," " Smolenskin," " Zionides," " Zionism "; JOSEPH, 165–8; KASTEIN; KOESTLER (2), 4–5, 287, 320–1; MIKARDO; PARKES (2), 103–7, 175, 181–6, 237–8; PINSKER, passim and N.B. 10, 46, 64; POLISH, 11–12, 22, 74–9, 115, 195–201, 209–10; RUSSELL, 383; SCHOLEM, 288–324; SCHWARZ-BART, 43, 49; SCHWARZS-CHILD; SPINOZA, 8, 47, 56, 69; *Standard Jewish Encyclopaedia,* arts. " Aliyah," " Alkalai," " Birnbaum," " Birobidjan," " Frankists," " Hess," " Judah Ha-Levi," " Kalischer," " Noah (Mordecai M.)," " Shabbetai Tzevi," " Zionism "; SYKES; WEIZMANN, 62–4, 74–5, 108–17, 138, 143, 156–7, 162–3, 168, 200, 322, 346, 362, 376–7, 390–1, 436; WILLIAMS, 22–4, 51–61, 67, 70–6, 100–5, 186, 212–13; WILSON, 103–13, 136, 310; WOUK, 35, 219–21, 231–6, 241, 262–3, 283, 324.

GENERAL BIBLIOGRAPHY

ALBRIGHT, W. F., (1) *The Archaeology of Palestine*. 1949.
    (2) *From the Stone Age to Christianity*. 1957 ed.
ANDERSON, Bernhard W., *The Living World of the Old Testament*. 1958.
ASHE, Isaac, *The Divine Origin of Christianity*. 1875.

BARKER, Ernest, *From Alexander to Constantine*. 1956.
BELLOC, Hilaire, *The Jews*. 1922.
BENTWICH, Norman, *The Jews in Our Time*. 1960.
BEVAN, Edwyn R., and SINGER, Charles, eds., *The Legacy of Israel*. 1928.
Bible and *Apocrypha*. Translations by Knox (1955), Moffatt (1926); and the
    Revised Standard Version (1952).
BORCHSENIUS, Poul, *The Son of a Star*. Trans. F. H. Lyon. 1960.
BRANDON, S. G. F., *Time and Mankind*. 1951.
BRASCH, R., *The Eternal Flame*. 1958.
BREWER, E. C., *Dictionary of Phrase and Fable*. Revised ed., 1959.
BRUCE, F. F., *Are the New Testament Documents Reliable?* 1953.
BUBER, Martin, *Israel and Palestine*. 1952.
BUTTERFIELD, H., *Christianity and History*. 1950.

CABROL, F., and LECLERCQ, H., eds., *Dictionnaire d'Archéologie Chrétienne*. 15 vols.
    1907, etc.
CHADWICK, H. M. and N. K., *The Growth of Literature*, vol. I. 1932.
CHARLES, R. H., *The Apocrypha and Pseudepigrapha of the Old Testament*. 2 vols.
    1913.
CHESTERTON, G. K., (1) *The Everlasting Man*. 1925.
    (2) *The New Jerusalem*. 1920.
COHEN, A., *Everyman's Talmud*. 1961.
COHEN, Israel, *Theodor Herzl*. 1959.
COLLINGWOOD, R. G. and MYRES, J. N. L., *Roman Britain and the English Settle-
    ments*. 1937.

General Bibliography

COTTRELL, Leonard, *The Anvil of Civilization*. 1957.
COULTON, G. G., and LUNN, Arnold, *Is the Catholic Church Anti-Social?* 1946.

DANIÉLOU, Jean, *The Lord of History*. 1958.
DANIEL-ROPS, *Israel and the Ancient World*. Trans. K. Madge. 1949.
DIRINGER, D., *Writing*. 1962.
DUCHESNE-GUILLEMIN, Jacques, *The Hymns of Zarathustra*. 1952.

EBAN, Abba, *Voice of Israel*. 1958.
ELDER, John, *Archaeology and the Bible*. 1961.
Encyclopaedia Britannica.

FINKELSTEIN, Louis, ed., *The Jews: their History, Culture and Religion*. 2 vols.
1961.

GASTER, Theodor H., *The Dead Sea Scriptures*. 1956.
GINSBURG, Christian D., *The Essenes and the Kabbalah*. 1955.
GINZBERG, Louis, *The Legends of the Jews*. 7 vols. 1947, etc.
GRAETZ, Heinrich, *Popular History of the Jews*. Trans. A. B. Rhine. 7 vols. 1930.
GRANT, Frederick C., *Roman Hellenism and the New Testament*. 1962.
GRAVES, Robert, *The White Goddess*. 1952.
GRAY, John, *Archaeology and the Old Testament World*. 1962.
GURNEY, O. R., *The Hittites*. 1954.

HA-AM, AHAD, *Ten Essays on Zionism and Judaism*. Trans. Leon Simon. 1922.
HERODOTUS, *History*. Trans. G. Rawlinson. 2 vols. 1907.
HERZL, Theodor, *The Jewish State*. 1946 ed., with biography.
HESS, Moses, *Rome and Jerusalem*. Trans. Meyer Waxman. 1918.
HOOKE, S. H., (1) *In the Beginning*. 1947.
    (2) Ed., *The Labyrinth*. 1935.
    (3) Ed., *Myth, Ritual, and Kingship*. 1958.
    (4) *The Siege Perilous*. 1956.
HOYLE, Fred, *The Nature of the Universe*. 1950.

JAMES, E. O., *The Ancient Gods*. 1960.
Jewish Encyclopaedia.
JOIN-LAMBERT, Michel, *Jerusalem*. 1958.
JOSEPH, Morris, *Judaism as Creed and Life*. 1958 ed.

JOSEPHUS, (1) *Antiquities of the Jews*. Trans. William Whiston. 1825.

    (2) *The Jewish War*. Trans. G. A. Williamson. 1959.

KASTEIN, Joseph, *The Messiah of Ismir*. 1931.

KAUFMANN, Yehezkel, *The Religion of Israel*. Trans. Moshe Greenberg. 1961.

KELLER, Werner, *The Bible as History*. Trans. William Neil. 1956.

KENT, Roland G., *Old Persian*. 1950.

KENYON, Kathleen, *Archaeology in the Holy Land*. 1960.

KLAUSNER, Joseph, *Jesus of Nazareth*. Trans. Herbert Danby. 1925.

KOESTLER, Arthur (1) *The Lotus and the Robot*. 1960.

    (2) *Promise and Fulfilment*. 1949.

KUHL, Curt, *The Old Testament: its Origins and Composition*. 1961.

LAMB, Harold, *Cyrus the Great*. 1961.

LEWIS, C. S., *Miracles*. 1947.

MANETHO. Trans. W. G. Waddell (Loeb Classical Library). 1940.

MIKARDO, Ian, "Living Socialism" (review of H. Darin-Drabkin, *The Other Society*). *Tribune*, 7th September, 1962.

MONTJUVIN, Jacques, *Panorama of Biblical History*. Trans. Terence White Gervais. 1958.

MORIARTY, Frederick L., "The Suffering Servant." *The Way* (Month Publications), April 1962.

NEIL, William, *The Rediscovery of the Bible*. 1954.

NORTH, Christopher R., (1) *Isaiah 40–55*. 1952.

    (2) *The Suffering Servant in Deutero-Isaiah*. 1948.

NOTH, Martin, *The History of Israel*. 1958.

OESTERLEY, W O. E., and ROBINSON, T. H., *A History of Israel*. 2 vols. 1932.

PARKES, James, (1) *The Foundations of Judaism and Christianity*. 1960.

    (2) *A History of the Jewish People*. 1962.

PARMITER, Geoffrey de C., *King David*. 1960.

PEDERSEN, J., *Israel: its Life and Culture*. Vols. I–II, 1926; vols. III–IV, 1940.

PHILO, *Works*. Trans. F. H. Colson and G. H. Whitaker (Loeb Classical Library). 1929, etc.

PINSKER, Leo, *Auto-Emancipation*. 1937 ed.

PLINY (the younger), *Letters.* Trans. W. Melmoth (Loeb Classical Library). 1915.

POLANO, H., *The Talmud: Selections.* 1876.

POLISH, David, *The Eternal Dissent.* n.d.

PRITCHARD, James B., *The Ancient Near East.* 1958.

RAPPOPORT, A., *The Folklore of the Jews.* 1937.

RASHI, *Commentary on the Pentateuch.* Trans. James H. Lowe. 1928.

RENAN, Ernest, *Life of Jesus.* 1935 (Thinker's Library).

ROBINSON, Theodore H., " Baal in Hellas." *Classical Quarterly*, vol. XI, 1917.

ROTH, Cecil, *A Short History of the Jewish People.* 1948.

ROWLEY, H. H., ed., *The Old Testament and Modern Study.* 1951.

RUSSELL, Bertrand, *A History of Western Philosophy.* 1946.

SCHOFIELD, J. N., *The Historical Background of the Bible.* 1938.

SCHOLEM, G. G., *Major Trends in Jewish Mysticism.* 1946.

SCHWARZ-BART, André, *The Last of the Just.* Trans. Stephen Becker. 1961.

SCHWARZSCHILD, Leopold, *The Red Prussian.* 1948.

SCHWEITZER, Albert, *The Quest of the Historical Jesus.* 1954 ed.

SMALLEY, Beryl, *The Study of the Bible in the Middle Ages.* 1952.

SNAITH, Norman H., *The Jews from Cyrus to Herod.* 1949.

SPENGLER, Oswald, *The Decline of the West.* Trans. Charles Francis Atkinson. 1959.

SPINOZA, Benedict de, *Tractatus Theologico-Politicus.* Trans. R. H. M. Elwes n.d.

Standard Jewish Encyclopaedia. 1959.

SUETONIUS, *The Lives of the Twelve Caesars.* Ed. Joseph Gavorse. 1931.

SYKES, Christopher, *Two Studies in Virtue.* 1953.

TACITUS, *Annals* and *Histories.* Ed. and trans. G. G. Ramsay. 1915.

Talmud. Soncino translation. Ed. J. Epstein. 35 vols. 1935, etc.

THOMAS, D. Winton, ed., *Documents from Old Testament Times.* 1958.

VAUX, Roland de, *Ancient Israel.* 1961.

VAWTER, Bruce, *A Path through Genesis.* 1957.

VON RAD, Gerhard, *Genesis.* Trans. John H. Marks. 1961.

WARMINGTON, B. H., *Carthage.* 1960.

WEIZMANN, Chaim, *Trial and Error*. 1949.

WHITE, Victor, *God and the Unconscious*. 1952.

WILLIAMS, L. F. Rushbrook, *The State of Israel*. 1957.

WILLIAMSON, Hugh Ross, *The Arrow and the Sword*. 1947.

WILSON, Edmund, *To the Finland Station*. 1960 ed.

WOLFSON, H. A., *Philo*. 2 vols. 1947.

WOUK, Herman, *This is my God*. 1960.

ZAEHNER, R. C., *The Dawn and Twilight of Zoroastrianism*. 1961.

INDEX

437

Index

Index

Index

Index

Index

447

Index